CONCERT
AND OPERA
SINGERS

Recent Titles in the Music Reference Collection
Series Advisers: Donald L. Hixon and Adrienne Fried Block

Music for Oboe, Oboe D'Amore, and English Horn: A Bibliography
of Materials at the Library of Congress
Compiled by Virginia Snodgrass Gifford

A Bibliography of Nineteenth-Century American Piano Music:
With Location Sources and Composer Biography-Index
John Gillespie and Anna Gillespie

The Resource Book of Jewish Music: A Bibliographical and Topical
Guide to the Book and Journal Literature and Program Materials
Compiled by Irene Heskes

American Vocal Chamber Music, 1945-1980: An Annotated Bibliography
Compiled by Patricia Lust

CONCERT AND OPERA SINGERS

A Bibliography of Biographical Materials

Compiled by Robert H. Cowden

Music Reference Collection, Number 5

Greenwood Press
Westport, Connecticut • London, England

Library of Congress Cataloging in Publication Data

Cowden, Robert H.
   Concert and opera singers.

   (Music reference collection, ISSN 0736-7740 ; no. 5)
   Includes index.
   1. Singers—Biography—Bibliography.   I. Title.
II. Series.
ML128.B3C7   1985   016.7821 '092 '2   85-12717
ISBN 0-313-24828-1 (lib. bdg. : alk. paper)

Library of Congress Catalog Card Number: 85-12717
ISBN: 0-313-24828-1
ISSN: 0736-7740

First published in 1985

Greenwood Press
A division of Congressional Information Service, Inc.
88 Post Road West, Westport, Connecticut 06881

Printed in the United States of America

The paper used in this book complies with the
Permanent Paper Standard issued by the National
Information Standards Organization (Z39.48-1984).

10 9 8 7 6 5 4 3 2 1

To my wife, Jacqueline, my children,
and my parents, without whom little of
value, including this book, would have
ever evolved!

Contents

Preface

The compiling of this work has been a true <u>Remembrance of Things
Past</u>, a remembrance which extends back almost an entire lifetime.
My mother, the youngest daughter of a Swedish immigrant family, was a
a student of Marie Sundelius in Boston, and as a child, I was often
told about her career and her voice studio. Marie was a cherished
visitor in my grandparent's home for she brought both worldliness and
compassion to what were humble but proud surroundings. As a student
at Princeton, I survived the elbow-to-elbow exhilaration of standing
room at the Metropolitan Opera where Sundelius had made her debut in
1916. How could I have imagined then, that as a member of the Metropolitan Opera National Company, I would rehearse in that historic
house? Along with my academics, I managed to schedule in voice les-
sons with Ann Lucky, who was one of the last students of the legendary Lilli Lehmann. Ann was a treasure house of both vocal knowledge
and memories and recollections of Europe between the two world wars.
A monumentally influential summer at The Tanglewood Music Center as
a scholarship student afforded me a personal involvement in music
making at the highest possible level; new career yearnings became
an option which simply had to be addressed. Several probing discus-
sions with Ann led to the Eastman School of Music and after graduating
from Princeton, I left for Rochester to join the studio of Julius
Huehn. By now the threads of tradition had begun to weave the fabric
that would inevitably tie me to the past. Julius had performed at the
old MET with some of the greatest voices of the twentieth century, including Kirsten Flagstad and Lauritz Melchoir. Beyond that, he was a
highly skilled and perceptive teacher. His mentor at the Julliard
School had been Anna Eugénia Schoen-René, herself a student of Pauline
Viardot-Garcia who had, in turn, been a student of her father, Manuel
del Popolo Garica. When my new wife, Jacqueline, and I went to Germany as Fulbright scholars, we both studied in Frankfurt am Main with
Gertrude Pitzinger. Gertrude was a protégée of the renowned recital-
ist Julia Culp, whose teacher, Etelka Gerster, was a highly respected
member of Mathilde Marchesi's studio. The legendary Marchesi was a
student of Manuel Garcia's son. One final historical note, my wife's
teacher in Italy was the famous Italian coloratura, Toti dal Monte.
All of these vocal luminaries, with the exception of Gerster, are
listed in this bibliography; their names have been assembled as the
result of both a scholar's and a collector's travels.

Like my father before me (or more likely because of my father), I
have always been an avid bibliophile. To the casual observer, all col-

lectors suffer from some misguided passion, indeed folly: a strong and unwavering commitment to possession, either of the object itself or of an enormous amount of information about it. The third edition of Webster's unabridged dictionary defines a collector as "an object or device that collects specimens." I have no way of knowing just which appercipient editor devised that definition, but truely one might tend to be suspicious of an individual who delights in leafing through rare books and who makes a point of walking through the stacks of famous libraries to see what is and isn't there. After all, Isaac D'Israeli did warn us that "bibliomania, or the collecting an enormous heap of books without intelligent curiosity, has, since libraries have existed, infected weak minds." On the other hand, notable collections have been carefully put together over time and with love by knowledgeable individuals in both the public and private sectors. The names of Oscar Sonneck, Alfred Cortot, and Paul Hirsch immediately come to mind, and there are a host of others. In his 1896 will, Edmond de Goncourt stated:

> My wish is that my drawings, my prints, my curiosities, my books—in a word, those things of art which have been the joy of my life—shall not be consigned to the cold tomb of a museum, and subjected to the stupid glance of the careless passer-by; but I require that they shall all be dispersed under the hammer of the auctioneer, so that the pleasure which the acquiring of each has given to me shall be given again, in each case, to some inheritor of my own tastes.

This statement represents the rationale for my particular explorations. One should know what has been added to the "enormous heap of books" and how to identify individual items in order to avoid the "follies of collectors." And each of us should pursue the quest with joy and dedication. This advice applies to both the professional and the serious amateur. Where does one look for information in order to pick the brains of some Wagnerian Wanderer, who has devoted a considerable amount of effort to understanding the world around him?

My interest in autobiographies and biographies on concert and opera singers began almost thirty years ago but really developed after I arrived in Rochester and began rummaging about in antiquarian bookstores. The magnificent resources of the Sibley Library also whetted my growing interest, and I compiled numerous lists of desiderata, which found their way into the hands of collectors, dealers, and scholars in North America and Europe. At that time, my only interest was to locate individual titles; my files of correspondence during that period include most, if not all, of the individuals involved in similar pursuits. Gradually my efforts became more organized, and in 1969, at the request of The National Association of Teachers of Singing, I compiled A Checklist of Books of a Biographical Nature by and about Singers (1st supplement, 1970). With the enthusiastic encouragement and support of Harvey Ringel, I began an "Annotated Bibliography of Singers," of which three initial parts appeared in The NATS Bulletin (December 1969, December 1970, and October 1971). Bill Moran, one of the very first to undertake such a compilation some years before, offered his full and unrestricted support as he always has to colleagues. My project quickly ran full tilt against the same obstacles he had encountered: time, access to source materials, and demands by family and profession. By the mid-1970s, I was firmly convinced that such a comprehensive bibliography would never see the light of day. Franz Stieger certainly suffered similar frustrations when he had to sell the manuscript of his opera catalogue to the Institute of Musical Research in Bueckenburg in 1918. But I persisted, and this book is the result of that commitment.

Thomas Wolfe once wrote that "we are the sum of all the moments of our lives--all that is ours is in them: we cannot escape or conceal it." In my particular case, countless moments were spent to fulfill a personal desire to examine as many of the titles listed herein as humanly possible. Although the completion of my bibliography depended on efficient hardware and software available from the Silicon Valley's fabulous computer industry, I personally compiled and annotated all of the entries because I felt that I had to interact with the material in order to appreciate the discoveries made. About ninety-eight percent of the entries have been held in my own hands; I have indicated when this was not possible. Anyone who has done research in a major library will quickly support the conclusion that card files and shelf lists cannot always be trusted. The rule of thumb should always be to look at each and every title yourself. Computerized data banks provide us with access to monumental amounts and types of information, but the question remains, is it correct? I have chosen to re-examine the material laboriously title by title. Any errors are clearly mine alone, and I accept that responsibility as being preferable to blind acceptance of either what comes up on the monitor or what is provided by colleagues in the field, both viable options which would have supplied me with information I could not have possibly checked.

One lasting joy of this past year of final research has been the discovery of several manuscripts which I had no prior knowledge of whatsoever. Similarly, I think that the appearance of this bibliography will result in an important number of discoveries. I will be very thankful to anyone who forwards additions or corrections to the publisher. After all, my compilation is only the first stage of an ongoing project. Already I am well into the next volume, which is a master index of concert and opera singers listed in major dictionaries, encyclopedias, and periodicals; works cited in this bibliography under COLLECTIVE WORKS: Books on Singers and COLLECTIVE WORKS: Related Books will be cross-indexed; those titles in APPENDIX I will also be cross-indexed. I intend to devote the final volume of this undertaking to a much needed biographical dictionary of concert and opera singers, a reference work needed for over three centuries. That was what I originally started out to create, but I had no idea at the beginning just what was involved. Now I do, and I honestly believe it to be possible. In 1975 Hans Schneider made a strong case for a general theatrical bibliography which would include a dictionary of actors and singers. Perhaps the time has finally come for a massive project to unite researchers in the field as there is very little in the way of fundamental bibliography.

Those in the information collecting business develop very meaningful obligations to numerous individuals in countless far-off and obscure places over a long period of time. Those with whom I have

shared information on this subject since the 1950s know well my deep
sense of thankfulness, not only for the details unobtainable anywhere
else but also for the mutual respect, professionalism, and warm
camaraderie which almost invariably accompanies the dialogue between
authors, collectors, dealers, librarians, and researchers. We are all
mutually interdependent! Many of these individuals are wonderfully
enthusiastic, sharing, and open; of the very special few among that
select group I wish to acknowledge William R. Moran, the late James F.
Dennis, Harvey Ringel, John C. Sicignano, and the late Leo Riemens.
To one particularly close friend and colleague, Lim M. Lai, who shares
perhaps more than anyone else I know my own enthusiasm and commitment
for this entire area of research, I acknowledge my deep appreciation
for his substantial contributions to this project.

   By their very nature, bibliographies are living entities—never
complete and always subject to change. The vast majority of titles
existing under my guidelines can be found in these pages; any brave
reader who wishes to create the elusive definitive bibliography of any
of the 708 singers listed, will find the basis to undertake such a
perilous venture in this volume. My sincerest prayer is that each
reader will share the joys of discovery, the frustrations of omission,
the victories of errors uncovered, and the exhilaration and commitment
of the never ending search!

Robert H. Cowden
Monte Sereno, California
December 1984

Introduction

Information on concert and opera singers seems to lurk in every corner, even in those beyond the imagination. Very early on in this endeavour, the need arose for tightly defined parameters that would limit the search and assure some degree of thoroughness. Anyone involved in the stormy, uncharted seas of bibliography will attest that completeness can be imagined perhaps, but never achieved. The field demands a touch of the Buddhist view of life as a never finalized continuum. As Vincent Duckles states in his introduction to the first edition of Music Reference and Research Materials: an Annotated Bibliography (New York, 1964): "Even as this edition goes to press, I am troubled by the submerged voices of would-be entries which may have been overlooked, and entries which may have been misplaced or misrepresented." And who else but the venerable musicologist and lexicographer Nicolas Slonimsky could have penned the following mea culpa: "Every time I approach my task I take a solemn vow to myself that this time over there will be no avoidable errors generated by a mysterious amblyopia, the cause of which may be hysteria, poisoning with ethyl or methyl alcohol, lead, arsenic, thallium, quinine, ergot, male fern, carbon disulfide, or Cannabis indica (the plant from which marijuana and hashish are derived)." If the master is troubled, then how vulnerable we all really are! But the desire and need to document far exceeds the fear of failure so attack we must. A number of years ago, I contributed to an exhibit catalog which was published by the Detroit Public Library. My thoughts now are as they were then. One innocently wanders into collecting and cataloging, not realizing the demands on time and energy that lurk silently in the shadows. The casual, "Isn't that interesting?" rapidly evolves into, "I must locate that title!" Irrevocably drawn into the whirlpool, one is converted to the preservation of human achievement.

CHOICE OF ARTISTS

Given the multitude of individuals who have pursued a vocal career since the seventeenth-century Italians inaugurated this popular and sophisticated indulgence, how does one limit the scope of research into the collective and individual comings and goings of these artists? In order to be considered for this volume, an artist had to be represented by either an autobiography or biography; the definition of these forms of recognition or self aggrandizement remained as broad as possible. Critical judgments, however, had to be made regarding those vocal performers who were concert artists in the most general

sense and who appeared occasionally in opera productions as well.
Fritzi Scheff certainly qualifies for the latter catagory based on
her three seasons with the Metropolitan Opera. The legendary Ella
Fitzgerald has overwhelmed concert audiences since the early 1930s!
And though the genres of operetta, Broadway, Hollywood, jazz, and
folk have nurtured their own special stars, this compilation is not
the place for the Gertrude Lawrences, the Gracie Fields, or Barbara
Streisands--no matter how abundant the published resources are.
Eventually someone will fulfill the unquestionable need for a bibliography concentrating on the available autobiographies, biographies, and periodical literature not to mention the impressive contributions of Leonard Feather, Roger D. Kinkle, Ray M. Lawless, and
Henry Pleasants, among others. The specialization of this volume,
however, only permitted the inclusion of artists, who became and remained famous as opera or concert singers.

Most research pleasantly results in determining its own parameters
and limitations; this effort was no exception. The published number
of autobiographies and biographies in this specialized field turned out
to be quite small. How was I to widen my fishing net to increase the
quantity as well as the value of the information collected? Vincent
Duckles was right when he stated that a bibliography must throw "the
essential patterns of a discipline into relief, casting light on what
has been accomplished and drawing attention to the shadows where work
still needs to be done." Music encyclopedias and dictionaries (as well
as certain periodicals) contain a wealth of material about performers.
My research clearly indicated a boundary--the magical number three.
Any combination of three or more entries or articles, with at least
one from a major encyclopedia or dictionary, qualified a singer for
inclusion. Why the requirement for at least one legitimate reference
work entry? Without passing judgement of the quality of the popular
press, the facts demonstrate that, almost without exception, singers,
who have been written about in two or more of the chosen periodicals
(discussed later) have also been recognized in the standard music
dictionaries or encyclopedias. Not unexpectedly, the exceptions were
primarily very young artists whose exploits, if prodigious enough, will
earn them a place in future volumes--perhaps even later editions of
this bibliography!

REFERENCE WORKS AND PERIODICALS

Initially twelve reference works in four languages and twelve periodicals in five languages were selected for inclusion; the final list
includes ten and nine respectively. My hope is that some future edition will expand on the number of references and periodicals included.
Each title has been assigned a bibliographical abbreviation, which
functions as a shorthand means of directing the reader to an entry
about a specific artist. (A coded list of abbreviations for these
books and periodicals immediately follows this introduction.)

FACTUAL DATA AND LANGUAGES

I have relied on the legendary lexicographer Nicolas Slonimsky, for
the spelling of names and the correct names and places. If the necessary data could not be found in BAKER 6, I then turned to GROVE 6 or

RIEMANN 12. The code KUTSCH 3 indicates that dates and/or places could
not be obtained from any other publication but this one. As expected,
some information could not be found or verified in the reference works
I was able to consult. Entries lacking that information will be very
quickly noticed. As I mentioned in the preface, any help from knowledgeable readers will be most appreciated. Slonimsky himself asked,
"who the hell cares? Well, nobody except a small band of benighted
chronologists who are determined to put things straight."

Regarding the choice of languages incorporated in this bibliography, I made a conscious effort to include all known material in the
Germanic and Italic branches of the Indo-European langauge family. A
few citations from the Balto-Slavic branch have been added because I
own a small sampling of these titles, but a comprehensive listing of
this material will have to await the efforts of a colleague more knowledgeable and conversant than I. Thus in this work, for example, the
massive amount of material in Russian on Chaliapin and Sobinov (to
mention only two of the most prominent artists) has not been included
at this time.

ORDER OF MATERIALS

The bibliography is divided into three major sections. The first,
COLLECTIVE WORKS: Books on Singers, includes one hundred twenty titles
devoted entirely or primarily to concert and opera singers. The entries are code numbered A0001 through A0120; authors, co-authors, and
editors in this section also appear in the Index. Those titles with
roughly forty or less artists include the name of each artist in the
annotation. Listing the artists by name enables the reader to select
appropriate titles for further investigation. As for my annotations,
I tried to avoid personal evaluations that could possibly influence
both present and future readers. I feel that a bibliographer's primary
obligation is to present, not comment on, information.

The second, COLLECTIVE WORKS: Related Books, contains one hundred
and fifty-four titles, with additional material on many of the singers
discussed in section one. As in the first section, the entries are
code numbered (B0001 through B0154), authors, co-authors, and editors
appear in the Index, and artists are listed in the annotation·if the
volume contains a total of forty or less artists.

In the final section, INDIVIDUAL SINGERS, A-Z, concert and opera
singers from Emma Abbott to Teresa Zylis-Gara are alphabetically listed
in the entries numbered C0001 through C0720 (including cross-references). Aside from the essential data, an entry can draw from five
different types of sources for a particular singer: (1) entries in any
of the ten reference works listed in the bibliographical abbreviations
section, including the edition and volume number if appropriate and
indicating the bibliographic references not duplicated in this book
(the exceptions are those titles I was personally able to inspect);
(2) articles of biographical or autobiographical nature from any of
the nine periodicals listed in the abbreviations section; (3) autobiographies or books by the singer directly related to pedagogy or
interpretation (except for novels, poetry, and the like); (4) biographies about the singer, including historical novels if there is

good reason to believe that the content was based on or influenced by the artist's life; and (5) other books containing important material (for example, because Maria Malibran was prominently mentioned in Louise Hériette-Viardot's autobiography, this information also appears under Maria Malibran's entry). The third section of this bibliography can act as its own index and, if used in conjunction with the earlier sections, should provide both scholar and amateur countless paths to pursue.

Because some of the critical material did not fit into any of the above categories, I included two appendixes which I trust will help readers searching for additional sources of information. The first, APPENDIX I: Reference Material, is a continuation of the bibliography and includes seventeen titles, providing a wealth of information not available anywhere else. The second, APPENDIX II: Index to Singers in GROVE 6, lists the 1,439 concert and opera singers accorded an entry in this basic reference work and cross-indexes them with the entries in PART C of this volume. This listing alone should save countless hours for innumerable readers.

I am delighted with the number of manuscripts, translations, and limited rare editions that surfaced during the many months and years of fascinating and frustrating involvement. Indeed, reflecting on Nicholas Slonimsky's earlier question, one might conclude that bibliographic efforts touch only "a small band," but over the years I have encountered too many individuals, for whom the vocal arts were an inspiration, to have the slightest doubt about the answer. If this is an obsession, it is a magnificent one. May each reader accept the challenge Shakespeare presented in The Tempest: "Lead off this ground; and let's make further search . . . ."

Bibliographical Abbreviations

The bibliographical abbreviations listed below are used in the text of this bibliography, particularly in the third section on individual singers. These abbreviations are widely used, and readers should find them easy to remember and use.

Encyclopedias and Dictionaries

BAKER 6
> Baker's Biographical Dictionary of Musicians. 6th edition. Completely revised by Nicolas Slonimsky. New York: G. Schirmer, Inc., 1978.

EdS
> Enciclopedia dello spettacolo. 9 vols. Roma: Casa Editrice le Maschere, 1954-62. Aggiornamento 1955-1965. Roma: Unione Editoriale, 1966.

EITNER
> Eitner, Robert. Biographisch-bibliographisches Quellen-Lexikon der Musiker und Musikgelehrten der christlichen Zeitrechnung bis zur Mitte des 19. Jahrhunderts.... 10 vols. Leipzig: Breitkopf & Haertel, 1898-1904. Miscellanea Musicae Bio-bibliographica; Musikgeschichtliche Quellennachweise als Nachtraege und Verbesserungen zu Eitner's Quellenlexikon. Leipzig: Breitkopf & Haertel, 1912-1914.

FETIS 2
> Fétis, Francois, J. Biographie universelle des musiciens et bibliographie générale de la music. 8 vols. 2me éd. Paris: Firmin Didot Frères, 1866-70. Supplément et complément. pub. sous la direction de M. Arthur Pougin. 2 vols. Paris, 1878-80.

GROVE 6
> Sadie, Stanley, ed., The New Grove Dictionary of Music and Musicians. 20 vols. London: Macmillan Publishers Limited, 1980.

KUTSCH 3
> Kutsch, K.J. and Leo Riemens. Unvergaengliche Stimmen: Saenger-lexikon. 3rd edition. Bern: Francke Verlag, 1975.

MENDEL
    Mendel, Hermann. Musikalisches Conversations-Lexikon: eine
    Encyklopaedie der gesammten musikalischen Wissenschaften. Fuer
    Gebildete aller Staende, unter Mitwirkung der Literarischen
    Commission des Berliner Tonkuenstlervereins.... 11 vols.
    Berlin: L. Heimann, 1870-79. CODE: MENDEL.

MGG
    Blume, Friedrich, ed. Die Musik in Geschichte und Gegenwart:
    allgemeine Enzyklopaedie der Musik.... 14 vols. Kassel: Baeren-
    reiter Verlag, 1949-67. Supplement. Kassel, 1973/1979.

RIEMANN 12
    Gurlitt, Wilibald, ed. Riemann Musik-Lexikon: Personenteil.
    2 vol. 12. voellig neubearbeitete Auflage. Mainz: B. Schott's
    Soehne, 1959-67. Ergaenzungsband. Mainz, 1972/1975.

SCHMIDL
    Schmidl, Carlo. Dizionario universale dei musicisti. 2 vols.
    Milano: Sonzogno, 1928-29. Supplemento. Milano, 1938.

Periodicals

GR   The Gramophone. Vol. 1 (1923-24) to Vol. 59 (1981-82).

MQ   Musical Quarterly. Vol. 1 (1915) to Vol. 45 (1959).

OPERA   Opera. Vol. 1 (1950) to Vol. 33 (1982).

OP   Opéra. Vol. 1 (1961) to Vol. 9 (1969). Publication ceased.

ON   Opera News. Vol. 1 (1936) to Vol. 47 (1982-83).

OW   Opernwelt. Vol. 1 (1960) to Vol. 23 (1982).

RNC   Record News Canada. Vol. 1 (1956) to Vol. 5 (1960). Publi-
        cation ceased.

RC   The Record Collector. January 1948 to Vol. 27 (1983).

RS   British Institute of Recorded Sound. As of 1961 the
        publication was called Recorded Sound. No. 1 (Summer 1956)
        to No. 63-64 (July-Oct 1976). No access to later issues.

CONCERT
AND OPERA
SINGERS

PART A.

COLLECTIVE WORKS:
Books on Singers

A0001. **Armstrong, William.** The Romantic World of Music. New York: E.P. Dutton & Company, 1922. ix, 239 p., 20 illus.

Articles based upon personal acquaintance with eighteen famous artists (exception Paderewski). Full of little known anecdotes. Patti, Nordica, Melba, Schumann-Heink, Garden, Caruso, McCormack, Hempel, Pasquale Amato, Galli-Curci, Jeritza, Jean Gordon, Ponselle, Lucy Gates, Bori, d'Alvarez, Florence Easton.

A0002. **Averkamp, Antoon.** De zangkunst en hare sterren. Graven-hage: J. Philip Kruseman, n.d. 272 p., 151 illus., 18-item bibliography, index of names.

Basic history of singers and singing. Particularly strong for 19th century and Dutch singers. A student of Messchaert, the author (b. February 18, 1861; d. June 1, 1934, Bussum) published a pedagogical treatise: Uit mijn practijk: wenken en raddgevingen bij het onderwigs en de studie van der solozang. Groningen, Den Haag, J.B. Wolters, 1916. 140 p., illus.

A0003. **Barker, Frank Granville.** Stars of the Opera. London: Lotus Press, 1949. 51 p., 9 illus.

Gigli, Turner, Melchoir, dal Monte, Luigi Infantino, Welitsch, Paolo Silveri, Constance Shacklock, Gobbi.

A0004. **Barker, Frank Granville.** Voices of the Opera. London: Arthur Unwin, 1951. 61 p., 10 illus.

Short biographical essays including nine singers written to appeal to the English opera public. Personal observations and anecdotes. Flagstad, Svanholm, Adriana Guerrini, Tagliavini, Hammond, Walter Midgley, Coates, Tajo, Christoff.

A0005. **Battaglia, Fernando.** L'arte del canto in romagna: i cantanti lirici romagnoli dell'Ottocento e del Novecento. Bologna: Bongiovanni Editore, 1979. 260 p., 33 illus., 26-item bibliography, index of names.

Over 700 singers mentioned. Substantial information on Bonci, Farneti, Forti, Masetti-Bassi, Masini, Melandri, Pagliughi, Parmeggiani, Pedrini, Pinza, Rossi-Morelli, Savorani-Tadolini,

Siboni, Simionato, Stignani, Tamburini, Tassinari.

A0006. **Baudissone, Bruno.** Un nido di memorie: interviste a 40 cantanti lirici. Torino: Edizioni Musicali Scomegna s.n.c., 1983. 168 p., 42 illus.

Actually there are interviews with forty-one contemporary singers. Bechi, Bergonzi, Bruscantini, Bruson, Caniglia, Christoff, Cigna, Cossotto, del Monaco, di Stefano, Domingo, Favero, Marion Filippeschi, Freni, Gencer, Ghiaurov, Rina Gigli, Gobbi, de Hidalgo, Kabaivanska, Kraus, Lauri-Volpi, Giovanni Manurita, Francesco Merli, Milnes, Montarsolo, Elena Nicolai, Olivero, Iva Pacetti, Tancredi Pasero, Pavarotti, Ginna Pederzini, Giacinto Prandelli, Katia Ricciarelli, Simionato, Tagliavini, Tajo, Tebaldi, Valdengo, Lucia Valentini Terrani, Carlo Zardo.

A0007. **Bazzetta de Vemenia, Nino.** Le cantanti italiane dell' Ottocento: ricordi - aneddoti - intimità - amori. Novara: Edizioni Giulio Volante, 1945. 298 p., 68 illus., bibliography at the end of each section.

103 18th and 19th century female singers. Some non-Italians such as Malibran are included. Useful reference for singers of secondary importance.

A0008. **Berutto, Gugliemo.** I cantanti piemontesi: dagli albori del melodrama ai nostri giorni. Torino: Italgrafica, 1972. 285 p., 250-item bibliography + 8 newspapers and the Enciclopedia dello spettacolo.

This is a biographical dictionary of over 300 singers from Lina Aimaro to Angiolina Zoja.

A0009. **Blaukopf, Kurt.** Grosse Oper grosse Saenger. Teufen: Arthur Niggli und Willy Verkauf, 1955. 172 p., 16 illus., music, opera discography, 31-item bibliography.

Short biographies of twenty-eight celebrated singers including Caruso, Callas, Della Casa, Christoff, Dermota, Fischer-Dieskau, Frick, Gigli, Goltz, Gueden, Hotter, Jurinac, Peter Klein, Kunz, London, Madeira, Metternich, Patzak, Schoeffler, Seefried, Siepi, di Stefano, Streich, Suthaus, Tebaldi, Uhde, Ludwig Weber, Windgassen.

A0010. **Brand-Seltei, Erna.** Bel canto: eine Kulturgeschichte der Gesangskunst. Wilhelmshaven: Heinrichshofen's Verlag, 1972. xii, 532, [64] p., 64 illus., index of names.

Perhaps most interesting for the outstanding singers who are not included, e.g. Tebaldi. Forty-two vocalists from the Garcias to Fischer-Dieskau are prominently mentioned, but many others are included. A complete listing is given in the Anhang Register pp. 510-532.

A0011. **Breslin, Herbert H.,** ed. The Tenors. New York: Macmillan

Publishing Co., Inc., 1974. xv, 203 p., 25 illus, index.

Selected were Pavarotti written by Stephen E. Rubin; Vickers by
John Ardoin; Tucker by William Bender; Corelli by Joan Downs;
Domingo by Alan Rich.

A0012. **Brook, Donald.** Singers of Today. 2nd revised and enlarged
edition. London: Rockliff, 1958 [1st edition 1949. Reprint 1971].
200 p., 41 illus.

Moderate, aproximately five pages each, coverage of the careers of
leading female and male singers (twenty each) during the period
after 1930. Based upon interviews.
Norman Allin, de los Angeles, Trevor Anthony, Isobel Baillie,
Bruce Boyce, Owen Brannigan, Callas, Coates, Cross, Henry Cummings,
Astra Desmond, Robert Easton, Keith Falkner, Fisher, Flagstad,
Franklin, Eric Greene, Gueden, Hammond, Roy Henderson, William
Herbert, Janet Howe, Parry Jones, Trefor Jones, Lewis, Walter
Midgley, Milanov, Morrison, Kenneth Neate, George Pizzey, Schwarz-
kopf, Constance Shacklock, Paolo Silveri, Sladen, René Soames,
Tebaldi, Turner, Jennifer Vyvyan, Norman Walker, Helen Watts.
The singers included many vary from the 1949 edition, a copy of
which I have not seen.

A0013. **Brower, Harriette.** Vocal Mastery: Talks with Master Singers
and Teachers. New York: Frederick A. Stokes Company, 1920. vi, 292 p.,
20 illus.

Conversational interviews with twenty-one famous singers and
five outstanding teachers.
Caruso, Farrar, Maurel, Lilli Lehmann, Galli-Curci, de Luca,
Tetrazzini, Scotti, Raisa, Homer, Martinelli, Anna Case, Easton,
d'Alvarez, Maria Barrientos, Muzio, Johnson, Reinald Werrenrath,
Breslau, Morgan Kingston, Hempel;
Bispham, Oscar Saenger, Witherspoon, Yeatman Griffith, Duval.

A0014. **Camner, James,** ed. The Great Opera Stars in Historic
Photographs. 343 Portraits from the 1850's to the 1940's. New
York: Dover Publications, Inc., 1978. ii, 199 p., 270 performers
from Tamburini to Thebom, index.

A0015. **Clayton, Ellen Creathorne.** Queens of Song: being Memoirs
of Some of the Most Celebrated Female Vocalists Who Have Performed
on the Lyric Stage from the Earliest Days of Opera to the Present
Time, to Which Is Added a Chronological List of All the Operas That
Have Been Performed in Europe. New York: Harper & Brothers, Publishers, 1865. Reprint 1972. xiv, 15-543 p., 10 portraits, 49-item
bibliography, chronological list of operas and their composers,
alphabetical list of dramatic composers not preeminent as operatic
writers, index.

Forty-two singers from Katherine Tofts to Teresa Tietjens. The
original two volume edition was published in London in 1863.

A0016. **Cooke, James Francis.** Great Singers on the Art of Singing.

Philadelphia: Theo. Presser Co., 1921. 304 p., 29 illus.

"A series of personal study talks with [27] of the most re-
knowned opera concert and oratorio singers of the time."
Alda, Amato, Bispham, Butt, Campanari, Caruso, Claussen,
Dalmores, Dippel, Eames, Easton, Farrar, Gadski, Galli-Curci,
Garden, Gluck, de Gogorza, Hempel, Melba, de Pasquale, Sembrich,
Schumann-Heink, Scotti, Scott, Thursby, Werrenrath, Williams.

A0017. **Davidson, Gladys**. A Treasury of Opera Biography. New
York: The Citadel Press, 1955. 352 p., 23 illus., 41-item bibliography, index of operas performed by the singers.

Short biographies of 119 singers from the 19th and 20th centuries. Especially strong for English singers. Published in
London the same year with the title: Opera Biographies.

A0018. **de Bossan, George S.** [pseud. for Sam Bottenheim]. Nederlandsche zangeressen. Amsterdam: Bigot & van Rossum N.V., n.d.
[1941]. 128 p., 87 small portraits, 4-item bibliography, index.

Short history of 111 of the Netherlands' leading female singers
from Sophie Offermans-van Hove to Elizabeth Rutgers.

A0019. **de Brémont, Anna**. The Great Singers. New York [origi-
nally published in London by W.W. Gibbings]: Brentano's, 1892. 228 p.

Biographical sketches of eighteen singers from Mrs. Billington
to Jenny Lind. No Americans included. Based in part on publi-
cations not always identified.
Braham, Billington, Catalani, Manual del Popolo Garcia, Giuglini,
Grisi, Hayes, Lablache, Lind, Malibran, Mario, Parepa-Rosa, Pasta,
Rubini, Ronconi, Schroeder-Devrient, Sontag, Tietjens.

A0020. **de Courzon, Emmanuel Henri Parent**. Croquis d'artistes.
Paris: Librairie Fishbacher, 1898. xiv, 252 p., 16 portraits,
iconography.

Valuable coverage of sixteen singers who performed in France.
Pauline Viardot-Garcia, Miolan-Carvalho, Nilsson, Faure, Krauss,
Jean Lassalle, Maurel, Edmond Vergnet, Caron, Renaud, Albert
Saleza, Galli-Marie, Fugere, Alexandre Taskin, Adele Isaac,
van Zandt.

A0021. **Eby, Gordon M.** From the Beauty of Embers: a Musical
Aftermath. New York: Robert Speller & Sons, Publishers, Inc.,
1961. xvii, [8], 5-144, [4] p., 63 illus., index.

"This is a book about people, events, music and memories." A
between-the-lines journalistic pot pourri. Portions reprinted
from Opera News.
Special attention paid to Bori, Ponselle, Werrenrath, Jepson,
Mabel Garrison, Alda.

A0022. **Edwards, Henry Sutherland**. The Prima Donna: Her History

and Surroundings from the Seventeenth to the Nineteenth Century.
2 vols. London: Remington and Co Publishers, 1883. Reprint 1978.
320 p.; 302 p., indices.

Written for the semi-serious opera buff. Conversational in tone.
Volume One: Robinson, Fenton, Cuzzoni, Bordoni, Mingotti,
Gabrielli, Arnould, Mara, Catalani, Colbran, Sontag.
Volume Two: Lind, Bosio, Titiens, Patti, Lucca, Nilsson, Albani.

A0023. **Ehrlich, A.** [pseud. for Albert Payne]. Beruehmte
Saengerinnen der Vergangenheit und Gegenwart. Leipzig: Verlag
von A.H. Payne, n.d. [1895]. ix, 228 p., 90 portraits.

Short but good biographies of ninety-one singers. Important for
the minor figures covered. The author anticipated a revised and
expanded second edition which was never published. Could his
notes still exist?

A0024. **Escudier, Marie Pierre** and **Léon Escudier.** Etudes biogra-
phiques sur les chanteurs contemporains, précédées d'une esquisse
sur l'art du chant. Paris: Chez Just Tessier, 1840. 248 p.

In 4 sections: (1) Sur l'art du chant; (2) Artistes du Théatre-
Italien: Lablache, Rubini, Tamburini, Grisi, Persiani, Pauline
Garcia; (3) Artistes de L'Académie Royal de Musique: Duprez,
Dorus-Gras; (4) Artistes du Théatre de l'Opéra-Comique: Cinti-
Damoreau, Eugénie Garcia.

A0025. **Escudier, Marie Pierre Yves** and **Léon Escudier.** Vie et adventures des cantatrices célèbres; précédées des musiciens de
l'empire et suivies de la vie anecdotique de Paganini. Paris: E.
Dentu, Libraire-Editeur, 1856. 381 p.

A selection of twenty-two famous vocalists of the age.
Maupin, Favart, Arnould, Gonthier, Dugazon, Saint-Huberty, Saint-
Aubin, Maillard, Gavaudan, Branchu, Phillips, Catarina Gabrielli,
Mara, Banti, Billington, Grassini, Catalani, Mainvielle Fodor,
Pisaroni, Pasta, Sontag, Malibran.

A0026. **Fantoni, Gabriele.** Storia universale del canto. 2 vols.
Milano: Natale Battezzati, 1873. 308 p., index; 318 p., index, appendix
of famous names divided by sex and period from Luigi Alberti to M.
Werner.

An historical curiosity in which the facts are reworked to fit the
author's partialities.

A0027. **Farga, Franz.** Die goldene Kehle: Meistergesang aus drei
Jahrhunderten. Wien: Verlag A. Franz Goeth & Co., 1947. 315 p.,
63 illus., index.

A general history of singers in a popular format.

A002. **Fernandez, Dominique** and **Charles Dupêchez.** L'universe des
voix - les divas. Paris: Editions Ramsay, 1980. 189, [3] p.,

numerous illus.

Thirteen contemporary artists.
Flagstad, Tebaldi, Sutherland, Vichnevskaya, Stich-Randall,
Caballé, Schwarzkopf, Della Casa, Jurinac, Seefried, Gueden,
Lipp, Streich.

A0029   **Ferris, George T.** Great Singers: Faustina Bordoni to
Henrietta Sontag. first series. new revised edition. New York:
D. Appleton and Company, 1907 [1st edition 1879. Reprint 1972].
xii, 220 p., 4 portraits.

Based entirely upon other sources. Aspects of the lives of seven
legendary female vocalists. Bordoni, Gabrielli, Arnould,
Billington, Catalani, Pasta, Sontag.

A0030. **Ferris, George T.** Great Singers: Malibran to Materna.
second series. new revised edition. New York: D. Appleton and
Company, 1907 [1st edition 1881. Reprint 1972]. xiii, 264 p.,
6 portraits.

Again based upon other sources with twelve additional artists.
Malibran, Schroeder-Devrient, Grisi, Pauline Viardot, Persiani,
Alboni, Lind, Cruvelli, Titiens, Patti, Nilsson, Materna.

A0031. **Ferro, Enzo Valenti.** Las voces Teatro Colón 1908-1982.
Buenos Aires: Ediciones De Arte Gaglianone, 1983. 499 p., 361 illus.,
index of names, list of operas performed 1908-1982, 22-item bibliography.

Brief comments on 692 singers who appeared at this famous house
during the 20th century.

A0032. **Foppa, Tito Livio.** Diccionario teatral del Rio de la Plata.
Buenos Aires: Ediciones Del Carro De Tespis, 1961. 1046, [11] p.

The singer's biographies are contained in the first part of this
massive work, pp. 43-704.

A0033. **Gajoni-Berti, Alberto.** Celebri cantanti veronesi del 700
e dell'800. Verona: Soc. An. Ed. M. Bettinelli, 1949. 87 p., 14
illus.

Short articles on twenty-three singers the most famous of whom
are Maria Labia and Giovanni Zenatello.
Daniel Barba, Gustavo Lazzarini, Adelaide Malanotto-Montresor,
Giovanni Corsi, Maria Spezia, Gottardo Aldigheri, Zenone Berto-
lasi, Chiarina Faccio, Luigi Maurelli, Amelia Conti-Foroni,
Giacomo Ferrari, Luigi Rossato, Achille Moro, Fausta Labia, Maria
Labia, Giovanni Zenatello, Lucia Crestani, Carlo Caffetto, Linda
Cannetti, Silvano Isalberti, Giulia Tess, Giuseppina Zinetti,
Amadeo Alemanni.

A0034. **Gara, Eugenio.** Cantarono alla Scala. Milano: Teatro alla
Scala/Electa Editrice, 1975. 180, [1] p., index of names and

operas, 104 illus.

A selection of masters of bel canto who were stars at La Scala.
Rubini, Pasta, Lablache, Malibran, Strepponi, Mirate, Kashmann,
Patti, Tamagno, Bellincioni, Gayarre, Borgatti, Bonci, Caruso,
Ruffo, Pertile.

A0035. **Gattey, Charles Nelson.** Queens of Song. London: Barrie &
Jenkins Ltd., 1979. 248 p., 37 period prints and photographs.
90-item select bibliography, index.

Prima donnas from Francesca Caccini to Luisa Tetrazzini. The
bulk of this engaging book is devoted to Malibran, Lind, Patti,
Melba, Tetrazzini.

A0036. **Gourret, Jean T.** Encyclopedie cantarices de l'Opéra de
Paris. Preface by Francois Lesure. Paris: Editions Menges, 1981.
317 p., numerous illus., index, 63-item bibliography.

Biographies of 1,727 singers!

A0037. **Gourret, Jean T.** Histoire de l'Opéra de Paris 1669-1971
(portraits de chanteurs). Paris: Edition Albatros, 1977. 192 p.,
8 illus., 21-item bibliography.

Ninety-six singers are afforded coverage; eight are highlighted.
Gabriel Bacquier, Ernest Blanc, Michel Dens, Christiane Eda-
Pierre, Andrea Guist, Robert Massard, Mady Mesplé, and Alain
Vanzo.

A0038. **Gourret, Jean T.** with **Jean Gireudeau.** Dictionnaire des
chauteurs de l'Opéra de Paris. Paris: Editions Ablatros, 1982. 331 p.,
102 illus., 39-item bibliography, index.

Included are over 1,500 singers!

A0039. **Gourret, Jean T.** and **Jean Giraudeau.** Les prestigieux
tenors de l'Opéra de Paris. Paris: Le Sycmore Editions, 1980.
146 p., 73 illus.

Biographies of 115 French tenors!

A0040. **Grew, Sydney.** Makers of Music: the Story of Singers and
Instrumentalists. London: G.T. Foulis & Co. Ltd., 1924. 365 p.,
index, 15 portraits of 10 singers.

Includes singers during the period 1650-1850.
Siface, Ferri, Grimaldi, Catherine Tofts, Margherita de l'Epine,
Senesino, Cuzzoni, Bordoni, Farinelli, Todi, Mara, Banti,
Grassini, Braham, Catalani, Pasta, the Garcias, Albertazzi,
Clara Novello.

A0041. **Haas, Walter.** Nachtigall in Samt und Seide: das Leben der
grossen Primadonnen. Hamburg: Marion von Schroeder Verlag, 1969.
403 p., 65 illus.

A clever and readable mixture of journalism and fact aimed
at the general public.

A0042. **Haebock, Franz.** Die Kastraten und ihre Gesangskunst:
eine Gesangsphysiologische kultur- und musikhistorische Studie.
Stuttgart: Deutsche Verlags-Anstallt, 1927. xvii, 510 p., 98-item
bibliography, index.

THE standard historical work on all aspects of this vocal phenom-
enon. Impeccable scholarship. Author died before he could
complete his research and writing. Do his notes still exist?

A0043. **Hartog, Jacques.** Beroemde zangeressen. Amsterdam: J.M.
Muelenhoff, 1916. 315 p., 21 portraits.

Well written articles about twenty-three of the most famous women
vocalists from the period 1850-1916.
Albani, Arnoldson, Artôt, Barbi, Kathi Bettaque, Culp, Engelen-
Sewing, de Hahn-Manifarges, Lillian Henschel, Hill, Huhn,
Jachmann-Wagner, Joachim, Koenen, Lilli Lehmann, Lind, Lucca,
Mara, Noordewier-Reddingius, Offermans-Van Hove, Malvina Schnorr
von Carolsfeld, Sembrich, Sontag.

A0044. **Hedberg, Frans.** Svenska operasangare: karateristiker och
portraetter. Stockholm: C.E. Fritze's K. Hofbokhandel, 1885.
320 p., 32 illus.

Important Swedish opera stars from Jenny Lind to Dina Edling.
The twenty-two artists include their forerunners as well as their
foreign competition.
Lind, Guenther, Mathilde and Wilhelmina Gelhaar, Olof and
Charlotte Strandberg, Sandstroem, Michaeli, Walin, Stenhammer,
Willman, Uddman, Hebbe, Oscar Arnoldson, Arlberg, Labatt, Grabow,
Oedmann, Janzon, Ek, Lundqvist, Edling.

A0045. **Henderson, William James.** The Art of Singing. New York:
The Dial Press, 1937. Reprint 1978. xviii, 509 p., index.

Collated articles and excerpts from articles edited by Irving
Kolodin and Oscar Thompson. Part I is a reissue of The Art of
the Singer. 1906. Part II, over 60% of the book, contains evalu-
ations of many of the important singers of the period by one of
America's greatest vocal critics. Many artists included, but
there is prominent mention of twenty-three.
Calvé, Tetrazzini, Maria Labia, Pauline Viardot, Galli-Curci,
Patti, Caruso, Farrar, Maurel, Jean de Reszke, Marion Talley,
Jeritza, Louis Graveure, Lilli Lehmann, Hauk, Ponselle, Pons,
Melba, Scotti, Renaud, Sembrich, Flagstad, Schumann-Heink.

A0046. **Heriot, Angus.** The Castrati in Opera. London: John Calder
Ltd., 1960 [1st published 1956 by Martin Secker and Warburg Ltd.
Reprint 1974]. 243 p., 11 illus., 101-item bibliography, index.

Well researched and authoritative, this is still a basic study!

A0047. **Herzfeld, Friedrich.** <u>Magie der Stimme: die Welt des
Singens, der Oper und der grossen Saenger</u>. Berlin: Verlag Ull-
stein, 1961. 263 p., 92 illus., 121 music examples, 124-item
bibliography, index.

> Discusses 295 singers by period, type, and country as his method
> of evolving a cultural history.

A0048. **Hines, Jerome.** <u>Great Singers on Great Singing</u>. Garden
City: Doubleday & Company, Inc., 1982. 356 p., glossary.

> Interviews with thirty-nine singers plus a short statement by the
> author. One is tempted to question the "greatness" of all of the
> singers included, but Hines does come up with some marvelous
> practical insights as to just what singing is all about.
> Albanese, Alexander, Arroyo, Baum, Castel, Corelli, Cossotto,
> Crespin, Cruz-Romo, Deutekom, Domingo, Elvira, Evangelista,
> Gedda, Giaiotti, Horn, MacNeil, McCracken, Milanov, Milnes,
> Moffo, Munsel, Nilsson, Olivero, Pavarotti, Peerce, Peters,
> Plishka, Ponselle, Quilico, Robinson, Sereni, Shane, Sills,
> Stevens, Sutherland, Talvela, Verrett, Zakariasen.

A0049. **Honolka, Kurt.** <u>Die grossen Primadonnen von der Bordoni
bis zur Callas</u>. Stuttgart: Cotta-Verlag, 1960. 288 p., 51 illus.

> Another attempt to place the singer in the broader context of
> cultural history.

A0050. **Jacobson, Robert M.** with photographs by **Christian
Steiner.** <u>Opera people</u>. Introduction by Michael Scott. New York:
The Vendome Press, 1982. 112 p.

> Gorgeous photographs, mostly in color, of twenty-nine well-known
> singers. A worthwhile coffee table conversation piece.
> Sutherland, Schwarzkopf, Domingo, Callas, Jessye Norman, de los
> Angeles, Horne, Carreras, Tebaldi, Price, Milnes, Verrett,
> Pavarotti, Scotto, Freni, Kraus, Sills, von Stade, Troyanos,
> Ludwig, Te Kanawa, Jones, Baker, Bumbry, Ghiaurov, Resnik,
> Tourel, Nilsson, Gedda.

A0051. **Klein, Herman.** <u>Great Woman-Singers of My Time</u>. Forward
by Ernest Newman. London: George Routledge & Sons, Ltd., 1931. Reprint
1968. vi, 244 p., 16 portraits, index.

> A prominent English critic shares his personal evaluations of
> twenty-six singers with a bias toward 19th century artists.
> Tietjens, Patti, Lucca, Nilsson, Di Murska, Trebelli, Albani,
> Nordica, Sembrich, Melba, Calvé, Alboni, Janet Patey, Sofia
> Scalchi, Giulia Ravogli, Schumann-Heink, Sterling, Materna,
> Brandt, Sucher, Vogl, Hedwig Reicher-Kindermann, Thérèse Malten,
> Lilli Lehmann, Klaksky, Ternina.

A0052. **Kobbé, Gustav.** <u>Ten Opera Singers: a Pictorial Souvenir with
Biographies of the Most Famous Singers of the Day</u>. 4th ed., Boston:
Oliver Ditson Company, 1906 [1st edition 1901]. 94 p., 152 portraits

and illustrations.

Biographies were furnished by the singers themselves. Excellent photographs, many from the studio of Aime Dupont and E.W. Histed. Caruso, Eames, and Ternina have been added to those who appeared in the original edition.
Calvé, Caruso, Eames, Melba, Nordica, Schumann-Heink, Sembrich, Ternina, Jean de Reszke, Edouard de Reszke.

A0053. **Kohut, Adolph**. Die Gesangskoeniginnen in den letzten drei Jahrhunderten. 2 vols. Berlin: Verlag Hermann Kuhz, n.d. [1906]. 236 p., 19 portraits; 255 p., 42 portraits.

Articles of some length about sixty-four singers from Marthe le Rochois to Schumann-Heink.

A0054. **Kopecký, Emanuel** and **Vilém Pospišil**. Slavní pěvci národního Divalda. Praha: Panton Praha, 1968. 223, [6] p., 120 illus.

Valuable information about thirty-two singers who are difficult to trace elsewhere.
Karel Burianovi, Emil Burianovi, Jan Konstantin, Ema Destinnová, Otakar Mařák, Gabriela Horvátová, Amálie Bobková, Kamila Ungrová, Theodor Schuetz, Richard Kubla, Miloslav Jeník, Otakar Masák, Jiří Huml, Emil Pollert, Olga Borová-Valoušková, Ada Nordenová, Vladimír Tomš, Karel Hruška, Mila Kočova, Stanislav Muž, Jan Berlík, Jindrich Blaziček, Ota Horáková, Marie Budikova, Marta Krásová, Zdeněk Otava, Marie Podvalová, Beno Blachut, Eduard Haken, Vaclav Bednár, Marja Tauberová, Vilem Zítek.

A0055. **Krause, Ernst**, ed. Opera Saenger: 44 Portraets aus der Welt des Musiktheaters. Berlin: Henschelverlag, 1963. 152 p., 44 portraits.

2nd edition 1965. 162 p., 48 portraits.
Biographies of singers who have starred in the opera houses of the DDR.

A0056. **Krause, Ernst** and **Marion Schoene**, eds. Opernsaenger: sechzig Portraets. Berlin: Henschelverlag, 1979. 183 p., 60 portraits, list of major roles for each artist.

This is actually the 3rd edition of A0055.

A0057. **Kuehner, Hans**. Grosse Saengerinnen der Klassik und Romantik: ihre Kunst, ihre Groesse, ihre Tragik. Stuttgart: Victoria Verlag Martha Koerner, 1954. 326 p., 10 portraits, 101-item bibliography, index.

Detailed articles of about sixty pages each on Mara, Sontag, Malibran, Schroeder-Devrient, Lind. There is an earlier edition, Genien des Gesanges aus dem Zeitalter der Klassik und Romantik, published in 1951 which I have not seen.

A0058. **Kutsch, K.J.** and **Leo Riemens.** Unvergaengliche Stimmen: Saengerlexikon. 3rd revised and enlarged edition. Bern: A. Francke AG Verlag, 1975 [1st edition 1962. 2nd edition 1966. See also A0059 and A0060]. 731 p.

> THE standard lexikon for over 2,000 concert and operatic artists who have recorded. Capsule biographies including the names of record companies with whom the artist has worked. Occasional bibliographic references. Information should be cross checked!

A0059. **Kutsch, K.J.** and **Leo Riemens.** Unvergaengliche Stimmen: Saengerlexikon. Erganzungsband. Bern: A. Francke AG Verlag, 1979. 263 p.

> Over 800 additional artists are included plus a fifty page section of addenda and corrigenda.

A0060. **Kutsch, K.J.** and **Leo Riemens.** A Concise Biographical Dictionary of Singers from the Beginning of Recorded Sound to the Present. Translated, expanded and annotated by Harry Earl Jones. Philadelphia: Chilton Book Company, 1969. xxiv, 487 p., notes for users, glossary of terms, abbreviations of record labels, principal operas, operettas, composers referred to in the text, principal "name" opera houses, principal music festivals.

> This expanded, almost 1,500 entries as opposed to 1,000+, version of the 2nd edition of A0058 must rate as a new work.

A0061. **Lahee, Henry C.** Famous Singers of Today and Yesterday. Boston: L.C. Page and Company, 1898 [revised and expanded edition, 1936]. ix, 337 p., 12 illus., preface includes nine bibliographic references, chronological table of famous singers, index.

> Concise, popular format history of singers based upon earlier sources.

A0062. **Lahee, Henry C.** The Grand Opera Singers of Today: an Account of the Leading Operatic Stars Who Have Sung During Recent Years, Together with a Sketch of the Chief Operatic Enterprises. new revised edition. Boston: The Page Company Publishers, 1922 [1st edition 1912]. x, 543 p., 48 illus., index.

> Traces the history of American opera houses from 1903 covering each leading singer as s/he appeared. Metropolitan Opera, Manhatten Opera, Boston Opera, and Chicago-Philadelphia Company.

A0063. **Lancellotti, Arturo.** Le voci d'oro. 3rd revised and enlarged edition [no record of 1st edition. 2nd edition 1942]. Roma: Fratelli Palombi Editori, n.d. [1953]. 407 p., 26 illus., 53-item bibliography.

> Biographies of twenty singers from Luigi Lablache to Rosetta Pampini.
> Lablache, Malibran, Mario, Cotogni, Patti, Gayarre, Masini, Tamagno, Giuseppe Kaschmann, Checco Marconi, Battistini, Fernando

de Figueiredo, M.M. Quintela, J.P. Quintela, O'Neill, Celestino,
Nilo, M. Quintela, Garrigues, M.P. Quintela, Miró, H. Lisboa,
Oliver, Lisboa, C. O'Neill, M.J. de Almeida, J. Vieira, Veiga,
Gazul, de Macedo, X. Vieira, A. de Andrade, Nascimento, F. d'
Andrade, Marcelo, D.J. de Almeida, Lopes, Conde, Raquete, Rosa.

A0076. **Natan, Alex.** Primadonna: Lob der Stimmen. Basil: Basilius
Presse, 1962. 142 p., 96 illus., discography of 33 1/3 and 45 rpm
releases as of April 1961.

Critical evaluations of fifty of the premiere female vocalists
of this century. Superb photographs.

A0077. **Natan, Alex.** Primo Uomo: grosse Saenger der Oper. Basil:
Basilius Presse, 1963. 154 p., 92 illus., biographical section
with an incomplete listing of biographies, discography.

Critical evaluation of fifty outstanding male singers who have
appeared on LP recordings. Again, the photographs are excellent
and the discography for 1963 merits some attention.

A0078. Onze musici: portretten en biografieën. Rotterdam:
Nijgh & Van Ditmar's Uitgevers-Mij. n.d. [c.1910]. 303 p.,
145 illus.

146 short biographies including singers. Excellent for obscure
Dutch artists.

A0079. Opera Stars. Moscow: State Publishing House, n.d. unpaginated
[18] p., 65 illus.

Twenty-six Soviet opera stars are represented.
Nadezhda Obukhova, Alexander Pirogov, Ivan Kozlovsky, Maxim
Mikhailov, Mark Reisen, Nikandr Khanaya, Mikhail Grishko, Sergi
Lemeshev, Sophia Preobrazhenskaya, Boris Gmyrya, Goar Gasparyan,
Halima Nasyrova, Byul-Byul Mamedov, Pavel Lisitsian, Tiit Kuusik,
Larisa Alexandrovskaya, Pystr Amiranashvili, Mamanjan Kulieva,
Ivan Petrov, Germaine Heine-Wagner, Lydia Myasnikova, Irina
Maslennikova, Yermek Serkebayev, Galina Vishnevskaya, Saira
Kiibayeva, Khanifa Mavlyanova.

A0080. **Padoan, Paolo.** Profili di cantanti lirici veneti.
Introduction by Giacomo Lauri-Volpi. Bologna: Bongiovanni
Editore, 1978. 209 p., 27 illus., individual discographies by
Daniele Rubboli.

Navarrini, Garbin, F. Labia, M. Labia, Agostini, Storchio, Adami,
Zenatello, Cannetti, Molinari, Galelli, Pertile, Martinelli,
Granforte, Rimini, Capuzzo, Dalla Rizza, Albanese, dal Monte,
Tocchio, Reali, Biasini, Lugo, Malapiero, Rasa, Rizzieri, Pobbe,
Carteri, Bruson.

A0081. **Pahlen, Kurt.** Grosse Saenger unserer Zeit. Wien: Bertelsmann Sachbuchverlag, 1972. 288 p., 21 illus., 40-item bibliography, index of names.

NOTE: There is an Argentinian edition, <u>Grandes cantantes de</u>
<u>nuestra tempo</u>. Buenos Aires: Emecé Editores, n.d. [1973].
334 p., 73 illustrations from private sources.
The original edition is a once-over-lightly. The Argentinian
version is an improvement because of the illustrations.

A0082. **Pavolini, Luisa**, ed. <u>Le grandi voci: dizionario critico-</u>
<u>biografico dei cantanti con discografia operistica</u>. Roma: Instituto
Per La Collaborazione Culturale, 1964. xiv, 1044 p., 48 illus., list
of recorded complete operas, list of recorded operatic excerpts.

Biographies of over 300 singers including essential career dates
and an up-to-date operatic discography. Each biography also has
a critical evaluation of vocal and artistic quality by a recognized authority. This is a STANDARD WORK of its kind.
NOTE: There exists an MS English translation of the greater
portion of this dictionary.

A0083. **Peltz, Mary Ellis**. <u>Spotlights on the Stars: Intimate</u>
<u>Sketches of Metropolitan Opera Personalities</u>. New York: The
Metropolitan Opera Guild, Inc., 1943. 114 p., 63 illus., index.

Material on forty-three artists on the 1942-43 MET roster plus a
paragraph each for forty-six other company personnel. Much of
this material originally appeared in <u>Opera News</u>.

A0084. **Phillipi, Felix**. <u>Die muenchener Oper: 12 Portraits mit</u>
<u>Text</u>. Muenchen: Verlagsanstalt fuer Kunst und Wissenschaft, 1884.
74, [12] p., 12 portraits.

Marie Basta, Victoria Blank, Lilli Dressler, Anton Fuchs, Eugen
Gura, Emilie Herzog, August Kindermann, Franz Nachbar, Gustav
Siehr, Heinrich Vogl, Therese Vogl, Mathilde Wekerlin.

A0085. **Pleasants, Henry**. <u>The Great Opera Singers from the Dawn of</u>
<u>Opera to Our Own Time</u>. New York: Simon and Schuster, 1966. 333 p.,
147 illus., glossary, 96-item bibliography, index.

Seventy great singers in historical perspective "who seem to have
contributed most importantly to the decisive phases in the evolu-
tion of the vocal art." Still THE basic history in English.

A0086. **Poessiger, Guenter**. <u>Die grossen Saenger und Dirigenten</u>.
Muenchen: Wilhelm Heyne Verlag, 1968. 220 p., 55 illus., 21-item
bibliography.

Small, popular lexicon which includes short biographies of 151
20th century recorded vocal artists. Understandably weighted to
German language singers. Fifty-five conductors are included.

A0087. **Pougin, Arthur**. <u>Figures d'Opéra-Comique: Madame Dugazon,</u>
<u>Elleviou, les Gavaduan</u>. Paris: Tresse, Editeur, 1875. Reprint 1973.
234 p., 3 portraits.

Sympathetic coverage of six late 18th century French singers. Les

Gavaduan include Adelaide, Alexandrinne-Marie, Emilie, and Jean-Baptiste-Sauveur.

A0088. **Pyjol, Ramon**. Mundo lirico: semblanzas biograficas de primerismas figuras de la opera. Barcelona: Ediciones Rondas, 1965. 206 p., 71 illus.

The thirty-five biographies are primarily devoted to singers who have appeared in Spain during the last four decades.
Caniglia, Caruso, Pederzini, Favero, Stignani, Caspir, Lázaro, Callas, Zeani, Gencer, Sutherland, Flagstad, Nilsson, Varnay, Lorenz, Windgassen, Tebaldi, Petrella, Barbieri, Simionato, Corelli, del Monaco, di Stefano, Tagliavini, Raimondi, Bergonzi, Guichandut, Vinay, Bechi, Guelfi, Rossi-Lemeni, Changalovich, Schwarzkopf, Stich-Randall, de los Angeles.

A0089. **Rasponi, Lanfranco**. The Last Prima Donnas. New York: Alfred A. Knopf, 1982. xv, [ii], 633 p., 56 portraits.

In-depth coverage of fifty-six singers by voice and/or role type. Certainly one of the finest more recent books of its kind.

A0090. **Reissig, Elisabeth**. Erlebte Opernkunst: Bilder und Gestalten der Berliner Staatsoper. erste und zweite folge. Berlin: Oesterheld Co. Verlag, 1928. 98 p., 12 illus.; 132, [1] p., 16 illus.

Edition limited to 500.
A musical connoisseur's observations of one of the great operatic ensembles of that time.
Erste folge: Barbara Kemp, Delia Reinhardt, Michael Bohnen, Josef Mann.
Zweite folge: Frieda Leider, Margarete Arndt-Ober, Fritz Soot, Friedrich Schoor, Heinrich Schlusnus, Tino Pattiera, Richard Tauber, Tilly de Garmo, Leo Schuetzendorf, Wlademar Henke.

A0091. **Rich, Maria F.**, ed. Who's Who in Opera: An International Biographical Dictionary of Singers, Conductors, Directors, Designers, and Administrators, also Including Profiles of 101 Opera Companies. New York: Arno Press, 1976. xxi, 684 p.

An absolutely monumental compilation which includes over 2,300 biographies from Abbado to Zylis-Gara. That last name always guarantees the final spot on the program! With the biographical information current as of the 1974-75 season, 1,553 singers are to be found with 497 sopranos, 197 mezzos, 351 tenors, and 508 baritones and basses. What more can anyone say?

A0092. **Rogers, Francis**. Some Famous Singers of the 19th Century. New York: The H.W. Gray Company, 1914. Reprint 1977. 128 p., 10 illus.

Conversational essays on fifteen singers which originally appeared in The New Music Reivew.
The Garcias (father, son, Maria, and Pauline), Catalani, Pasta,

Lablache, Rubini, Nourrit, Duprez, Sontag, Lind, Grisi, Mario, Tamburini.

A0093. **Rosenthal, Harold.** Sopranos of Today: Studies of Twenty-five Opera Singers. London: John Calder, 1956. 103 p., 64 illus.

Artists admired by the editor of Opera. Portions of the text are from previously published material. A brief list of records follows each study.
de los Angeles, Borkh, Brouwenstijn, Callas, Della Casa, Cross, Fisher, Flagstad, Goltz, Gruemmer, Gueden, Hammond, Jurinac, Adele Leigh, Milanov, Moedl, Elsie Morrison, Pons, Schwarzkopf, Seefried, Shuard, Steber, Tebaldi, Varnay, Welitsch.

A0094. **Rosenthal, Harold.** Great Singers of Today. London: Calder and Boyars Ltd., 1966. Reprint 1977. 212 p., 226 illus.

General observations on fifty-five female and forty-five male artists who were personally heard and evaluated by the author. The commentary on the sopranos was reprinted from entry A0093. The author himself correctly suggests that this particular work falls between a "book of reference and a book of critical studies."

A0095. **Rosenthal, Harold.** The Golden Age of Singing. London: The Gramophone Company Limited, n.d. [c.1956]. 36 p., 55 illus.

Short biographical notes on fifty-six singers ranging from Caruso to Leonard Warren.

A0096. **Rubboli, Daniele.** Chronache de voci modenesi. Milano: nuove edizioni, 1981. 101, [6] p., 46 illus., discographies for 20 singers, index.

114 singers mentioned. Very important for at least eight artists. Luigia Boccabadati, Teresina Chelotti, Aristide Aneschi, Vincenzo Guicciard, Arrigo Pola, Anni Cinquanta, Freni, Pavaroti.

A0097. **Rubboli, Daniele.** Le voci raccontate (Ferrara 1200-1977). Bologna: Bongiovanni Editore, 1976. 202, [14] p., 48 illus.,

Twenty-six individual discographies by Gino Bergamasco. Coverage of 226 singers.

A0098. **Sánchez-Torres, Enrique.** Fleta, Lázaro, Schipa, Anselmi: críitica y versos con opiniones importantes. Madrid: Imp. B. Izaguirre, 1924. 120 p., numerous illustrations.

Of little importance. Discusses a "Conferencia-concierto" which took place in Madrid December 29, 1922. Some performance details and comparisons. Theodorini, Massini, Stagno, and Gayarre are among the more famous artists mentioned.

A0099. **Sargeant, Winthrop.** Divas. New York: Coward, McCann & Geoghegan, Inc., 1973. 192 p., 44 illus.

Most of this material is adapted from articles which first appeared in The New Yorker.
Sutherland, Horne, Sills, Nilsson, Price, Farrell.

A0100. **Scanzoni, Signe von**. Richard Strauss und seine Saenger: eine Plauderei ueber das Musiktheater in den Wind gesprochen. Muenchen: Walter Ricke, 1961. 95 p.

Fascinating insights into the vocal ideas of Strauss in relation to the singers with whom he worked. Incorporates interviews. Horst Taubmann, Franz Klarwein, Hans Hotter, Annelies Kupper, Hildegarde Ranczak, Viorica Ursuleac.

A0101. **Scott, Michael**. The Record of Singing to 1914. New York: Charles Scribner's Sons, 1977. xii, 243 p., 209 illus. from the Stuart-Liff Collection, glossary of vocal terms, 123-item select bibliography, index.

Another absolutely monumental work which is already a classic in the field. Patti through Chaliapin.

A0102. **Scott, Michael**. The Record of Singing, Volume II: 1914–1925. London: Gerald Duckworth & Co., Ltd., 1979. 262 p., 191 illus. from the Stuart-Liff Collection, 129-item bibliography, notes, index of names.

Continues the high quality of A0101. Makes one seriously question whether or not the author can complete his magnum opus in one more volume as projected.

A0103. **Seeger, Horst** (Mitarbeit fuer die Gebeite Opernfiguren und -zitate: **Eberhard Schmidt**). Opern Lexikon. Wilhelmshaven: Heinrichshofen's Druck, 1979. 6, 11–598 p.

This dictionary is included as opposed to a number of others which are perhaps better known and more widely available because of the extensive coverage of Communist Block artists about whom information is not readily available.

A0104. **Sguerzi, Angelo**. Le stirpi canore. Bologna: Edizioni Bongiovanni, 1978. 223 p., index of names.

Over 500 singers mentioned. Thirty-two artists highlighted. Berganza, Bergonzi, Bruscantini, Callas, Christoff, Corelli, Cossotto, Dalla Rizza, dal Monte, di Stefano, Domingo, Favero, Flagstad, Freni, Gedda, Gencer, Gigli, Lauri-Volpi, Nilsson, Olivero, Pagliughi, Pertile, Schipa, Schwarkopf, Siepi, Simionato, Stabile, Stignani, Taddei, Tebaldi, Varrett, Warren.

A0105. **Simpson, Harold**. Singers to Remember. Lingfield (Surrey): The Oakwood Press, n.d. [1972]. 223 p.

Brief articles on ninety-eight singers with suggested recordings. Quite helpful for lesser known artists.

A0106. **Smântânescu, Dan,** ed. Portrete se autoportrete: cintăreti români. Bucuresti: Editura Muzicala, 1974. 230 p., 33 illus.

 Zina De Nori, Aca de Barbu, Jenu Ciolac, Maria Snejina, Alexander Alger, D. Mihailescu-Toscani, Pia Igy-Delin.

A0107. **Steane, J.B.** The Grand Tradition: Seventy Years of Singing on Record. New York: Charles Scribner's Sons, 1974. xii, 628 p., 138 illus., appendix, select bibliography, composer's index, index of names.

 A real labor of competency and love. Indispensible.

A0108. **Steinitzer, Max.** Meister des Gesangs. Berlin: Schuster & Loeffler, 1920. 230 p., 38-item bibliography, index of names.

 High quality, gentlemanly tour through the arena of notable singers.

A0109. **Stephens, Robert N.** Queens of Song. Troy: Nims and Knight, n.d. [1889]. unpaginated.

 A series of ten etched portraits (mounted India proof) by Kirk-patrick, F.L. & C.A. Worrall. Each portrait has a two page literary sketch of the artist by Stephens. This is a high class souvenir of the time with beautiful engravings.

A0110. **Strantz, Ferdinand von.** Persoenliche Erinnerungen an beruehmte Saengerinnen des XIX. Jahrhunderts. Berlin: Hermann Lazarus, 1906. 44 p.

 Schroeder-Devrient, Grisi, Persiani, Stoltz, Lind, Sontag, Viardot-Garcia, Mara, Johanna Wagner [-Jachmann], Ken, Lucca, Patti, Materna, Artôt, Mallinger, Reicher-Kindermann, Renaud, Sucher, Brandt, Lilli Lehmann.

A0111. **Tegani, Ulderico.** Cantanti di una volta. Milano: Valsecchi Editore, 1945. 334 p.

 Journalistic coverage of a personal selection of forty-one artists only some of whom were personally heard by the author. Tamagno, Battistini, Scialiapin, Malibran, Mario, Barbara Marchesio, Carlotta Marchesio, Patti, Maurel, Isabella Galletti-Gianoli, Caruso, Tetrazzini, Strepponi, Tamberlik, Gayarre, Romilda Pantaleoni, Cotogni, Bellincioni, Stagno, Marconi, Pisaroni, Pasta, Frezzolini, Brambilla, Erminia Borghi-Mamo, Masini, Stolz, Rubini, Ruffo, Zenatello, Stracciari, Barbieri Nini, Pietro Cesari, Edoardo Garbin, Sontag, Felice Varesi, Fancelli, Maddalena Mariani-Masi, Cavalieri, Borgati, Giuseppe Krismer.

A0112. **Thompson, Oscar.** The American Singer: a Hundred Years of Success in Opera. New York: The Dial Press, 1937. 426 p., 108 illus., 4 appendices concerning first appearances of American singers.

A landmark work which put the emergence of the American singer into perspective.

A0113. **Thurner, A.** Les reines de chant. Paris: A. Hennuyer, Imprimeur-Editeur, 1883. 335 p., 4 engravings by E. Abot.

A basic study of sixty-one 17th, 18th, and 19th century vocalists from Francesca Caccini to the author's contemporaries.

A0114. **Tubeuf, André.** Le chant retrouvé: sept divas, renaissance de l'Opéra. Paris: Librairie Arthème Fayard, 1979. 271 p., illus., discography.

Caballé, Crespin, Jurinac, Rysanek, Swarzkopf, Sutherland, and Varnay are individually saluted for reviving the 19th century 'bel canto' school of singing.

A0115. **Tubeuf, André,** ed. Les introuvables du chant wagnérien. Paris: L'Avant-Scène Opéra, 1984. 189, [6] p., illus.

Forty-four Wagnerian singers are covered to a greater or lesser degree plus an interview with Hans Hotter ("Hans Hotter, le long voyage de Wotan") by the author.
Austral, Bockelmann, Arthur Endrèze, Flagstad, Fuchs, Anny Helm, Hotter, Husch, Janssen, Alfred Jerger, Journet, Kipnis, Klose, Larsen-Todsen, Rudolf Laubenthal, Lawrence, Lehmann, Leider, Lemnitz, List, Lorenz, Lubin, Martinelli, Melchoir, Maria Muller, Hans Nissen, Herrmann, Maria Olszewska, Pertile, Gotthelf Pistor, Ralf, Maria Reining, Rethberg, Rosvaenge, Emil Schipper, Schorr, Schumann, Meta Seinemeyer, Singer, Hina Spani, Thill, Ludwig Weber, Walter Widdop, Marcel Wittrisch, Fritz Wolff.

A0116. **Tuggle, Robert.** The Golden Age of Opera with the Photographs of Herman Mishkin. Forward by Anthony Bliss. New York: Holt, Rinehart and Winston, 1983. x, 246 p., 181 illus., notes on newspaper citations, index.

Includes ninety-nine singers from Bonci to Bori. A coffee table delight for the centennial year of the Metropolitan Opera.

A0117. **Ulrich, Homer.** Famous Women Singers. New York: Dodd, Mead & Company, 1953. 127 p., 15 illus., index.

Fifteen life stories from Jenny Lind to Dorothy Kirsten geared to the younger reader.
Lind, Patti, Nordica, Sembrich, Calvé, Melba, Schumann-Heink, Garden, Farrar, Galli-Curci, Flagstad, Anderson, Pons, Stevens, Kirsten.

A0118. **Van Hemel, Viktor.** De zangkunst. tweede vermeerderde druk. Antwerpen: Cupids-Uitgaven, n.d. [1958]. 112 p., 20 illus., discography, index, 50-item bibliography.

Elementary biographies of eighty-five singers from seventeen countries. Leo Riemens mentioned an earlier edition published during the 1940's which I have never seen.

A0119. **Van Vechten, Carl.** <u>Interpreters</u>. revised edition. New
York: Alfred A. Knopf, 1920 [1st edition 1917. Reprint 1977].
201 p., 16 illus.

   A highly sensible evaluation of the strengths and weaknesses of
   six singers (plus Nijinsky) by one of America's more articulate
   and intelligent critics.
   Fremstad, Farrar, Garden, Chaliapine, Mariette Mazarin, Yvette
   Guilbert.

A0120. **Weissmann, Adolf.** <u>Die Primadonna</u>. Berlin: Paul Cassirer,
1920. 228 p., 31 illus., index.

   This is more in the way of a general history of singers and is not
   strictly confined to women. The plates are excellent.

PART B.

COLLECTIVE WORKS:
Related Books

B0001. **Alcari, C.** Parma nella musica. Parma: M. Fresching, 1931.
259 p.

Biographical dictionary of famous musicians from Parma including
singers.

B0002. **Aldrich, Richard.** Concert Life in New York 1902-1923. New
York: G.P. Putnam's Sons, 1941. Reprint 1971. 795 p., index, list of
Sunday New York Times articles.

Reviews of all important vocalists who concertized in New York
City between 1902 and 1923 by a highly respected professional.
The index references most of the reviews.

B0003. **Arditi, Luigi.** My Reminiscences. 2nd edition. London:
Skeffington and Son, 1896. Reprint 1977. xxv, 352 p., 38 illus.,
appendices include a complete list of Arditi's compositions up to
the year 1896, arrangements, operas produced, singers who appeared
under his direction.

All indications are that this is an edited translation with
additions from Arditi's notes in Italian by Baroness von
Zedlitz. Very valuable source for singers during the last
half of the 19th century.

B0004. **Armitage, Merle.** Accents on Life. Forward by John Charles
Thomas. Ames: The Iowa State University Press, 1964. xv, 386 p.,
53 illus.

Memoirs of a multi-talented impresario who was an associate of
Charles L. Wagner.
McCormack, Galli-Curci, Ponselle, Garden, Chaliapin, Guilbert,
Jeritza.

B0005. **Batten, Joe.** The Story of Sound Recording. London:
Rockliff, 1956. xiv, 201 p., 30 illus., 3 appendices including
"Recording Artistes' First Engagements, 1904-1914," index.

Memoirs of a pioneer recording manager.

B0006. **Bennett, John R.** Smetana on 3000 Records. London: The

Oakwood Press, 1974. 465 p., portrait, musical examples, instrumental and choral recordings, singers register, instrumental and
choral register.

 Biographies of fifty-one famous and obscure Czech singers in
 the section "Singers Recordings," pp. 279-408. Most of this
 material is unavailable in English elsewhere.

B0007. **Bennett, Joseph.** Forty Years of Music 1865-1905. London:
Methuen & Co., 1908. xvi, 415 p., 24 illus., index.

 Rather boring but it does provide necessary background for the
 period which includes some outstanding vocalists.

B0008. **Bernhardt, Adelheid.** Aus dem Dresdner Hoftheater: biographische Skizzen. Dresden: Commissions-Verlag von E. Pierson's
Buchhandlung, 1882. iv, 154 p.

 Includes the biographies of thirteen mostly unknown singers.
 Wuellner, Otto-Alvsleben, Schuch-Proska, Prochaska, Reuther,
 Riese, Gudehus, Eichberger, Marchion, Degele, Decarli, Bulss, Erl.

B0009. **Blaze de Bury, Ange Henri.** Musiciens contemporains. Paris:
Michel Lévy frères, 1856. xvi, 289 p.

 Nourrit, Pasta, Malibran, Sontag.

B0010. **Bragaglia, Leonardo.** Verdi e i suoi interpreti (1839-1978):
vita scenica delle opere del cigno di busseto attraverso una antologia
critica e uno studio delle ventotto opere di Giuseppe Verdi. Roma:
Bulzoni Editore, 1979. 375, [3] p., numerous illus., index of names.

 Over 500 important interpreters of Verdian roles.

B0011. **Brown, Maynard,** ed. Operatic and Dramatic Album. London: E.
Matthews & Sons, n.d. [c.1877]. unpaginated, 61 illus.

 Thirty-one singers are included among fifty-three artists. Large
 folio with a full-page lithograph of each artist. This appears to
 be a subscription publication.
 Patti, Campanini, Tietjen, Santley, Sterling, Nilsson, Fauré,
 Albani, Ostava Torriani, Lemmens-Skeirington, Reeves, Cora Stuart,
 Allan James Foli, Zélea Terbelli, Gayarre, Zare Talberg, Sophie
 Scalchi, Kate Santley, Gerster, Anna d'Angeri, Blanche Cole,
 Julia Gaylord, Hortense Synnerberg, La Ferriere, de Belocca, del
 Puente, Giuseppe Francelli, Marie Roze, Alwina Valleria, Edward
 Lloyd, John Howson.

B0012. **Buffen, Frederick F.** Musical Celebrities. London: Chapman
& Hall, Limted, 1889. 116 p., 18 illus.

 Journalism. Based upon interviews which first appeared in The
 Lady. Quality souvenir with outstanding portraits.
 Patti, Sembrich, Reeves, Henschel.

B0013. **Buffen, Frederick, F.** <u>Musical Celebrities. second series</u>.
London: Chapman & Hall, Limited, 1893. viii, 125 p., 25 illus.

    Twenty-five articles which include Albani, Melba, Nordica,
Ella Russell, Edward B. Scovel, Marie Rôze, Zélie de Lussan,
Eames, Fanny Moody, Ernestina Ponti, Alwina Valleria, Hauk,
Calvé, Marie Brema, Emma Nevada, Giulia Ravogli, Sophia
Ravogli, Jean de Reszke, Edouard de Reszke.

B0014. **Burney, Charles.** <u>A General History of Music from the
Earliest Ages to the Present Period</u>. vol. 4. London: Payne and
Son, 1789. ii, 685, [2], [13], [1] p., list of music books,
index, errata.

    First-hand observations about singers during the end of the
Baroque Italian opera.

B0015. **Cairns, David.** <u>Responses: Musical Essays and Reviews.</u>
New York: Alfred A. Knopf, Inc., 1973. xiv, 266 p., musical
examples.

    Expanded and edited from previously published articles, the author
shares his sensitive understanding and penetrating analysis of a
few vocal artists.
Geraint Evans, Brouwenstijn, Vickers, Hotter, Sutherland,
Fischer-Dieskau, Elisabeth Schumann.

B0016. **Caputo, Pietro.** <u>Cotogni, Lauri-Volpi e ...: breve storia
della scuola vocale romana</u>. Bologna: Edizioni Bongiovanni, 1980. 151
p., 16 illus., list of appearances of 34 major artists at the Rome
Opera, 26-item bibliography.

    Among many singers, the folowing are given special attention:
Battistini, Corelli, Cotogni, Fineschi, Lauri-Volpi, Raimondi,
Rossi-Lemeni, Stabile, Taddei, Tucci.

B0017. **Cattaeno, Pieralberto.** <u>Il bel canto</u>. Bergamo: Grafica
Gutenberg Editrice, 1979. 157, [2] p., 129 illus., 59-item bibliography.

    There are bibliographic notes with each chapter. Devoted to the
outstanding vocalists who performed with the Teatro alla Scala
during the past two hundred years.

B0018. **Chorley, Henry F.** <u>Music and Manners in France and Germany: a Series of Travelling Sketches of Art and Society</u>. 3 vols.
London: Longman, Brown, Green, and Longmans, 1844. Reprint 1983.
viii, 299 p.; viii, 302 p.; xii, 299 p.

    First-hand accounts of such artists as Mara, Nourrit, Schroeder-
Devrient, Tichatschek.

B0019. **Chorley, Henry F.** <u>Thirty Years' Musical Recollections</u>.
Edited by Ernest Newman. New York: Alfred A. Knopf, 1926. Reprint
1983. xxv, 411 p., portrait, index.

Invaluable for mid-19th century (1830-1859) singers. Remarks
about thirteen major and many lesser figures. The original two
volume edition was published in London in 1863.
Malibran, Lablache, Rubini, Grisi, Pasta, Persiani, Mario, Lind,
Alboni, Ronconi, Pauline Viardot, Sontag, Ristori.

BO020. **Cook, Ida** and **Louise Cook**. We Followed Our Stars. New
York: William Morrow & Comapny, 1950. 246 p., 17 illus.

The story of two opera lovers out to have a good time. Interesting
insights. Lack of an index unfortunate. Period from Galli-Curci
to World War II. The authors extended their story in an update
published in Toronto in 1976 which I have not seen.

BO021. **Cox, Rev. T.J.** Musical Recollections of the Last Half
Century. 2 volumes. London: Tinsley Brothers, 1872. xv, 345 p.;
vi, 370 p.

Much of this material was first published in Tinsley's Magazine
and covers the period 1818-1867. Not the result of personal
observations and evaluations, the author depended upon these
publications: Quarterly Musical Magazine and Review (1818-1828);
The Harmonicon (1823-1833); and The Athenaeum, the Times, and
the Spectator for the remaining years.

BO022. **Culshaw, John.** Ring Resounding: the Recording in Stereo of
'Der Ring des Nibelungen'. London: Secker & Warburg, 1967. 284 p.,
20 illus., cast listings, index.

An overview of the artistic, financial, political, and technical
problems surrounding this unique and unprecedented undertaking.
A MUST to understand 20th century singers and singing. Reissued
in 1972 in a special edition with numerous new illustrations.
Flagstad, Hotter, London, Fischer-Dieskau, Nilsson, Ludwig and
their supporting casts.

BO023. **Culshaw, John.** Putting the Record Straight: the Autobiography of John Culshaw. Edited posthumously by Erik Smith.
New York: The Viking Press, 1968. 362 p., index.

The author worked closely with many of the most famous singers
of the last two decades.
Björling, del Monaco, Flagstad, Gueden, McCracken, Nilsson,
Price, Sutherland, Tebaldi.

BO024. **Davison, Henry,** ed. From Mendelsson to Wagner Being the
Memoirs of J.W. Davidson Forty Years Music Critic of "The Times."
London: Wm. Reeves, 1912. xviii, 539 p., 61 illus., list of
articles [incomplete], index.

The critic's son compiled this from documents and memoranda.
Covers the period 1835-1885 in England.

BO025. **de Boigne, Charles.** Petits mémoires de l'Opéra. Paris:
Librairie Nouvelle, 1857. iii, 368 p.

Nourrit, Stolz, Duprez, Falcon, Alboni.

B0026. **de Curzon, Henri.** L'Oeuvre de Richard Wagner a Paris et ses interpretes (1850-1914). Paris: Maurice Senart et Cie, Editeurs, n.d. 92, [2] p., 24 illus., index of names.

Renaud, Caron, Van Dyck, Litvinne, Louise Grandjean, Dalmas, Breval, Alvarez, Gresse, Jean de Reszke, Franz, Demougeot.

B0027. **della Corte, Andrea.** L'Interpretazione musicale e gli interpreti. Torino: Unione Tipografico-Editrice Torinese, 1951. xvi, 574 p., 12 portraits, 263 illus.

Using quotations from contemporary sources, the author discusses the singers of Rossini, Bellini, Donizetti, Verdi, and Wagner. This broad 19th century coverage allows few specifics.

B0028. **Desarbres, Nérée.** Deux siecles a l'Opéra (1669-1868). Paris: E. Dentu, Editeur, 1868. 297 p.

Included are short biographies of 130 singers.

B0029. **Diósy, Béla,** ed. Ungarischer kuenstler Almanach: das Kuenstler Ungarns in Wort und Bild. Budapest: Koeniglich Ungarische Universitaetsdruckerei, 1929. 383 p., numerous illus., index of names.

Fifty-seven singers, each with a picture, biography and/or repertoire and/or press notices. See B0145.

B0030. **Downes, Irene,** ed. Olin Downes on Music: a Selection of His Writings during the Half-Century 1906-1955. New York: Simon and Schuster, 1957. xxxi, 473 p., index.

Includes evaluations of nine singers by a very powerful critic. Calvé, Garden, Hayes, Jeritza, Lotte Lehmann, Chaliapin, de Lucca, Novotna, Anderson.

B0031. **Duey, Philip A.** Bel Canto in Its Golden Age: a Study of Its Teaching Concepts. New York: King's Crown Press, 1951. Reprint 1980. vii, 222 p., notes, 317 item bibliography, index.

Although the thrust of this book is pedagogical rather than biographical, the excellent bibliography is a MUST for those interested in the castrati.

B0032. **Duval, John H.** Svengali's Secrets and Memoirs of the Golden Age. New York: Robert Speller & Sons, 1958. 181 p., 17 portraits.

Reminiscences of an opera coach.
Maurel, Patti, Melba, del Puente, Ruffo, Flagstad, Chaliapin, Calvé, Caruso among others.

B0033. **Ebers, John.** Seven Years of the King's Theater. London: William Harrison Ainsworth, 1828. Reprint 1979. xxviii, 395 p., 6 plates.

As manager from 1821 to 1827, Ebers provides important background for the period.

BO034. **Edwards, H. Sutherland**. Idols of the French Stage. London:
Remington & Co., Publishers, 1889. 2 vols. 284 p.; 279 p.

Madame Favart, Arnould, Dugazon, Saint-Huberty.

BO035. **Elson, Louis C.**, ed. Modern Music and Musicians for
Vocalists. 2 vols. New York: The University Society, Inc., 1918.
Vol. I The Singer's Guide. ix, 316 p., 2 illus.; Vol. II Opera:
History and Guide. viii, 319-640 p., numerous illus.

Vol. I includes articles by Blance Marchesi, Melba, Maurel, Lilli
Lehmann, Butt, Caruso.
Vol. II includes an article by Nordica and biographical material
on twenty-four "Great Vocalists."
Cuzzoni, Farinelli, Gabrielli, Arnould, Pacchierotti, Mara,
Saint-Huberty, Billington, Catalani, Lablache, Rubini, Pasta,
Sontag, Mario, Malibran, Grisi, Lind, Patti, Nilsson, Materna,
Jean de Reszke, Edouard de Reszke, Melba, Sembrich.

BO036. **Estavan, Lawrence**, ed. W.P.A. Project 10677: the History
of Opera in San Francisco. 2 vols. San Francisco: The W.P.A., 1938.
136 p., 41-item bibliography; 164 p., 41-item bibliography.

Vol. I includes Eliza Biscaccianti, Hayes, Bishop, Nevada, Fay.
Vol. II includes Tetrazzini.

A0037. **Ewen, David**. Men and Women Who Make Music. New York: Thomas
Y. Crowell Company, 1939. xiv, 274 p., 16 illus., index.

A number of singers are mentioned, but this is especially inter-
esting for:
Flagstad, Lotte Lehmann, Melchoir, Pinza.
The 1945 edition adds Anderson, Moore, Pons, Thomas, and Tibbett.
The 1949 edition deletes Moore and adds Lawrence, Pearce, and
Traubel.

A0038. **Ewen, David**. Musicians Since 1900: Performers in Concert and
Opera. New York: H.W. Wilson Company, 1978. ix, 974 p., numerous
portraits.

Over 200 singers are included among the 432 performers mentioned.
The magazine and newspaper citations are tantalizing limited.
Ninety-nine sopranos, fourteen mezzos, thirteen contraltos, forty-
one tenors, twenty-seven baritones; six bass-baritones, and seventeen basses.

BO039. **Fabian, Imre**, ed. Oper 1977: grosse Saenger - ein
Stueck Operngeschichte. Velber: Friedrich Verlag, 1977.
132 p., numerous illus.

Ursuleac, Ahlersmeyer, Schmitt-Walter, Kipnis, Korjus, Giannini,
Berger, Gueden, Seefried, Dermota, Simionato, del Monaco.

There is a continuation of this title which I have not seen
that includes an additional sixteen singers.
Callas, Tebaldi, Albanese, Erich Kunz, Welitsch, Jurinac, Clara
Ebers, Varnay, Hotter, Boehme, Greindl, Schoeffler, Frick,
Gruemmer, Ernster, Della Casa.

B0040. **Fabian, Monroe H.** On Stage: 200 Years of Great Theatrical
Personalities. New York: Mayflower Books, Inc., 1980. 224 p.,
numerous illus., index of artists.

Lind, Caruso, Chaliapin, Farrar, McCormack, Melchoir, Robeson,
Leyna, Callas, Resnik, Horne.

B0041. **Fenner, Theodore.** Leigh Hunt and Opera Criticism: the
"Examiner" Years, 1808-1821. Lawrence: The University Press of
Kansas, 1972. xiv, 253 p., 20 illus., notes, 163-item select
bibliography, general index, performers index, operas index.

Belloc, Billington, Braham, Catalani, Fodor-Mainvielle, Manuel
del Popolo Vicente Garcia, Pasta, Vestris prominently mentioned.

B0042. **Finck, Henry T.** My Adventures in the Golden Age of Music.
New York: Funk & Wagnalls Company, 1926. Reprint 1971. xvi, 462 p.,
31 illus., index.

Autobiography of the New York Evening Post critic. Very brief
evaluations of twenty-five singers from Patti to Galli-Curci.
Jean de Reszke, Eames, de Gogorza, Materna, Brandt, Lilli
Lehmann, Niemann, Alvary, Fischer, Calvé, Melba, Sembrich,
Nordica, Schumann-Heink, Homer, Fremstad, Farrar, Caruso, Renaud,
Garden, Raisa, Jeritza, Bori, Easton, Galli-Curci.

B0043. **Finck, Henry T.** Success in Music and How It is Won. New
York: Charles Scribner's Sons, 1909. xiv, 471 p., index.

Short articles which attempt to pinpoint the reasons for thirty-
two artists' success.
Lind, Nilsson, Patti, Catalani, Pasta, Tetrazzini, Viardot-
Garcia, Malibran, Mara, Sontag, Schroeder-Devrient, Lilli Lehmann,
Brandt, Schumann-Heink, Lucca, Sembrich, Melba, Garden, Calvé,
Nordica, Eames, Farrar, Rubini, Mario, Tamagno, Campanini,
Caruso, Jean de Reszke, Santley, Maurel, Renaud, Wuellner.

B0044. **Firner, Walter**, ed. Wir von der Oper: ein kritisches
Theaterbildbuch. Muenchen: Verlag F. Bruckmann AG, 1932. 126 p.,
40 portraits.

Short articles written by twenty-eight singers who were famous
in Germany before the Second World War. Personal and revealing.
Alpar, Domgraf-Fassbaender, Eisinger, Fidesser, Hofmann, Jeritza,
Janssen, Ivoguen, Lotte Lehmann, Leider, List, Melchoir, Mueller,
Onegin, Pattiera, Piccaver, Reinhardt, Rode, Roswaenge, Scheidl,
Schmidt, Schoene, Schumann, Slezak, Stiedry, Tauber, Willer,
Wolff.

B0045. **Flor, Kai.** Store tonekunstnere jeg mødte. København:
Berlingske Forlag, 1954. 117 p., illus.

Gigli, Chaliapin, Forsell, Battistini.

B0046. **Foreman, Edward,** ed. Giambattista Mancini's Practical
Reflections on Figured Singing. Champaign: Pro Musica Press, 1967.
vi, 159 p.

Appendix III of this publication includes biographical notes
about seventy-seven 17th and 18th century singers.

B0047. **Furiosi, Nicola.** Note biografiche de alcuni celebri cantanti
e musicisti (1800-1900): divagazioni musicali in VI puntate. Roma:
Litografia Marves, n.d. [c.1955]. 33 p.

Giuseppe Capponi, Giovanni Balisardi, Valeria Manna.

B0048. **Gaisberg, F.W.** Music on Record. London: Robert Hale
Limited, 1946. Reprint 1977. 269 p., 33 illus., index.

Originally published 1942 in New York as The Music Goes Round.
Mentions most of the important singers who recorded before World
War Two. Important material on five singers.
Tetrazzini, Melba, Melchoir, Chaliapin, Schumann.

B0049. **Ganz, Wilhelm.** Memories of a Musician: Reminiscences of
Seventy Years of Musical Life. London: John Murray, 1913. xv, 357 p.,
19 illus., list of compositions, index.

Mentions over forty singers from Jenny Lind to Maggie Teyte.
Worthwhile information on Patti.

B0050. **Gatti-Casazza, Giulio.** Memories of the Opera. New York:
Charles Scribner's Sons, 1941. Reprint 1977. xii, 326 p., 18 illus.,
index.

Published posthumously from a MS approved by the General Manager
of the Metropolitan Opera in 1933. Far from the record we would
like to have had, but informative for a handful of artists.
Caruso, Destinn, Farrar, Fremstad, Homer, Ponselle, Scotti,
Tibbett.

B0051. **Genast, Eduard.** Aus Weimars klassischer und nachklassischer
Zeit: Erinnerungen eines alten Schauspielers. Stuttgart: Verlag von
Robert Lutz, 1904. 374 p., portrait.

Sophie Schroeder, Schroeder-Devrient, Lind, Sontag, Roger.

B0052. **Gérold, Théodore.** L'art du chant en France au XVIIe siècle.
Strasbourg: L'Imprimerie Strasbourgeoise, 1921. xv, 279 p., musical
examples, index of names, 172-item bibliography.

Edition of 500 copies.
Although primarily a style manual, this work contains limited

information about important 17th century French singers.

B0053. **Gollancz, Victor**. Journey Towards Music: a Memoir. New York: E.P. Dutton & Company, Inc., 1965. 238 p., 36 illus., appendix (9 months' opera season), index of names and places.

  Six singer-actors are accorded special attention.
  Callas, Chaliapin, Destinn, Lotte Lehmann, Mayr, Schumann.

B0054. **Gourret, Jean**. Vivre l'opéra avec les chanteurs. Paris: Editions Albatros, 1975. 191 [3] p., 27 illus.

  Primarily a book on singing with occasional brief mention of a number of singers who performed in Paris.

B0055. **Graf, Max**. Die Wiener Oper. Wien: Humboldt-Verlag, 1955. 384 p., 28 illus.

  A famous critic reminisces in celebration of the reopening of the Staatsoper.
  Winkelmann, Materna, Renaud, Papier, Gutheil-Schoder, Jeritza, Mayr, Battistini.

B0056. **Graves, Charles L**. Post-Victorian Music With Other Studies and Sketches. Port Washington: Kennikat Press, 1971 [1st edition 1911]. xi, 369 p., index.

  Landi, Sterling, Patti, Stockhausen, Santley, Garcia (son), Melba, Viardot-Garcia.

B0057. **Gregor, Hans**. Die Welt der Oper - die Oper der Welt: Bekenntnisse. Berlin: Ed. Bote & G. Bock, 1931. x, 3-423 p., 25 illus., index.

  Recollections of famous singers who performed between the world wars from Caruso to Lotte Lehmann.

B0058. **Grew, Sydney**. Favorite Musical Performers. London: T.N. Foulis Limited, 1923. 266 p., 10 illus.

  Rosina Buckman, Frank Mullings, Robert Radford, John Coates.

B0059. **Hadden, J. Cuthbert**. Modern Musicians. Edinburgh: T.N. Foulis, 1918 [1st edition 1913]. 267 p., 21 illus.

  Fifteen singers included in this piece of popular journalism. Melba, Tetrazzini, Caruso, Butt, Calvé, and Kirkby-Lunn are in the first edition. The nine added singers are Green, Coates, Radford, Watkin Mills, Ada Crossley, McCormack, Agnes, Nicholls, and Edna Thornton.

B0060. **Hanslick, Eduard**. Aus dem Opernleben der Gegenwart. Berlin: Allgemeiner Verein fuer deutsche Litteratur, 1889. 379 p.

  Six singers reviewed by one of the most famous/infamous critics.

Roger, Duprez, Nilsson, Faure, Dustmann, Ungher.

B0061. **Hanslick, Eduard.** Tagebuch eines Musikers. Berlin: Allgemeiner Verein fuer deutsche Litteratur, 1892. 360 p.

Lind, Nilsson, Spies, van Zandt, Sembrich, Lucca, Barbi, Brandt, Scheidemantel, Gura.

B0062. **Hartmann, Rudolf.** Das geliebte Haus: mein Leben mit der Oper. Muenchen: Deutscher Tashenbuch Verlag, 1979 [1st edition 1975]. 456 p., 56 illus., repertoire list 1952-1967, index.

Memoirs of the famous director and Intendant of the Bayerischen Staatstheater.
Bjoner, Borkh, Cebotari, Della Casa, Fischer-Dieskau, Hille-brecht, Hotter, Roswaenge, Rysanek, Toepper, Ursuleac, Wunderlich.

B0063. **Hawkins, John.** A General History of the Science and Practice of Music. vol. 5. London: T. Payne and Son, 1776. 482, [57], [1] p., errata, portraits, plates, musical examples.

Important for singers of the Handelian era. It is interesting to compare his thoughts with Burney's first-hand observations (B0014).

B0064. **Heylbut, Rose** and **Aimé Gerber.** Backstage at the Opera. New York: Thomas Y. Crowell Company, 1937. Reprint 1977 as Back-stage at the Metropolitan Opera. ix, 325 p., 19 illus., index.

These are highly personal observations and recollections. Calvé, Caruso (a chapter), Chaliapin, Crooks, Eames, Farrar, Flagstad, Fremstad, Johnson, Lilli Lehmann, Nordica, Plancon, Edouard de Reszke, Jean de Reszke, Schumann-Heink, Scotti, Sembrich.

B0065. **Hines, Dixie** and **Harry Prescott Hanaford**, eds. Who's Who in Music and Drama: an Encyclopedia of Biography of Notable Men and Women in Music and the Drama. New York: H.P. Hanaford Publisher, 1914. 560 p.

The professional biographies are found in pp. 17-334. There are valuable cast lists from the Metropolitan Grand Opera Company (Nov. 14, 1910-April 19, 1913); Boston Grand Opera Company (Nov. 7, 1910-March 29, 1913); Chicago Grand Opera Company (Nov. 3, 1910-Feb. 1, 1913); Metropolitan Opera House Company Philadelphia (Dec. 13, 1910-March 25, 1913).

B0066. **Hogarth, George.** Memoirs of the Musical Drama. 2 vols. London: Richard Bentley, 1838. xii, 465 p., 2 portraits; viii, 464 p., 6 portraits.

Invaluable commentary on 18th and 19th century performers by a contemporary. "...a critical view of the qualities and merits of the most distinguished...performers...interwoven...with many details, anecdotes, and circumstances..."

B0067. **Houssaye, Arsène.** Princesses de comédie et déesses d'opéra: portraits, camées, profils, silhouettes. Paris: Henri Plon, 1860. vi, 452 p., portrait.

Includes chapters on Arnould, Carmago, Favart, Guimard, Sylvia.

B0068. **Hurst, P.G.** The Golden Age Recorded: a Collector's Survey. Henfield, Sussex: p.p. at Eaton Thorne, 1946. 175 p., appendix of recordings by artist.

I have not seen the revised edition published in 1963. Revealing insights into fifty-nine sopranos, fifteen mezzo-sopranos, thirty-three tenors, thirty-six baritones, and thirteen basses by a professional with a large following of supporters.

B0069. **Jacobson, Robert.** Reverbrations: Interviews with the World's Leading Musicians. New York: William Morrow & Company, Inc., 1974. 308 p.

Seventeen renowned vocalists are among those interviewed. Arroyo, Baker, Domingo, Farrell, Kirsten, Lear, Milnes, Nilsson, Price, Rysanek, Schwarzkopf, Sills, Stewart, Thomas, Tourrel, Vickers, Welitsch.

B0070. **Klampfl, Eduard.** Richard Wagners 'Parsifal' und seine Bayreuther Darsteller. Wien: Huber & Lahme Nachfg., 1908. 162 p., 12 illus.

Winkelmann, Gudehus, Jaeger, van Dyck, Gruening, Birrenkoven, Gerhaeuser, Bergstaller, Schmedes, von Bary, Remond, Hadwiger.

B0071. **Klein, Herman.** Thirty Years of Musical Life in London 1870-1900. New York: The Century Company, 1903. Reprint 1978. xvii, 483 p., 106 illus., index.

A noted critic recalls many of the great artists who appeared in London. "Most of the purely personal incidents related in these pages appear in print for the first time." The index reads like a Who's Who of that era.

B0072. **Klein, Herman.** The Golden Age of Opera. London: George Routledge & Sons, Ltd., 1933. Reprint 1979. xxvi, 275 p., 12 illus., index.

Extends B0071 to the era of Destinn and Caruso. Klein was a voice student of Manuel Patricio Garcia and co-authored the 1894 London edition of Hints on Singing.

B0073. **Kloss, Erich,** ed. Richard Wagner an seine Kuenstler. Zweiter Band der 'Bayreuther Briefe' (1872-1883). Leipzig: Schuster & Loeffler, 1908. 414 p., index of names.

Materna, Lilli Lehmann, Niemann, Neumann.

B0074. **Kohut, Adolph.** Beruehmte israelitische Maenner und Frauen

in der Kulturgeschichte der Menschheit: Lebens- und Charakter-
bilder aus Vergangenheit und Gegenwart. 2 vols. Leipzig-Reudnitz:
Druck und Verlag von A.H. Payne, n.d. 433 p., illus.; 432 p.,
illus.

> The first volume includes eighteen opera and concert singers.
> Alberti, Braham, Demuth, Goldberg, Gumbert, Henskel, Kalisch,
> Landau, Lasalle, Lederer, Liebau, Muehlmann, Ney, Oberlaender,
> Robinson, Rothmuehl, Sontheim, Strakosch.

B0075. **Kohut, Adolph**. Das Dresdner Hoftheater in der Gegenwart.
Dresden: E. Pierson's Verlag, 1888. vii, 520 p., 142 portraits.

> A comprehensive overview which includes twenty-nine singers.
> von Chavanne, Friedmann, Hummel, Jahn, Loeffler, Malton, Otto-
> Alvsleben, Reuther, Saak, Schacko, Schuch, Sigler, Bulss,
> Daeseler, Decarli, Eichberger, Erl, Gudehus, Gutzschbach, Jensen,
> Kruis, Lurgenstein, Marchion, Meincke, Richter, Reise, Scheide-
> mantel, Schrauff, Ueberhorst.

B0076. **Krehbiel, Henry Edward**. Chapters of Opera Being Historical
and Critical Observations and Records Concerning the Lyric Drama
in New York from Its Earliest Days down to the Present Time. New
York: Henry Holt and Company, 1908. Reprint 1980. xvii, 435 p., 72
illus., index.

> Innumerable singers mentioned by an unsympathetic critic viewing
> the first twenty-five years of the Metropolitan Opera.

B0077. **Krehbiel, Henry Edward**. More Chapters of Opera Being
Historical and Critical Observations and Records Concerning the
Lyric Drama in New York from 1908 to 1918. New York: Henry Holt
and Company, 1919. xvi, 474 p., 43 illus., appendix of performance records at the Met and the Manhatten Opera, index.

> This is primarily a rewrite of articles printed in the New York
> Tribune between 1908 and 1918. A sequel to B0076.

B0078. **Kuhe, Wilhelm**. My Musical Recollections. London: Richard
Bentley nd Son, 1896. xxviii, 394 p., 17 illus., index.

> A concert pianist's comments on his vocal contemporaries demon-
> strate a great deal of sensitivity and insight.
> Albani, Giulia Grisi, Lablache, Lind, Mario, Patti, Reeves,
> Nilsson, Trebelli.

B0079. **Laget, Auguste**. Le chant et les chanteurs. Paris: Heugel
& Cie. n.d. [1874]. 364 p.

> A collection of previously printed material which is largely a
> mixture of anecdote and reality. Chapters on six singers.
> Garat, Elleviou, Ponchard, Nourrit, Duprez, Roger.

B0080. **Lengyel, Cornel**, ed. W.P.A. Project 10377: the History
of Music in San Francisco. vol. 4. Celebrities in El Dorado 1850-

1906. New York: AMS Press, 1972 [1st edition 1938 with illus.].
270 p., selected bibliography, index.

Biographies of musicians who visited San Francisco between 1850
and 1906 including forty-six singers. Surprisingly enough this
encompassed many of the great vocalists of the age, e.g. Melba,
Scotti, Sontag, and Bishop.

B0081. **Lengyel, Cornel**, ed. W.P.A. Project 10377: the History
of Music in San Francisco. vol. 6. Early Music Teachers. San
Francisco: W.P.A., 1940. 149 p., 6 illus., appendices.

Eugenio Bianchi, Margaret Alverson, Inez Fabri, Giovanna Bianchi.

B0082. Le nouvel opéra: le monument - les artistes par x,y,z.
edition d'artiste. Paris: Michel Lévy Frères, 1875. 339 p., portraits.

Includes biographies with a portrait of twenty-nine singers.
Villaret, L. Achard, Sylvas, Basquin, Grisy, Vergnet, Hayet,
Salomon, Faure, Gailhard, Lassalle, Caron, J. Belval, Bataille,
F. Dieu, Menu, Anguez, Krauss, Gueymard-Lauters, Ferrucci, Bloch,
Mauduit, M. Belval, Moisset, Fouquet, Daram, Arnaud, Geismard,
Nilsson.

B0083. **Lewinsky, Josef**. Theatralische Carrieren: biographische
Skizzen. Leipzig: J.B. Klein'sche Buchhandlung, 1881. 268 p.,
25 illus.

Brandt, Lehmann, Lucca, Gerster.

B0084. **Liebermann, Rolf**. Opernjahre: Erlebnisse und Erfahrungen
vor, auf und hinter der Buehne grosser Musiktheater. Translated by
Eva Schoenfeld from Actes et entractes. Paris, 1976. Muenchen:
Scherz Verlag, 1977. 320 p., index.

Insights from a General Director including seven singers.
Callas, Corelli, Domingo, Freni, Ghiaurov, Nilsson, Margaret
Price.

B0085. **Linfield, John H.** Singers of Bygone Days: a Retro-
spective of Fifty Years - 1894-1944, and Some of the Sleeping
Memories It Awakens of Those Who Sang and Charmed in These Far-
off Yesterdays. Cleckheaton: p.p. by John Siddall Ltd., 1950.
20 p., index.

Reminiscences and reflections written in 1949. They may indeed
bring back "the vanished past in relation to singers I had heard."

B0086. **Lombardo, Giuseppe A.** Annuario della arte lirica e coreo-
grafica italiana 1897-98. prima edizione. Milano: Arturo Demarchi,
1898. iv, 310 p., numerous illus.

128 singer's biographies with a portrait of each.
NOTE: There are apparently other volumes of this publication.

B0087. **Lumley, Benjamin.** <u>Reminiscences of the Opera</u>. London:
Hurst and Blackett, 1864. Reprint 1976. xx, 448 p., portrait.

As the manager of Her Majesty's Theater between 1842 and 1858,
he engaged many of the famous singers of that time.

B0088. **Machabey, Armand.** <u>Le bel canto</u>. Paris: LaRousse, 1948.
124 p., chronology du bel canto, index of names, 165-item bibliography.

Very brief and general coverage of 18th and 19th century singers.

B0089. **Mann Ernest** and **Bruno Vogler, Heinz Voss, Hans Gerloff.**
<u>Deutschlands Oesterreich-Ungrarns und der Schweiz: Musiker in Wort</u>
<u>und Bild. Eine illustrierte Biographie der gesamten alldeutschen</u>
<u>Musikwelt</u>. 1. ausgabe 1909/10. Leipzig-Gohlis: Bruno Vogler Verlags-
buchhandlung, 1909. vi, 525 p.

A variety of singers among the other musicians.

B0090. **Mapleson, James Henry.** <u>The Mapleson Memoirs 1848-1888</u>.
New York: Belford, Clarke & Co., 1888. 2 vols. xi, 372 p., portrait;
viii, 319 p., appendix of singers and operas, index.

He produced opera between 1858 and 1888. Although the facts are
questionable, this is an important period source for eleven noted
singers. Harold Rosenthal edited and annotated a new edition in
1966.
Campinini, Fohstroem, Gerster, Hauk, Nicolini, Nilsson, Nordica,
Patti, del Puente, Tietjens, Trebelli.

B0091. **Maretzek, Max.** <u>Crochets and Quavers: or, Revelations of an</u>
<u>Opera Manager in America</u>. New York: S. French, 1855. Reprint 1966
with Preface by Jan Popper. Reprint 1968. viii, 11-346 p.

The leading impresario in America prior to the opening of the Met.
The unabridged reprint published in 1968 has an index and also
includes the sequel, <u>Sharps and Flats</u>, originally published in
New York in 1890.
Unusual material on Lind, Parodi, Hayes, Sontag, Mario, Patti,
and Alboni.

B0092. **Marks, Edward B.** <u>They All Had Glamour from the Swedish</u>
<u>Nightingale to the Naked Lady</u>. New York: Julian Messner, Inc.,
1944. Reprint 1972. xvii, 448 p., 269 illus., index.

Highly readable and nostalgic blend of immagination and reality.
Malibran, Grisi, Bishop, Sontag, Lind, Alboni, Tietjens, Picco-
lomini, Nilsson, Adelina Patti, Carlotta Patti, Lucca, Kellogg,
Hauk.

B0093. **Martin, Jules.** <u>Nos artistes: annuaire des théâtres et</u>
<u>concerts 1901-1902</u>. Paris: Société d'Editions Litteraires et
Artistiques. Librairie Paul Ollendorf, 1901. 410 p., 375
portraits.

Numerous singers. Are there other publications in this series?

B0094. **Martin, Jules.** Nos artistes: portraits et biographies suvis d'un notice sue les droits d'auteurs, l'Opéra, la Comédie-Francaise, les associations artistiques, etc.... Paris: Librairie de l'Annuaire Universal, 1895. 448 p., 369 portraits.

Good for obscure 19th century performers.

B0095. **von Mensi-Klarbach, Alfred.** Alt-Muenchner Theater-erinnerungen: Bildnisse aus der Glanzzeit der Muenchner Hofbuehnen. zweite, stark vermehrte auflage. Muenchen: Verlag von Knorr & Hirth, G.M.B.H., 1924. 255 p., 32 illus.

Materials on thirty-two singers.
Heinrich Vogl, Therese Vogl, Nachbaur, Mikorey, Schlosser, Walter, Gura, Brulliot, Bausewein, Brucks, Bertram, Moran-Olden, Kloepfer, Kindermann, Alvary, Ternina, Wekerlin, Dressler, Borchers, Basta, Frank, Blank, Bender, Bauberger, Brodersen, Knote, Wolf, Ivoguen, Bosetti, Willer, Morena, Fassbender.

B0096. **Meyer, Torben** and **Josef Mueller-Marein, Hannes Reinhardt.** Musikalske selvportraetter. København: Jul. Gjellerups Forlag, 1966. 325 p., 40 illus.

Ten singers are included among the other artists.
Bjoner, Borg, Callas, Lovberg, Merriman, Nilsson, Schwarzkopf, Seefried, Soederstroem, Ulfung.

B0097. **Mildberg, Bodo.** Das Dresdner Hoftheater in der Gegenwart: Biographien und Charakteristiken. Dresden: F. Piersons Verlag, 1902. 270 p., 112 portraits.

Twenty-seven singers are among the other company personnel.
Abendroth, Authes, Brag, von Chavanne, Decarli, Erl, Forchhammer, Froehlich, Giessen, Gutzschbach, Hoepfl, Jaeger, Krammer, Kruis, Krull, Malten, Rast, Rebuschka, Better, Berron, Blaschke, Rains, Ruebsan, Scheidmantel, Wachter, Wedekind, Wittich.

B0098. **Milke, S.J. Auais.** Algo de la opera: guia practica del aficianado al teatro lirico. Mexico, D.F.: Ediciones Selectas, 1982. 2 vols. 672, [4] p., numerous illus.; 673-1352, [4] p., numerous illus., index of composers, 49-item bibliography.

An impressive compilation which quite probably depends upon sources other than those listed in the bibliography. The critical part, "Compositores y Cantantes Famosos", begins on page 627 of the first volume.

B0099. **Monaldi, Gino.** Ricordi viventi di artisti scomparsi. Campobasso: Tipografica Molisana, 1927. 249 p., 12 illus.

Brief articles on a number of artists including three singers.
Giorgio Ronconi, Antonio Cotogni, Roberto Stagno.

B0100. **Moogk, Edward B.** Roll Back the Years: History of Canadian Recorded Sound and Its Legacy, Genesis to 1930. Ottawa: National Library of Canada, 1975. xii, 443 p., numerous illus., discography, 8 appendices, 15-item bibliography, index.

> Albani, Craig Campbell, Donalda, Dufault, Easton, Edvina, Ferrari-Fontana, Firth, Fischer, Gauthier, Gordon, Heather, Hollinshead, Howard, Johnson, Pavloska, Plamondon.

B0101. **Moore, Gerald.** Am I Too Loud? A Musical Autobiography. New York: The Macmillan Company, 1962. viii, 288 p., 12 illus.

> The premiere accompanist of his generation discusses the artists with whom he worked. Marvelous insights into ten singers. Coates, Chaliapin, Gerhardt, Schumann, Teyte, McCormack, Ferrier, Schwarzkopf, de los Angeles, Fischer-Dieskau.

B0102. **Moore, Gerald.** Farewell Recital: Further Memories. London: Hamish Hamilton, 1978. [v], 178 p., 13 illus., index.

> de los Angeles, Baker, Fischer-Dieskau, Gerhardt, Pears, Schwarz-kopf are all prominently mentioned.

B0103. **Mount-Edgcumbe, [Richard] 2nd Earl of.** Musical Reminiscences of an Old Amateur Chiefly Respecting the Italian Opera in England for Fifty Years from 1773 to 1823: the Second Edition Continued to the Present Time. London: W. Clarke, 1827 [1st edition 1823]. xii, 13-183 p.

> The period of Rauzzini to Catalani with forty-five singers mentioned, eighteen of them prominently.
> Rauzzini, Gabrielli, Pozzi, Galli, Giorgi, Pacchierotti, Lebrun, Todi, Mara, Babbini, Mengozzi, Marchesi, Billington, Grassini, Catalani, Braham, Pasta, Velluti.

B0104. **Mueller-Marein, Josef** and **Hannes Reinhardt.** Das musikalische Selbstportrait von Komponisten, Dirigenten, Instrumentalisten, Saengerinnen und Saengern unserer Zeit. Hamburg: Nannen-Verlag GmbH, 1963. 508 p., 55 illus., select bibliography, index of names.

> Fifty well-known artists including twenty-three singers were asked to provide autobiographical insights and commentary. Ivoguen, Berger, Streich, Seefried, Lorenz, Leider, Bollmann, Lemnitz, Rosvaenge, Klose, Schlusnus, Melchoir, Varnay, Winters, Hotter, Windgassen, Moedl, Gruemmer, Goltz, Kunz, Ludwig, Koeth, Bockelmann.

B0105. **Nanquette, Claude.** Anthologie des interprètes. Paris: Editions Stock, 1979. 745, [4] p., index.

> Pages 11-249 are devoted to seventy singers from Theo Adam to Fritz Wunderlich whose careers flourished after 1945.

B0106. **Nanquette, Claude.** Les grands interprètes romantiques.

Paris: Librairie Arthème Fayard, 1982. 367 p., 60 illus., 406-item
bibliography.

> Principal singers, conductors, and instrumentalists from the
> early 19th century through Lauritz Melchoir. Short articles
> on twenty-four singers.
> Rubini, Lablache, Pasta, Cinti-Damoreau, Nourrit, Schroeder-
> Devrient, Sontag, Duprez, Malibran, Giulia Grisi, Falcon, Lind,
> Pauline Viardot, Schneider, Patti, Lilli Lehmann, Jean de Reszké,
> Caron, Calvé, Melba, Caruso, Garden, Chaliapine, Melchoir.

B0107. **Newton, Ivor.** At the Piano - Ivor Newton: the World of an
Accompanist. London: Hamish Hamilton, 1966. viii, 309 p., 21 illus.,
index.

> Commentary on 15 outstanding singers among many, many others.
> de Groot, Rosing, Tetrazinni, Chaliapin, Melba, Calvé,
> Slobodskaya, dal Monte, Turner, Hammond, d'Alvarez, Ferrier,
> Supervia, Flagstad, Moore.

B0108. **Niggli, Paul.** Musiker Medaillen. Hofheim am Taunus: Verlag
Friedrich Hofmeister, 1965. 268 p., illus.

> Ninety singers from Faustina Bordoni to Grace Bumbry are listed.
> Edition of 1,500 copies.

B0109. **Noble, Helen.** Life with the Met. New York: G.P. Putnam's
Sons, 1954. 250 p., index.

> As a secretary at the Met she was in a unique position to observe.
> Bori, Farrar, Flagstad, Johnson, Ponselle, and Talley.

B0110. **Null, Gary** and **Carl Stone.** The Italian Americans. Harris-
burg: Stackpole Books, 1976. 220 p., 132 item bibliography, index
of names.

> Caruso, Albanese, del Monaco, Giannini, Lanza, Moffo, Carmela
> Ponselle, Rosa Ponselle, Siepi, Tebaldi, Tozzi.

B0111. **O'Connell, Charles.** The Other Side of the Record. New
York: Alfred A. Knopf, 1947. Reprint 1970. xi, 332, xi p., index.

> The former Music Director at RCA Victor recalls fifteen artists
> including five singers.
> Moore, Pons, Melchoir, Flagstad, Traubel.

B0112. **O'Donnell, Josephine.** Among the Covent Garden Stars.
London: Stanley Paul & Co., Ltd., 1936. 295 p., 49 illus., index.

> As secretary to the director she was in a position to know.
> Lotte Lehmann, Leider, Melba, Melchoir, and Supervia among a
> host of others.

B0113. **Parker, H.T.** Eighth Notes: Voices and Figures of Music and
the Dance. New York: Dodd, Mead and Company, 1922. 238 p.

Originally printed in the <u>Boston evening transcript</u>, our critic
shares "...the impressions received and recorded by a reviewer..."
Garden, Farrar, Jeritza, Renaud, Chaliapin, Caruso, Fremstad,
Tetrazzini, Galli-Curci, Ruffo, McCormack, Rosing, Culp, Gerhardt,
Hempel, Destinn, Teyte, Gauthier, Schumann-Heink.

BO114. **Phipson, T.L.** <u>Voice and Violin: Sketches, Anecdotes, and</u>
<u>Reminiscences</u>. London: Chatto & Windus, 1898. xvi, 226 p., index.

Banti, Alboni, Tamburini.

BO115. **Piccini, Giulio** [pseud. **Jarro**]. <u>Autori, cantanti, con-</u>
<u>certisti, acrobati. ritratti, macchiette, anecdoti: memorie</u>
<u>umoristiche</u>. terza edizione corretta e aumentata. Firenze: R.
Bemporad & Figlio, 1898. 351 p., index.

I have not seen the 1st edition of 1887 which apparently contains
similar articles by the critic on these same five vocalists.
Tamberlick, Stagno, Bellincioni, Nevada, Arnoldson.

BO116. **Pougin, Arthur.** <u>Acteurs et actrices d'autrefois: historie</u>
<u>anecdotique des théatres a Paris depuis trois cent ans</u>. Paris: F.
Juven et cie, Editeurs, n.d. [c.1912]. 278 p., 109 illus.

Thirty-one singers are among those singled out for attention.
Maupin, Favart, Laruette, Dugazon, Camargo, Arnould, Saint-
Huberty, Elleviou, Les Gavaudan (see A0087), Ponchard, Nourrit,
Duprez, Malibran, Lablache, Sontag, Tamburini, Giulia Grisi,
Giuditta Grisi, Rubini, Mario, Stoltz, Roger, Pauline Garcia,
Alboni, Caron, Faure, Patti, Tamberlick.

BO117. **Pougin, Arthur.** <u>Un ténor de l'Opéra au XVIIIe siècle: Pierre</u>
<u>Jélyotte et les chanteurs de son temps</u>. Paris: Librairie Fischbacher.
1905. Reprint 1973. 239 p., 22 illus.

As the title implies, there is a great deal of information about
18th century singers besides Jélyotte.
Marie Antier, Pelissier, Catherine-Nicole Lamaure, Petitpas, Fel,
Chevalier, Bourbonnais, Coupe, La Camargo, and Salle.

BO118. **Rambaud, Yveling** and **E. Coulon.** <u>Les théatres en robe de</u>
<u>chambre</u>. Paris: Achille Faure, Libraire-Editeur, 1866. 276 p.,
index of names.

Short biographies of fifty-seven singers are included.

BO119. <u>Rassegna internazionale del teatro lirico</u>. Roma: R.I.T.L.
Direzione Generale, 1959. 310, [3] p., 101 portraits.

Although the decision was made to exclude publicity materials
generated by agents and impresarios, this particular publication
includes 101 singers with biographical materials and portraits
from Belen Amparan to Giuseppe Zecchillo, and much of this
material is difficult if not impossible to find elsewhere.
And, after all, any rule deserves an appropriate exception.

B0120. **Reichelt, Johannes.** Erlebte Kostbarkeiten: Begegungen mit
Kuenstlern in Bekenntnisstunden. zweite, gaenzlich erneuerte auflage.
Dresden: Verlag Wodni & Lindecke, 1941. 421 p., 44 illus., index of
names.

   Five singers among twenty German and Austrian artists.
   Perron, Scheidemantel, Burrian, Vogelstrom, Malten.

B0121. **Riemens, Leo.** Uren der zangkunst: opera's beroemde zangers
en zangeressen. Amsterdam: Uitgave De Bezige Bij, 1954. 178 p., 17
illus.

   Short articles for popular consumption by a noted vocal critic.
   Caruso, Tauber, Hayes, Melba, Ferrier, Urlus, Brouwenstijn.

B0122. **Roeder, Ernst.** Das Dresdner Hoftheater der Gegenwart:
Biographisch-kritische Skizzen der Mitglieder. neue folge. Dresden:
E. Pierson's Verlag, 1896. viii, 216 p., 61 portraits.

   Anthes, Bossenberger, Bruns, Dibbern, Edel, Froelich, Herms,
   Hofmueller, Huhn, Joachim, Krug, Nebruschka, Perron, Szirovatka,
   Telekn, Wachter, Wedekind, Wittich.

B0123. **Rosenberg, Charles G.** You Have Heard of Them, by Q. New
York: Redfield, 1894. vi, 8-353 p., portrait.

   Balfe, Grisi, Hayes, Jullien, Lablache, Lind.

B0124. **Rushmore, Robert.** The Singing Voice. New York: Dodd, Mead
& Company, 1971. xx, 332 p., 37 illus., Appendix by Karl Trump,
glossary, reference notes, 277-item bibliography, index.

   The bibliography includes seventy-two titles by or about singers
   as well as ten titles which involve more than one artist.
   Prominently mentioned in the text are Björling, Caruso, Eames,
   Farrar, Flagstad, Fremstad, Garcia (son), Lilli Lehmann, Lotte
   Lehmann, Patti, Ponselle, Price, and Jean de Reszke.

B0125. **Russell, Henry** and **Kathleen Sullivan.** The Passing Show.
Boston: Little, Brown, and Company, 1926. 295 p., 9 illus., index.

   Frank observations by an impresario. Particular mention is made
   of Caruso and Melba, but many others are touched upon in passing.

B0126. **Ryan, Thomas.** Recollections of an Old Musician. New York:
E.P. Dutton & Company, 1899. Reprint 1979. xvi, 274 p., 46 illus.

   Lind, Hayes, Sontag, Alboni, Nilsson.

B0127. **Sáenz, Gerardo,** ed. Ecos teatrales by Luis G. Urbina.
México: Instituto Nacional de Bellas Artes, 1963. 257 p., 56 page
bibliography.

   Barrientos, Carreno, Enzo Leliva, Tetrazzini.

BO128. **Saleski, Gdal.** <u>Famous Musicians of a Wandering Race: Bio-graphical Sketches of Outstanding Figures of Jewish Origin in the Musical World.</u> New York: Block Publishing Company, 1927. xiv, 463 p., photo of each musician.

> Max Block, Braslau, Dalmores, Dalossy, Demuth, Gabor, Gluck, Nanette Guilford, Henschel, Jadlowker, Kalish, Kipnis, Isa Kremer, Kurz, Jean Louis Lasalle, Hilda Lashanska, Lilli Lehmann, Lucca, Anna Meitschik, Pasta, Raisa, Marie Rappold, Renaud, Rimini, Saenger, Lazar Samoiloff, Schumann-Heink, Schwarz, Sibiriakoff, Slobodskaya, Sontheim, Strakosch, Tartakoff, Weil, Walfe.

> 2nd edition: <u>Famous Musicians of Jewish Origin.</u> New York, 1949. Forty-two singers are included with some additions to and some deletions from the original thirty-five artists selected. Kurt Baum, Sidor Belarsky, Mario Bernini, Desi Halban, Brenda Lewis, Regina Resnik, Robert Merrill, Richard Tucker, Jennie Tourel. Both editions must be consulted!

BO129. **Salvucci, Antonio.** <u>Confidenze e aneddoti de cantanti celebri e maestri compositori.</u> Roma: Demer, 1964. 134 p., numerous illus.

> Amato, Storchio, Anselmi, Stracceari, Caruso, Georgini, Lauri-Volpi, Scheavazzi, Gigli, Galeffi, de Lucca.

BO130. **Schoen-René, Anna Eugénie.** <u>America's Musical Inheritance: Memories and Reminiscences.</u> New York: G.P. Putnam's Sons, 1941. xi, 244 p., 18 illus., index.

> Especially important for the Garcia family, but there is also extensive commentary on Schumann-Heink, Sembrich, Lilli Lehmann, Melba, and Caruso.

BO131. **Schonberg, Harold.** <u>Facing the Music.</u> New York: Summit Books, 1981. 464 p., index.

> Newspaper critics seem unable to resist republishing their work, and that is all to the benefit of this sort of bibliography. Tebaldi, Warren, Nilsson, Garden, Farrar, Ponselle, Melchoir among a galaxy of stars.

BO132. **Schwaiger, Egloff,** ed. <u>Warum der Applaus: beruehmte Interpreten ueber ihre Musik.</u> Muenchen: Ehrenwirth Verlag: 1968. 349 p., 48 illus., section of short biographies.

> Twenty-one singers are among those chosen to discuss their pro-fessional lives. Edited from radio interviews, these articles provide valuable autobiographical material.
> Berry, Della Casa, Dermota, Engen, Fischer-Dieskau, Gedda, Hotter, Janowitz, Koeth, Ludwig, Prey, Rothenberger, Rysanek, Silja, Streich, Thomas, Toepper, Varnay, Watson, Windgassen, Wunderlich.

BO133. **Seidl, Anton,** ed. <u>The Music of the Modern World Illustrated in the Lives and Works of the Greatest Modern Musicians and in Repro-</u>

ductions of Famous Paintings, etc.... 2 vols. New York: D. Appleton and Company, 1895 [originally issued in 25 fascicles for subscribers 1895]. xi, 236 p., 52 illus.; vii, 348 p., 27 illus.

An absolutely overwhelming publication and a gold mine of information. Articles written by Maurel (2), Kellogg, Tamagno, Eames, Plancon, Alvary, Lilli Lehmann, Jean de Reszke, Edouard de Reszke, Scalchi, Calvé, Mathilde Marchesi, and Melba.

There are biographies of thirty-two outstanding vocal artists. Patti, Nordica, Sontag, Malibran, Tamagno, Grisi, Catalani, Lind, Lablache, Ronconi, Alboni, Mario, Pasta, Tietjens, Parepa-Rosa, Roze, Albani, Nilsson, Capoul, Lucca, Foure, Campanini, Nicolini, Hauk, Wachtel, Cary, Phillipps, Henschel, Whitney, Galli-Marie, Gerster, Viardot-Garcia.

B0134. **Shaw, George Bernard.** London Music in 1888–89 as Heard by Corna di Bassetto (later known as Bernard Shaw) with some Further Autobiographical Particulars. London: Constable and Company Limited, 1950 [1st edition 1937]. 420 p., index.

d'Andrade, Henschel, Nordica, Patti, Edouard de Reszke, Jean de Reszke.

B0135. **Shaw, George Bernard.** Music in London 1890–94. 3 vols. London: Constable and Company Limited, 1956. 302 p.; 325 p.; 320 p., index.

This particular set is based upon the revised edition of 1932. Shaw's writings are de rigueur for connoiseurs of witty, inteligent, and penetrating criticism. Reprinted from The World, these selections include comments on Albani, Alvary, Calvé, van Dyck, Eames, Henschel, Lassalle, Maurel, Melba, Plancon, Edouard and Jean de Reszke.

B0136. **Sheean, Vincent.** First and Last Love. New York: Random House, 1956. 305 p., index.

An autobiography in which penetrating observations are made about famous artists from Garden to Flagstad.
Caruso, Chaliapin, Flagstad, Garden, Leider, Lotte Lehmann.

B0137. **Sheean, Vincent.** Oscar Hammerstein I: the Life and Exploits of an Impresario. New York: Simon and Schuster, 1936. xx, 363 p., 17 illus., index.

Very helpful regarding artists who appeared with the Manhatten Opera Company which Hammerstein ran in competition with the Met. Bonci, Caruso, Cavalieri, Farrar, Garden, Melba, Nordica, Renaud, Sammarco, Sembrich, Tetrazzini.

B0138. **Smith, William Charles.** The Italian Opera and Contemporary Ballet in London 1789-1820: a Record of Performances and Players with Reports from the Journals of the Time. London: Society for Theatre Research, 1955. xviii, 191 p., illus.

B0139. **Spark, William.** <u>Musical Memories</u>. London: Swan Sonnenschein & Co., 1888. viii, 439 p., portrait.

Grisi, Mario, Titiens, Giuglini, Patti.

B0140. **Strakosch, Maurizio.** <u>L'impresario in angustie: Adelina Patti e altre stelle fuori della leggenda (1886-1893)</u>. Versione, introduzione e note de Eugenio Gara. Milano: Valentino Bompiani, 1940. 381 p., illus.

Gara has based this version on the 2nd edition, <u>Souvenirs d'un imprésario</u>, published in Paris in 1887 and has included a translation of the memoirs of the impresario Schuermann: <u>Les etoiles en voyage: la Patti - Sarah Bernhardt - Coquelin</u>. 2nd edition. Paris: Tresse & Stock, Editeurs, 1893. 206 p.

Patti, Pasta, Alboni, Nilsson, Mario, Krauss among others.

B0141. **Taullard, A.** <u>Historia de nuestros viejos teatros</u>. Buenos Aires: Imprenta López, 1932. 500 p., numerous illus.

Anselmi, Darclée, Carelli, Gayarre, Tamagno, Stagno, Massini, Patti.

B0142. **Trotter, James M.** <u>Music and Some Highly Musical People...</u> [including]<u>...Sketches of the Lives of Remarkable Musicians of the Colored Race</u>. Boston: Lee and Shepard, Publishers, 1881. Reprint 1968. 352, 152 p., 12 illus., index of music.

Early, basic source about the careers of Black American artists. Elizabeth Taylor Greenfield, the Lucca family, Thomas J. Bowers, ("The American Mario"), Anna Madah Hyers, Emma Louise Hyers, Nellie E. Brown.

B0143. **Uda, Michele.** <u>Arte e artisti</u>. Compiled by Mary Scott-Uda. 2 vols. Napoli: Stab. Tip. Pierro e Veraldi nell'Istituto Casanova. 1900. 317 p., portrait; 292 p.

Galli-Marie, Gayarre, de Lucca, Marconi, Masini, Maurel, Nevada, Patti, Stagno, Bellincioni.

B0144. **Upton, George P.** <u>Musical Memories: My Recollections of Celebrities of the Half Century 1850-1900</u>. Chicago: A.C. McClurg & Co., 1908. xiv, 345 p., 47 illus., index.

Among the many artists who performed in Chicago, eight singers are given special notice.
Lind, Sontag, Hays, Patti, Nilsson, Lucca, Hauk, Kellogg.

B0145. **Vásárhelyi, Julius.** <u>Ungarn ein Land der Musik: Ungarischer Kuenstleralmanach</u>. Budapest: Koeniglich Ungarische Universitaetsdruckerei, 1930. 340 p., numerous illus.

Fifty-five singers each with a portrait and a short biographical sketch. This could well be the second edition of B0029 which

omits some artists and adds others. There is an alphabetical
listing of artists at the end of this volume.

B0146. **Vehanen, Kosti.** Rapsodia elaemaestae. Helsinki: Werner
Soederstroem Osakeyhtioe, 1944. 249, [2] p., 18 illus., major
career dates.

Marian Anderson's Finnish accompanist comments on twelve singers.
Ruffo, Caspir, Cahier, Anderson, Urlus, Crooks, Carlo, Tervani,
Jaernefelt, Ackté, Ravenna, Piltti.

B0147. **Wagnalls, Mabel.** Opera and Its Stars: a Description of the
Music and Stories of the Enduring Operas and a Series of Interviews
with the World's Famous Sopranos. New York: Funk & Wagnalls Company,
1924. xiv, 410 p., 24 illus.

Galli-Curci, Jeritza, Garden, Hempel, Sembrich, Farrar, Melba,
Eames, Calvé, Nordica, Lilli Lehmann.

B0148. **Wagnalls, Mabel.** Stars of the Opera. revised and enlarged
edition. New York: Funk & Wagnalls Company, 1907 [1st edition 1899].
402 p., 19 illus.

Description of thirteen operas and "approved" interviews with
seven divas. Geraldine Farrar is added to the 1899 edition.
Sembrich, Eames, Calvé, Nordica, Lilli Lehmann, Melba, Farrar.

B0149. **Wagner, Alan.** Prima Donnas and Other Wild Beasts. Larchmont: Argonaut Books, 1961. 250 p., cast of characters.

The immature operatic beginners' journalistic delight. Although
a total of 139 singers are mentioned, there is little substance.

B0150. **Wagner, Charles L.** Seeing Stars. New York: G.P. Putnam's
Sons, 1940. Reprint 1977. ix, 403 p., 11 illus., index.

The manager for McCormack, Garden, and Galli-Curci talks about
McCormack, Garden, Galli-Curci, Alda, Melba, and Tibbett.

B0151. **Watkins, Mary Fitch.** Behind the Scenes at the Opera:
Intimate Revelations of Back-Stage Musical Life and Work. New York:
Frederick A. Stokes, 1925. vii, 328 p.

Journalistic vignettes including eleven singers employed at
the Met during the 1920's. Little depth or insight.
Scotti, Jeritza, Alda, Howard, Bori, Whitehill, Johnson, Garden,
Chaliapin, Farrar, Sembrich.

B0152. **Weinschenk, H.F.** Kuenstler Plaudern. Berlin: Wilhelm
Limpert Verlag, 1938. 338 p., 177 illus.

The author includes twenty-three singers among the fifty artists
he has asked to discuss their lives and careers. All of them
were well-known in Germany at the time, but the information
given is particularly welcome for those who did not achieve

international status.
Baknaloff, Bockelmann, Bohnen, Bollmann, Giannini, Gigli, Ivoguen, Kiepura, Leider, Leisner, Lorenz, dal Monte, Mueller, Onegin, Prohaska, Rode, Roswaenge, Sack, Slezak, Chaliapin, Schlusnus, Voelker, Wittrich.

BO153. **Whelbourn, Hubert.** Standard Book of Celebrated Musicians, Past and Present. revised and enlarged edition. New York: Garden City Publishing Co., Inc., 1937. xiii, 305 p., 7 illus.

This was originally published in London as Celebrated Musicians, Past and Present in 1930. 344 musicians are included, but the coverage is very elementary.

BO154. **Wyndham, Henry Saxe.** Stories of the Operas and the Singers Containing the Plots of the Operas and Biographical Sketches with Portraits of the Artists. London: John Long, Ltd., 1910. 96 p., 61 illus.

Biographical notes for fifty-two Covent Garden singers.

PART C.
Individual Singers, A-Z

This brief headnote is intended for those readers who bypassed the Introduction which contains a detailed explanation of the type of information one will encounter in PART C: INDIVIDUAL SINGERS, A-Z. The entries are alphabetical, are code numbered C0001 through C0720, and include at least two of the five possible sources of material which relate to that individual. These distinct catagories will always be listed in the following order: (1) A coded entry which indicates one of ten major dictionaries or encyclopedias. The titles and codes are listed in Bibliographical Abbreviations which follows the Introduction. Titles were chosen for their reliability and availability, and each entry will give the edition and volume number where appropriate. To alert the reader to additional bibliographic references NOT DUPLICATED in this work, the entry "(Bibliography)" will appear after the code, e.g. BAKER 6 (Bibliography); (2) A coded entry which refers to one of nine periodicals which have been checked for articles of a biographical or autobiographical nature. These details are also in Bibliographical Abbreviations; (3) Autobiographies and books written by the singer which relate directly to pedagogy or interpretation; (4) Biographies about a singer including historical novels if there was good reason to believe that the content was based upon or influenced by actual happenings; (5) Additional sources as well as cross-references.

C0001.
ABBOTT, EMMA. American Soprano. b. December 9, 1850, Chicago; d. January 5, 1891, Salt Lake City.

1. BAKER 6; GROVE 6/1; SCHMIDL/Supp.

2. ON 12/3, 22/16.

4. Greenwood, Grace. Emma Abbott: Prima Donna. London: Grand English Opera Company, 1879. 17 p.

    There are variations of this pamphlet published both in London where she made her professional debut on May 2, 1876 and in New New York which saw her in the same Donizetti role (Maria in La Fille du regiment) on February 8, 1877.

    Martin, Sadie E. The Life and Professional Career of Emma Abbott. Minneapolis: L. Kimball Printing Company, 1891. 192 p., 28 illus., biographical appendix.

This was begun as a collaboration in October 1890 and was then finished after Abbott's death on the basis of consultations with the singer's family.

Moore, E.W. and W.A. Story. A Souvenir in Remembrance of the Late Emma Abbott. Portland: W.A. Story & S.H. Friedlander, 1891. 76 p., 7 illus., musical examples.

C0002.
ABELL, JOHN. Scottish Tenor. b. 1652, Aberdeenshire; d. 1724, Cambridge.

1. BAKER 6; GROVE 6/1; RIEMANN 12.

5. Farmer, Henry George. "A King's Musician for the Lute and Voice John Abell (1652/3-1724)." In Hinrichsen's Musical Year Book. pp. 445-456. London: Hinrichsen Edition Limited, 1957.

C0003.
ABENDROTH, IRENE. Austrian Soprano. b. July 14, 1872, Lemberg; d. September 1, 1932, Weidling bei Wien.

1. EdS 1/1; SCHMIDL.

2. RC 6/4.

4. Gedenkblatt zum bevorstehenden 60. Geburtstag der ehemaligen K. K. hofopern- und kgl. saechs. Kammersaengerin a d. Irene Abendroth. n.p., n.d. [1932]. 7 p. (mimeograph).

    Thaller, Thomas. Irene Abendroth: ein Fragment ihrer Kuenstlerlaufbahn. Dresden: E. Pierson's Verlag, 1904. viii, 95 p., 56 illus., list of studied and performed roles.

    Taller was the singer's husband.

C0004.
ACKTE, AINO. Finnish Soprano. b. April 23, 1876, Helsinki; d. August 8, 1944, Nummela.

1. BAKER 6; EdS 1/1; GROVE 6/1; MGG 1/15 (Bibliography).

2. ON 40/22; RNC 5/3.

3. Ackté, Aino. Minnen och fantasier. Translated by Bertel Gripenberg. Stockholm: Albert Bonniers Foerlag, 1916. 128 p.

    Ackté, Aino. Minnen och upplevelser. Helsingfors: Soederstrom & C:O Foerlags-aktiebolag, 1925. 340 p., 47 illus., review excerpts.

    Ackté, Aino. Musitojeni kirja I: kuvitettu. Helsingissae: Kustannusosakeyhtioe Otava, 1925. 330 p., numerous illus., reviews.

These memoirs include information through 1904.
NOTE: She wrote a book about her second husband, Bruno Jalander,
which contains no information germane to the selection process.

Ackté, Aino. Taiteeni taipaleelta. Helsingissae: Kustannusosa-
keyhtise Otava, 1935. 212 p., numerous illus.

Memoirs from the period 1905-1920.

4. Wennervirta, Ludwig. Aino Ackté - Albert Edelfelt: eraes
    taiteemime episodi. Porvoo: Werner Soederstroem Osakeyhtioe,
    1944. 99 p., 17 illus.

5. Primus-Nyman, K.E. "Aino Ackté pa scenen 'Salome' a Covent Garden
    London." In Einsk tidskrift. 74:359-64. Helsingfors, n.d.

C0005.
ADAM, THEO. German Baritone. b. August 1, 1926, Dresden.

1. BAKER 6; GROVE 6/1; RIEMANN 12 + Supp. (Bibliography).

2. ON 33/18; OP 9/5; OW 6/3.

3. Adam, Theo. Seht, hier ist Tinte, Feder, Papier...aus der
    Werkstatt eines Saengers. Berlin: Henschelverlag Kunst und
    Gesellschaft, 1980. 225, [2] p., 54 illus., career chronology,
    complete list of roles, discography, index of names.

4. Olivier, Philippe. Theo Adam. "Les trésors de l'Opéra, no. 2."
    Paris: Opéra International, 1979. 61 p., illus., list of roles,
    discography.

C0006.
ADAMI-CORRADETTI, IRIS. Italian Soprano. b. March 14, 1909, Milano.
No lexicon listing.

4. Padoan, Paolo. Iris Adami-Corradetti: fra storia e critica.
    Bologna: Bongiovani Editore, n.d. [c.1979]. 103 p., illus.,
    chronology, repertoire, discography, index.

C0007.
ADELINE, MARIE-MADELEINE. French Soprano. b. December 15, 1760,
Venice; d. February 3, 1841, Versailles.

1. EdS 1/1; SCHMIDL/Supp. (under Riggieri).

4. Stern, J. Mesdemoiselles colombe de la Comédie-Italienne.
    Paris, 1923.

    No copy located.

C0008.
ADRIANA. SEE: BASILE-BARONI, ADRIANA. (C0042).

C0009.
ALBANESE, LICIA. Italian Soprano. b. July 22, 1913, Bari.

1. BAKER 6; EdS 1/1; RIEMANN 12 + Supp. (Bibliography).

2. ON 22/15, 39/1.

5. Musicisti e cantanti lirici Baresi. Bari: Biblioteca Dell'
   Archivio Delle Tradizioni Popolari Baresi, 1968. 63 p., illus.

C0010.
ALBANI, EMMA. Canadian Soprano. b. November 1, 1847, Chambley, near
Montreal; d. April 3, 1930, London.

1. BAKER 6; EdS 1/1; FETIS 2 + Supp.; GROVE 6/1; MGG 1/15; RIEMANN
   12; SCHMIDL.

2. GR 30/6; OPERA 23/4; RC 12/4-5, 8-9, 14/9-10; RNC 1/5.

3. Albani, Emma. Forty Years of Song. London: Mills & Boon, Limited,
   1911. Reprint 1977 with a discography by W.R. Moran. 285 p., 17
   illus. + 2 letters in facsimilie.

5. SEE: William Earl Brown entry under **MARCELLA SEMBRICH** (C0582).

C0011.
ALBONI, MARIETTA. Italian Mezzo-Soprano. b. March 6, 1823, Cesena;
d. June 23, 1894, Ville d'Avray, France.

1. BAKER 6; EdS 1/1; GROVE 6/1; MGG 1/16 (Bibliography); SCHMIDL.

4. Acloque, Elisa. Marietta Alboni. Paris: Moquet, 1848. 26 p.,
   portrait.

   Charbonneau, Hélène. L'Albani: sa carrière artistique et
   triomphale. Montréal: Imprimerie Jacques-Cartier, 1938. 171 p.,
   illus., index.

   Pougin, Arthur. Marietta Alboni. Paris: Plon-Nourrit & Cie,
   1912. 269 p., 6 illus., 6-part appendix which includes a list
   of her roles and her will.

5. Adami, Giuseppe. Tre romanzi dell'Ottocento: con sedici tavole
   fuori testo. Milano: Rizzoli e C., 1943. 254 p., 30 illus.

C0012.
ALCAIDE, TOMAZ de ACQUINO CARMELO. Portuguese Tenor. b. February
16, 1901, Estremoz; d. November 9, 1967, Lisbon.

1. EdS 1/1; GROVE 6/1.

3. Alcaide, Tomáz. Un cantor no palco e na vida: memórias. Lisboa:
   Publicacőes Europa-America, 1961. 295 p., 22 illus., chart of
   performances by year.

4. Exposição Tomaz Alcaide. Lisboa: Teatro Da Trindade, 1968. 77 p., 8 illus., chronology, catalogue of the exhibit (433 items).

CO013.
ALDA, FRANCES. New Zealand Soprano. b. May 31, 1883, Christchurch; d. September 18, 1952, Venice.

1. BAKER 6; EdS 1/1; GROVE 6/1; RIEMANN 12.

2. ON 27/24; RC 6/10.

3. Alda, Frances. Men Women and Tenors. Boston: Houghton Mifflin Company, 1937. Reprint 1970, 1971. 307 p., 30 illus.

   She wrote almost as well as she sang, and her memoirs are full of recollections about the Met between 1908 and 1929.

CO014.
AMATO, PASQUALE. Italian Baritone. b. March 21, 1878, Naples; d. August 12, 1942, New York City.

1. BAKER 6; EdS 1/1; GROVE 6/1; SCHMIDL.

2. RC 21/1-2, 5-6; RNC 1/1, 2.

CO015.
AMSTAD, MARIETTA. Swiss Soprano. b. May 31, 1882, Beggenried; d. August 7, 1972, Beggenried. No lexicon listing.

3. Amstad, Marietta. Erinnerungen einer nidwaldner Saengerin. Beckenried: p.p. by Martha Amstad, 1973. 116 p., 8 illus., 7 articles and manuscripts authored by the singer.

CO016.
ANDERS, PETER. German Tenor. b. July 1, 1908, Essen; d. September 4, 1954, Hamburg.

1. RIEMANN 12.

2. GR 32/5; OW 23/1; RNC 3/1, 4/6.

4. Pauly, Friedrich W. Peter Anders. Berlin: Rembrandt Verlag, 1963. 64 p., 32 illus., list of recordings.

CO017.
ANDERSON, MARIAN. American Mezzo-Soprano. b. February 17, 1902, Philadelphia.

1. BAKER 6; GROVE 6/1; RIEMANN 12.

2. ON 20/5.

3. Anderson, Marian. My Lord, What a Morning. New York: The Viking Press, 1956. viii, 312 p., 11 illus.

Howard Taubman provided editorial and critical assistance.

4. Albus, Harry T. The 'Deep River' Girl: the Life of Marian
    Anderson in Story Form. Grand Rapids: Wm. B. Eerdmans Publishing
    Company, 1949. 85 p., illus.

    Newman, Shirlee P. Marian Anderson: Lady from Philadelphia.
    Philadelphia: The Westminister Press, 1966. 175 p., 21 illus.,
    42-item bibliography, biography of the author, index.

    Sims, Janel L. Marian Anderson: an Annotated Bibliography and
    Discography. Westport: The Greenwood Press, 1981. viii, 243 p.,
    illus., discography, index, appendix.

    Spivey, Lenore. Singing Heart: a Story Based On the Life of
    Marian Anderson. Largo: Community Service Foundation, 1963.
    65 p., 14 illus., 12-item bibliography.

    Stevenson, Janet. Singing to the World: Marian Anderson.
    Chicago: Encyclopedia Britannica Press, Inc., 1963. 191 p.,
    17 illus.

    Tobias, Tobi. Marian Anderson. New York: Thomas Y. Crowell
    Company, 1972. 42 p., 22 illus.

    Intended for school children as is the previous entry.

    Vehanen, Kosti. Marian Anderson: a Portrait. New York: Whitt-
    lesley House, 1941. Reprint 1970. [iii], 270 p., 13 illus.,
    3-part appendix which includes four important reviews and signifi-
    cant dates.

    A recollection of the period 1931-41 when the author was her
    accompanist. Written with the assistance of George J. Barnett.

    Westlake, Nedda M. and Otto E. Albrecht. Marian Anderson: a
    Catalog of the Collection at the University of Pennsylvania
    Library. Philadelphia: University of Pennsylvania Press, 1981.
    vii, 89 p., illus.

    The singer donated her papers and memorabilia to the University
    of Pennsylvania in 1977.

5. Dobrin, Arnold. Voices of Joy, Voices of Freedom. New York:
    Coward, McCann & Geoghegan, 1972. 127 p., 12 illus., 13-item
    bibliography, index.

    Hughes, Langston. Famous Negro Music Makers. New York: Dodd, Mead
    & Company, 1955. 179 p., 23 illus., index.

    Hurok, Sol & Ruth Goode. Impresario: a Memoir. London: Mac-
    donald & Co., Ltd., 1947. Reprint 1976. x, 11-272 p., 35 illus.

    Richardson, Ben Albert. Great American Negroes. New York: Thomas
    Y. Crowell Company, 1947. viii, 223 p.

Rollins, Charlemae. <u>Famous Negro Entertainers of Stage, Screen, and TV</u>. New York: Dodd, Mead & Company, 1967. 122 p., 16 illus., index.

C0018.
d'ANDRADE, FRANCESCO. Portuguese Baritone. b. January 11, 1859, Lisbon; d. February 8, 1921, Berlin.

1. BAKER 6; EdS 1/1; MGG 1/15; RIEMANN 12; SCHMIDL.

2. RNC 3/7.

4. <u>Andenken an die erste Gastspielreise d'Andrade in Deutschland und Holland</u>. Elberfeld: Verlag Sam. Lucas, n.d. [c.1889]. 146 p., 8 illus.

C0019.
ANITUA, FANNY. Mexican Mezzo-Soprano. b. January 22, 1887, Durango; d. April 4, 1968, Mexico City.

1. RIEMANN 12/Supp.

5. Garcia, Francisco Moncada. <u>Pequeñas biografias de grandes musicos mexicanos</u>. México, D.F.: Ediciones Framong, 1966. 291 p.

C0020.
ARNOULD, MADELEINE SOPHIE. French Soprano. b. February 14, 1740, Paris; d. October 18, 1802, Paris.

1. BAKER 6; EdS 1/1; FETIS 2 + Supp.; GROVE 6/1; RIEMANN 12 (Bibliography); SCHMIDL.

2. MQ 6/1.

4. Billy, Andre. <u>La vie amoureuse de Sophie Arnould (avec des documents inédits)</u>. Paris: Ernest Flammarion, 1929. 191 p.

Deville, Pierre Francois Albérie. <u>Arnoldiana, ou Sophie Arnould et ses contemporaines; recueil choisi d'anecdotes piquantes, de réparties et de bons mots de Mlle. Arnould; précédé d'une notice sur sa vie et sur l'académie impériale de musique</u>. Paris: Gerard, 1813. 380 p., portrait.

Douglas, Robert B. <u>Sophie Arnould Actress and Wit</u>. Paris: Charles Carrington, 1898. x, 272 p., 7 engravings by Adolphe Lalauze.

Edition of 500 copies. A French edition of 425 copies was published in Paris the same year.

Dussane, Beatrix. <u>Sophie Arnould: la plus spirituelle des bacchantes</u>. Paris: Editions Albin Michel, 1938. 256 p.

Fayolle, Francois Joseph Marie. <u>Esprit de Sophie Arnould</u>. Paris: Chez F. Louis, Libraire, 1813. 106 p.

Goncourt, Edmond and Jules de Goncourt. Sophie Arnould d'áprés sa correspondence et ses mémoirs inédits. 3rd ed., Paris, G. Charpentier et Cie, 1885 [1st edition 1857]. xv, 327 p., dated list of operas performed in Paris 1758-1776, iconography.

The first edition was published by Poulet-Malassis et de Broise, and the second edition dated 1877 was published by Ernst Dentu.

5. Williams, H. Noel. Later Queens of the French Stage. New York: Charles Scribner's Sons, 1906. [iii], 360 p., 8 illus., index.

C0021.
ARROYO, MARTINA. American Soprano. b. February 2, 1940, New York City.

1. BAKER 6; GROVE 6/1 (Bibliography); RIEMANN 12/Supp.

2. ON 36/3, 41/8; OW 20/2.

C0022.
ASZTALOS, ELISA. German Soprano. No lexicon listing.

3. Asztalos, Elisa. Memorien aus meinem Kuenstlerleben als Prima-donna in Deutschland, Oesterreich und Italien. Hamburg: Verlags-anstalt und Druckerei Aktien-Gesellschaft, n.d. [1901]. 272 p., portrait.

C0023.
ATHANASIU, JEAN. Romanian Baritone. b. 1885, Bucharest; d. 1938, Bucharest.

1. EdS 1/1.

4. Istratty, Ella. Jean Athanasiu. Bucureşti: Editura Muzicală, 1966. 149 p., 12 illus., list of repertoire.

C0024.
AUSTRAL, FLORENCE. Australian Soprano. b. April 26, 1894, Melbourne; d. May 15, 1968, Sydney.

1. BAKER 6; EdS 1/1; GROVE 6/1; RIEMANN 12 + Supp.

2. GR 15/2, 21/4; RC 14/1-2, 7-8.

C0025.
BABINI, MATTEO. Italian Tenor. b. February 19, 1754, Bologna; d. September 22, 1816, Bologna.

1. BAKER 6; EdS 1/1; SCHMIDL.

4. Brighenti, Pietro. Elogio de Matteo Babini detto al Liceo filarmonico di Bologna. Bologna: Per le Stampe de Annesio Nobili, 1821. 28 p., portrait.

A favorite at the French court prior to the Revolution.

C0026.
BACCALONI, SALVATORE. Italian Bass. b. April 14, 1900, Rome;
d. December 31, 1969, New York City.

1. BAKER 6; EdS 1/1; GROVE 6/1 (Bibliography); RIEMANN 12/Supp.

2. ON 28/20, 34/17; OPERA 21/3.

C0027.
BACHMANN, CHARLOTTE WILHELMINE. German Soprano. b. November 2, 1757,
Berlin; d. August 19, 1817, Berlin.

1. MENDEL 1/1; MGG 1/15 (Bibliography); SCHMIDL.

4. Hartung, A. and K.W. Klipfel. Zur Erinnerung an Charlotte
   Wilhelmine Karoline Bachmann. Berlin, 1818.

   No copy located.

C0028.
BADESCU, DINU. Romanian Tenor. b. October 17, 1904, Craiova.

3. Bădescu, Dinu. Pe cărările unei vieti de boem: evocări.
   Bucureşti: Editura Muzicalá, 1973. 186 p., 38 illus.

C0029.
BADIA, CONCHITA. Spanish Soprano. b. November 14, 1897, Barcelona;
d. May 2, 1975, Barcelona.

1. GROVE 6/2.

4. Alavedra, Juan. Conxita Badia: una vida d'artista. Barcelona:
   Editorial Pòrtic, 1975. 254 p., 16 illus., discography, index.

C0030.
BAHR-MILDENBURG, ANNA. Austrian Soprano. November 29, 1872, Vienna;
d. January 27, 1947, Vienna.

1. EdS 1/1; GROVE 6/2; RIEMANN 12; SCHMIDL/Supp.

2. OPERA 4/1,3,4,5.

3. Bahr-Mildenburg, Anna. Erinnerungen. Wien: Wiener Literarische
   Anstalt, 1921. 231 p., 3 illus.

   Bahr-Mildenburg, Anna and Hermann Bahr. Bayreuth. Leipzig: Ernst
   Rowohlt Verlag, 1912. 114 p.

   The first 3 chapters (pp. 9-41) are by the singer.

   Bahr-Mildenburg, Anna. Tristan und Isolde: Darstellung des
   Werkes aus dem Geiste der Dichtung und Musik. Leipzig: Musik-
   wissenschaftlicher Verlag, 1936. 115 p., illus.

4. Kraus, Candida. Richard Wagner und Anna Bahr-Mildenburg. Wien:

University Dissertation, 1946. 130 p.

Stefan, Paul. <u>Anna Bahr-Mildenburg</u>. Wien: Wiener Literarische
Anstalt Gesellschaft m.b.H., 1922. 38 p., portrait.

5. Bach, R. "Im memoriam." In <u>Der Theater-Almanach</u>. Monaco, 1947.

C0031.
BAILEY, NORMAN. English Baritone. b. March 23, 1933, Birmingham.

1. GROVE 6/2; RIEMANN 12/Supp.

2. ON 41/15; OPERA 24/9.

C0032.
BAJENARU, IOAN. Romanian Tenor. b. 1863; d. October 30, 1921. No
lexicon listing.

4. Massoff, Ioan. <u>Tenorul Ioan Băjenaru si vremea lui</u>. Bucuresti:
    Editura Muzicală, 1970. 232 p., 30 illus., 41-item bibliography.

C0033.
BAKER, JANET. English Mezzo-Soprano. b. August 21, 1933, York.

1. BAKER 6; GROVE 6/2; RIEMANN/Supp.

2. GR 45/5; ON 34/19, 42/1; OPERA 21/5, 27/11.

3. Baker, Janet. <u>Full Circle: an Autobiographical Journal</u>. photo-
    graphs by Zoe Dominic. New York: Franklin Watts, Inc., 1982.
    xiv, 270 p., 56 illus., appendix of operatic roles compiled by
    Paul Hirschman.

4. Blyth, Alan. <u>Janet Baker</u>. Shepperton: Ian Allan Ltd., 1973.
    64 p., 47 illus., discography by Malcolm Walker.

C0034.
BALATRI, FILIPPO. Italian Baritone. b. 1676, Alfea; d. 1756.

1. Eitner 1/1.

3. Balatri, Filippo: <u>Frutti del mondo, esperimentati da Filippo
    Balatri nativo dell'alfea in toscana</u>. This MS was edited by
    Karl Vossler and published in Palermo in 1924 by Remo Sandron
    Editore. 292 p.

    A fairly complete version of one of the very earliest known
    singer's autobiographies. Balatri was a singer at the Hof-
    kapelle in Munich and resigned on April 22, 1721 over a salary
    dispute. The editor separated Balatri's text into chapters
    and added a table of contents as well as a preface which in-
    cludes a number of quotations from the singer's will <u>Testa-
    mento o sia ultima volonta di Filippo Balatri, nativo Alfea</u>.
    Balatri mentioned other writings in this will, but Vossler
    was unable to locate any of them.

C0035.
BALFE, MICHAEL WILLIAM. Irish Baritone. b. May 15, 1808, Dublin;
d. October 20, 1870, Rowney Abbey, Hertfordshire.

1. BAKER 6; EdS 1/1; FETIS 2/1 + Supp.; GROVE 6/2 (Bibliography);
    MGG 1/1; RIEMANN 12; SCHMIDL.

2. GR 3/4.

3. Balfe, Michael William. Indispensible Studies for a Soprano
    Voice. London, 1852.

    Balfe, Michael William. Method of Singing. London, 1855.

    No copies located of these two pedagogical manuals.

4. Barrett, William Alexander. Balfe: His Life and Work. London:
    Remington and Co., 1882. v, 313 p., 6 illus., index.

    Kenney, Charles Lamb. A Memoir of Michael William Balfe.
    London: Tinsley Brothers, 1875. Reprint 1978. 309 p., 3 illus.

C0036.
BAMPTON, ROSE. American Soprano. b. November 28, 1908, Cleveland.

1. BAKER 6; EdS 1/1 (Bibliography); GROVE 6/2; RIEMANN 12 + Supp.

2. RC 8/11-12.

C0037.
BANTI-GIORGI, BRIGIDA. Italian Soprano. b. c.1759, Monticelli
d'Ongina, near Crema; d. February 18, 1806, Bologna.

1. BAKER 6; EdS 1/1; GROVE 6/2; SCHMIDL.

4. Banti, Giuseppe. Vita di Brigida Banti. Bologna: n.p., 1869.

    Lozzi, Carlo. "Brigida Banti, regina del teatro lirico nel secolo
    XVIII." In Rivista Musicale Italiana 11 (1904): 64-76.

5. SEE: T.L. Phipson (B0114).

C0038.
BARBI, ALICE. Italian Mezzo-Soprano. b. June 1, 1862, Modena;
d. September 4, 1948, Rome.

1. BAKER 6; SCHMIDL (Bibliography).

5. Hanslick, Eduard. Fuenf Jahre Musik 1891-1895. Berlin: All-
    gemeiner Verein fuer deutsche Litteratur, 1896. 402 p.

    Rokitansky, Victor. Ueber Saenger und Singen. Wien: A.
    Hartleben's Verlag, 1891. xvi, 191 p.

C0039.
BARBIERI, FEDORA. Italian Mezzo-Soprano. b. June 4, 1920, Trieste.

1. BAKER 6; EdS 1/1; GROVE 6/2; RIEMANN 12/Supp.

2. ON 17/13, 41/16.

C0040.
BARDI, MITZI. Czechoslovakian Soprano. No lexicon listing.

3. Aus dem Repertoire Mitzi Bardi. Prague: Im Selbstverlag, 1910.
   24 p.

C0041.
BARONI, LEONORA. Italian Soprano. b. December 1611, Mantua;
d. April 6, 1670, Rome.

1. EdS 1/1 (Bibliography); FETIS 2/1; GROVE 6/2 (Bibliography);
   SCHMIDL.

4. Costaguti, Vincenzo. Applausi poetici alle glorie della signora
   Leonora Baroni. Roma: n.p., 1639.

   Apparently the earliest publication of a biographical nature
   about a singer. Leonora, the daughter of 'La bella Adriana,'
   was the greatest vocalist of her time. No copy located.

C0042.
BASILE-BARONI, ADRIANA ('La bella Adriana'). Italian Soprano. b.
c.1580, Posillipo, near Naples; d. c.1640, Rome.

1. EdS 1/2 (Bibliography); GROVE 6/2 (Bibliography): SCHMIDL (Bibliography).

4. Ademollo, Alessandro. La bell'Adriana a Milano (1611). Milano:
   R. Stabilimento Musicale Ricordi, n.d. [1885]. 14 p., portrait.

   Ademollo, Alessandro. La bell'Adriana ed altre virtuose del suo
   tempo alla corte di mantova. Città di Castello: S. Lapi Tipografo Editore, 1888. ix, 359 p., illus., index of names.

C0043.
BASILIDES, MARIA. Hungarian Mezzo-Soprano. b. November 11, 1886,
Jolsva; d. September 26, 1946, Budapest.

1. EdS 1/2; GROVE 6/2.

4. Molnár, Jenö Antal. Basilides Mária. Budapest: Zenemükiadó,
   1967. 92 p., 36 illus., list of opera roles, list of oratorios,
   2 LP records with 12 selections.

C0044.
BATHY, ANNA. Hungarian Soprano. b. June 13, 1901, Beregszasz;
d. May 20, 1962, Budapest.

1. GROVE 5/2.

4. Somogyi, Vilmos & Imre Molnár. Báthy Anna. Budapest: Zene-
    mükiadó, 1969. 76 p., 20 illus., list of opera roles, 2 LP
    records with 6 selections.

C0045.
BATTISTINI, MATTIA. Italian Baritone. b. February 27, 1856, Rome;
d. November 7, 1928, Collebaccaro, near Rome.

1. BAKER 6; EdS 1/2 (Bibliography); GROVE 6/2; MGG 1/15 (Biblio-
    graphy); RIEMANN 12; SCHMIDL.

2. GR 4/3; ON 22/4; OPERA 8/5; OW 23/12; RC 2/9, 3/5, 8/11-12;
    RNC 5/7, 8, 9.

4. Fracassini, Gino. Mattia Battistini: profilo artistico illus-
    trato. Milano: Carlo Barbini, 1914. 160 p., 10 illus.

    Palmegiani, Francesco. Mattia Battistini (il re dei baritoni).
    Milano: Stampa D'Oggi, n.d. [1949]. Reprint 1977 with discog-
    raphy by W.R. Moran. 199 p., 10 illus., 13-item bibliography.

    Shawe-Taylor, Desmond. Mattia Battistini (1856-1928): a Biogra-
    phical Sketch. London: The Gramophone Company, n.d. [1960].
    16, [2] p., 2 illus., recording details.

    One of a series of pamphlets for "Great Recordings of the Century."

    NOTE: A study of the singer by Tom Sillanpa is in preparation.

5. SEE: LINA CAVALIERI (C0109).

    SEE: Celestino Sarobe entry under MIGUEL FLETA (C0207).

C0046.
BEDFORD, PAUL JOHN. English Bass. b. c.1792, Bath; d. January 11,
1871, Chelsea.

1. EdS 1/2.

3. Bedford, Paul John. Recollections and Wanderings of Paul Bedford:
    Facts, Not Fancies. London: Routledge, Warne, & Routledge, 1864.
    160 p., portrait.

    A minor figure who performed with Malibran, Schroeder-Devrient,
    and Lablache. Of slight biographical significance, "...it may
    amuse my numerous friends and multitudinous acquaintances, and
    may be the medium of passing a weary half hour..."

C0047.
BELLINCIONI, GEMMA. Italian Soprano. b. August 18, 1864, Monza;
d. April 23, 1950, Naples.

1. BAKER 6; EdS 1/2 (Bibliography); GROVE 6/2; MGG 1/15 (Bibliog-

raphy); RIEMANN 12; SCHMIDL + Supp.

2. ON 14/5, 41/9; RC 16/9-10, 18/5-6.

3. Bellincioni, Gemma. Io e il palcosenico: (trenta e un anno di vita artistica). Milano: Societa Anonima Editoriale, 1920. Reprint 1974 (together with the next entry) with a discography by W.R. Moran. 137 p.

    Stagno-Bellincioni, Bianca. Roberto Stagno e Gemma Bellincioni: intimi. Firenze: Casa Editrice Monsalvato, 1943. Reprint 1977. 172 p., 22 illus.

    Bianca is the daughter of this famous couple (b. January 23, 1888 Budapest). SEE: EdS 1/9 (Bibliography). The 1977 reprint includes both this title and the earlier 1920 edition of Gemma Bellincioni's autobiography with a discography by W.R. Moran.

5. SEE: Eduard Hanslick entry under ALICE BARBI (C0038).

C0048.
BELLOC-GIORGI, MARIA TERESA. Italian Mezzo-Soprano. b. July 2, 1784, San Benigno, near Turin; d. May 13, 1855, San Giorgio Cavanese.

1. BAKER 6 (Bibliography); EdS 1/2 (Bibliography); GROVE 6/2; SCHMIDL + Supp.

4. Della Croce, Vittorio. Una giacobina piemontese alla scala: la primadonna Teresa Belloc. Torino: Edizioni Eda, 1978. 222 p., 14 illus., iconography, repertorie, Rossini era discography, 80-item bibliography, index.

C0049.
BENDER, PAUL. German Bass. b. July 28, 1875, Driedorf; d. November 25, 1947, Munich.

1. BAKER 6; EdS 1/2; GROVE 6/2; RIEMANN 12.

2. RC 17/11, 18/1-2.

C0050.
BENTON, JOSEPH. American Tenor. b. September 10, 1900, Sayre, California; d. April 4, 1975, Oklahoma City.

1. BAKER 6; RIEMANN 12.

3. Benton, Joseph. Oklahoma Tenor: Musical Memories of Giuseppe Bentonelli. Norman: University of Oklahoma Press, 1973. xiii, 150 p., 16 illus.

C0051.
BERGANZA, TERESA. Spanish Mezzo-Soprano. b. March 16, 1935, Madrid.

1. GROVE 6/2 (Bibliography); EdS/Supp.; RIEMANN 12/Supp.

2. ON 31/18; OPERA 18/3; OW 10/5, 19/4.

4. Segalini, Sergio. Teresa Berganza. Paris: Librairie Arthème
   Fayard, 1982. 94, [16] p., 103 illus., chronology, discography.

C0052.
BERGER, ERNA. German Soprano. b. October 19, 1900, Dresden.

1. BAKER 6; GROVE 6/2; MGG 1/15 (Bibliography); RIEMANN 12.

4. Hoecker, Karla. Erna Berger: die singende Botschafterin. Berlin:
   Rembrandt Verlag, 1961. 63 p., 33 illus., list of roles.

C0053.
BERGMAN, BLANCHE. Dutch Soprano. b. August 15, 1955, Gaud; d. December 30, 1974, Hartheim, near Freibourg-en-Brisgau. No lexicon listing.

4. DuBois, J.P. Blanche Bergman: une etoile pour trois saisons.
   privately printed, 1975. unpaginated [21 p.], 3 illus.,
   contents of a memorial recording.

C0054.
BERGONZI, CARLO. Italian tenor. b. July 13, 1924, Parma.

1. BAKER 6; EdS/Supp. (Bibliography); GROVE 6/2 (Bibliography);
   RIEMANN 12/Supp.

2. ON 24/22, 43/4; OPERA 29/3; OP 7/2.

C0055.
BERNAC, PIERRE. French Baritone. b. January 12, 1899, Paris;
d. October 17, 1979, Villeneuve-les-Avignon.

1. BAKER 6; GROVE 6/2 (Bibliography); RIEMANN 12.

2. ON 41/13; RS 18 (April 1965).

3. Bernac, Pierre. Francis Poulenc, the Man and His Songs. Translated by Winifred Radford. New York: B. Norton, 1977. 233 p.,
   bibliography, index of titles, index of first lines.

   Bernac, Pierre. The Interpretation of French Song. New York:
   Praeger, 1970. xiv, 326 p., index of titles, index of first lines,
   index of composers.

5. Gelatt, Roland. Music Makers: Some Outstanding Musical Performers of Our Day. New York: Alfred A. Knopf, 1953. xvi, 286,
   xiv p., 21 illus., index.

   Based upon personal interviews and live performances, these
   articles include studies of Bernac, Flagstad, and Lotte Lehmann.
   "Each chapter attempts to analyze its subject's special gifts,
   the reasons why he performs as he does, and his influence on
   other musicians."

C0056.
BERRY, WALTER. Austrian Baritone. b. April 8, 1929, Vienna.

1. EdS/Supp. (Bibliography); GROVE 6/2; MGG 1/15; RIEMANN 12/Supp.

2. ON 31/8, 38/23; OW 2/8, 9/6, 15/10.I

4. SEE: Paul Lorenz entry under **CHRISTA LUDWIG** (C0373).

C0057.
BETETTO, JULIJ. Yugoslavian Bass. b. August 27, 1885, Ljubljana;
d. January 14, 1963, Ljubljana.

1. EdS 1/2 (Bibliography); RIEMANN 12/Supp.

4. Ukmar, V. Srečanja z Julijem Betetto. Lubjljana: Drzvana zalozba
    Slovenije, 1961. 126 p., 19 illus., list of roles.

C0058.
BILLINGTON, ELIZABETH. English Soprano. b. c.1765 London; d. August
25, 1818, near Venice, Italy.

1. BAKER 6; EdS 1/2 (Bibliography); GROVE 6/2 (Bibliography);
    RIEMANN 12; SCHMIDL (Bibliography).

4. Ridgway, James, ed. Memoirs of Mrs. Billington, from Her Birth:
    containing a Variety of Matter, Ludicrous, Theatrical, Musical,
    and ---; with Copies of Several Original Letters, Now in the
    Possession of the Publisher, written by Mrs. Billington, to her
    Mother, the Late Mrs. Weichsel: a Dedication; and a Prefatory
    Address. London: J. Ridgway, 1792. [4], xv, 78 p., portrait.

    A libelous attack on the singer rather typical of the journal-
    istic practices of the time. A rebuttal, Answer to the Memoirs
    of Mrs. Billington (London 1792), was printed immediately.
    BAKER 6 states that this defense was "written by a gentleman."
    I have not seen a copy nor have I seen the French translation
    of Ridgway's book (Paris 1822) mentioned in FETIS 2/1.

5. Parker, John R. Musical Biography: or Sketches of the Lives
    and Writings of Eminent Musical Characters interspersed with
    an Epitome of Interesting Musical Matter. Boston: Stone &
    Fovell, 1824. vii, 250 p.

    SEE: Quarterly Musical Magazine and Review 1 (1818):164-90.

C0059.
BISPHAM, DAVID SCULL. American Baritone. b. January 5, 1857, Philadelphia; d. October 2, 1921, New York City.

1. BAKER 6; EdS 1/2; GROVE 6/2; SCHMIDL/Supp.

2. ON 31/12; RC 6/1, 12/8-9.

3. Bispham, David Scull. A Quaker Singer's Recollections. New York:

The Macmillan Company, 1920. Reprint 1977. vii, 401 p., 19 illus., index.

BAKER 6 notes that Bispham's career records were left to the New York Public Library.

C0060.
BJOERLING, JUSSI. Swedish Tenor. b. February 2, 1911, Stora Tuna; d. September 9, 1960, Siaroe, near Stockholm.

1. BAKER 6; EdS 1/2; GROVE 6/2 (Bibliography); MGG 1/15; RIEMANN 12.

2. GR 38/6; ON 24/7, 25/3, 36/14; OPERA 11/11; OW 14/4; RNC 4/4, 5.

3. Bjoerling, Jussi. Med bagaget i strupen. Stockholm: Wahlstroem & Widstrand, 1945. 175, [10] p., 10 illus., discography, list of roles.

4. Bjoerling, Goesta. Jussi: boken om storebor. Stockholm: Steinsviks Bokfoerlag, 1945. 224 p., 113 illus., discography.

   Hagman, Bertil, ed. Jussi Bjoerling: en minnesbok. Stockholm: Albert Bonniers foerlag AB, 1960. 214 p., 81 illus., list of stage repertoire sung in Sweden, discography by Carl L. Brunn.

   Memorial articles by thirty-nine colleagues.

   Lund, Eyvind Skandrup and Herbert Rosenberg. Jussi Bjoerling: a Record List. Copenhagen: Nationaldiskoteket, 1969. 82 p., index.I

   Porter, Jack W. and Harald Henrysson. A Jussi Bjoerling Discography. Indianapolis, Jussi Bjoerling Memorial Archive, 1982. 190 p., 21-item bibliography, title index, performer index.

   Seemungal, Rupert P. A Complete Discography of Jussi Bjoerling. 3rd edition [1st edition 1959]. Trinidad: n.p., 1964. 55 p.

C0061.
BJONER, INGRID. Norwegian Soprano. b. November 8, 1927, Krakstad.

1. EdS/Supp.; GROVE 6/2; RIEMANN 12/Supp.

2. ON 29/8; OW 11/4, 22/12.

C0062.
BLACHUT, BENO. Czechoslovakian Tenor. b. June 14, 1913, Ostrava-Vítkovice.

1. EdS 1/2; GROVE 6/2 (Bibliography); RIEMANN 12.

4. Brožovská, Jarmila. Beno Blachut. Bratislava: Panton Praha, 1964. 66, [18] p., 23 illus., list of roles, discography.

C0063.
BLAKE-ALVERSON, MARGARET. American Mezzo-Soprano. b. June 12, 1836,
Mt. Carmel, Indiana; d. ? No lexicon listing.

3. Blake-Alverson, Margaret. <u>Sixty Years of California Song</u>. San
    Francisco: privately printed by Sunset Publishing House, 1913.
    x, 275 p., 321 illus., list of pupils.

C0064.
BLASIS, VIRGINIA de. Italian Soprano. b. August 5, 1804, Marseille;
d. May 11-12, 1838, Florence.

1. EdS 1/2 (Bibliography); RIEMANN 12; SCHMIDL.

4. Cominazzi, P. <u>Biografia di Virginia Blasis e onori poetici</u>.
    Milano: Centenarie e Cie., 1853.

    No copy located.

C0065.
BLEGEN, JUDITH. American Soprano. b. April 23, 1941 Missoula,
Montana.

1. BAKER 6; GROVE 6/2.

2. ON 39/6, 46/7.

C0066.
BOCKELMANN, RUDOLF. German Baritone. b. April 2, 1892, Bodenteich;
d. October 9, 1958, Dresden.

1. BAKER 6; EdS 1/2; GROVE 6/2; MGG 1/15; RIEMANN 12 + Supp.

3. Bockelmann, Rudolf. "Die Rolle des Hans Sachs." In <u>Sammelbaende</u>
    <u>der Robert Schumann Gesellschaft</u> II (1967).

    No copy located.

4. Wessling, Berndt W. <u>Verachtet mir die Meister nicht! ein Buch der</u>
    <u>Erinnerung an Rudolf Bockelmann</u>. Celle: Schweiger & Pick Verlag,
    1963. 120 p., 25 illus., 11-item bibliography, discography,
    calendar of important dates, index of names.

C0067.
BOEHME, KURT. German Bass. b. May 5, 1908, Dresden.

1. GROVE 6/2; RIEMANN 12.

4. Richter, Karl. <u>Kurt Boehme: selbstverstaendlich emfaengt mich</u>
    <u>ihro Gnaden!</u> Augsburg: Schroff-Druck Verlagsgesellschaft mbH,
    1977. 239 p., 66 ilus., complete list of roles, discography.

C0068.
BOHNEN, MICHAEL. German Bass. b. May 2, 1888, Cologne; d. April 26,
1965, Berlin.

1. BAKER 6; EdS 1/2 (Bibliography); GROVE 6/2 (Bibliography);
    MGG 1/15 (Bibliography); RIEMANN 12.

2. ON 34/14; RC 27/9-10, 11-12.

C0069.
BONCI, ALESSANDRO. Italian Tenor. b. February 10, 1870, Cesena;
d. August 9, 1940, Viserba, near Rimini.

1. BAKER 6; EdS 1/2 (Bibliography); GROVE 6/3; RIEMANN 12;
    SCHMIDL.

2. RC 11/7, 9-10, 12/4-5, 18/1-2.

4. Bannenta, D. Alessandro Bonci: impressioni. Ferrara: Tipo-
    grafia Zuffi, 1901.

    No copy located.

C0070.
BONINSEGNA, CELESTINA. Italian Soprano. b. February 26, 1877, Reggio
Emilia; d. February 14, 1947, Milan.

1. EdS 1/2 (Bibliography); GROVE 6/3 (Bibliography); SCHMIDL/Supp.

2. RC 12/1-2, 3, 8-9, 10-11, 12.

C0071.
BORDONI-HASSE, FAUSTINA. Italian Mezzo-Soprano. b. c.1700, Venice;
d. November 4, 1781, Venice.

1. BAKER 6 (under Hasse); EdS 1/2 (Bibliography); GROVE 6/3 (Bib-
    liography); MGG 1/5 (under Johann Adolf Hasse); RIEMANN 12
    (under Johann Adolf Hasse); SCHMIDL (under Faustina Hasse).

2. MQ 29/2 (article also includes Susannah Maria Cibber, Francesca
    Cuzzoni, Margherita Durastanti, and Anastasia Robinson).

4. Hoegg, Margarete. Die Gesangskunst der Faustina Hasse und das
    Saengerinnenwesen ihrer Zeit in Deutschland. Koenigsbrueck: A.
    Pabst, 1931. 95 p., list of repertoire.

    Niggli, A. Faustina Bordoni-Hasse: eine Primadonna des acht-
    zehnten Jahrhunderts. Leipzig: Breitkopf & Haertel, 1880.
    57 p. (pp. 261-318), 20-item bibliography.

    Although issued separately, this is actually Nr. 21/22 of the
    Sammlung Musikalischer Vortraege.

    Polko, Elise. Faustina Hasse: musikalischer Roman. Leipzig:
    Verlag von B. Elischer Nachfolger, 1895 [1st edition 1860].
    vii, 654 p.

    Urbani de Gheltof, G.M. La nuova sirena ed il caro Sassone: note
    biografiche. Venezia, M. Fontana, 1890. 81 p.

5. Rochlitz, Friedrich. <u>Fuer Freunde der Tonkunst</u>. 4 vol. dritte auflage. Leipzig: Carl Cnobloch, 1868 [1st edition 1824]. Vol. 4, pp. 161-76.

CO072.
BORGATTI, GIUSEPPE. Italian Tenor. b. March 19, 1871, Cento; d. October 18, 1950, Reno, Lago Maggiore.

1. BAKER 6; EdS 1/2 (Bibliography); GROVE 6/3 (Bibliography); SCHMIDL.

2. ON 26/9; RC 8/11-12.

3. Borgatti, Giuseppe. <u>La mia vita d'artista: ricordi e aneddoti</u>. Bologna: L. Cappelli-Editore, 1927. 182 p., 13 illus.

   There is an MS translation in English by the late George L. Nyklicek.

CO073.
BORGIOLI, DINO. Italian Tenor. b. February 15, 1891, Florence; d. September 12, 1960, Florence.

1. BAKER 6; EdS 1/2; GROVE 6/3; RIEMANN 12.

2. GR 15/1; OPERA 11/11.

CO074.
BORI, LUCREZIA. Spanish Soprano. b. December 24, 1887, Valencia; d. May 14, 1960, New York City.

1. BAKER 6; EdS 1/2 (Bibliography); GROVE 6/3 (Bibliography); RIEMANN 12; SCHMIDL/Supp.

2. ON 8/8, 25/1; RC 3/10, 4/1, 5, 9/5, 21/7-8; RNC 4/2.

4. Marion, John Francis. <u>Lucrezia Bori of the Metropolitan Opera</u>. New York: P.J. Kenedy & Sons, 1962. 192 p., 10 illus., index.

5. SEE: autobiographies of **GIACOMO LAURI-VOLPI** (CO347).

CO075.
BOUE, GEORI. French Soprano. b. October 16, 1918 Toulouse. No lexicon listing.

1. KUTSCH 3.

2. OP 2/10.

4. Mancini, Roland. <u>Géori Boué</u>. Paris: Sodal, 1967. 32 p., 26 illus.

   Special supplement to the French periodical, <u>Opéra</u>.

C0076.
BOVY, VINA. Belgian Soprano. b. May 22, 1900, Ghent.

1. BAKER 6; GROVE 6/3; RIEMANN 12.

2. ON 15/21.

4. Deleersnyder, Jacques. Vina Bovy. Ghent: privately printed, 1965. 128 p., 40 illus., list of roles by year and theater.

C0077.
BRAHAM, JOHN. English Tenor. b. March 20, 1774, London; d. February 17, 1856, London.

1. BAKER 6; EdS 1/2; GROVE 6/3 (Bibliography); RIEMANN 12 (Bibliography); SCHMIDL.

4. Gilliland, Thomas. Jack in Office: containing Remarks on Mr. Braham's Address to the Public.... London: C. Chapple, n.d. [1805]. 40 p.

   Levien, John Mewburn. The Singing of John Braham. London: Novello and Company Limited, 1944. 40 p., 5 illus.

C0078.
BRANDT, MARIANNE. Austrian Mezzo-Soprano. b. September 12, 1842, Vienna; d. July 9, 1921, Vienna.

1. BAKER 6; GROVE 6/3 (Bibliography); RIEMANN 12.

5. La Mara [pseud. for Ida Maria Lipsius]. Die Frauen im Tonleben der Gegenwart: musikalische Studienkoepfe. vol. 5. Leipzig: Breitkopf & Haertel, 1875-82.

   No copy seen.

C0079.
BRIGHENTI, MARIA GIORGI. SEE: GIORGI-BRIGHENTI (C0244).

C0080.
BRIZZI-GIORGI, MARIA. Italian Soprano. b. August 7, 1775, Bologna; d. January 18?, 1812, Bologna.

1. SCHMIDL (Bibliography).

4. Bacchetti, Antonio. Elogio funebre di Maria Brizzi Giorgi detto nella Chiesa delle Muratelle in Bologna nel giorno de' suoi funerali 22 gennajo 1812. Bologna: Tipografia Masi e Comp., n.d. [1812]. viii, 40 p.

   Giordani, Pietro. Elogio a Maria Brizzi Giorgi nelle solenni esequie a lei fatte dall'Academia Filarmonica in San Giovanni in Monte di Bologna. Bologna: Tipografia de Franceschi, 1813.

   No copy located.

C0081.
BROSCHI, CARLO. SEE: **FARINELLI** (C0188).

C0082.
BROUWENSTIJN, GRE. Dutch Soprano. b. August 26, 1915, Den Helder.

1. EdS/Supp.; GROVE 6/3 (Bibliography); MGG 1/15; RIEMANN 12 +
    Supp. (Bibliography).

2. OPERA 10/7.

3. van Swol-Brouwenstijn, Gré and A.C. van Swol. Gré Brouwenstijn
    met en zonder make-up. Bussum: Telebock nv, 1971. 224 p., 187
    illus., list of major appearances, discography.

5. Bieb in Holland. Utrecht: A.W. Brunna En Zoon, 1958. 191 p.,
    12 illus.

    Thirty-Two articles reprinted from Vrij nederland which include
    Brouwenstijn and Julia Culp. Popular journalism.

C0083.
BROWNLEE, JOHN. Australian Baritone. b. January 7, 1900, Geelong;
d. January 10, 1969, New York City.

1. BAKER 6; EdS 1/2; GROVE 6/3; RIEMANN 12 + Supp.

2. ON 33/18; OPERA 20/3; RC 8/11-12.

C0084.
von BRUCKMANN, HANNA. German Soprano. b. December 16, 1870,
Wiesbaden. No lexicon listing.

3. von Bruckmann, Hanna. Dreissig Jahre aus meinem Leben. Muenchen:
    "als Privatdruck hergestellt," Verlag Karl Thiemig KG, n.d.
    (preface suggests that the writing began in 1950). 275 p.,
    45 illus.

    Her maiden as well as stage name was **HANNA BORCHERS**. She
    married the diplomat Alfred von Bruckmann in 1900 after she
    left the stage.

C0085.
BRUSON, RENATO. Italian Baritone. b. January 13, 1936, Este, near
Padua.

1. GROVE 6/3.

2. ON 46/18; OPERA 30/3.

C0086.
BUMBRY, GRACE. American Mezzo-Soprano. b. January 4, 1937, St. Louis,
Missouri.

1. BAKER 6; GROVE 6/3; RIEMANN/Supp.

2. ON 26/2, 32/7, 46/4; OPERA 21/6; OW 4/5, 20/7.

C0087.
BURKE, THOMAS ASPINALL. English Tenor. b. March 2, 1890, Leigh,
Lancashire; d. September 13, 1969, Sutton, Surrey.

1. GROVE 6/3 (Bibliography).

4. Vose, John D. The Lancashire Caruso. Blackpool: John D. Vose,
   1982. 201 p., 40 illus., list of performances, list of films,
   discography.

C0088.
BUTT, CLARA. English Mezzo-Soprano. b. February 1, 1873, Southwick,
Sussex; d. January 23, 1936, Worthsloke, Oxford.

1. BAKER 6; GROVE 6/3 (Bibliography).

2. ON 37/13.

4. Ponder, Winifred. Clara Butt: Her Life Story. London: George
   G. Harrap & Co., Ltd., 1928. Reprint 1978. 262 p., 24 illus.,
   index.

5. SEE: **ROLAND FOSTER** (C0214).

C0089.
CABALLE, MONTSERRAT. Spanish Soprano. b. April 12, 1933, Barcelona.

1. GROVE 6/3 (Bibliography); RIEMANN 12/Supp.

2. GR 51/2; ON 30/1, 38/18; OPERA 26/4; OP 6/7; OW 17/4.

4. Farret, Georges. Monserrat Caballé. "Les Trésors de l'Opéra No.
   6." Paris, Opéra International, n.d. [1980]. 62 p., 46 illus.,
   chronological repertoire list, chronology.

C0090.
CAFFARELLI. Italian Mezzo-Soprano Castrato. b. April 12, 1710,
Bitonto; d. January 31, 1783, Naples.

1. BAKER 6; EdS 1/2 (Bibliography); GROVE 6/3 (Bibliography);
   MGG 1/15 (Bibliography); RIEMANN 12 (Bibliography) + Supp.
   (Bibliography); SCHMIDL.

4. Faustini-Fasini, E. Gli astri maggiori del "Bel Canto" napole-
   tano: Gaetano Majorano, detto "Cafarelli". Roma: Edizioni
   Psalterium, 1939.

   No copy seen.

   Giovine, Alfredo. Il musico gaetano maiorano detto cafarelli,
   non era barese ma bitontino (cenni biografici, elenco de
   rappresentazioni, bibliografia, indici vari e iconografia).
   Bari: n.p., 1969. 44 p., 13 illus., 114 item bibliography, list

of operas with casts, index of names.

C0091.
CALLAS, MARIA. American Soprano. b. December 3, 1923, New York City;
d. September 16, 1977, Paris.

1. BAKER 6; EdS 1/7 (under Meneghini-Callas with Bibliography);
   GROVE 6/3 (Bibliography); MGG 1/12 (under Meneghini-Callas with
   Bibliography); RIEMANN 12 (under Meneghini-Callas).

2. GR 31/10, 37/2, 55/5; ON 21/4, 29/19, 34/7, 36/21, 42/5, 43/2,
   44/2; OPERA 3/2, 21/9-10, 24/4, 28/11; OW 12/12, 14/6, 18/11.

4. Ardoin, John & Gerald Fitzgerald [a double publication].
   Callas: the Art and the Life by John Ardoin; The Great Years
   by Gerald Fitzgerald. New York: Holt, Rinehart and Winston,
   1974. 282 p., numerous illus., chronology 1938-1974, index.

   Ardoin, John. The Callas Legacy. London: Duckworth, 1977. xi,
   224 p., recorded interviews, recorded performances, 51-item
   bibliography (especially important for articles), index of names.

   Ardoin, John. The Callas Legacy: a Biography of a Career.
   revised edition. New York: Charles Scribner's Sons, 1982 [1st
   edition 1977]. 240 p., illus., recorded interviews, filmed performances, 51-item bibliography, index of names.

   This is a corrected version of the author's 1977 publication with
   a limited number of additional recordings which are evaluated in
   the spirit of the earlier work.

   Bragaglia, Leonardo. L'arte dello stupore: omaggio a Maria Callas.
   Un saggio con bibliografia, discografia, cronologia della vita e
   dell'arte. Antologia critica. Presentazione di Giacomo Lauri Volpi
   con due lettere inedite di Maria Callas a Lauri Volpi. Roma:
   Bulzoni Editore, 1977. 81 p., 32 illus., bibliography, discography,
   chronology.

   No copy seen.

   Callas, Evangelia & Lawrence G. Blochman. My Daughter Maria
   Callas. New York: Fleet Publishing Corporation, 1960. Reprint
   1977. 186 p., 20 illus.

   Cederna, Camilla. Callas. Milano: Longanesi e C., 1968. 149
   p., discography by Mario Pasi.

   Galatopoulos, Stelios. Callas, la divina: Art that Conceals
   Art. revised and enlarged edition. London: J.M. Dent & Sons
   Ltd., 1966 [1st edition 1963]. 218 p., 31 illus., list of
   concerts, list of recordings, index.

   Galatopoulas, Stelios. Callas: prima donna assoluta. London:
   W.H. Allen & Co. Ltd., 1976. xviii, 353 p., 103 illus., list
   of recordings, annals of Maria Callas' performances, index.

Gara, Eugenio: _Maria Callas_. Translated by Barbara Wall. Geneva:
Rene Kister, 1958 [1st edition 1957]. 32 p., 19 portraits by
Roger Hauert, 1 facsimilie, list of recordings.

Goise, Denis. _Maria Callas: la diva scandale_. Paris: G. Authier,
n.d. [c.1978]. 196 p., 8 illus.

Herzfeld, Friedrich. _Maria Meneghini-Callas oder die grosse
Primadonna_. Berlin: Rembrandt-Verlag, 1959. 61 p., 32 illus.

Jellinek, George. _Callas: Portrait of a Prima Donna_. New York:
Ziff-Davis Publishing Company, 1960. 354 p., 64 illus., repertoire list with recordings, index.

Jurik, Marian. _Maria Callas_. Praha: Supraphon, 1975. 73 p.,
9 illus., discography, LP recording.

Linakis, Steven. _Diva: the Life and Death of Maria Callas_.
London: Peter Owen, 1980. 169 p., 5 illus.

Mancini, Roland and Jean-Louis Caussou. _Maria Callas_. Paris:
Sodal, 1964. 33 p., 15 illus., discography.

Special supplement to the French periodical, _Opera_.

"Maria Callas: ses récitals 1954-1969." In _l'Avant-Scène Opéra_ 44
(1982). 191, [3] p., numerous illus., 26-item bibliography,
discography, list of televised operas.

Meneghini, Giovanni Battista and Renzo Allegri. _My Wife Maria
Callas_. Translated with an introduction by Henry Wisneski.
New York: Farrar, Strauss and Giroux, Inc., 1982 [1st edition
1981]. xiv, 331 p., 42 illus., index.

Picchetti, María Teresa and Marta Teglia. _El arte de Maria Callas
como metalenguaje_. Buenos Aires: Editorial Bocarte, n.d.
[1969]. 97 p.

Remy, Pierre-Jean. _Maria Callas: a Tribute_. Forward by Lord
Harwood. Translated by Catherine Atthill. New York: St. Martin's
Press, 1978. 192 p., 80 illus., list of roles including number/
place/conductor/principal singers, discography.

Riemens, Leo. _Maria Callas_. Utrecht: A.W. Bruna & Zoon, 1960.
156 p., 17 illus., list of roles, discography.

Segalini, Sergio. _Callas imágenes de una voz_. Barcelona:
Ediciones Daimon, Manuel Tamayo, 1980 [1st edition 1979].
171 p., numerous illus., complete chronology 1938-1974,
discography.

Basically a photographic study by the music critic of _Matins
de Paris_.

Stassinopoulos, Arianna. _Maria Callas: the Woman Behind the_

Legend. New York: Simon and Schuster, 1981. 383 p., 61 illus., source notes including 12-item bibliograhy.

Tortora, Giovanna and Paolo Barbieri, eds. Per Maria Callas. Bologna: Edizioni Recitar Cantando, n.d. 365 p., numerous illus., chronology.

A memorial tribute which is primarily a collection of illustrations and reviews.

Wisneski, Henry. Maria Callas: the Art Behind the Legend. performance annals 1947-1974 by Arthur Germond. New York: Doubleday & Company, Inc., 1975. x, 422 p., 152 illus., discography of private recordings, 46-item bibliography, index, index to artists appearing in the performance annals.

5. Celli, Teodoro. "A Song from Another Century." In Opera Annual 6:13-30. London: John Calder, 1965.

    SEE: Memoirs under ELISABETH SCHWARZKOPF (C0576).

C0092.
CALVE, EMMA. French Soprano. b. August 15, 1858, Decazeville; d. January 6, 1942, Millau.

1. BAKER 6; EdS 1/2 (Bibliography); GROVE 6/3 (Bibliography); MGG 1/15 (Bibliography); RIEMANN 12; SCHMIDL + Supp.

2. ON 23/4, 35/15; OPERA 6/4; RNC 2/2, 3; RS 59 (July 1975).

3. Calvé, Emma. My Life. Translated by Rosamond Gilder. New York: D. Appleton and Company, 1922. Reprint 1977 with discography by W.R. Moran. xiii, 280 p., 21 illus., index.

    Calvé, Emma. Sous tous les ciels j'ai chanté...: souvenirs. Paris: Librarie Plon, 1940. 297 p., 16 illus.

    This is the second volume of her memoirs.

    Gallus, Arthur [pseud. for Arthur Wisner]. Emma Calvé: Her Artistic Life with Numerous Autograph Pages especially written by Mlle. Calvé. New York: R.H. Russell, 1902. 76 p., 78 illus.

    Girard, Georges. Emma Calvé: la cantatrice sous tous les ciels. Millau: Editions Grands Causses, 1983. 295 p., 51 illus., iconographie, discography, 76-item bibliography.

    Limited edition of 310 copies.

    Kobbé, Gustav. Signora. New York: Thomas Y Crowell & Co., Publishers, 1907. 205 p., 3 illus.

    A children's novel thought to be based on Calvé's life.

C0093.
CAMPANINI, ITALO. Italian Tenor. b. June 30, 1845, Parma; d.
November 14, 1896, Vigatto, near Parma.

1. BAKER 6; EdS 1/2 (Bibliography); GROVE 6/3; SCHMIDL + Supp.

4. Ferrarini, Mario. Cantanti celebri parmensi del secolo XIX
    (il primo "Lohengrin" e il primo "Vasco di Gama"). Parma: La
    Bodoniana, 1938. 10 p., 2 illus.

    Italo Campanini and Emilio Naudin.

C0094.
CANIGLIA, MARIA. Italian Soprano. b. May 5, 1905, Naples; d. April
15, 1979, Rome.

1. GROVE 6/3 (Bibliography); EdS 1/2 (Bibliography); RIEMANN 12 +
    Supp.

2. ON 24/21, 37/5, 44/1.

C0095.
CAPECCI, RENATO. Italian Baritone. b. November 6, 1923, Cairo, Egypt.

1. GROVE 6/3; EdS/Supp.; RIEMANN 12/Supp.

2. OW 10/4, 16/9, 19/12.

C0096.
CAPOUL, JOSEPH-AMEDEE-VICTOR. French Tenor. b. February 27,
1839, Toulouse; d. February 18, 1924, Pujaudran-du-Gers.

1. BAKER 6 (Bibliography); EdS 1/2 (Bibliography); SCHMIDL + Supp.

4. Grand, Georges. Victor Capoul. Paris: Imprimerie de E. Donnaud,
    1877. 15 p., portrait.

C0097.
CARBONE, AGOSTINO. Italian Baritone. No lexicon listing.

4. Memoriale artistico del baritono buffo Agostino Carbone. Genova:
    Tipografia Dei Tribunali, 1889. 11 p., list of repertoire.

C0098.
CARELLI, EMMA. Italian Soprano. b. May 12, 1877, Naples; d. August
17, 1928, Montefiascone.

1. EdS 1/3 (Bibliography); RIEMANN 12/Supp.; SCHMIDL/Supp.

2. RC 11/8, 12/1-2.

4. Carelli, Augusto. Emma Carelli: trent'anni di vita del teatro
    lirico. Roma: Casa Libraria Maglione, 1932. 327 p., 16 illus.

CO099.
CARELLI, GABOR. Romanian Tenor. b. 1917, Budapest. No lexicon
listing.

3. Carelli, Gábor. Utam a metropolitanbe. Budapest: Zenemukiadó,
    1979. 207 p., 54 illus.

CO100.
CARON, ROSE. French Soprano. b. November 17, 1857, Monerville;
d. April 9, 1930, Paris.

1. BAKER 6; EdS 1/3 (Bibliography); SCHMIDL + Supp.

4. Solenière, Eugène. Rose Caron: monographie critique. Paris:
    Bibliothèque d'Art de la Critique, 1896. 47 p., 10 illus., list
    of roles in Brussles and Paris, concerts, 25-item bibliography,
    iconography.

CO101.
CARPI, VITTORIO. Italian Baritone. b. 1846; d. March 27, 1917,
Florence.

1. SCHMIDL.

3. Carpi, Vittorio. Al di qua e al de la dell'Atlantico: impres-
    sioni di un artista di canto. Firenze: Francesco Lumachi,
    1901. 298 p.

    Carpi, Vittorio. Ancora qualche apprezzamento sull'arte del
    canto. Milano: G. Ricordi & Co., 1902.

    No copy seen.

CO102.
CARRENO, MARIA TERESA. Venezuelan Soprano. b. December 22, 1853,
Caracas; d. Jume 12, 1917, New York City.

1. BAKER 6 (Bibliography); FETIS 2/Supp.; GROVE 6/3 (Bibliography);
    MGG 1/2; RIEMANN 12 + Supp. (Bibliography); SCHMIDL.

4. Milinowski, Marta. Teresa Carreño "by the grace of God." New
    Haven: Yale University Press, 1940 [reprint 1977]. xvii, 410
    p., 29 illus., chronology, 98-item bibliography, index.

    Peña, Israel. Teresa Carreño (1853-1917). Caracas: Ediciones
    de la "Fundación Eugenio Mendoza," 1953. 64 p., illus.

    Teresa Carreño o un esayo sobre su personalidad a los 50 años
    de su muerte. Carracas: Inciba Musica, 1966. 28 p., 8 illus.

    Travieso, Carmen Clemente. Teresa Carreño (1853-1917): ensayo
    biografica. Caracas: Editorial "Ancora," 1953. 80 p., 4-item
    bibliography.

    An MS translation by the late George L. Nyklicek exists.

C0103.
CARRERAS, JOSE. Spanish Tenor. b. December 5, 1946, Barcelona.

1. GROVE 6/3.

2. ON 42/14; OW 20/8.

C0104.
CARUSO, ENRICO. Italian Tenor. b. February 27, 1873, Naples;
d. August 2, 1921, Naples.

1. BAKER 6; EdS 1/3 (Bibliography); GROVE 6/3; MGG 1/2; RIEMANN 12
    (Bibliography) + Supp.; SCHMIDL + Supp.

2. GR 2/2, 4, 8/7–11, 9/6, 11/8, 12/10, 14/10, 17/4, 21/8; ON 24/9,
    37/16 (A Century of Caruso), 45/1, 46/2; OW 2/11, 3/4, 12/8,
    20/6; RC 4/5–6, 7, 9, 11, 12, 5/1, 3, 5, 7, 6/10, 11, 12, 7/6–7,
    12, 22/3–4.

3. Caruso, Enrico. Wie Man singen soll! praktische Winke. Trans-
    lated by August Spanuth. Leipzig: B. Schott's Soehne, n.d.
    61 p., portrait.

    The first American edition was published in 1909, reprint 1974.
    The first English edition was published in 1913, reprint 1973.
    Caruso always denied having written this work!

    Gerbi, Ernesto, ed. L'altro Caruso (80 caricatures). Milano:
    Eliot – nuova editrice internazionale, 1961. 163 p., 80 illus.

    The singer's famous caricatures were first printed as, Caruso's
    Book: Being a Collection of Caricatures and Character Studies
    from Original Drawings of the Metropolitan Opera Company. New
    York: R.G. Cooke, 1906. 47 p., illus.

4. Armin, George [pseud. for George Hermann]. Enrico Caruso: eine
    Untersuchung der Stimme Carusos und ihre Verhaeltnis zum Stau-
    prinzip. Berlin: Gesellschaft fuer Stimmkultur, 1929. 111 p.

    A comparison of Caruso's method of singing with that of other
    tenors such as Gigli, Piccaver, and Slezak. Armin was responsible
    for at least five other books on singing.

    Barát, Endre and Endre Lévay. La vie fantastique de Caruso.
    Translated by Jacques Ancelot. Paris: Les Editions Ardo, 1946.
    224 p., 2 illus.

    There is an edition of this work published in Budapest in 1957.
    218 p., 8 illus., list of roles.

    Barthelemy, Richard. Memories of Caruso. Translated by Constance
    S. Camner. Plainsboro, La Scala Autographs, 1979. [2], 15 p.,
    3 illus.

    Caruso's accompanist and coach. Edition limited to 500 copies.

Bello, John. Enrico Caruso: a Centennial Tribute. Providence: Universal Associates, 1973. unpaginated [83 p.], numerous illus., titles recorded by Caruso, Met performances on tour, list of exhibit items.

This is a catalog of the "Caruso Centennial Exhibit" compiled by the author.

Bolig, John Richard. The Recordings of Enrico Caruso. Dover, Delaware: The Eldridge Reeves Johnson Memorial, n.d. 96 p.

Comprehensive study of 496 recordings.

Caruso, Dorothy. Enrico Caruso: His Life and Death. New York: Simon and Schuster, 1945. ix, 303 p., 43 illus., high points in Caruso's life, repertoire, discography by Jack L. Caidin.

Caruso, Dorothy and Torrance Goddard. Wings of Song: the Story of Caruso. New York: Minton, Balch & Company, 1928. 218 p., 16 illus.

Daspuro, Nicola. Enrico Caruso. Milano: Casa Editrice Sonzogno, 1938. 79 p., 16 illus., 19 caricatures.

There is an expanded [124 p.] Spanish translation by Arrigo Coen Antiua published in Mexico City, n.d. [c.1938]. This book is actually the 9th chapter of an unpublished book, Memorie postume, devoted to Edoardo Sonzogno, his times and his contemporaries. A personal recollection of the singer which dates from the time Daspuro convinced Sonzogno to engage Caruso at the beginning of his career.

de Bry, Michel. Enrico Caruso: "the Young Caruso". London: The Gramophone Company, n.d. [1961]. 16, [2] p., 2 illus. recording details.

One of a series of pamphlets for "Great Recordings of the Century."

de Maria y Campos, Armando. El canto del cisne (una temporada de Caruso en 1919): recuerdo de un cronista. Mexico: Editorial Arriba El Telon, 1952. 159, [4] p.

Favia-Artsay, Aida. Caruso on Records. Valhalla: The Historic Record, 1965. 218 p., portrait, index, 60 cps and 50 cps Caruso stroboscopes.

Flint, Mary H. Impressions of Caruso and His Art as Portrayed at the Metropolitan Opera House. New York: privately printed by J.P. Paret & Co., 1917. 22 p., 12 illus.

Francillo-Kauffmann, Hedwig and Eugen Gottlieb-Hellmesberger. Von Caruso zu dir: Gesangstechnisches aus der Praxis und fuer die Praxis. Wien: Universal Edition A.G., 1935. 54, [1] p., portrait, 51 musical exercises.

Includes a four page autobiographical introduction by Francillo-Kauffmann who became a Kammersaengerin in Vienna after studies with **AGLAJA ORGENI** (C0460).

Freestone, J. & H.J. Drummond. Enrico Caruso: His Recorded Legacy. London: Sedgwick and Jackson, 1960. Reprint 1968 [from the 1961 Minneapolis edition]. x, 130 p., portrait, list of reissues, index.

Fucito, Salvatore and Barnet J. Beyer. Caruso and the Art of Singing including Caruso's Vocal Exercises and His Practical Advice to Students and Teachers of Singing. New York: Friederick A. Stokes Company, 1922. xi, 219 p., 13 illus., vocal exercises.

Fucito was Caruso's accompanist and coach 1915-1921.

Gara, Eugenio. Caruso: storia di un emigrante. con trentadue tavole fuori testo e dieci autocaricature del tenore. Milano: Rizzoli, 1947. 285 p., 32 illus., chronology, repertoire, discography, geographical list of appearances, bibliographic notes, index of names.

Greenfield, Howard. Caruso. New York: G.P. Putnam's Sons, 1983. 275 p., 34 illus., repertoire list by year, 125-item bibliography, index.

Hacker, Werner. Enrico Caruso: ein Lebensroman. Berlin: Paul Neff Verlag, 1944. 183 p.

Jackson, Stanley. Caruso. New York: Stein and Day Publishers, 1972. xiii, 302 p., 21 illus., 67-item bibliography, index.

Key, Pierre V.R. and Bruno Zirato. Enrico Caruso: a Biography. Boston: Little, Brown and Company, 1922. Reprint 1972. xv, 455 p., 35 illus., list of decorations, list of repertoire, list of all appearances, index.

Ledner, Emil. Caruso Erinnerungen. Hannover: Paul Steegemann Verlag, 1922. 93 p., 16 illus.

These are articles reprinted from the Berliner Tageblatt.

Lehrmann, Johannes. Caruso singt! Ernstes und Lustiges um Caruso und die Gastspielzeit vor 30 Jahren in Wort und Bild. Leipzig: Johannes Lehrmann Verlag, 1940. 80 p., 74 illus.

Marafioti, P. Mario. Caruso's Method of Voice Production: the Scientific Culture of the Voice. Preface by Victor Maurel. New York: D. Appleton & Company, 1922. 308 p.

This book has little if anything to do with Caruso.

Mouchon, Jean-Pierre. Enrico Caruso 1873-1921, sa vie et sa voix: etude psycho-physiologique, physique, phonetique et esthetique. Langres: Petit-Cloître a Langres, 1966. 106 p.,

37 illus.

Mouchon, Jean-Pierre. Enrico Caruso: His Life and Voice. Gap: Editions Ophrys, n.d. [1974]. 74 p., illus., bibliographic references.

This is an edited, reduced version of the previous entry.

Petriccione, Diego. Caruso nell'arte e nella vita. Napoli: Edizione Santojanni, 1939. 63 p., 37 illus., song.

Reis, Kurt. Caruso, Triumph einer stimme: Roman nach zeitgenoess-ischen Quellenwerken und Memorien frei bearbeitet. Duesseldorf: Deutsche Buchvertriebs- und Verlags-Gesellschaft, 1955. 352 p.

Robinson, Francis. Caruso: His Life in Pictures. New York: The Studio Publications, Inc., 1957. 160 p., 244 illus., discography by John Secrist.

Steen, Hans. Caruso. Eine Stimme erobert die Welt. Essen-Steele: Verlag Willi Webels, 1946. 105 p.

Thiess, Frank. Caruso: Roman einer Stimme. Hamburg: P. Zsolnay Verlag, 1952 [1st edition 1942]. 719 p.

Thiess, Frank. Caruso: Vortrag gehalten am 26. Februar 1943 in der Deutsch-Italienischen Gesellschaft in Frankfurt am Main. Wien: Karl H. Bischoff Verlag, 1943. 56 p.

Thiess, Frank. Caruso in Sorrent. Wien: Paul Zsolnay Verlag Gesellschaft m.b.H., 1949. 346 p.

Thiess, Frank. Il tenore de Trapani. Torino: Frassinelli Tipografo Editore, n.d. xi, 196 p.

Thiess, Frank. Neapolitanische Legende. Wien: Paul Zsolnay Verlags-GmbH, 1952. 209 p.

Tortorelli, Vittorio. Enrico Caruso nel centenario della nascita. Prefazione di Ivan Martynov. Rimini: Artisti asso-ciati, 1973. 188 p., 4 illus., repertoire, 27-item biblio-graphy.

Wagenmann, Josef Hermann. Caruso und das Problem der Stimm-bildung: Umsturz in der Stimmbildung (Loesung das Stimmbildungs-und Carusoprobleme). Schrift fuer Saenger, Schauspieler, Redner und Jedermann. dritte vemehrte auflage. Leipzig: Arthur Felix, 1922 [1st edition 1911]. 107 p., portrait.

Ybarra, Thomas R. Caruso: the Man of Naples and the Voice of Gold. New York: Harcourt, Brace and Company, 1953. 315 p., 10 illus., appendix of 1st performances at the Met, 33-item bibliography.

5. Caruso, Dorothy: Dorothy Caruso: a Personal History. New York: Hermitage House, 1952. 191 p., 12 illus.

SEE: Bracale, Adolfo. Mis memorias. Caracas, 1931.

SEE: **LINA CAVALIERI** (C0109).

SEE: **ROLAND FOSTER** (C0214).

SEE: Bedouins by Huneker under **MARY GARDEN** (C0232).

SEE: Huneker, James. Variations. New York: Charles Scribner's Sons, 1921. viii, 279 p.

SEE: Mathewson, Anna. The Song of the Evening Stars. Boston: The Gorham Press, 1911.

   Caruso did the fourteen caricatures for this book of poetry.

SEE: Young, Patricia. Great Performers. London: Oxford University Press, 1964. 55 p., illus.

C0105.
CARVAHLO-MIOLAN, CAROLINE-MARIE-FELIX. French Soprano. b. December 31, 1827, Marseilles; d. July 10, 1895, near Dieppe.

1. BAKER 6; EdS 1/3 (Bibliography); FETIS 2/Supp.; GROVE 6/3; RIEMANN 12; SCHMIDL.

4. Spoll, Edouard-Accoyer. Mme. Carvalho: notes et souvenirs. Paris: Librairie des Bibliophiles, 1885. 104 p., portrait.

C0106.
THE CASTRATI.

1. EdS 1/3 (under "Evirato" with Bibliography); GROVE 6/3 (Bibliography).

2. MQ 5/4; OPERA 1/3, 4; OW 8/11, 20/1, 22/6.

4. NOTE: A0042, A0046, A0074, A0085, B0014, B0032, B0046, B0063, C0090, C0188, C0198, C0380, C0383, C0462, C0583, C0646, and C0692.

5. d'Ancillon, Charles. Traite des eunuques, dans le quel on explique toutes les différentes fortes d'eunuques, quel rang ils ont tenu, et quel cas on en a fait.... Paris: n.p., 1707. Annonymous English translation: Eunuchism displayed. London, 1718. xviii, 187 p.

A thorough analysis of eunuchs by the French lawyer who was engaged to formulate a legal opinion as to the marriage rights of the castrati.

Franca, Ida. <u>Manuel of Bel Canto</u>. New York: Coward-McCann, 1959. xviii, 142 p., index, appendix on vocal defects.

Part III, "The Castrated Singers and Their Role in Bel Canto," includes short biographies of twenty-nine castrati. The author was a student of **MATTIA BATTISTINI** (C0045).

Henderson, William James. <u>Early History of Singing</u>. New York: Longmans, Green and Co., 1921. 201 p., index.

C0107.
CATALANI, ANGELICA. Italian Soprano. b. May 10, 1780, Sinigaglia; d. June 12, 1849, Paris.

1. BAKER 6; EdS 1/3 (Bibliography); FETIS 2/2; GROVE 6/4; MGG 1/2 (Bibliography); RIEMANN 12 + Supp. (Bibliography); SCHMIDL (Bibliography).

4. Satter, Heinrich. <u>Angelica Catalani: Primadonna der Kaiser und Koenige</u>. Frankfurt am Main: Verlag Frankfurter Buecher, 1958. 512 p., portrait.

    Scudo, P. "Angelica Catalani: histoire d'un cantatrice de l'Opéra." In <u>Nouvelle période</u> 4 (1849).

5. SEE: John R. Parker under ELIZABETH BILLINGTON (C0058).

    SEE: <u>Quarterly Musical Magazine and Review</u> under ELIZABETH BILLINGTON (C0058).

    SEE: Scudo, P. <u>Critique et littérature musicales</u>. Paris: Victor Lecou, 1852. xi, 346, [1] p.

    SEE: Sievers, Georges Louis Pierre. "Ueber Madame Valabregue Catalani als Sangerin, Schauspielerin und mimische Darstellerin." In <u>Zeitgenossen I</u> (1816):115-132.

    SEE: Simpson, Arthur. <u>Secret Memoirs of Madame Catalani</u>. Bath: privately printed by M. Gye, 1811. 46 p.

C0108.
CATLEY, ANNE. English Soprano. b. 1745, London; d. October 14, 1789, near Brentford.

1. EdS 1/3; GROVE 6/4.

2. GR 28/5.

4. <u>The Life of Miss Anne Catley Celebrated Singing Performer of the Last Century including an Account of Her Introduction to Public Life, Her Personal Engagements in London, and Her Various Adventures and Intrigues with Well-Known Men of Quality and Wealth</u>. London: n.p., 1888. 78 p., list of repertoire, portrait.

5. SEE: Charles E. Pearce under **LAVINIA FENTON** (C0196). Pearce's
    bibliography lists a Life of Miss Catley by Ambross
    which I have never seen.

C0109.
CAVALIERI, LINA. Italian Soprano. b. December 25, 1874, ·Viterbo;
d. February 8, 1944, Florence.

1. BAKER 6; EdS 1/3 (Bibliography); GROVE 6/4 (Bibliography);
    SCHMIDL + Supp.

2. ON 24/13

3. Cavalieri, Lina. La mie verità. Redatte da Paolo D'Arvanni.
    Roma: S.A. Poligrafica Italiana, 1936. 201 p., 91 illus.

    Chapters on Chaliapin and Farrar as well as extensive material
    on Battistini and Caruso.

C0110.
CEBOTARI, MARIA. Austrian Soprano. b. February 10, 1910, Kishinev,
Bessarabia; d. June 9, 1949, Vienna.

1. BAKER 6; EdS 1/3; GROVE 6/4; MGG 1/15; RIEMANN 12.

2. GR 27/2; ON 38/9; OW 20/1.

4. Maria Cebotari Kammersaengerin. Bremen: n.p., n.d. [c.1934].
    22 p., 7 illus., repertoire list, reviews.

    Mingotti, Antonio. Maria Cebotari: das Leben einer Saengerin.
    Salzburg: Hellbrunn-Verlag, 1950. Reprint 1977. 145 p., 22
    illus., list of operatic roles and films.

C0111.
CHANOVSKY, GEORGE. Russian Baritone. b. April 14, 1892, St.
Petersburg.

1. BAKER 6.

2. ON 25/21, 43/18.

C0112.
CHALIAPIN, FEODOR IVANOVITCH. Russian Bass. b. February 13, 1873,
Kazan; d. April 12, 1938, Paris.

Chaliapin, along with Enrico Caruso and Jenny Lind, has been the
uninvited beneficiary of an enormous amount of research and published material of a biographical nature. Many of the titles,
rather than being valid translations or updated versions, seem to
reflect the changing political orientations and alliances during
the singer's lifetime and up to the present year, the most recent
being the massive study edited by Elena Grosheva. Much of this
material is in Russian, a language which was excluded for reasons
articluated in the Introduction to this bibliography. Therefore,

only those titles are listed which I have personally been able to
annotate. A colleague with the appropriate language background will
undoubtedly unravel the mysteries presently surrounding these publications, and we shall have to wait, hopefully not too long, until
this is done. For information and sources beyond what I have been
able to list, the reader is referred to the Library of Congress
classification ML420;S53 as well as to the following title:

Grosheva, Elena Andreevna, ed. Fedor Ivanovich Shaliapin. 3rd
edition. Moskva, Iskusstvo, 1976-79. 3 vols. (index in vol. 3).

1. BAKER 6 (Bibliography); EdS 1/3 (Bibliography); GROVE 6/17
   (under Shalyapin with Bibliography); MGG 1/11 (under Schaljapin with Bibliography); RIEMANN 12 (under Schaljapin with
   Bibliography); SCHMIDL + Supp. (under Scialapin).

2. GR 2/3, 11/4, 15/12, 33/8; ON 18/16, 37/15; OPERA 3/2, 33/1;
   OW 3/4, 12/3, 20/11; RC 5/6, 6/8, 10/11, 12/3, 7, 20/8-10.

3. Chaliapin, Feodor Ivanovitch. Pages From My Life: an Autobiography. Edited by Katharine Wright and translated by H.M.
   Buck. New York: Harper & Brothers Publishers, 1927. 345 p.,
   18 illus.

   Chaliapin, Feodor Ivanovitch. Man and Mask: Forty Years in the
   Life of a Singer. Translated from French [Paris 1932] by
   Phyllis Megroz. New York: Alfred A. Knopf, 1932. Reprint 1970.
   Reprint 1973. xxvi, 358 p., 17 illus.

   Chaliapin, Feodor Ivanovitch. Chaliapin: an Autobiography as
   Told to Maxim Gorky. Translated and edited by Nina Froud and
   James Hanley. London: Mcdonald, 1968 [American edition 1967].
   320 p., 89 illus., repertoire list, 33-item bibliography,
   notes on persons mentioned, index.

4. Feschotte, Jacques. Ce géant: Féodor Chaliapine. Paris: La
   Table Ronde, 1968. 228 p., 9 illus., discography.

   Goury, Jean. Feodor Chaliapine: iconographie, biographie,
   discographie. Paris: Societe de Diffusion d'Art Lyrique, n.d.
   [1969]. 80 p., 25 illus., discography, 11-item bibliography.

   Semeonoff, Boris. Feodor Chaliapin (1873-1938). London: The
   Gramophone Company, n.d. [1958]. Printed "By permission of the
   Editor of 'The Record Collector.'" 12 p., 2 illus., recording
   details.

   Included in the same publication:
   Shawe-Taylor, Desmond. Chaliapin on the Stage and in the Record-
   ing Studio. 1958.
   One of a series of pamphlets for "Great Recordings of the Century."

5. SEE: Merle Armitage under MARY GARDEN (C0232).

   SEE: autobiography by LINA CAVALIERI (C0109).

SEE: Sol Hurok under **MARIAN ANDERSON** (C0017).

SEE: Strakhova-Ermans, Varvara. Le chant. Paris: E. Vinck, Imprimeur, 1946. 115, [5] p., 15 illus.

C0113.
CHOLLET, JEAN-BAPTISTE. French Tenor. b. May 20, 1798, Paris; d. January 10, 1892, Nemours.

1. EdS 1/3 (Bibliography).

4. Laget, August. Jean-Baptiste Chollet: premier sujet du théatre de l'Opéra-Comique. Toulouse, 1880.

No copy located.

C0114.
CHRISTOFF, BORIS. Bulgarian Bass. b. May 18, 1914, Plovdiv.

1. BAKER 6 (Bibliography); EdS 1/3; GROVE 6/4 (Bibliography); MGG 1/15 (Bibliography); RIEMANN 12.

2. ON 27/2, 47/10; OPERA 9/11; OW 5/7.

4. Goury, Jean. Boris Christoff. Paris: Sodal, 1970. 32 p., 23 illus.

Special supplement to the French periodical, Opéra.

C0115.
CIGNA, GINA. French Soprano. b. March 6, 1900, Paris.

1. BAKER 6; EdS 1/3 (Bibliography); GROVE 6/4 (Bibliography); RIEMANN 12.

2. ON 29/10, 43/17; OPERA 21/1.

C0116.
CLAUSEN, JULIA. Swedish Mezzo-Soprano. b. June 11, 1879, Stockholm; d. May 1, 1941, Stockholm.

1. BAKER 6; EdS 1/3; RIEMANN 12.

3. Clausen, Julia. Tristan og Isolde. København: n.p., n.d. [c.1939]. 132 p.

Edition of 200 copies.

C0117.
COLLIER, MARIE. Australian Soprano. b. April 16, 1927, Ballarat; d. December 8, 1971, London.

1. GROVE 6/4; RIEMANN 12/Supp.

2. OPERA 19/12, 23/2.

CO118.
CORELLI, FRANCO. Italian Tenor. b. April 8, 1923, Ancona.

1. BAKER 6; EdS/Supp.; GROVE 6/4 (Bibliography); RIEMANN 12/Supp.

2. ON 25/17, 30/14; OP 3/5; OW 5/2.

CO119.
CORNELIUS, PETER. Danish Tenor. b. January 4, 1865, Labjerggaard Jutland; d. December 30, 1934, Snekkersten.

1. EdS 1/3; GROVE 6/4.

2. RNC 2/5, 6.

4. Skjerne, Gotdfred. <u>Peter Cornelius</u>. København: NYT Nordisk Forlag, 1917. 48 p., 15 illus.

CO120.
COSMA, LUCIA. Romanian Soprano. b. 1875; d. 1972. No lexicon listing.

3. Itu, Ion. <u>Destinul unei artiste</u>. Bucureşti: Editura Muzicală, 1976. 143 p., 6 illus.

CO121.
COSSOTTO, FIORENZA. Italian Mezzo-Soprano. b. April 22, 1935, Crescentino, Vercelli, near Turin.

1. BAKER 6; EdS/Supp.; GROVE 6/4 (Bibliography); RIEMANN 12/Supp.

2. ON 47/8; OW 8/11.

CO122.
COTOGNI, ANTONIO. Italian Baritone. b. August 1, 1831, Rome; d. October 15, 1918, Rome.

1. EdS 1/3 (Bibliography); SCHMIDL.

2. RC 8/11-12.

4. Angelucci, Nino. <u>Ricordi di un artista (Antonio Cotogni)</u>. Roma: Tipografia Editrice "Roma," 1907. 131 p., 51 illus., list of titles and honors, music dedicated to him, list of roles.

CO123.
COTRUBAS, ILLEANA. Romanian Soprano. b. June 9, 1939, Galati.

1. GROVE 6/4.

2. OPERA 27/5, 45/16; OW 13/1, 16/3.

CO124.
COX, JEAN. American Tenor. b. January 14, 1922, Gadsden, Alabama.

1. GROVE 6/5; RIEMANN 12/Supp.

2. ON 36/9; OW 14/7.

4. Held, Gerhard and Brigitte Held, eds. <u>Jean Cox zum 16. Januar</u>
   <u>1982</u>. Laaber: Laaber-Verlag, 1982. 302 p., 67 illus., list of
   roles, discography.

   A homage by sixty-one colleagues.

C0125.
CRABBE, ARMAND. Belgian Baritone. b. April 23, 1883, Brussels;
d. July 24, 1947, Brussels.

1. BAKER 6; EdS 1/3; GROVE 6/5; RIEMANN 12/Supp. (Bibliography).

2. RC 24/5-6; RNC 3/2, 4/3.

3. Crabbé, Armand. <u>Conversation et conseils sur l'art du chant:</u>
   <u>quelques anecdotes et souvenirs de 25 années de carrière lyrique</u>
   <u>international</u>. Bruxelles: Editions Schott, 1931. 76 p.,
   portrait.

   Crabbé, Armand. <u>L'art d'Orphée: la physiologie du chant: dis-</u>
   <u>sertations, commentaires et souvenirs de quarante années de</u>
   <u>carrière lyrique internationale. Lexique musical et exercices</u>
   <u>vocaux</u>. Bruxelles, Editions Inter-Nos, 1946 [1st edition
   1933]. 126, [8] p., portrait, musical examples + 8 page
   folding plate of exercises.

   This is an updated and expanded version of the previous entry.

C0126.
CRESPIN, REGINE. French Soprano. b. February 23, 1927, Marseilles.

1. BAKER 6; EdS/Supp.; GROVE 6/5 (Bibliography); RIEMANN 12/Supp.

2. ON 30/22, 40/7, 43/10; OPERA 14/3; OP 1/2, 3/3.

3. Crespin, Régine. <u>La vie et l'amour d'une femme</u>. Paris: Librairie
   Arthème Fayard, 1982. 318 p., 77 illus., career highlights,
   discography.

C0127.
CRISTOFOREANU, FLORICA. Romanian Soprano. b. May 16, 1887, Rimnicul
Sarat; d. March 1, 1960, Rio de Janeiro.

1. EdS 1/3; GROVE 6/5 (Bibliography); SCHMIDL/Supp.

3. Cristoforeanu, Florica and H. Barbu. <u>Amintiri din cariera mea</u>
   <u>lirică</u>. Bucureşti, Editura Muzicală, 1964. 362 p., 36 illus.

C0128.
CROIZA, CLAIRE. French Mezzo-Soprano. b. September 14, 1882, Paris;
d. May 27, 1946, Paris.

1. EdS 1/3; GROVE 6/5 (Bibliogrphy).

2. RS 41 (January 1971).

4. Abraham, Hélène. Un art de l'interprétation: Claire Croiza. --
   Les cashiers d'une auditrice -- avec la lettre a madame C...
   de Paul Valéry. Paris: Office de Centralisation D'OUVRAGES,
   1954. 368 p., 11 illus., index.

   Edition of 1,000 copies.

CO129.
CROOKS, RICHARD. American Tenor. b. June 26, 1900, Trenton, New
Jersey; d. September 29, 1972, Portola Valley, California.

1. BAKER 6; GROVE 6/5 (Bibliography); RIEMANN 12.

2. ON 30/23; RC 12/6, 7, 10-11, 20/11-12; RNC 2/9.

CO130. CROSS, JOAN. English Soprano. b. September 7, 1900 London.

1. EdS 1/3 (Bibliography); GROVE 6/5 (Bibliography); RIEMANN 12.

2. OPERA 1/1, 28/2, 31/9.

CO131.
CROUCH, ANNA MARIA. English Soprano. b. April 20, 1763, London;
d. October 2, 1805, Brighton.

1. GROVE 6/5.

4. Young, Mary Julia. Memoirs of Mrs. Crouch including a Retrospect
   of the Stage during the Years She Performed. 2 vol. London:
   Printed for J. Asperne, 1806. ii, 284 p., portrait; 328 p.

5. SEE: autobiography of MICHAEL KELLY (CO316).

CO132.
CRUVELLI, SOPHIE. German Soprano Sophie Cruewell. b. March 12, 1826,
Bielefeld; d. November 6, 1907, Monaco.

1. EdS 1/3 (Bibliography); GROVE 6/5; SCHMIDL + Supp.

4. Favre, Georges. Une grande cantatrice nicoise: La Vicomtesse
   Vigier (Sophie Cruvelli) 1826-1907. Paris: Editions A. et J.
   Picard, 1979. 113 p., 12 illus., 18-item bibliography, index
   of names.

CO133.
CUENOD, HUGUES-ADHEMAR. Swiss Tenor. b. June 26, 1902, Corseaux-sur-
Vevey.

1. BAKER 6; GROVE 6/5; RIEMANN 12 + Supp.

4. Spyckert, Jérôme. Un diable musicien: Hughes Cuénod. Lausanne:

Editions Payot, 1979. 231 p., 37 illus., discography.

C0134.
CULP, JULIA. Dutch Mezzo-Soprano. b. October 6, 1880, Groningen;
d. October 13, 1970, Amsterdam.

1. BAKER 6; GROVE 6/5; MGG 1/15; RIEMANN 12 + Supp., SCHMIDL.

2. GR 5/4; RC 2/7; RS 47 (July 1972).

5. SEE: Bieb in Holland under **GRE BROUWENSTIJN** (C0082).

C0135.
CUNELLI, GEORGES. Russian? Baritone? No lexicon listing.

3. Cunelli, Georges. Voice No Mystery: Half a Century of Recol-
    lections in the Arts of Singing and S6eaking. Preface by Paul
    Robeson. London: Stainer & Bell Ltd., 1973. xiii, 160 p.,
    17 illus., 2 questionnaires.

C0136.
dalla RIZZA, GILDA. Italian Soprano. b. October 2, 1892, Verona;
d. July 4, 1975, Milan.

1. EdS 1/4; GROVE 6/5 (Bibliography); SCHMIDL/Supp.

2. ON 34/14, 40/9.

4. Rizzi, F.G.. Gilda dalla Rizza: verismo e bel canto. Venezia:
    Tipografia Commerciale, 1964. 142 p., 23 illus., facsimiles,
    list of operatic roles.

C0137.
dal MONTE, TOTI. Italian Soprano. b. June 27, 1893, Mogliano, near
Treviso; d. January 26, 1975, Pieve di Soligo.

1. BAKER 6; EdS 1/4 (Bibliography); GROVE 6/5 (Bibliography);
    RIEMANN 12 + Supp. (Bibliography); SCHMIDL/Supp.

2. GR 32/4; ON 40/1; OP 8/6; OW 9/6; RC 4/9.

3. dal Monte, Toti. Una voce nel mondo. Milano: Longanesi E C.,
    1962. 381 p., 55 illus.

    Too bad her autobiography is not half as interesting as her
    real life!

C0138.
d'ALVAREZ, MARGUERITE. English Mezzo-Soprano. b, c.1886, Liverpool;
d. October 18, 1953, Alassio, Italy.

1. EdS 1/1 (under Alvarez).

3. d'Alvarez, Marguerite. All the Bright Dreams. New York: Har-
    court, Brace and Company, 1956 [1st edition Forsaken Alters.

London, 1954]. 313 p., 8 illus., epilogue.

C0139.
DAMBRAUSKAITE, ANTANINA. Lithuanian Soprano. No lexicon listing.

3. Dambrauskaite, Antanina. Antanina Dambrauskaite: the Book about One Lithuanian Opera Singer. Munich: F. Bruckmann KG, 1949. 74 p., 46 illus. of the artist.

    115 copies printed for the singer.

C0140.
van DAM, JOSE. SEE: VAN DAM, JOSE (C0676).

C0141.
DANCO, SUZANNE. Belgian Soprano. b. January 22, 1911, Brussels.

1. BAKER 6; EdS 1/4; GROVE 6/5; RIEMANN 12.

3. Danco, Suzanne. Suzanne Danco's Opera Repertoire 1949-1950. Rome: Il Povero Bibliofilo, 1949. 57 p., 54 illus.

    Projected at "1,000 copies," this is quite probably an agent's brainstorm. The name of the publisher is marvelous! "We have received so many requests from so many different quarters..." So reads the introduction to:

    Preliminary Outline for the New Edition of the Testimonials to Suzanne Danco. Roma: Il Povero Bibliofilo, n.d. [1950].

C0142.
DANNSTROEM, JOHAN ISIDOR. Swedish Tenor. b. December 15, 1812, Stockholm; d. October 17, 1897, Stockholm.

1. GROVE 6/5 (Bibliography), RIEMANN 12; SCHMIDL/Supp.

4. Nagra blad ur Isidor Dannstroems minnes-anteckningar. Stockholm: Central-Tryckeriet, 1896. 97 p., portrait, song.

C0143.
DARCLEE, HARICLEA. Romanian Soprano. b. 1860, Bucharest; d. January 12, 1939, Bucharest.

1. EdS 1/4 (Bibliography); GROVE 6/5 (Bibliography): SCHMIDL.

2. ON 23/23.

4. Sbârcea, George and Ion Hartulari-Darclée. Darclée. Bucureşti: Editura Muzicală, 1972. 228, [3], [56] p., 86 illus., list of repertoire.

C0144.
D'AUBIGNY von ENGELBRUNNER, NINA. German Mezzo-Soprano. b. 1777, Kassel; d. ?

1. FETIS 2/1 (Bibliography). The earliest listing is to found in Ernst Ludwig Gerber's Neues historisch-biographisches Lexikon der Tonkunst. Leipzig, 1812.

3. D'Aubigny von Engelbrunner, Nina. Briefe an Natalie ueber den Gesang, als Befoerderung der haeuslichen Glueckseligkeit und des geselligen Vergnuegens: ein Handbuch fuer Freunde des Gesangs. Leipzig: Boss und Compagnie, 1803. xiv, 234 p., musical exercises and examples.

C0145.
DAVID, LEON. French Tenor. b. December 18, 1867, Sables-d'Olonne; d. October 27, 1962, Sables-d'Olonne.

1. BAKER 6.

3. David, Léon. La vie d'un ténor. Fontenay-Le-Comte: P. & O. Lussand Freres, 1950. ix, 405 p., 8 illus.

C0146.
DAWSON, PETER. Australian Baritone. b. 1882, Adelaide; d. September 26, 1961, Sydney. No lexicon listing.

1. KUTSCH 3.

2. GR 10/8, 13/4, 39/6.

3. Dawson, Peter. Fifty Years of Song. London: Hutchinson & Co., Ltd., 1951. 239 p., 16 illus., 3 appendices including his repertoire of songs, index.

C0147.
de BELOCCA, ANNA. French Mezzo-Soprano. b. January 4, 1854; d. ? No lexicon listing.

4. Berlioz, Victor. Anna de Belocca. Paris: Librairie Nouvelle, 1874. 28 p., portrait.

C0148.
de BIDOLI, EMI. Italian Baritone. No lexicon listing.

3. de Bidoli, Emi. Reminiscences of a Vocal Teacher. Cleveland: privately printed by Edwards Brothers, Inc. [Ann Arbor], 1946. xi, 97 p., 5 illus.

    Studied with AGLAJA ORGENI (C0460); VIARDOT-GARCIA (C0684).

C0149.
de BLASIS, VIRGINIA. Italian Soprano. b. August 5, 1804, Marsiglia; d. May 12?, 1838, Florence.

1. EdS 1/2 (under Blasis with Bibliography).

4. Biografia de Virginia de Blasis tratta dal 'Figaro' di Milano e ristampata con correzioni e aggiunte. Firenze: n.p., 1838.

CO150.
DELLA CASA, LISA. Swiss Soprano. b. February 2, 1919, Burgdorf, near Bern.

1. EdS 1/4 (Bibliography); GROVE 6/5 (Bibliography); MGG 1/15; RIEMANN 12 + Supp.

2. ON 27/9; OPERA 19/3; OW 3/6.

4. Debeljevic, Dragan. Ein Leben mit Lisa della Casa oder, "in dem Schatten ihrer Locken". Zuerich: Atlantis-Verlag, 1975. 268 p., 55 illus.

CO151.
DELLER, ALFRED. English Countertenor. b. May 30, 1912, Margate; d. July 16, 1979, Bologna, Italy.

1. BAKER 6; GROVE 6/5 (Bibliography); MGG 1/15; RIEMANN 12 + Supp. (Bibliography).

4. Hardwick, Michael and Mollie Hardwick. Alfred Deller: a Singularity of Voice. London: Cassell & Company Ltd., 1968. xi, 204 p., 30 illus., discography, appendix on the countertenor voice, index.

CO152.
DEL MONACO, MARIO. Italian Tenor. b. July 27, 1915, Florence.

1. BAKER 6; EdS 1/4; GROVE 6/5 (Bibliography); MGG 1/15; RIEMANN + Supp. (Bibliography).

2. GR 31/12; ON 16/18, 23/13, 45/10; OPERA 13/6; OP 3/6; OW 2/2, 23/12.

3. Del Monaco, Mario. La mia vita e i miei successi. Milano: Rusconi Libri S.p.A., 1982. 137 p., 24 illus., list of roles, index of names, index of operas, index of theaters.

4. Chédorge, André. Mario Del Monaco. Paris: Sodal, 1963. 33 p., 19 illus.

    Special supplement to the French periodical, Opéra.

    Segond, André and Daniel Sébille. Mario Del Monaco ou un ténor de legénde. Lyon: Editions Jacques-Marie Laffont et Associes, 1981. 263 p., 40 illus., selective chronology, repertoire, discography, list of films, 20-item bibliography.

CO153.
de LOS ANGELES, VICTORIA. SEE: LOS ANGELES, V. de (CO369).

CO154.
DE LUCA, GIUSEPPE. Italian Baritone. b. December 25, 1876, Rome; d. August 26, 1950, New York City.

1. BAKER 6; EdS 1/4 (Bibliography); GROVE 6/5; RIEMANN 12 + Supp.
    (Bibliography); SCHMIDL.

2. OW 9/3; RC 5/3, 5, 6/7, 11/6, 7, 12/8-9; RNC 5/5.

C0155.
DE LUCIA, FERNANDO. Italian Tenor. b. October 11, 1860, Naples;
d. February 21, 1925 Naples.

1. EdS 1/4 (Bibliography); GROVE 6/5 (Bibliography); SCHMIDL.

2. OPERA 6/7; RC 11/6.

4. de Giorgio, Achemenide. Fernando de Lucia. Milano: Capriolo e
    Massimino, 1897. 14 p.

C0156.
DE MURO, BERNARDO. Italian Tenor. b. November 3, 1881, Tempio
Pausania, Sassiri; d. October 27, 1955, Rome.

1. EdS 1/4 (Bibliography); SCHMIDL/Supp.

2. RC 18/3, 11, 19/3-4, 20/6-7.

3. De Muro, Bernardo. Quand'ero folco. Milano: privately printed,
    1955. 95 p.

    There exists an MS English translation by the late George L.
    Nyklicek.

4. Fresi, Franco. Bernardo De Muro: una voce, una fabia. Bologna:
    Edito Dall'Associazione Turistica Pro Loco, n.d. [c.1981]. xvi,
    116 p., 9 illus.

C0157.
DE MURO LOMANTO, ENZO. Italian Tenor. b. April 11, 1902, Canosa di
Puglia; d. March 15, 1952, Naples. No lexicon listing.

1. KUTSCH 3.

4. Giovine, Alfredo. Enzo De Muro Lomanto, cenni biografici:
    bibliografia e iconografia. Bari: n.p., 1970. 20 p., 23 illus.,
    61-item bibliography, operatic repertoire, discography.

C0158.
DENS, MICHEL. French Baritone. b. June 22, 1914, Roubaix. No lexicon
listing.

1. KUTSCH 3.

2. OP 3/3.

4. Caussou, Jean-Louis. Michel Dens. Paris: Sodal, 1964. 32 p.,
    27 illus., discography.

Special supplement to the French periodical, Opéra.

CO159.
DE RESZKE, EDOUARD. Polish Bass. b. November 22, 1853, Warsaw;
d. May 25, 1917, Garnek.

1. BAKER 6 (Bibliography); EdS 1/8 (under Retzske); GROVE 6/5;
    MGG 1/11 (under Reszke with Bibliography); RIEMANN 12 + Supp.
    (under Reszke with Bibliography); SCHMIDL.

2. ON 18/7; OPERA 6/1; OW 21/5; RC 6/5, 8.

CO160.
DE RESZKE, JEAN. Polish Tenor. b. January 14, 1850, Warsaw;
d. April 3, 1925, Nice, France.

1. BAKER 6; EdS 1/8 (under Retzske with Bibliography); GROVE 6/5;
    MGG 1/11 (under Reszke); RIEMANN 12 + Supp. (under Reszke with
    Bibliography); SCHMIDL.

2. GR 17/12; ON 9/16, 14/11, 15/9, 19/21; OPERA 6/1; OW 21/5;
    RC 5/1; RNC 5/11.

4. De Lys, Edith. Jean De Reszke Teaches Singing to Edith De Lys:
    a True Copy of the Lesson Notebooks of Edith De Lys. San
    Francisco: Leon Volan, Publisher, 1979. 79 p., 5 illus.,
    musical examples.

    Hurst, P.G.. The Age of Jean De Reszke: Forty Years of Opera
    1874-1914. New York: Robert M. McBride Co., 1959 [1st edition
    London 1958]. 256 p., 28 illus., 2 indices.

    Leiser, Clara. Jean De Reszke and the Great Days of Opera.
    New York: Minton, Balch & Company, 1934. Reprint 1975. xiv,
    337 p., 32 illus., appendix, 35-item bibliography, index.

5. SEE: autobiography of **GEORGES CUNELLI** (CO135).

    SEE: autobiography of **MAGGIE TEYTE** (CO651).

CO161.
DERMOTA, ANTON. Austrian Tenor. b. June 4, 1910, Kropa.

1. EdS 1/4; GROVE 6/5 (Bibliography); RIEMANN 12 + Supp.

3. Dermota, Anton. Tausendundein Abend: mein Saengerleben. Wien:
    Paul Neff Verlag, 1978. 358 p., 40 illus., repertoire list,
    list of honors and titles, discography by Juergen E. Schmidt,
    index of names.

CO162.
DERNSCH, HELGA. Austrian Soprano. b. February 3, 1939, Vienna.

1. GROVE 6/5; RIEMANN 12/Supp.

2.   ON 35/26; OPERA 24/5; OW 22/4.

C0163.
DESCHAMPS. French Soprano. b. 1730; d. 1764. No lexicon listing.

4.   Capon, G. and R. Yve-Plessis. Fille d'Opéra, vendeuse d'amor:
     histoire de Mlle. Deschamps (1730-1764) racontée d'aprés des
     notes de police et des documents inédits. Paris: Plessis,
     Libraire, 1906. 257 p., 5 illus., index of names.

C0164.
DE SOUZA, ANTOINETTA. Brazilian Mezzo-Soprano. No lexicon listing.

4.   Antonietta De Souza. Rio de Janiero: Typ. Baptista de Souza,
     1928. 103 p., 2 illus.

C0165.
DESTINN, EMMY. Czechoslovakian Soprano. b. February 26, 1878, Prague;
d. January 28, 1930, Budejovice.

1.   BAKER 6; EdS 1/4 (Bibliography); GROVE 6/5 (Bibliography);
     RIEMANN 12; SCHMIDL + Supp.

2.   GR 7/11, 16/10; ON 26/8; OPERA 6/9; OW 23/5; RC 20/1-2, 4.

4.   Bajerova, Marie. O Emě Destinnové. Praha: Vysehrad, 1979.
     143 p., 35 illus., chronological career record, 7-item bib-
     liography.

     Brieger-Wasservogel, Lothar. Emmy Destinn. Maria Labia. Berlin:
     Virgil Verlag, 1908. 32 p., 2 illus.

     Holzknecht, Vaclav and Trita Bohumil. Ema Destinnova. Praha:
     Panton, 1972. 306 p., 204 illus., chronology, discography.

     Text is in Czech, English, and German. There exists another MS
     English translation.

     Martínková, Marie. Život Emy Destinnové. 2nd edition. Plzni:
     Emil Kosnar, 1946. 171 p., 28 illus.

     Pospíšil, Miloslav. Veliké srdce: život a umení Emy Destinnové.
     Praha: Supraphon, 1974. 175, [1] p., 32 illus., discography,
     list of roles, bibliography.

C0166.
DIAZ, JUSTINO. American Bass. b. January 29, 1940, San Juan, Puerto
Rico.

1.   GROVE 6/5.

2.   ON 31/9, 36/11.

C0167.
DIDUR, ADAM. Polish Bass. b. December 24, 1874, Sanok, Galacia;

d. January 7, 1946, Katowice.

1. BAKER 6; EdS 1/4; GROVE 6/5; RIEMANN 12 + Supp. (Bibliography);
   SCHMIDL.

2. RC 16/1, 23/7-8.

CO168.
DI STEFANO, GIUSEPPE. Italian Tenor. b. July 24, 1921, Catania.

1. BAKER 6; EdS 1/4 (Bibliography); GROVE 6/5 (Bibliography),
   RIEMANN 12 + Supp.

2. GR 32/1; OW 4/6.

4. Eggers, Heino. Giuseppe Di Stefano. Berlin: Rembrandt-Verlag,
   1967. 64 p., 30 illus., list of 10 selected recordings.

CO169.
DOMINGO, PLACIDO. Spanish Tenor. b. January 21, 1941, Madrid.

1. BAKER 6; GROVE 6/5 (Bibliography).

2. GR 49/7; ON 41/20, 44/3, 46/16; OPERA 23/1, 33/11; OP 10/1;
   OW 11/5, 15/9, 22/8-9.

3. Domingo, Placido. My First Forty Years. New York: Alfred A.
   Knopf, 1983. 256 p., 51 illus., performance list 1959-March
   1983, discography, index.

CO170.
DONALDA, PAULINE. Canadian Soprano. b. March 5, 1882, Montreal;
d. October 22, 1970, London, England.

1. BAKER 6.

2. RC 2/9, 10/12.

4. Brotman, Ruth C. Pauline Donalda: the Life and Career of a
   Canadian Prima Donna. Montreal: The Eagle Publishing Co.,
   Ltd., 1975. 125 p.

   Donalda's extensive personal library was donated to McGill
   University.

CO171.
DRAGULINESCU-STINGHE, ELENA. Romanian Soprano. b. 1881. No lexicon
listing.

3. Dragulinescu-Stinghe, Elena. Amintiri. Bucureşti: Editura
   Muzicală, 1965. 189 p., 43 illus.

CO172.
DUGAZON, LOUISE ROSALIE. French Soprano. b. June 18, 1755, Berlin;
d. September 22, 1821, Paris.

1. BAKER 6; EdS 1/4 (Bibliography); MGG 1/15 (Bibliography);
   SCHMIDL/Supp. (Bibliography).

4. Le Roux, Hughes and Alfred Le Roux. La Dugazon. Paris:
   Librairie Félix Alcan, 1926. vi, 139 p., 8 illus.

   Oliver, Jean-Jacques. Mme. Dugazon de la Comédie-Italienne
   (1755-1821). Paris: Société Française d'Imprimerie et de
   Librairie, 1917. 129 p., illus., repertoire, bibliography,
   iconography.

5. SEE: H. Noel Williams under SOPHIE ARNOULD (C0020).

C0173.
DUPREZ, LOUIS-GILBERT. French Tenor. b. December 6, 1806, Paris;
d. September 23, 1896, Paris.

1. BAKER 6; EdS 1/4 (Bibliography); GROVE 6/5 (Bibliography);
   MGG 1/3 (Bibliography); RIEMANN 12; SCHMIDL + Supp.

2. ON 47/8.

3. Duprez, Louis-Gilbert. Souvenirs d'un chanteur. Paris:
   Ancienne Maison Michel Lévy Frères, 1880. 280 p.

   NOTE: EdS 1/4 mentions two additional autobiographies, neither
   of which I have seen.

   Duprez, Louis-Gilbert. L'Art du chant. Paris: Heugel et Cie,
   1845. 212 p.

   Duprez, Louis-Gilbert. Le mélodie: études...de l'art du chant.
   Paris Heugel et Cie, 1846. xxiv, 221 p., illus.

   Duprez, Louis-Gilbert. Sur la voix et l'art du chant, essai rimé.
   Paris, Tresse, 1882. 24 p.

4. Elwart, A.A. Duprez: sa vie artistique avec une biographie
   authentique de son maitre, Alexandre Choron. Paris: Victor
   Magen, Editeur, 1838. vii, 219 p., portrait.

C0174.
DURIGO, ILONA. Romanian Mezzo-Soprano. b. May 13, 1881, Budapest;
d. December 25, 1943, Budapest.

1. RIEMANN 12.

4. Weidenmann, Jakobus. Ilona Durigo, 1881-1943. St. Gallen:
   Buchdruckerei H. Tschudy, 1944. 21 p., portrait.

C0175.
DUTHE, CATHERINE-ROSALIE GERARD. French Soprano. No lexicon listing.

4. Ginisty, Paul, ed. Souvenirs de Mllé. Duthe de l'Opéra (1748-
   1830). Paris: Louis-Michaud, n.d. 320 p., 33 illus.

C0176.
DVORAKOVA, LUDMILA. Czechoslovakian Soprano. b. July 11, 1923, Kolin.

1. GROVE 6/5; RIEMANN 12/Supp.

2. OPERA 22/9; OW 6/1.

4. Jiráskova, Jiřina. Ludmila Dvořáková. Praha, Supraphon, 1978.
    58 p., illus., one LP record.

C0177.
van DYCK, ERNEST. SEE: VAN DIJCK, ERNEST (C0677).

C0178.
EAMES, EMMA. American Soprano. b. August 13, 1865, Shanghai, China;
d. June 13, 1952, New York City.

1. BAKER 6; EdS 1/4 (Bibliography); GROVE 6/5 (Bibliography);
    SCHMIDL.

2. ON 17/2; OPERA 8/1; RC 8/4; RS 59 (July 1975).

3. Eames, Emma. Some Memories and Reflections. New York: D.
    Appleton and Company, 1927. Reprint 1977 with discography by
    W.R. Moran. x, 311 p., 29 illus., index.

4. Lawrence, Edward. A Fragrance of Violets: the Life and Times
    of Emma Eames. New York: Vantage Press, 1973. 186 p., 25 illus.,
    30-item bibliography.

C0179.
EASTON, FLORENCE. English Soprano. b. October 24, 1884, Middles-
brough-on-Tees, Yorkshire; d. August 13, 1955, New York City.

1. BAKER 6; EdS 1/4; GROVE 6/5; RIEMANN 12.

2. ON 32/11; RC 21/9-10, 11-12, 27/2-3; RNC 4/9, 10, 5/4.

C0180.
ELLEVIOU, JEAN. French Tenor. b. June 14, 1769, Rennes; d. May 5,
1842, Paris.

1. BAKER 6; EdS 1/4 (Bibliography); FETIS 2/3; GROVE 6/6 (Bibliog-
    raphy); RIEMANN 12; SCHMIDL/Supp.

4. de Courzon, Henri. Elleviou. Paris: Librairie Felix Alcan, 1930.
    124 p., 8 illus.

C0181.
von ELSNER, MARIE EUGENIA. No lexicon listing.

4. Scott, John M. Litta, an American Singer: a Sketch of Marie
    Eugenia von Elsner. Bloomington, 1897. 170 p.

    She was a member of the Strakosch Opera Company 1878-80.

C0182.
ELWES, GERVASE. English Tenor. b. November 15, 1866, Billinghall, near Northampton; d. January 12, 1921, Boston.

1. BAKER 6; GROVE 6/6; RIEMANN 12.

2. GR 2/10; RC 17/8.

4. Elwes, Winefride and Richard Elwes. Gervase Elwes: the Story of His Life. London: Grayson & Grayson, 1935. vii, 320 p., 10 illus., 3 appendices including a list of recordings, index.

C0183.
ELY, SALLY FROTHINGHAM. b. 1863; d. June 23, 1917. No lexicon listing.

3. Ely, Sally Frothingham. A Singer's Story. Stanford: The University Press [privately printed by Leonard W. Ely], n.d. [c.1918]. 151 p., 4 illus.

C0184.
ERB, KARL. German Tenor. b. July 13, 1877, Ravensburg; d. July 13, 1958, Ravensburg.

1. EdS 1/4; GROVE 6/6; MGG 1/3, 1/16 (Bibliography); RIEMANN 12 + Supp. (Bibliography).

2. OW 21/3; RC 24/3-4, 9-10.

4. Mueller-Goegler, Maria. Karl Erb: das Leben eines Saengers. Offenburg, Verlag Franz Huber, 1948. 190 p., 19 illus.

5. Giesen, Hubert. Am Flugel, Hubert Giessen: meine Lebenserin- nerungen. Frankfurt/M., S. Fischer Verlag, 1972. 300, [2] p., 28 illus., discography by Ute Mayer, index.

    SEE: entries under **MARIA IVOGUEN** as they were married 1921-32.

    Mueller, Martin and Wolfgang Mertz, eds. Diener der Musik: un- vergessene Soloisten und Dirigenten unserer Zeit im Spiegel der Freunde. Tuebingen, Rainer Wunderlich Verlag Hermann Leins, 1965. 275 p., 20 illus., bibliography, selected discography.

    Gerd Schneider wrote the article on Erb, pp. 197-211.

C0185.
ERNSTER, DEZSO. Hungarian Bass. b. November 23, 1898, Pecs; d. February 15, 1981, Zuerich.

1. RIEMANN/Supp.

2. ON 11/6; OW 22/3.

4. Fábián, Imre. Ernster Dezsö. Budapest: Zenemuekiadó, 1969. 69 p., 33 illus., list of roles by season, 2 LP records; 8 selections.

CO186.
EVANS, GERAINT. Welsh Baritone. b. February 16, 1922, Pontypridd.
pridd.

1. BAKER 6; EdS/Supp.; GROVE 6/6 (Bibliography); RIEMANN 12/Supp.

2. GR 52/6; OPERA 12/4, 24/2.

3. Evans, Geraint and Noël Goodwin. Sir Geraint Evans: a Knight at the Opera. London: Michael Joseph, 1984. xi, 276 p., 91 illus., chronology of roles, debut performances, discography, honors and awards, index.

CO187.
FALCON, MARIE-CORNELIE. French Soprano. b. January 28, 1814, Paris; d. February 25, 1897, Paris.

1. BAKER 6; EdS 1/4; FETIS 2/3; GROVE 6/6; RIEMANN 12 + Supp. (Bibliography), SCHMIDL.

2. ON 31/9.

4. Bouvet, Charles. Cornélie Falcon. Paris: Librairie Félix Alcan, 1927. ii, 151 p., 8 illus.

CO188.
FARINELLI (Carlo Broschi). Italian Castrato Soprano. b. January 24, 1705, Andria; d. September 16, 1782, Bologna.

1. BAKER 6; EdS 1/5 (Bibliography); GROVE 6/6 (Bibliography); MGG 1/3; RIEMANN 12 + Supp. (Bibliography); SCHMIDL.

4. Bouvier, René. Farinelli: le chanteur des rois. Paris: Editions Albin Michel, 1943. 285 p., 16 illus., 75-item bibliography.

Crudeli, Tommaso. In lode del signor Carlo Broschi detto Farinello musico celebre: ode. Firenze: Anton Maria Albizzini, 1734. 18 p., portrait.

Giovine, Alfredo. Perche Carlo Broschi di Andria e non napolitano era soprannominato Farinelli? Bari: Biblioteca Dell' Archivio Delle Tradizioni Popolari Baresi, 1971. 16 p., 9 illus.

Goldman, Lawrence Louis. The Castrato. New York: The John Day Company, 1973. xxiv, 264 p., 59-item bibliography.

An interesting novel based on Farinelli and the 18th century.

Haebock, Franz. Die Kunst des Cavaliere Carlo Broschi Farinelli. Wien: Universal Edition, 1923. lvii, 227 p., illus.

The preface includes a complete list of known roles and performances.

Ricci, Corrado. Burney, Casanova e Farinelli in Bologna. Milano:

G. Ricordi & C., 1890. 44 p., illus.

Sacchi, Giovenale. Vita del cavaliere Don Carlo Broschi.
Vinegia: Nella Stamperia Colletti, 1784. 48 p.

C0189.
FARRAR, GERALDINE. American Soprano. b. February 28, 1882, Melrose,
Massachusets; d. March 11, 1967, Ridgefield, Connecticut.

1. BAKER 6; EdS 1/5; GROVE 6/6; MGG 1/3; RIEMANN 12; SCHMIDL/Supp.

2. GR 17/11, 12; ON 4/3, 24/7, 26/12, 30/13, 31/25, 38/21, 47/1;
   OW 11/3, 21/6; RC 13/9-10, 11-12, 14/7-8, 20/6-7.

3. Farrar, Geraldine. The Story of an American Singer by Herself.
   Boston: Houghton Mifflin Company, 1916. x, 115 p., 44 illus.

   Farrar, Geraldine. Geraldine Farrar Memorien. Uebersetzt und
   bearbeitet von Adelina Sacerdoti-Thomin. Mainz: Zaberndruck-
   Verlag, 1928. viii, 255 p., 41 illus., index.

   An expanded version of the 1916 autobiography.

   Farrar, Geraldine. Such Sweet Compulsion. New York: The Grey-
   stone Press, 1938. Reprint 1970. xii, 303 p., 88 illus., list
   of roles, index.

4. Nash, Elizabeth. Always First Class: the Career of Geraldine
   Farrar. Maryland: University Press of America, 1982. ix, 281 p.,
   306-item bibliography, index of people, productions, and roles.

   Wagenknecht, Edward Charles. Geraldine Farrar: an Authorized
   Record of Her Career. Seattle: University Book Store, 1929.
   91 p., 3 illus., list of operatic roles, list of films, list
   of recordings, selected bibliography of 33 books and articles.

   Limited edition of 350 autographed copies.

5. SEE: autobiography of LINA CAVALIERI (C0109).

   Tellegren, Lou. Women have been Kind: the Memoirs of Lou
   Tellegren. New York: Vanguard Press, 1931. 305 p., illus.

C0190.
FARRELL, EILEEN. American Soprano. b. February 13, 1920, Willimantic,
Connecticut.

1. BAKER 6; GROVE 6/6; RIEMANN 12/Supp.

2. ON 25/14, 32/6.

C0191.
FASSBAENDER, Brigitte. German Mezzo-Soprano. b. July 3, 1939, Berlin.

1. GROVE 6/6; RIEMANN 12/Supp.

2. OPERA 32/8; OW 7/12, 16/7.

CO192.
FAURE, JEAN-BAPTISTE. French Baritone. b. January 15, 1830, Moulins,
Allier; d. November 9, 1914, Paris.

1. BAKER 6 (Bibliography); EdS 1/5 (Bibliography); FETIS 2/Supp.;
    GROVE 6/6 (Bibliography); RIEMANN 12; SCHMIDL.

2. MQ 4/2.

3. Faure, Jean-Baptiste. Aus jeunnes chanteurs, notes et conseils:
    extraits de traité practique la voix et le chant. Paris: Henri
    Heugel, n.d. [c.1898]. 83 p.

    Faure, Jean-Baptiste. La voix et le chant: traité pratique.
    Paris: Au Menestral. Henri Heugel, 1886. 255 p., portrait,
    musical examples and exercises.

4. de Curzon, Henri. Une gloire francaise de l'art lyrique: J.-B.
    Faure 1850-1914. Paris: Librairie Fischbacher, 1923. 183 p.,
    15 illus., list of roles by year.

CO193.
FAVART, MARIE-JUSTINE-BENOITE. French Soprano. b. June 15, 1727,
Avignone; d. April 21, 1772, Paris.

1. EdS 1/5 (bibliography); FETIS 2/3; GROVE 6/6 (Bibliography);
    MGG 1/3 (Bibliography).

4. Dumoulin, Maurice. Favart et Madame Favart: un ménage
    d'artistes au XVIIIe siècle. Paris: Louis-Michaud Editeur,
    n.d. [1912]. 191 p., 39 illus., 27-item bibliography.

    Iacazzi, Alfred. The European Vogue of Favart: the Diffusion
    of the Opéra-Comique. New York: Publications of the Institute
    of French Studies, Inc., 1932. xiii, 410 p., list of works,
    selective bibliography, index.

    Letainturier-Fradin, Gabriel. Les amours de Madame Favart: roman
    historique. Paris: Ernest Flammarion, Editeur, n.d. [c.1907].
    496 p., 85-item bibliography, list of portraits.

    Pougin, Arthur. Madame Favart: etude théatrale, 1727-1772.
    Paris: Librairie Fischbacher, 1912. 62 p., 13 illus., list of
    first appearances.

5. Williams, H. Noel. Queens of the French Stage. New York:
    Charles Scribner's Sons, 1905. vii, 365 p., 9 illus., index.

CO194.
FAVERO, MAFALDA. Italian Soprano. b. January 6, 1905, Porto-maggiore,
near Ferrara; d. September 3, 1981, Milan.

1. EdS 1/5 (Bibliography); GROVE 6/6 (Bibliography); RIEMANN 12/Supp.

2. ON 42/14.

4. Buscaglia, Italo. Mafalda Favero nella vita e nell'arte.
    Milano: Editoriale Italiana, 1946. 95 p., 11 illus., opera
    repertoire.

C0195.
FAY SYMINGTON, MAUDE. American Soprano. b. May 21, 1844, Bayou Goula,
Louisiana; d. February 28, 1928, Watertown, Maine.

1. BAKER 6.

3. Fay Symington, Maude. Living in Awe. Edited by Marshall Dill,
    Jr. San Francisco: privately printed for members of the family,
    1968. 173 p., portrait.

    Reduced and revised from the original MS by Fay's nephew in an
    edition of 125 copies.

    NOTE: There is a book, Music Study in Germany from the Home
    Correspondence of Amy Fay, which is occasionally mistaken for
    the work of Maude Fay. Amy Fay was a painist.

C0196.
FENTON, LAVINIA. English Soprano. b. c.1708, London; d. January ?,
1760, West Combe Park, Greenwich.

1. EdS 1/5 (Bibliography).

4. Pearce, Charles E.. Polly Peachum: the Story of Lavinia Fenton
    and the Beggar's Opera. New York: Benjamin Blom, Inc., 1968
    [1st edition London. 1913]. xvi, 382 p., 47 illus., appendix,
    82-item bibliography, index.

    The Life of Lavinia Fenton Beswick, Alias Fenton, Alias Polly
    Peachum.... London: A. Moore, 1728. 48 p.

C0197.
FERRANI, CESIRA. Italian Soprano. b. May 8, 1863, Torino; d. May 6,
1943, Pollone.

1. EdS 1/5; SCHMIDL.

2. ON 22/15; RC 20/6-7; RNC 3/5.

C0198.
FERRI, BALDASSARRE. Italian Castrato Soprano. b. December 9, 1610,
Perugia; d. November 18, 1680, Perugia.

1. BAKER 6; EdS 1/5 (Bibliography); FETIS 2/3; GROVE 6/6 (Biblio-
    graphy); MGG 1/4 (Bibliography); RIEMANN 12; SCHMIDL.

4. Conestabile, Giancarlo. Notizie biografiche de Baldassarre Ferri.
    Perugia: Dalla Tipografia Bartelli, 1846. 16 p.

CO199.
FERRIER, KATHLEEN. English Mezzo-Soprano. b. April 22, 1912, Higher
Walton, Lancashire; d. October 8, 1953, London.

1. BAKER 6; EdS 1/5 (Bibliography); GROVE 6/6 (Bibliography); MGG
   1/16; RIEMANN 12 + Supp. (Bibliography).

2. GR 28/10, 31/6, 9, 33/9, 38/5; OPERA 4/12.

4. Cardus, Neville, ed. Kathleen Ferrier: a Memoir. New York:
   G. P. Putnam's Sons, 1955 [1st edition London 1954]. 125 p.,
   32 illus., list of recordings.

   Six major essays by colleagues.

   Ferrier, Winifred. Kathleen Ferrier: Her Life. Harmondsworth:
   Penguin Books Ltd., 1959 [1st edition London 1955]. 319 p., 40
   illus., 2 appendices; repertoire and recordings.

   This book includes the above title.

   Lethbridge, Peter. Kathleen Ferrier. London: Cassell & Company
   Ltd., 1959. 122 p., 3 illus.

   Ramberg, Ruth. Kathleen Ferrier fra 14 ar gammel yrkeskvinne
   til sanger av verdensformat. Oslo: n.p., 1974. 190, [1] p.,
   17 illus., discography.

   Rigby, Charles. Kathleen Ferrier: a Biography. London: Robert
   Hale Limited, 1955. xvii, 198 p., 52 illus., index.

5. SEE: Mueller & Mertz under **KARL ERB** (CO184). Article by
   Bruno Walter.

CO200.
FFRANGCON-DAVIES, DAVID THOMAS. English Baritone. b. December 11,
1855, Bethesda, Caernarvon; d. April 13, 1918, London.

1. BAKER 6; EdS 1/5 (under his daughter, Gwen); RIEMANN 12 +
   Supp.; SCHMIDL.

4. Ffrangcon-Davies, Marjorie. David Ffrangcon-Davies: His Life and
   Book. London: John Lane, The Bodley Head, 1938. xxi, 192 p.,
   6 illus., index.

   This book by the singer's daughter includes The Singing of the
   Future. [1st edition London 1905. Reprint 1968].

CO201.
FIGNER-MEI, MEDEA IVANOVNA. Italian Mezzo-Soprano. b. April 4, 1859,
Florence; d. July 8, 1952, Paris.

1. BAKER 6; EdS 1/5 (under Nikoloj Figner with Bibliography); GROVE
   6/6 (under Nikolay Figner with Bibliography).

2. RC 4/3.

3. Figner-Mei, Medea Ivanovna. Moi vospominaniia. St. Petersburg:
   n.p., 1912. 44 p., illus.

4. Moore, Jerrold Northrop. Medea Mei-Figner. Woodbridge: privately
   printed. 16 p., 9 illus.

   Pamphlet in "The Rubini Collection" LP release RS301.

C0202.
FIGNER, NICOLAY. Russian Tenor. b. February 21, 1857, Nikiforovka;
d. December 13, 1919, Kiev.

1. BAKER 6; EdS 1/5 (Bibliography); GROVE 6/6 (Bibliography);
   RIEMANN 12 + Supp. (Bibliography).

3. Figner, Nicolay. Vospominaniia: pisma, materialy. Compiled by
   L.M. Kontateladze. Leningrad: Muzyka, 1968. 191 p., illus.,
   discography, bibliography, index.

   There is an MS translation in English by the late George L.
   Nyklicek titled: Nicolay Figner: Recollections, Letters,
   Materials.

C0203.
FINKENSTEIN, JETTKA. No lexicon listing.

4. Wilda, Oscar. Jettka Finkenstein, grossherzogli hessische Kammersaengerin: eine biographische Skizze zum 25 jaehrigen Kuenstler-
   jubilaeum. Breslau: Schletter'sche Buchhandlung, n.d. [1906].
   31 p., 8 illus.

C0204.
FISCHER-DIESKAU, DIETRICH. German Baritone. b. May 28, 1925, Berlin.

1. BAKER 6; EdS 1/5; GROVE 6/6; MGG 1/16; RIEMANN 12 + Supp.
   (Bibliography).

2. GR 30/5, 48/7; ON 25/12, 33/12, 40/5; OPERA 16/1; OP 3/8;
   OW 1/5; RNC 5/11.

3. Fischer-Dieskau, Dietrich. Auf den Spuren der Schubert-Lieder:
   Werden-Wesen-Wirkung. Wiesbaden: F.A. Brockhaus, 1971. 371 p.,
   76 illus., 38-item bibliography, index of sing titles, index of
   names.

   Fischer-Dieskau, Dietrich. Texte deutscher Lieder: ein Handbuch.
   Muenchen: Deutscher Taschenbuch Verlag GmbH & Co. KG, 1968.
   474 p., 10-item bibliography, index of songs by composer, index
   of authors and translators, index of titles and opening text.

4. Demus, Joerg, Karla Hoecker, Wolf-Eberhard von Lewinski and
   Werner Oehlmann. Dietrich Fischer-Dieskau. Berlin: Rembrandt
   Verlag, 1966. 88 p., 67 illus., opera roles, discography.

Florent, Francois. Dietrich Fischer-Dieskau. Paris: Sodal, 1967. 32 p., 24 illus., discography.

Special supplement to the French periodical, Opéra.

Herzfeld, Friedrich. Dietrich Fischer-Dieskau. Berlin: Rembrandt Verlag, 1958. 63 p., 27 illus.

Whitton, Kenneth S.. Dietrich Fischer-Dieskau, Mastersinger: a Documented Study. Forward by Gerald Moore. New York: Holmes & Meier Publishers, Inc., 1981. 342 p., 47 illus., 107-item bibliography, index of names, discography compiled by Maurice R. Wright.

5. Hoecker, Karla. Gespraeche mit Berliner Kuenstlern. Berlin: Stapp Verlag, 1964. 132 p., 23 illus., lebensdaten.

   Interviews with sixteen artists including Fischer-Dieskau and Elisabeth Gruemmer.

CO205.
FLAGSTAD, KIRSTEN. Norwegian Soprano. b. July 12, 1895, Hamar; d. December 7, 1962, Oslo.

1. BAKER 6; EdS 1/5 (Bibliography); GROVE 6/6; MGG 1/4; RIEMANN 12 + Supp. (Bibliography).

2. GR 16/12, 31/6, 40/9; ON 15/15, 27/10; OPERA 1/3, 14/2; RC 7/8.

3. Biancolli, Louis. The Flagstad Manuscript: an Autobiography Narrated to Louis Biancolli. New York: G.P Putnam's Sons, 1952. Reprint 1977. xix, 293 p., 20 illus., list of roles, index.

   Flagstad, Kirsten. Remember Me: utsyn over en kunstnergjerning: Kirsten Flagstad i radiosamtale med Torstein Gunnarson i norsk rikskringkasting 29. Desember 1961. Oslo: Gyldendal, n.d. [1975]. 44 p., illus.

   Text is in English and Norwegian.

   McArthur, Edwin. Flagstad: a Personal Memoir. New York: Alfred A. Knopf, 1965. Reprint 1980. xvii, 343, ix p., 25 illus., 2 appendices, appearances in opera, index.

   Rein, Aslaug. Kirsten Flagstad. Oslo: Ernst G. Mortensens Forlag, 1967. 287 p., 49 illus., 10-item bibliography, list of roles, list of recordings 1914-1959, index.

   Sanborn, Pitts. David Ewen in Living Musicians (New York, The H. W. Wilson Company, 1940) mentions a work I have not located. "An authorized biography of Flagstad was written by Pitts Sanborn and published in the fall of 1940." Do Sanborn's notes still exist? Refer to DO009 for a complete citation.

Sanner, Jr., Howard C. <u>Kirsten Flagstad Discography</u>. University of Maryland M.M. Thesis, 1981. vi, 244 p., 121-item bibliography, appendix of Flagstad's known broadcasts, artist index, composer/title index.

5. SEE: Roland Gelat under **PIERRE BERNAC** (C0055).

C0206.
FLANNERY, MARY. SEE: MELLISH, MARY (C0410).

C0207.
FLETA, MIGUEL. Spanish Tenor. b. December 28, 1893, Albalate; d. May 30, 1938, La Coruna.

1. BAKER 6; EdS 1/5 (Bibliography); GROVE 6/6 (Bibliography); RIEMANN 12; SCHMIDL/Supp.

2. RC 15/5-6.

4. Sarobe, Celestino. <u>Venimécum del artista lírico</u>. Barcelona: Imp. Comas, 1947. 191 p., illus.

   Torres, Luís and Andrés Ruiz Castillo. <u>Miguel Fleta: el hombre, el "divo", y su musa</u>. Zaragoza, El Heraldo de Aragón, 1940. 282 p., illus.

C0208.
FODOR-MAINVIELLE, JOSEPHINE. French Soprano. b. October 13, 1789, Paris; d. August 14, 1870, St. Genis-Laval.

1. EdS 1/5; FETIS 2/3; GROVE 6/6 (Bibliography); MGG 1/4; SCHMIDL (Bibliography) + Supp.

3. Fodor-Mainvielle, Joséphine. <u>Réflections et conseils sur l'art du chant</u>. Paris: Perrotin et Cie, 1857. 15 p.

4. Unger, Johann Karl. <u>Joséphine Mainville Fodor: precis historique sur sa vie...</u>. Vienne: Chez Charles Ferdinand Beck, 1823. 24 p. (pp. 1-12 in French; pp. 15-24 in German).

C0209.
FOHSTROEM, ALMA. Finnish Soprano. b. January 2, 1856, Helsinki; d. February 20, 1936, Helsinki.

1. RIEMANN 12.

4. Erve, Paul [pseud. for V. von Rode]. <u>Alma Fohstroem</u>. Helsingissae: Kustannusosakeyhtioe Otava, 1920. 123 p., 11 illus., list of roles.

C0210.
FOLESCU, GHEORGHE. Romanian Bass. b. September 17, 1884; d. ? No lexicon listing.

4. Buescu, Corneliu. <u>Gheorghe Folescu</u>. Bucureşti: Editura Muzicală,

1966. 141 p., 26 illus., repertoire list, 8-item bibliography.

CO211.
FORMES, KARL JOHANN. German Bass. b. August 7, 1815, Muehlheim; d. December 15, 1889, San Francisco, California.

1. BAKER 6; EdS 1/5 (Bibliography); GROVE 6/6 (Bibliography).

3. Formes, Karl Johann. My Memoirs: Autobiography of Karl Formes published in His Memory. San Francisco: Jas. H. Barry, 1891. 240 p.

    This is an expanded version of the next entry.

    Formes, Karl Johann. Aus meinem Kunst- und Buehnenleben: Erinner- ungen des Bassisten. Koeln: Gehly, 1888. 122 p., illus.

    Formes, Karl Johann. Karl Formes Method of Singing for Soprano and Tenor. 2nd edition. San Francisco, n.p., n.d., [c.1885]. 165 p.

CO212.
FORRESTER, MAUREEN. Canadian Mezzo-Soprano. b. July 25, 1930, Montreal.

1. BAKER 6; GROVE 6/6 (Bibliography); RIEMANN 12/Supp.

2. ON 31/3.

CO213.
FORSELL, JOHN. Swedish Baritone. b. May 8, 1868, Stockholm; d. May 30, 1941, Stockholm.

1. BAKER 6; GROVE 6/6 (Bibliography); RIEMANN 12.

2. GR 15/4; RNC 2/7, 4/7, 8.

4. Boken om John Forsell: utgiven av operan pa John Forsells 70- arsdag den 6 nov. 1938. Stockholm: P.A. Norstedt & Soener, 1938. 112 p., 56 illus.

    Elmblad, Sigrid. John Forsell, halfsekelmannen foer dagen: nagra ord till lifsjubileet. Stockholm: n.p., 1918. 4 p.

    Ljungberger, Erik. John Forsell. Stockholm: H.W. Tullberg, 1916. 43 p., illus.

CO214.
FOSTER, ROLAND. Australian Bass. No lexicon listing.

3. Foster, Roland. Come Listen to My Song: Reminiscences of Music and Travel in Two Worlds and Two Eras. Sydney: William Collins Ltd., 1949. 288 p., 34 illus.

CO215.
FRANCI, BENVENUTO. Italian Baritone. b. July 1, 1891, Pienza, Siena.

1. EdS 1/5 (Bibliography); GROVE 6/6 (Bibliography); RIEMANN 12/Supp.

4. Benvenuto Franci visto da se stesso. Roma: Fratelli Palombi Editori, 1938. 32 p., 9 illus.

CO216.
FRANKENBERG, FRANZ. German Bass. b. 1759, Mattighofen; d. September 10, 1789, Berlin.

1. FETIS 2/3.

4. Leben und Charakter Frankerbergs. Berlin, 1789.

   Published in remembrance of his sudden and unexpected death. I have not seen a copy.

CO217.
FRANKLIN, DAVID. English Bass. No lexicon listing.

3. Franklin, David. Basso Cantante: an Autobiography. London: Gerald Duckworth, 1969. 232 p., 13 illus., index.

CO218.
FREMSTAD, OLIVE. Swedish Soprano. b. March 14, 1871, Stockholm; d. April 21, 1961, Irvington-on-Hudson, New York.

1. BAKER 6; EdS 1/5 (Bibliography); GROVE 6/6; RIEMANN 12.

2. ON 16/9, 20/23; RC 7/3.

4. Cather, Willa Sibert. The Song of the Lark. Boston: Houghton Mifflin Company, 1915. 490 p.

   This is novel based upon the life of the singer.

   Cushing, Mary Watkins. The Rainbow Bridge. New York: G.P. Putnam's Sons, 1954. Reprint 1977 with discography by W.R. Moran. 318, [1] p., 19 endpaper illus., index.

   The singer's private secretary romanticizes her recollections.

CO219.
FRENI, MIRELLA. Italian Soprano. b. February 27, 1935, Modena.

1. BAKER 6; EdS/Supp.; GROVE 6/6; RIEMANN 12/Supp.

2. ON 31/6, 42/4; OPERA 18/4; OP 5/6; OW 6/2, 15/1.

4. Chédorge, André. Mirella Freni. "Les Trésors de l'Opéra No. 5." Paris: Opéra International, n.d. [1979]. 64 p., 21 illus., discography.

CO220.
FRICK, GOTTLOB. German Bass. b. July 28, 1906, Olbronn, Wuerttemberg.

1. GROVE 6/6; RIEMANN/Supp.

2. OPERA 17/3 (reprinted from OW); OW 1/1, 7/1.

4. Hey, Hans A. Gottlob Frick. Muenchen: Harald Herbrecht Verlag.
   1968. 35 p., 20 illus.

CO221.
FRIEDLEIN, CHRISTINE. German Mezzo-Soprano. b. January 7, 1862,
Regensburg; d. ? No lexicon listing.

3. Friedlein, Christine. Erinnerungen einer Hofopernsaengerin:
   Erinnerungsblaetter. Karlsruhe: Verlag C.F. Mueller, 1923. 59 p.

CO022.
FUENTES, JOVITA. Philippine Soprano. No lexicon listing.

4. Hernandez-Chung, Lilia. Jovita Fuentes: a Lifetime of Music.
   Manila: The Jovita Fuentes Musicultural Society, 1979. 184 p.,
   62 illus., appendix of reviews, notes, 10-item bibliography.

CO223.
FUGERE, LUCIEN. French Baritone. b. July 22, 1848, Paris; d. January
15, 1935, Paris.

1. BAKER 6; EdS 1/5 (Bibliography); GROVE 6/7; RIEMANN 12; SCHMIDL/
   Supp. (Bibliography).

2. RC 8/5.

3. Fugère, Lucien and Raoul Duhamel. Nouvelle méthode pratique de
   chant francais par l'articulation. Paris: Enoch et Cie, 1929.
   xii, 90 p., illus.

4. Duhamel, Raoul. Lucien Fugère chanteur scénique français. Paris:
   Bernard Grassett, 1929. 203 p., 4 illus.

   Edition of 1,100 copies.

5. SEE: Boschot, Adolphe. Chez les musiciens (du XVIIIe siècle à nos
   jours). Paris: Plon-Nourrit, 1922. 285 p.

CO224.
GABRIELESCU, GRIGORE. Romanian Tenor.

1. SCHMIDL/Supp. (no dates).

4. Massoff, Ioan. Glorioasa existentă a tenorúlui Grigore
   Gabrielescu. Bucureşti: Editura Muzicală a Uniunii Compozi-
   torilor, 1974. 143 p., 14 illus.

CO225.
GABRIELLI, CATERINA. Italian Soprano. b. November 12, 1730, Rome;
d. February 16, 1796, Rome.

1. BAKER 6; EdS 1/5 (Bibliography); FETIS 2/3; GROVE 6/7 (Bibliog-
    raphy); MGG 1/4 (Bibliography); RIEMANN 12; SCHMIDL + Supp.
    (Bibliography).

4. Ademollo, Alessandro. La piu famosa delle cantanti italiane
    nella seconda meta del Settecento. Milano, 1890.

    No copy located.

CO226.
GADSKI, JOHANNA. German Soprano. b. June 15, 1872, Anclam; d.
February 22, 1932, Berlin.

1. BAKER 6; EdS 1/5 (Bibliography); GROVE 6/7 (Bibliography);
    RIEMANN 12 (under Gadsky).

2. RC 11/9-10, 11-12, 12/1-2.

CO227.
GALEFFI, CARLO. Italian Baritone. b. June 4, 1882, Malamocco; d.
September 22, 1961, Rome.

1. EdS 1/5; GROVE 6/7 (Bibliography); SCHMIDL.

2. OPERA 12/12.

4. Celletti, Rodolfo. Carlo Galeffi e la Scala. Milano: Teatro
    alla Scala/Electa Editrice, 1977. 102 p., 76 illus., chronology,
    discography, index of names, index of illus., general index.

    Guimarães, Beatriz Leas. A deslumbrante carreira do célebre
    barítono Carlo Galeffi. Rio di Janeiro: Iguassú, 1962. 74 p.,
    6 illus.

    Marchetti, Arnoldo. Carlo Galeffi: una vita per il canto. Roma:
    Casa Editrice Stabilimento Aristride Staderini, 1973. 108 p.,
    26 illus., discography, index of names.

CO228.
GALLI-CURCI, AMELITA. Italian Soprano. b. November 18, 1882, Milano;
d. November 26, 1963, La Jolla, California.

1. BAKER 6, EdS 1/5 (Bibliography); GROVE 6/7; RIEMANN 12.

2. GR 1/2, 41/8; ON 22/22, 28/1, 47/6; RC 4/10.

4. Le Massena, C.E. Galli-Curci's Life of Song. New York: The
    Paebar Company, 1945. Reprint 1978 with discography. 336 p.,
    46 illus., list of roles, list of recordings.

5. SEE: Merle Armitage under **MARY GARDEN** (CO232).

CO229.
GARAT, PIERRE-JEAN. French Baritone. b. April 25, 1762, Ustaritz, Bas-Pyrenees; d. March 1, 1823, Paris.

1. BAKER 6; EdS 1/5 (Bibliography); FETIS 2/3; GROVE 6/7 (Bibliography); MGG 1/4 (Bibliography); RIEMANN 12 + Supp. (Bibliography); SCHMIDL.

4. de Fagoaga, Isidoro. Pedro Garat "El Orfeo de Francia". Buenos Aires: Editorial Vasca Ekin, S.R.L., 1948. 280 p., 10 illus., 75-item bibliography.

    Lafond, Paul. Garat 1762-1823. Paris: Calmann Lévy, Editeur, n.d. [c.1890]. xi, 363 p., portrait.

    Miall, Bernard. Pierre Garat Singer and Exquisite: His Life and His World (1762-1823). New York: Charles Scribner's Sons, 1913. 364 p., 35 illus., index.

CO230.
GARCIA, MANUEL del POPOLO VICENTE. Spanish Tenor. b. January 22, 1775, Seville; d. June 9, 1832, Paris.

1. BAKER 6; EdS 1/5 (Bibliography); FETIS 2/3; GROVE 6/7 (Bibliography); MGG 1/4; (Bibliography); RIEMANN 12/Supp. (Bibliography); SCHMIDL.

2. ON 15/8.

3. Garcia, Manuel del Popolo Vicente. 340 exercises, thèmes variés et vocalises: composés pour ses élèves par Manuel Garcia (père). 4th edition. Paris: Heugel et Cie, 1868. 101 p.

4. see: listings under **MANUEL PATRICIO GARCIA** (CO231).

5. see: listings under **MANUEL PATRICIO GARCIA** (CO231).

CO231.
GARCIA, MANUEL PATRICIO. Spanish Baritone. b. March 17, 1805, Madrid; d. July 1, 1906, London.

1. BAKER 6; EdS 1/5 (Bibliography); FETIS 2/3; GROVE 6/7 (Bibliography); RIEMANN 12 (Bibliography); SCHMIDL.

2. OW 22/5; RC 4/11.

3. Garcia, Manuel. Mémoire...des sciences en 1840: réimpression augmentée de quelques observations nouvelles sur les sons simultanés et suivie du rapport de la commission de l'Académie des sciences du 12 avril 1841. Paris: E. Duverger, 1847. 39 p.

    Garcia, Manuel. Traité complet de l'art du chant. Paris: Heugel et Cie, 1841.

    The editions of 1848 and 1872 were reprinted in 1975 in an edition

collated, edited, and translated by Donald V. Paschke. The
editions of 1847 and 1872, published in 1983, were also collated,
edited, and translated by Paschke. A more available English
translation of some of this material, Hints on Singins, was
published in London and New York in 1894; Reprint 1970.

Heaven only knows how many variations and editions in how many
different languages have resulted from Garcia's pedagogical
writings. The question remains as to how probing the research
to achieve what result at what cost!

4.   Garcia, Albert. Garcia's Treatise on the Art of Singing: a
     Compendious Method of Instruction, with Examples and Exercises
     for the Cultivation of the Voice. London: Leonard & Co., 1924.
     75 p.

     MacKinlay, M. Sterling. Garcia the Centenarian and His Times
     being a Memoir of Manuel Garcia's Life and Labours for the
     Advancement of Music and Science. Edinburgh: William Blackwood
     and Sons, 1908. Reprint 1975; 1976. 335 p., 18 illus., 31-item
     bibliography, index.

     Malvern, Gladys. The Great Garcias. New York: Longmans, Green
     and Co., 1958. 210 p., 2 illus.

5.   SEE: Desternes and Chandet under MARIA MALIBRAN (C0378).

     Fuchs, Viktor. "Manuel Garcia, Centenarian." In Opera Annual 5
     London: John Calder, 1958. pp. 67-76.

     Héritte de la Tour, Louis. Une famille de grands musiciens.
     Paris: Delamain, Boutelleau et cie, Editeurs, 1922. xi, 266 p.,
     11 illus.

     The grandson of Pauline Viardot attempts to correct inaccurate
     information about the 5 Garcias. Partially based upon Louise
     Hériette-Viardot's autobiography (C0281).

     Héritte-Viardot, Louise. Memories and Adventures. Translated
     from the German MS by E.S. Buchheim. London: Mills & Boon,
     Limited, 1913. xiii, 271 p., 20 illus., index.

     SEE: Herman Klein under ADELINA PATTI (C0473).

     SEE: autobiography of ANNA EUGENIA SCHOEN-RENE (C0566).

C0232.
GARDEN, MARY. Scottish Soprano. b. February 20, 1874, Aberdeen; d.
January 3, 1967, Aberdeen.

1.   BAKER 6; EdS 1/5; GROVE 6/7 (Bibliography); RIEMANN 12; SCHMIDL.

2.   GR 29/11; ON 18/22, 31/15; OPERA 13/5; OW 9/3.

3.   Garden, Mary and Louis Biancolli. Mary Garden's Story. New York:

Simon and Schuster, 1951. xii, 302 p., 47 illus., index.

4. Barnes, Jr., Harold M. Mary Garden on Records. San Angelo: The Holcombe-Blanton Printery, 1947. 20 p.

5. Armitage, Merle. Accents on Life. Forward by John Charles Thomas. Ames: The Iowa State University Press, 1964. xv, 386 p., 53 illus.

Canaille, Caro. Etoiles en pantoufles. Givors: A. Martel, n.d. [1954]. 270 p.

Material on Mary Garden and Lily Pons.

Huneker, James. Bedouins. New York: Charles Scribner's Sons, 1920. viii, 271 p., 6 illus.

Includes critical reviews of Mary Garden and Enrico Caruso by one of America's most brilliant writers on the arts.

Kahn, Otto Hermann. Of Many Things: being Reflections and Impressions of International Affairs, Domestic Topics and the Arts. New York: Boni & Liveright, 1926. 437 p.

Robinson-Duff, Sarah. Simple Truths used by Great Singers. Boston: Oliver Ditson Company, 1919. [iii], 113 p., 2 illus.

Wagenknecht, Edward. Seven Daughters of the Theater. Norman: University of Oklahoma Press, 1964. x, 234 p., 30 illus., index.

CO233.
GAYARRE, JULIAN. Spanish Tenor. b. January 9, 1844, Valle de Roncal, Navarra; d. January 2, 1890, Madrid.

1. EdS 1/5 (Bibliography); SCHMIDL.

4. Beramendi, E.F. Julián Gayarre y Pablo Sarasate. Buenos Aires: Sebastián de Amorrortu e Hijos, 1944. 182, [1] p., 13 illus.

de Arrendondo, Máximo. Julián Gayarre! Estudio critico-bio-grafico. Madrid: Edición Minuesa de los Rios, 1890. 75 p., illus.

Enciso, Julio. Memorias de Julián Gayarre. Pamplona: Editorial Gomez, 1955. 276 p., portrait.

Gonzalez, Anselmo. Gayarre. Paris: Casa Editorial Franco-Ibero-Americana, n.d. [c.1926]. 213 p., 13 illus.

NOTE: Series, "Vida anecdótica de los grandes artistas líricos y dramáticos," lists La Malibran by A. Munoz Parez as printed, and, as in preparation, other biographies of Caruso, Patti, Tamagno, Tamberlick, and Rubini.

Hernández-Girbal, F. Julián Gayarre: el tenor de la voz de ángel. New York: Arno Press, 1977. [Reprint of 1955 edition

published by Ediciones Lira, Barcelona. 608, [49] p., 49
illus.]. 605 p., 28 illus., bibliography, index.

Hernández-Girbal, F. Una vida triumfal: Julián Gayarre, bio-
grafiá novelesca. Madrid: Atlántico Biblioteca, 1931. 356 p.,
repertoire list.

Historia artistica y apuntes biográficos del eminente tenor
español Julián Gayarre. Habana: La Universal, 1890. 69 p.

Peramos, Francisco. Gayarre, el tenor portentoso. Madrid:
Publicaciones Españolas, 1959. 29 p., 5 illus.

Sunjuan Urmeneta, José María. Gayarre. Pamplona: Diputación Foral
de Navarra-Direccion de Turismo, 1968. 31 p., illus.

5. Carmena y Millán, Luis. Coras del pasado: música, literatura,
   y tauromaquia. Madrid: Imprenta Ducazal, 1904. pp. 3-18.

   Ribera, Salvador A. & Luis Alberto Aguila. La opera. Santiago
   De Chile: Imprenta Y Encuadernación Roma, 1895.

CO234.
GAZZANIGA, MARIETTA. Italian Soprano. b. 1824, Voghera; d. January
2, 1884, Milano.

1. SCHMIDL.

4. Un recuerdo a Marietta Gazzaniga. Habana: La Habanera, 1858.
   16 p.

CO235.
GEDDA, NICOLAI. Swedish Tenor. b. July 11, 1925, Stockholm.

1. BAKER 6; EdS/Supp.; GROVE 6/7 (Bibliography); MGG 1/16 (Bibliography); RIEMANN 12 + Supp. (Bibliography).

2. GR 44/12; ON 25/10, 32/24, 42/15, 47/5; OPERA 17/12; OW 12/10,
   23/2.

3. Gedda, Nicolai and Aino Sellermark. Gavan är inte gratis:
   Nicolai Gedda beraetar sitt liv foer Aino Sellermark. Stockholm: Albert Bonnier Foerlag, 1977. 227 p., 8 illus.

CO236.
GENCER, LEYLA. Turkish Soprano. b. October 10, 1924, Istanbul.

1. EdS/Supp.; GROVE 6/7 (Bibliography).

2. OPERA 23/8; OW 7/6, 15/3.

CO237.
GERHARDT, ELENA. German Mezzo-Soprano. b. November 11, 1883, Leipzig;
d. January 11, 1961, London.

1. BAKER 6; GROVE 6/7 (Bibliography); MGG 1/16; RIEMANN 12 + Supp.
    (Bibliography).

2. GR 2/10, 10/5, 6, 11/3, 38/10; RS 40 (October 1970).

3. Gerhardt, Elena. Recital. London: Methuen & Co. Ltd., 1953.
    Reprint 1972. xi, 183 p., 16 illus., "Elena Gerhardt and the
    Gramophone" by Desmond Shawe-Taylor with a list of recordings.

4. Ertel, Paul. Kuenstlerbiographie: Elena Gerhardt. Berlin, 1907.

    Ertel was music critic of the Berliner Lokal Anzeiger and a
    fan of the singer. I have not seen a copy.

CO238.
GERVILLE-REACHE, JEANNE. French Mezzo-Soprano. b. March 26, 1882,
Orthez; d. January 15, 1915, New York City.

1. BAKER 6.

2. RC 21/3-4, 7-8.

CO239.
GHIAUROV, NICOLAI. Bulgarian Bass. b. September 13, 1929, Velingrad.

1. GROVE 6/7 (Bibliography); EdS/Supp.; MGG 1/16; RIEMANN 12/Supp.

2. ON 30/4; OPERA 28/10; OP 4/6; OW 6/4, 21/5.

4. Grenèche, Philippe. Nicolai Ghiaurov. "Les Trésors de l'Opéra
    No. 3." Paris: Opéra International, 1979. 61 p., illus., list
    of roles, discography.

CO240.
GIANNINI, DUSOLINA. American Soprano. b. December 19, 1902, Philadelphia.

1. BAKER 6; EdS 1/5; GROVE 6/7 (Bibliography); RIEMANN 12 + Supp.

2. ON 44/8; RC 9/2.

CO241.
GIBELIUS, OTTO. German Cantor. b. 1612, Borg; d. October 20, 1682,
Minden.

1. RIEMANN 12 (Bibliography) + Supp. (Bibliography).

4. Ganse, Albrecht. Der Cantor Otto Gibelius (1612-1682): sein
    Leben und seine Werke unter besonderer Beruecksichtigung seiner
    Schriften zur Schulgesangsmethodik. Leipzig: Frommhold &
    Wendler, 1934. 98 p., illus.

1931 University Dissertation, Kiel.

C0242.
GIGLI, BENIAMINO. Italian Tenor. b. March 20, 1890, Recanati; d.
November 30, 1957, Rome.

1. BAKER 6; EdS 1/5 (Bibliography); GROVE 6/7; MGG 1/5 (Bibliography) + 1/16 (Bibliography); RIEMANN 12 + Supp. (Bibliography), SCHMIDL + Supp.

2. GR 12/1, 16/1, 7, 22/1, 25/9; ON 22/8; OPERA 9/2; OW 20/12;
   RC 2/3, 4, 9/9-10, 11-12, 13/7-8; RNC 2/4.

3. Gigli, Beniamino. Confidenze. seconda edizione aumentata. Roma:
   Consorzio Editoriale Italiano S.A., 1942. 213 p.

   Gigli, Beniamino. La verità sul mio "caso". Roma: Società Tipografia Editrice Italiana, 1945. 35 p.

   Gigli, Beniamino. Memorie. Verona: Arnoldo Mondadori Editore,
   1957. 355 p., 8 illus.

   Gigli, Beniamino. The Memoirs of Beniamino Gigli. Translated by
   Darina Silone. London: Cassell & Company, 1957. Reprint 1977.
   x, 277 p., 52 illus., operatic repertorie with town, theater,
   and date, discography by Mark Ricaldone, list of recorded titles,
   index.

4. Calderon, Elda. Gigli: explica su triunfo. Buenos Aires:
   Editorial Mundo Moderno, 1952. 159 p., 6 illus.

   de Rensis, Raffaello. Beniamino Gigli: sein Leben, seine Kunst,
   seine Persoenlichkeit. Translated by Ivo Striedinger [from Il
   cantore del popolo, Beniamino Gigli]. Muenchen: Verlag H.
   Hugendubel, 1936. 152 p., 23 illus.

   Foschi, Franco. Omaggio a Beniamino Gigli primavera del tenore.
   Roma: Bulzoni Editore, 1982. unpaginated [aprox. 265 p.].
   numerous illus., index of appearances by year/city/theater/
   date/type.

   Hahn, Herbert. Un'anima cantava, eine Seele sang: Begegnungen
   mit Beniamino Gigli. Stuttgart: J. Ch. Mellinger Verlag, 1953.
   144 p., 5 illus.

   NOTE: This appears to be an expansion of: Heute wird es nicht
   regnen -- es singt ja Gigli. Stuttgart: Waldorf-Verlag, 1940.

   Herbert-Caesari, E.. Tradition and Gigli 1600-1955: a Pane-
   gyric. 2nd edition. London: Robert Hale Limited, 1963 [1st
   edition 1958]. 160 p., 2 illus., index.

   Rosner, Robert. Beniamino Gigli und die Kunst des Belcanto.
   Wien: Verlag Carl Haslinger Qdm. Tobias, 1929. 29 p.

   Silvestrini, Domenico. Beniamino Gigli e l'anima delle folle.
   Bologna: Tipografia Aldina Editrice, 1937. 95 p.

5. SEE: autobiography of **GABOR CARELLI**. (CO099).

CO243.
GILLY, DINH. French Baritone. b. July 19, 1877, Algiers; d. May 19, 1940, London.

1. GROVE 6/7.

2. GR 18/2; RC 5/7, 21/3-4.

CO244.
GIORGI-BRIGHENTI, MARIE (stage name: Righetti). Italian Mezzo-Soprano. b. 1793, Bologna; d. ?

1. FETIS 2/2 (under Brighenti); SCHMIDL (under Giorgi-Righetti, Geltrude).

4. Cenni di una donna già cantante sopra il maestro Rossini, in riposta a ciò che ne serisse, nella state dell'anno 1822, il giornalista inglese in Parigi, e fu riportato in una gazetta di Milano dello stesso anno. Bologna: Tipografia Sassi, 1823.

    No copy seen.

CO245.
GIRARDI, ANTON MARIA. Austrian Tenor. b. December 5, 1850, Gratz; d. April 20, 1918, Vienna. No lexicon listing.

4. Das Schicksal setz den Hobel an: der Lebensroman Alexander Girardis. Braunschweig: Verlag Friedr. Vieweg & Sohn, 1941. 415 p., portrait.

    Lunzer, Eduard. Girardinetto: gesammelte Skizzen aus Alexander Girardis Kuenstler-laufbahn. Wien: Selbstverlag des Verfasser, 1894. 46 p., 2 illus.

CO246.
GLESS, JULIUS. German Bass. b. March 24, 1886, Oltingen; d. December 24, 1967, Colone. No lexicon listing.

1. KUTSCH 3.

4. Zentner, Wilhelm. Erinnerungen an Kammersaenger Julius Gless zum 90. Geburtstag. Koeln: privately printed, 1976. 6 p., portrait.

CO247.
GLOSSOP, PETER. English Baritone. b. July 6, 1928, Sheffield.

1. GROVE 6/7; RIEMANN 12/Supp.

2. OPERA 20/5; OW 10/9.

CO248.
GLUCK, ALMA. American Soprano. b. May 11, 1884, Bucharest; d. October

October 27, 1938, New York City.

1. BAKER 6; GROVE 6/7; RIEMANN 12.

2. GR 2/12; RC 1/8, 6/2, 3.

4. Davenport, Marcia. Of Lena Geyer. New York: Grosset & Dunlap
    Publishers (rights owned by Charles Scribner's Sons), 1936.
    473 p.

    Alma Gluck's daughter dedicated this novel to her mother, and
    there is every reason to believe that it was both inspired by
    and based upon the singer's life.

    Davenport, Marcia. Too Strong for Fantasy. New York: Charles
    Scribner's Sons, 1967. 483 p., 12 illus., index.

    Davenport's autobiography with invaluable material on Gluck.

CO249.
GOBBI, TITO. Italian Baritone. b. October 24, 1913, Bassano del
Grappa.

1. BAKER 6; EdS 1/5; GROVE 6/7 (Bibliography); MGG 1/16 (Biblio-
    graphy); RIEMANN 12 + Supp.

2. GR 34/10, 46/6; ON 31/3, 36/19, 45/8; OPERA 6/10, 16/11;
    OP 6/4, 8/5; OW 7/2, 16/1.

3. Gobbi, Tito. My Life. New York: Macdonald & James, 1980 [1st
    edition London 1979]. 224 p., numerous illus., discography.

    Gobbi, Tito. Tito Gobbi on His World of Italian Opera. New York:
    Franklin Watts Inc., 1984. 265 p., 49 illus., index.

C250.
GOMPERZ-BETTELHEIM, CAROLINE. Austrian Mezzo-Soprano. b. June 1,
1845, Pest; d. January 24, 1926, Vienna. No lexicon listing.

4. Caroline von Gomperz-Bettelheim: biographische Blaetter zum 1.
    Juni 1915 fuer Freunde gedruckt. Wien: Carl Fromme, 1915 [1st
    edition 1905]. viii, 41 p., 6 illus.

CO251.
GORR, RITA. Belgian Mezz-Soprano. b. February 18, 1926, Zelzaete.

1. EdS/Supp.; GROVE 6/7; RIEMANN 12/Supp.

2. ON 30/3; OPERA 12/10; OP 2/5.

CO252.
GRANDI, MARGHERITA. Australian Soprano. b. October 4, 1894, Hobart.

1. GROVE 6/7

2. RC 25/3-4, 27/7-8.

CO253.
GRASSINI, JOSEPHINA. Italian Mezzo-Soprano. b. April 8, 1773, Varese;
d. January 3, 1850, Milan.

1. BAKER 6 (Bibliography); EdS 1/5 (Bibliography); FETIS 2/4;
    GROVE 6/7; MGG 1/5; RIEMANN 12/Supp. (Bibliography); SCHMIDL
    (Bibliography).

2. ON 39/14.

4. Gavoty, André. <u>La Grassini première cantatrice de S.M. l'Empereur
    et Roi</u>. Paris: Editions Bernard Grasset, 1947. 255 p., 10 illus.,
    14 appendices, section of sources with more than 90 references.

    Pougin, Arthur. <u>Une cantatrice 'amie' de Napoléon: Giuseppina
    Grassini 1773-1850</u>. Paris: Librairie Fischbacher, 1920. 73 p.,
    20 illus.

5. SEE: Jeanne, René. <u>Les oeuvres libres, nouvelle série</u> 34 (1949):
    131-96.

CO254.
GREENE, HENRY PLUNKET. Irish Baritone. b. June 24, 1865, near Dublin:
d. August 19, 1936, London.

1. BAKER 6; GROVE 6/7 (Bibliography); RIEMANN 12.

2. GR 14/4.

3. Greene, Henry Plunket. <u>From Blue Danube to Shannon</u>. London:
    Philip Allan, 1934. viii, 179 p.

    Greene, Henry Plunket. <u>Interpretation in Song</u>. Introduction by
    Dorothy Uris. New York: Da Capo Press, Inc., 1979 [1st edition
    London, 1912]. xiii, xii, 307 p., musical examples.

    Greene, Henry Plunket. <u>Where the Bright Waters Meet</u>. 3rd
    edition, revised and enlarged. London: Philip Allan, 1936
    [1st edition 1924]. 210 p., 15 illus.

CO255.
GREENFIELD, ELIZABETH T. American Mezzo-Soprano. b. 1819, Natchez.
Mississippi; d. March 31, 1876, Philadelphia. No lexicon listing.

4. La Brew, Arthur. <u>The Black Swan, Elizabeth T. Greenfield Song-
    stress: Biographical Study Annotated and Compiled by Arthur La
    Brew</u>. Detroit: privately printed, 1969. 89 p., 3 illus., appendix.

    Edition of 1,500 copies.

    <u>The Black Swan at Home and Abroad: or, a Biographical Sketch
    of Miss Elizabeth Taylor Greenfield, the American Vocalist</u>.
    Philadelphia: W.S. Young, Printer, 1855. 64 p.

C0256.
GREINDL, JOSEF. German Bass. b. December 23, 1912, Munich.

1. GROVE 6/7; RIEMANN 12 + Supp.

2. OW 1/10.

C0257.
GRISI, GIUDITTA. Italian Mezzo-Soprano. b. July 28, 1805, Milan; d. May 1, 1840, Robecco d'Oglio, near Cremona.

1. BAKER 6; EdS 1/5 (Bibliography); FETIS 2/4 + Supp.; GROVE 6/7 (Bibliography); MGG 1/5 (Bibliography); RIEMANN 12; SCHMIDL.

2. ON 18/20.

5. Weatherson, Alexander. The Donizetti Society Journal 4. Eynsham: Oxford, 1980. 261 p., 12 illus.

    The section on Grisi includes a chronology and repertoire.

    SEE: Cecilia Maria de Candia Pearce under **MARIO** (C0389).

C0258.
GRIST, RERI. American Soprano. b. 1932, New York City.

1. GROVE 6/7; RIEMANN 12/Supp.

2. ON 30/20; OW 8/9.

C0259.
GROZAVESCU, TRAIAN. Romanian Tenor. b. 1894, Klausenberg; d. February 15, 1927, Vienna. No lexicon listing.

1. KUTSCH 3.

4. Demeter-Grozăvescu, Mira. Traian Grozăvescu. Bucureşti: Editura Muzicală, 1965. 268 p., 38 illus., discography, repertoire, 20-item bibliography.

C0260.
GRUEMMER, ELISABETH. German Soprano. b. March 31, 1911, Niederjeutz bei Diedenhofen.

1. GROVE 6/7 (Bibliography); RIEMANN 12 + Supp.

2. ON 31/22.

5. SEE: Karla Hoecker under **DIETRICH FISCHER-DIESKAU** (C0204).

C0261.
GUEDEN, HILDA. Austrian Soprano. b. September 15, 1922, Vienna.

1. BAKER 6; EdS 1/6; GROVE 6/7 (Bibliography); RIEMANN 12 + Supp.

2. ON 22/10.

CO262.
GUENTHER, CARL. German Tenor. b. November 22, 1885, Ottensen bei
Buxtehude; d. September 9, 1958, Hamburg. No lexicon listing.

1. KUTSCH 3.

4. von Wiese, Eberhard. <u>Nach den Sternen muss man greifen, vom
Kupferschmied zum Kammersaenger: Erinnerungen des Kammersaengers
Carl Guenther von der Hamburgischen Staatsoper</u>. Hamburg: Hans
Christians Verlag, 1956. 238 p., 17 illus.

CO263.
GULBRANSON, ELLEN. Swedish Soprano. b. March 4, 1863, Stockholm;
d. January 2, 1947, Oslo.

1. BAKER 6; EdS 1/6 (Bibliography); GROVE 6/7; RIEMANN 12.

4. Elsta, Fanny. <u>Boken om Ellen Gulbranson</u>. Oslo: Cammermeyers
Boghandel, 1950. 190 p., 54 illus., index of names.

CO264.
GURA, EUGEN. German Baritone. b. November 8, 1842, Saatz, Bohemia;
d. August 26, 1906, Aufkirchen, Bavaria.

1. BAKER 6; EdS 1/6 (Bibliography); GROVE 6/7 (Bibliography);
MGG 1/5 (Bibliography); RIEMANN 12 + Supp. (Bibliography);
SCHMIDL/Supp.

3. Gura, Eugen. <u>Erinnerungen aus meinem Leben</u>. Leipzig: Breitkopf
und Haertel, 1905. 124 p., 5 illus.

CO265.
GUTHEIL-SCHODER, MARIE. German Mezzo-Soprano. b. February 10, 1874,
Weimar; d. October 4, 1935, Weimar.

1. BAKER 6; EdS 1/6 (Bibliography); RIEMANN 12 (Bibliography).

2. ON 42/10.

3. Gutheil-Schoder, Marie. <u>Erlebtes und Erstrebtes</u>. Wien, Krey
(Veroeffentlichungen des Verlages der Museumfreunde in Wien),
1937. 58 p.

4. Andro, L. [pseud. of Therese Rie]. <u>Marie Gutheil-Schoder</u>.
Wien: Wiener Literarische Anstalt, 1923. 31 p., portrait.

CO266.
HACKETT, CHARLES. American Tenor. b. November 4, 1889, Worcester,
Massachusets; d. January 1, 1942, New York City.

1. BAKER 6.

2. RC 22/8-9, 10-11.

C0267.
HAGMAN, SOPHIE. Swedish Soprano. b. 1761; d. 1826. No lexicon
listing.

4. Forsstrand, Carl. <u>Sophie Hagman och hennes samtida: nagra</u>
   <u>anteckningar fran det gustavianska stockholm</u>. Stockholm:
   Wahlstroem & Nidstrand, 1911. 211 p., 8 illus., index of
   259 names with dates.

C0268.
HAMLIN, GEORGE JOHN. American Tenor. b. September 20, 1868, Elgin,
Illinois; d. January 20, 1923, New York City.

1. BAKER 6.

4. Hamlin, Anna M. <u>Father was a Tenor</u>. Hicksville: New York,
   Exposition Press, n.d. [c.1978]. 96 p., 2 illus.

   Trott, Josephine. <u>George Hamlin American Singer 1868-1923: a</u>
   <u>Resume of His Career</u>. Denver: privately printed, 1925. 53 p.,
   7 illus.

C0269.
HAMMOND, JOAN. New Zealand Soprano. b. May 24, 1912 Christchurch.

1. GROVE 6/8 (Bibliography); RIEMANN 12 + Supp.

2. OPERA 10/2.

3. Hammond, Joan. <u>A Voice, a Life</u>. London: Victor Gollancz Ltd.,
   1970. 264 p., 29 illus., list of repertoire, discography, index.

C0270.
HARPER, HEATHER. English Soprano. b. May 8, 1938, Belfast.

1. BAKER 6; GROVE 6/8; RIEMANN 12/Supp.

2. ON 42/7; OPERA 22/7.

C0271.
HASSE, FAUSTINA BORDONI-. SEE: **BORDONI-HASSE, F.** (C0071).

C0272.
HAUK, MINNIE. American Soprano. b. November 16, 1851, New York City;
d. February 6, 1929, Triebschen, by Lucerne, Switzerland.

1. BAKER 6 (Bibliography); EdS 1/6 (Bibliography); GROVE 6/8 (Bibliography); RIEMANN 12; SCHMIDL/Supp.

2. ON 9/20.

3. Hauk, Minnie. <u>Memories of a Singer</u>. Collated by E.B. Hitchcock.
   London: A.M. Philpot, Ltd., 1925. Reprint 1977. 295 p., 16
   illus.

She married Baron Ernst von Hesse-Wartegg in 1881 and her autobiography is sometimes listed under Hesse-Wartegg or de Wartegg.

CO273.
HAYES, CATHERINE. Irish Soprano. b. October 25, 1825, Limerick; d.
August 11, 1861, London.

1. GROVE 6/8 (Bibliography); EdS 1/6.

4. Memoir of Miss Catherine Hayes, "The Swan of Erin," by a contri-
    butor to the Dublin University Magazine. London: Cramer, n.d.
    [c.1861]. 9 p., illus.

CO274.
HAYES, ROLAND. American Tenor. b. June 3, 1887, Curryville, Georgia;
d. January 1, 1977, Boston, Massachusets.

1. BAKER 6 (Bibliography); GROVE 6/8; RIEMANN 12 (Bibliography) +
    Supp.

2. RC 10/2, 12/3-4, 8-9.

4. Harris, Charles. Reminiscences of My Days with Roland Hayes.
    Orangeburg: privately printed, 1944. 27 p., portrait.

    Helm, Mackinley. Angel Mo' and Her Son Roland Hayes. Boston:
    Little, Brown and Company, 1944. Reprint 1974. ix, 289 p.
    portrait.

5. SEE: Langston Hughes under **MARIAN ANDERSON** (CO017).

CO275.
de HEGERMANN-LINDENCRONE, LILLIE. American Mezzo-Soprano. b. 1844;
d. 1916. No lexicon listing.

2. ON 33/23.

3. de Hegermann-Lindencrone, Lillie. In the Courts of Memory 1858-
    1875 from Contemporary Letters. New York: Harper & Brothers
    Publishers, 1912. Reprint 1980. viii, 450 p., 27 illus., index.

    Student of Garcia. Sang under the name of **LILLI MOULTON**.

    de Hegermann-Lindencrone, Lillie. The Sunny Side of Diplomatic
    Life 1875-1912. New York: Harper & Brothers Publishers, 1914.
    x, 337 p., 34 illus.

    Moulton, Mrs. Charles. A Sketch of Her Musical Career with
    Reminiscences of Her Life. New York: Baker & Goodwin, 1871.
    15 p.

CO276.
HEINRICH, WILHELM. American Tenor. b. 1865; d. December 26, 1911.
No lexicon listing.

4. Winn, Edith Lynwood. <u>Wilhelm Heinrich Musician and Man: a Tribute</u>. Boston: C.W. Thompson & Co., 1914. 235 p., 5 illus., list of important dates.

C0277.
HEMING, PERCY. English Baritone. b. September 6, 1883, Bristol; d. January 11, 1956, London.

1. GROVE 6/8.

2. OPERA 5/4, 7/4.

C0278.
HEMPEL, FRIEDA. German Soprano. b. June 26, 1885, Leipzig; d. October 7, 1955, Berlin.

1. BAKER 6; EdS 1/6 (Bibliography); GROVE 6/8; MGG 1/6; RIEMANN 12.

2. GR 3/2, 33/7; ON 20/15; RC 10/3.

3. Hempel, Frieda. <u>Mein Leben dem Gesang: Erinnerungen</u>. Berlin: Argon Verlag, 1955. 319 p., 31 illus., opera repertoire, index of names.

    There is an MS translation in English by the late George L. Nyklicek.

C0279.
HENSCHEL, GEORGE. German Baritone. b. February 18, 1850, Breslau; d. September 10, 1934, Aviemore, Scotland.

1. BAKER 6 (Bibliography); GROVE 6/8 (Bibliography); MGG 1/6 (Bibliography); RIEMANN 12; SCHMIDL.

2. RS 62 (April 1976).

3. Henschel, George. <u>How to Interpret a Song</u>. Philadelphia: Theodore Presser, 1929.

    No copy located.

    Henschel, George. <u>Musings and Memories of a Musician</u>. London: Macmillan and Co., Limited, 1918. Reprint 1979. 400 p., portrait, index.

    The singer also authored a book of personal recollections of Johannes Brahms.

4. Henschel, Helen. <u>When Soft Voices Die: a Musical Biography</u>. London: John Westhouse Limited, 1944. 216 p., 10 illus., index.

C0280.
HERFORD, JOHANN JOSEPH. German Tenor. b. 1771; d. May 27, 1829, Tilsit. No lexicon listing.

4. Grunwald, Fritz. Aus dem Leben des Tilsiter Cantors Johann
   Joseph Herford. Koenigsberg i. Pr.: privately printed, 1934.
   90, unpaginated genealogy tables, [1x] p., list of roles in
   Breslau and Danzig, 91-item bibliography, index of names.

CO281.
HERITTE-VIARDOT, LOUISE. French Mezzo-Soprano. b. December 14, 1841,
Paris; d. January 17, 1918, Heidelberg.

1. BAKER 6; GROVE 6/19 (under Pauline Viardot); RIEMANN 12 (under
   Viardot-Garcia); SCHMIDL (under Viardot).

3. Héritte-Viardot, Louise. Die Natur in der Stimmbildung fuer
   Redner und Saenger. Heidelberg: O. Pelters Verlag, 1906. 29 p.

   Héritte-Viardot, Louise. Memories and Adventures. Translated
   and arranged by E.S. Buchheim. London: Mills & Boon, Limited,
   1913. Reprint 1978. xiii, 271 p., 20 illus., index.

   This book was edited from the original MS in German. There
   is a French edition published in Paris in 1923 which I have
   not seen.

5. SEE: Louis Héritte de la Tour under **MANUEL PATRICIO GARCIA**
         (CO231).

CO282.
HEROLD, VILHELM KRISTOFFER. Danish Tenor. b. March 19, 1865, Hasle,
Bornholm; d. December 15, 1937, Copenhagen.

1. GROVE 6/8; RIEMANN 12.

2. GR 15/9; RNC 1/10.

4. Ipsen, Arne. Sangern fra Hasle: folkebeg om Vilhelm Herold og
   hans bornholmske barndomsby i 1870'erne. Rønne: Bornholmern,
   1979. 63 p., illus., bibliography.

   Vilhelm Herold 1893-1915. København: Erslev & Hasselbalch,
   n.d. [c.1916]. unpaginated [28 p.], 49 illus.

   Vilhelm Kristoffer Herold Discography. Copenhagen: Copenhagen
   Nationale Diskoteket Katalog, No. 8. n.d. [1961].

5. Fønss, Johannes. Friske erindringer: fra livets og det andet
   teater. København: Verden Vts. Forlag, 1921.

CO283.
HIDALGO, ELVIRA de. Spanish Soprano. b. December 27, 1892, Aragón;
d. January 21, 1980, Milan.

1. GROVE 6/8 (Bibliography); EdS 1/6 (Bibliography); RIEMANN 12/Supp.

2. ON 32/26.

C0284.
HILLEBRECHT, HILDEGARD. German Soprano. b. November 26, 1927, Hanover.

1. GROVE 6/8; RIEMANN 12/Supp.

2. OW 3/4, 8/6.

C0285.
HINES, JEROME. American Bass. b. November 8, 1921, Los Angeles, California.

1. BAKER 6; EdS/Supp.; GROVE 6/8; RIEMANN 12/Supp.

2. ON 11/7, 27/22, 32/23, 45/5.

3. Hines, Jerome. This is My Story, This is My Song. Westwood: Fleming H. Revell Company, 1968 [Spanish edition translated by Arnoldo Canclini 1974]. 160 p., 12 illus.

    NOTE: A0048 in which he interviews thirty-nine singers.

C0286.
HISLOP, JOSEPH. Scottish Tenor. b. April 5, 1884, Edinburgh; d. May 6, 1977, Upper Largo, Fife.

1. GROVE 6/8 (Bibliography); RIEMANN 12 + Supp.

2. RC 23/9-10, 25/1-2.

C0287.
HOFFMANN, BAPTIST. German Baritone. b. July 9, 1864, Garitz bei Kissingen; d. July 5, 1937, Gratz. No lexicon listing.

1. KUTSCH 3.

4. Hoffmann-Kuesel, G. Baptist Hoffmann: ein Leben fuer die Kunst. Berlin: Afas-Musikverlag Hans Duennebeil, 1949. 75 p., 14 illus., opera repertoire.

C0288.
HOLLWEG, ILSE. German Soprano. b. February 23, 1922, Solingen.

1. RIEMANN 12 + Supp.

4. Ruhrberg, Karl. Ilse Hollweg. Duisburg: Walter Braun Verlag, 1971. 75 p., 49 illus., list of recordings, lists of repertoire.

C0289.
HOLM, EMIL. Danish Bass. No lexicon listing.

4. Erindringer og todsbilleder fra midten of forrige aarhundrede til vor tid. 2 vols. København: Berlingske Forlag, 1938/39. 157 p., 52 illus., index of names; 216 p., 103 illus., index of names.

C0290.
HOMER, LOUISE. American Mezzo-Soprano. b. April 28, 1871, Shady-side, near Pittsburgh; d. May 6, 1947, Winter Park, Florida.

1. BAKER 6; GROVE 6/8; RIEMANN 12.

2. ON 28/10, 33/19; RC 2/7.

4. Homer, Anne. Louise Homer and the Golden Age of Opera. New York: Wm. Morrow & Co., Inc., 1974. 439 p., 62 illus., 30-item select bibliography, index.

   Homer, Sidney. My Wife and I: the Story of Louise and Sidney Homer. New York: The Macmillan Company, 1939. Reprint 1977. xiii, 269 p., 18 illus.

5. Vermorcken, Elizabeth Moorhead. These Too were Here. Pittsburgh: University of Pittsburgh Press, 1950. Reprint by The Folcroft Press, n.d., and Norwood Editions 1977. 62 p.

C0291.
HOENGEN, ELISABETH. German Mezzo-Soprano. b. December 7, 1906, Gevelsberg, Westphalia.

1. GROVE 6/8; RIEMANN 12 + Supp.

4. Wurm, Ernst. Elisabeth Hoengen. Wien: Oesterreichischer Bundesverlag fuer Unterricht, Wissenschaft und Kunst, 1966. 72 p., 24 illus., list of performances, discography.

C0292.
HOPPE, HEINZ. German Tenor. b. January 26, 1924, Saerbeck, Kreis Muenster.

1. Riemann 12/Supp.

4. Hoppe-Linzen, Carla. Willst du dein Herz mir schenken . . .: mein Leben mit Hienz Hoppe. Emsdetten: Verlag Lechte, 1972. 152 p., 58 illus., discography, repertoire list.

C0293.
HORNE, MARILYN. American Mezzo-Soprano. b. January 16, 1934, Bradford, Pennsylvania.

1. BAKER 6; EdS/Supp.; GROVE 6/8 (Bibliography -- birthyear listed as 1929); RIEMANN 12/Supp. (Bibliography).

2. ON 34/9-10, 37/18, 45/12, 45/15; OPERA 18/12.

3. Horne, Marilyn and Jane Scovell. Marilyn Horn: My Life. New York: Atheneum, 1983. 258 p., illus., discography, index.

4. Dodge, Emelie Ruth. Marilyn Horne. New York: Gloria Enterprises Inc., 1979. unpaginated [20 p.]., 51 illus.

5. Phillips, Harvey E. The Carmen Chronicle: the Making of an Opera.
    New York. Stein and Day Publishers, 1973. 288 p., 36 illus., index.

    A reporter's detailed documentation and log of rehearsals, per-
    formances and recording sessions of the late Goeran Genrele's
    Metropolitan Opera opening night!

C0294.
HOTTER, HANS. German Baritone. b. January 19, 1909, Offenbach
am Main.

1. BAKER 6; EdS 1/6; GROVE 6/8 (Bibliography); MGG 1/16; RIEMANN 12
    + Supp.

2. GR 52/8; OPERA 4/10, 17/1, 27/7; OW 3/7-8, 15/3.

3. Hotter, Hans. "Die Oper, das unmoegliche Kunstwerk." In Oester-
    reichische Musikzeitschrift 20 (1965).

    No copy seen.

4. Turing, Penelope. Hans Hotter: Man and Artist. London: John
    Calder, 1983. 280 p., 44 illus., chronology, operatic repertiore,
    operas produced, discography, index.

    Wessling, Berndt W. Hans Hotter. Bremen: Carl Schuenemann
    Verlag, 1966. 142 p., 36 illus., repertoire, 17-item bibliog-
    raphy, discography.

C0295.
HOWARD, KATHLEEN. American Mezzo-Soprano. b. July 17, 1884, Clifton,
Canada; d. August 15, 1956, Hollywood, California.

1. BAKER 6; RIEMANN 12.

3. Howard, Kathleen. Confessions of an Opera Singer. New York:
    Alfred A. Knopf, 1918. 273 p., 8 illus., opera repertoire.

C0296.
HUEHN, JULIUS. American Baritone. b. January 12, 1904, Revere,
Massachusetts; d. June 8, 1971, Rochester, New York.

1. BAKER 6.

3. Huehn, Julius. An American Wotan at the Met. MS compiled and
    edited by Robert H. Cowden. Detroit, 1972. iv, 270, [11] p.,
    performed operatic repertoire, 18-item related reading list,
    list of illus., index of names, list of opera and oratorio
    appearances.

C0297.
HUNNIUS, MONIKA. German Soprano. No lexicon listing.

3. Hunnius, Monika. Mein Weg zur Kunst. Heilbronn: Eugen Salzer,
    1924. 352 p., portrait, index of names.

Hunnius, Monika. Wenn die Zeit erfuellt ist . . . Briefe und Tagebuchblaetter. Edited by Anne-Monika Glasow. Heilbronn: Eugen Slazer Verlag. 1959 [1st edition 1936]. 335 p., stammbaum.

C0298.
IBOS, GUILLAUME. French Tenor. b. July 10, 1860, Muret, near Toulouse; d. ? No lexicon listing.

4. Loiseau, Georges. Notes sur le chant. Paris: privately printed for the author by Durand et Cie, 1947. 193 p., 5 illus.

Ibos created the role of Werther in Paris (January 16, 1893) after Van Dyck had done the premiere in Vienna (February 16, 1892). Some very amusing comments on his career and on the critics.

C0299.
ISLANDI, STEFAN. Icelandic Tenor. b. October 6, 1907, Iceland. No lexicon listing.

1. KUTSCH 3.

4. Indrioei, G. Áfram veginn: sagan um Stefán Islandi. Akureyri: Bjoernsson, 1975. 264 p., 16 illus., discography, index.

C0300.
ISORI, IDA. No lexicon listing.

4. Batka, Richard. Ida Isori et son art du "Bel Canto". Paris: Chez Costallat e Cie, n.d. [c.1912]. 26 p., portrait.

C0301.
ISTRATTY, EDGAR. Romanian Bass. No lexicon listing.

4. Istratty, Ella. De vorbă cu Edgar Istratty. Bucureşti: Editura Muzicală, 1969. 193 p., 17 illus.

C0302.
IVOGUEN, MARIA. Hungarian Soprano. b. November 18, 1891, Budapest.

1. BAKER 6; EdS 1/6; GROVE 6/9; MGG 1/6; RIEMANN 12.

2. RC 20/5, 12.

5. SEE: Maria Mueller-Goegler under KARL ERB (C0184).

C0303.
JADLOWKER, HERMANN. Latvian Tenor. b. July 17, 1877, Riga; d. May 13, 1953, Tel Aviv.

1. BAKER 6; EdS 1/6 (Bibliography); GROVE 6/9; RIEMANN 12.

2. OW 12/1; RC 19/1-2.

C0304.
JAGEMANN, HENRIETTE KAROLINE. German Soprano. b. January 25, 1777,
Weimar; d. July 10, 1848, Dresden.

1. EdS 1/6 (Bibliography).

4. Bamberg, Eduard von. Die Erinnerungen der Karoline Jagemann nebst
   zahlreichen unveroeffentlichten Dokumenten aus der Goethezeit.
   2 vols. Dresden: Im Sibyllen-Verlag, 1926. 282 p., 18 illus.,
   286-624 p., 26 illus., index of names.

C0305.
JANACOPULOS, VERA. Brazilian Soprano. b. December 20, 1892,
Petropolis; d. December 5, 1958, Rio de Janeiro.

4. Franca, Eurico Nogueira. Memorias de Vera Janacópulos. Rio de
   Janeiro: Ministerio da educacao e cultura, 1959. 83 p., 4 illus.

C0306.
JANOWITZ, GUNDULA. German Soprano. b. February 8, 1939, Berlin.

1. GROVE 6/9; RIEMANN 12/Supp. (Birthyear 1937).

2. ON 32/1; OP 5/10; OW 15/4.

C0307.
JANSSEN, HERBERT. German Baritone. b. September 22, 1895, Cologne;
d. June 3, 1965, New York City.

1. BAKER 6; EdS 1/6 (Bibliography); GROVE 6/9; RIEMANN 12 + Supp.

2. OPERA 16/8; RC 16/11-12, 21/3-4.

C0308.
JELYOTTE, PIERRE. French Counter Tenor. b. April 13, 1713, Lassoube;
d. October 12, 1797, Chateau d'Estos.

1. EdS 1/6; FETIS 2/4; GROVE 6/9 (Bibliography); MGG 1/6 (Bibliography); RIEMANN 12 (Bibliography).

4. Pougin, Arthur. Un ténor de l'opéra au XVIIIe siecle Pierre
   Jélyotte et les chanteurs de son temps. Paris: Librairie Fischbacher, 1905. Reprint 1973. 239 p., 22 illus.

   NOTE: Also listed as B0117 because of the detailed information
   about Marie Antier, Pélissier, Catherine-Nicole Lamaure,
   Petitpas, Fel, Chevalier, Bourbonnais, Coupé, La Camargo, and
   Sallé.

5. Imbert, Hugues. Médaillons contemporains. Paris: Librairie
   Fischbacher, 1902. 406, [1] p., index of names.

C0309.
JERITZA, MARIA. Czechoslovakian Soprano. b. October 6, 1887, Bruenn;
d. July 10, 1982, Orange, New Jersey.

1. BAKER 6; EdS 1/6 (Bibliography); GROVE 6/9 (Billiography); MGG
   1/7 (Bibliography); RIEMANN 12 + Supp.; SCHMIDL.

2. GR 2/7; ON 10/23, 25/15, 47/3; OW 13/10, 23/8-9.

3. Jeritza, Maria. Sunlight and Song: a Singer's Life. Translated
   by Frederick H. Martens. New York: D. Appleton and Company, 1924.
   Reprint 1977. 262 p., 39 illus.

4. Decsey, Ernst. Maria Jeritza. Wien: J. Fischer-Verlag, 1931.
   75 p., 57 illus.

   Text is in English and German.

   Werba, Robert. Maria Jeritza Primadonna des Verismo. Wien:
   Oesterreichischer Bundesverlag Gesellschaft m.b.H., 1981.
   188 p., 23 illus., list of roles, 311-item bibliography,
   chronology.

   von Wymetal, Wilhelm. Maria Jeritza. Wien: Wiener Literarische Anstalt, 1922. 52 p., portrait.

5. SEE: Merle Armitage under MARY GARDEN (CO232).

CO310.
JOACHIM, AMALIE. German Soprano. b. May 10, 1839, Marburg; d.
February 3, 1899, Berlin.

1. BAKER 6; GROVE 6/9 (Bibliography under Joseph Joachim);
   RIEMANN 12.

4. Plaschke, Olga. Amalie Joachim: Blaetter der Erinnerung. Berlin:
   Harmonie Verlagsgesellschaft fuer Literatur und Kunst, 1899.
   39 p., portrait.

5. SEE: Heinrich Riemann under JENNY LIND (CO360).

CO311.
JOHNSON, EDWARD. Canadian Tenor. b. August 22, 1878, Guelph,
Ontario; d. April 20, 1959, Guelph, Ontario.

1. BAKER 6; EdS 1/4 (under Di Giovanni with Bibliography); GROVE
   6/9 (Bibliography); RIEMANN 12 + Supp. (Bibliography);
   SCHMIDL/Supp.

2. ON (numerous references during his tenure as Director of the
   Metropolitan Opera 1935-1950) 14/23, 24/2; RNC 2/6.

4. Mercer, Ruby. The Tenor of His Time: Edward Johnson of the
   Met. Toronto: Clarke, Irwin & Company Limited, 1976. xv,
   336 p., 48 illus., discography by J.B. McPherson and W.R.
   Moran, awards, index.

5. Simon, Robert Edward. Be Your Own Music Critic: the Carnegie
   Hall Anniversary Lectures.... Garden City, Doubleday, Doran

and Co., 1941. xiv, 300 p.

C0312.
JONES, SISSIERETTA. American Soprano. b. January 5, 1868, Portsmouth,

Virginia; d. June 24, 1933, Providence, Rhode Island.

1. BAKER 6.

4. Sissieretta Jones, the Black Patti. MS in the 'Hackley
    Collection' at the Detroit Public Library, Michigan.

    NOTE: There is also original material about this singer in
    the Boston Conservatory Library, Massachusetts.

C0313.
JONES, GWYNETH. Welsh Soprano. b. November 7, 1937 Pontnewynydd.

1. GROVE 6/9; RIEMANN 12/Supp.

2. GR 50/1; ON 31/5, 37/7, 45/11; OPERA 21/2; OP 10/3; OW 9/8,
    13/4.

4. Mutafian, Claude. Gwyneth Jones. Paris: Opéra International,
    1980. 63 p., illus., chronology, discography, list of films.

C0314.
JURINAC, SENA. Yugoslavian Soprano. b. October 24, 1921, Travnik.

1. BAKER 6; EdS 1/6 (Bibliography); GROVE 6/9 (Bibliography);
    RIEMANN 12 + Supp.

2. ON 32/26; OPERA 1/5, 17/4; OW 4/3

4. Tamussino, Ursula. Sena Jurinac. Augsburg: Schroff-Druck Verlags-
    gesellechaft mbH, 1971. 211 p., 146 illus., complete list of roles
    and films, discography.

C0315.
KELLOGG, CLARA LOUISE. American Soprano. b. July 9, 1842, Sumter-
ville, North Carolina; d. May 13, 1916, New Hartford, Connecticut.

1. BAKER 6; GROVE 6/9 (Bibliography); RIEMANN 12; SCHMIDL/Supp.

3. Kellogg, Clara Louise. Memoirs of an American Prima Donna. New
    York, G.P. Putnam's Sons, 1913. Reprint 1978. xiii, 382 p., 40
    illus., index.

4. Clara Louise Kellogg and English Opera. n.p., n.d. 13 p.

    A release for the English Opera Company which she founded in 1873.

C0316.
KELLY, MICHAEL. Irish Tenor. b. December 25, 1762, Dublin; d. October
9, 1826, Margate.

1. BAKER 6; GROVE 6/9 (Bibliography); MGG 1/7; RIEMANN 12 + Supp. (Bibliography); SCHMIDL.

3. Kelly, Michael. <u>Reminiscences of Michael Kelly, of the King's Theater, and Theater Royal Drury Lane, including a Period of Nearly Half a Century: with Original Anecdotes of Many Distinguished Persons, Political, Literary, and Musical</u>. 2 vols. London: Henry Colburn, 1826. Reprint 1968 with introduction by A. Hyatt King; Reprint 1975 edited with an introduction by Roger Fisk. 354 p., portrait; 404 p., history of the King's Theater.

   Historically one of the most famous of all singer's autobiographies, this was edited and arranged for publication by Theodore Hook.

4. Ellis, S.M. <u>The Life of Michael Kelly Musican, Actor, and bon viveur 1762-1826</u>. London: Victor Gollancz Ltd., 1930. 400 p., 24 illus., index.

CO317.
KEMBLE, ADELAIDE. English Soprano. b. 1814; d. August 4, 1879, London.

1. GROVE 1/2.

2. ON 29/11.

3. Kemble, Adelaide. <u>A Week in a French Country House</u>. London: n.p., 18 ?.

   No copy located.

5. SEE: William Appleton under **LUCIA ELIZABETH VESTRIS** (CO683).

CO318.
KEMP, BARBARA. German Soprano. b. December 12, 1881, Cochem an der Mosel; d. April 17, 1959, Berlin.

1. BAKER 6; GROVE 6/9; RIEMANN 12.

4. Bie, Oskar. <u>Barbara Kemp</u>. Berlin: E. Reiss, n.d. [1921]. 47 p., 5 illus.

CO319.
KENNEDY, DAVID. Scottish Tenor. b. April 15, 1825, Perth; d. October 12, 1886, Stratford, Ontario.

1. GROVE 6/9; RIEMANN 12.

4. Kennedy, Marjory. <u>David Kennedy the Scottish Singer: Reminiscences of His Life and Work and Singing Round the World. a Narrative of His Colonial and Indian Tours by David Kennedy, jun.</u> London: Alexander Gardner, 1887. 95, 11-379 p., 16 illus.

   The second section (pp. 11-379) is a revision and condensation

by the singer before his death of three books already published.
I have seen none of the original editions.

CO320.
KENNEDY-FRASER, MARJORY. Scottish Soprano. b. October 1, 1857, Perth;
d. November 21, 1930, Edinburgh.

1. BAKER 6; GROVE 6/9 (Bibliography); RIEMANN 12; SCHMIDL.

3. Kennedy-Fraser, Marjory. A Life of Song. London: Oxford
    University Press, 1929. 199 p., 4 illus.

CO321.
KIEPURA, JAN. Polish Tenor. b. May 16, 1902, Sosnowiec; d. August
15, 1966, Rye, New York.

1. BAKER 6; GROVE 6/10 (Bibliography); RIEMANN 12.

2. OW 21/4.

4. Ramage, Jean. Jan Kiepura. Paris: Opéra, 1968. 32 p., 20 illus.

    Special supplement to the French periodical, Opéra.

    Waldorff, Jerzy. Jan kiepura. Kraków: Polskie Wydaw. Muzyczne,
    1974. 93, [3 + 28] p., 28 illus., repertoire, list of films.

CO322.
KING, JAMES. American Tenor. b. May 22, 1925, Dodge City, Kansas.

1. GROVE 6/10; RIEMANN 12/Supp.

2. ON 36/8; OP 8/1; OW 9/2, 14/6, 21/3.

CO323.
KIPNIS, ALEXANDER. Russian Bass. b. February 13, 1891, Zhitomir;
d. May 14, 1978, Westport, Connecticut.

1. BAKER 6; GROVE 6/10; MGG 1/7; RIEMANN 12.

2. ON 10/18, 19, 25/9; RC 22/3-4, 23/7-8.

CO324.
KIRSTEN, DOROTHY. American Soprano. July 6, 1917, Montclair,
New Jersey.

1. BAKER 6; GROVE 6/10.

2. ON 35/19, 40/9.

3. Kirsten, Dorothy with Lanfranco Rasponi. A Time to Sing.
    Forward by Robert Jacobson. Garden City: Doubleday & Company,
    Inc., 1982. xiv, 247 p., awards/degrees/citations/etc., dis-
    cography by Stanley A. Bowker, index.

CO325.
KLAFSKY, KATHARINA. Hungarian Soprano. b. September 19, 1855, St. Johann; d. September 22, 1896, Hamburg.

1. BAKER 6; EdS 1/6 (Bibliography); GROVE 6/10 (Bibliography); RIEMANN 12 + Supp. (Bibliography); SCHMIDL/Supp.

4. Ordemann, Ludwig. <u>Katharina Klafsky</u>. Leipzig: Verlag von Theodore Fuendling, 1903 [Hameln 1905]. vii, 90 p., portrait.

CO326.
KNAUER-HAAS, MATHILDE. German Mezzo-Soprano. b. 1863; d. 1930. No lexicon listing.

4. Knauer, Alfred M., ed. <u>Mathilde Knauer-Haas, Grosshess. Kammer-saengerin: dem Andenken meiner lieben Frau</u>. Mainz: privately printed by Firma Zaberndruck, 1931. unpaginated, 53 illus., musical examples, reviews.

   Edition of 250 copies.

CO327.
KNOTE, HEINRICH. German Tenor. b. November 26, 1870, Munich; d. January 12, 1953, Garmisch.

1. BAKER 6; GROVE 6/10; RIEMANN 12.

4. Wagenmann, Josef Hermann. <u>Der sechzigjaerige deutsche Meister-saenger Heinrich Knote in seiner stimmbildnerischen Bedeutung und im Vergleich mit anderen Saengern</u>. Muenchen: Erich Hecht Verlagsbuchhandlung, 1931. 253 p., 4 illus.

   A fascinating study for anyone interested in tenors as the author compares Knote with twenty-seven other singers including Erb, Melchoir, Pattiera, Tauber, Urlus, Soot, Voelker, Slezak, Piccaver, Roswaenge, and Kiepura!

CO328.
KOETH, ERIKA. German Soprano. b. September 15, 1927, Darmstadt.

1. GROVE 6/10; RIEMANN 12 + Supp.

2. OW 1/12.

4. Adam, Klaus. <u>Herzlichst! Erika Koeth</u>. Darmstadt: Justus von Liebig Verlag, 1969. 296 p., 66 illus., index of names.

CO329.
KOLLO, RENE. German Tenor. b. November 20, 1937, Berlin.

1. GROVE 6/10; RIEMANN 12/Supp.

2. ON 41/6; OW 15/4, 19/6.

4. Fabian, Imre. <u>Imre Fabian im gespraech mit René Kollo</u>. Zuerich:

Orell Fuessli Verlag, 1982. 171, [1] p., 34 illus., career
dates, list of roles, discography.

C0330.
KONETZNI, HILDE. Austrian Soprano. b. February 12, 1902, Vienna;
September 6, 1968, Vienna.

1. GROVE 6/10; RIEMANN 12 + Supp.

2. ON 42/19.

C0331.
KONYA, SANDOR. Hungarian Tenor. b. September 23, 1923, Sarkad.

1. EdS 1/Supp.; GROVE 6/10; RIEMANN 12/Supp.

2. ON 26/12, 30/16; OW 3/5.

C0332.
KOROLEWICZ-WAYDOWA, JANINA. Polish Soprano. b. February 8, 1875,
Warsaw; d. July ?, 1957, Krakow. No Lexicon listing.

1. KUTSCH 3.

3. Korolewicz-Waydowa, Janina. Sztuka i zycie: moj pamietnik.
    Wroclaw: Zaklad Narodowy im. Ossolińskich, 1969 [1st edition
    1958. 421 p., 28 illus.]. xiv, 426 p., 40 illus., chronology,
    Polish premieres with casts, biographies of artists, index.

C0333.
KOSCHAT, THOMAS. Austrian Bass. b. August 8, 1845, Viktring, near
Klagenfurt; d. May 19, 1914, Vienna.

1. BAKER 6; RIEMANN 12 (Bibliography); SCHMIDL.

4. Krobath, Karl. Thomas Koschat der Saenger Kaerntens: seine
    zeit und sein Schaffen. Leipzig: Verlag von F.E.C. Leuckart,
    1912. 136 p., 20 illus., musical examples.

C0334.
KRASOVA, MARTA. Czechoslovakian Mezzo-Soprano. b. March 16, 1901,
Protivin; d. February 20, 1970, Vraz u Berouna.

1. BAKER 6; GROVE 6/10 (Bibliography); RIEMANN 12 + Supp. (Bibliog-
    raphy).

4. Národni umělkyne marta krásová: ze života nelké pěvkyně. Praha:
    Vladimír Solín, 1960. 39 p., 26 illus., discography, repertoire.

C0335.
KRAUS, ALFREDO. Spanish Tenor. b. 1927, Canary Islands.

1. EdS 1/Supp.; GROVE 6/10.

2. ON 31/14, 43/13; OPERA 26/1; OW 19/9.

C0336.
KRAUSE, TOM. Finnish Baritone. b. July 5, 1934, Helsinki.

1. GROVE 6/10; RIEMANN 12/Supp.

2. OW 13/11, 21/8-9.

C0337.
KRAUSS, GABRIELLE. Austrian Soprano. b. March 24, 1842, Vienna;
d. January 6, 1906, Paris.

1. BAKER 6; EdS 1/6 (Bibliography); FETIS 2/Supp.; GROVE 6/10;
   RIEMANN 12; SCHMIDL.

4. de Charnacé, Guy. Gabrielle Krauss. Paris: Henri Plon,
   Imprimeur-Editeur, 1869. 28 p., portrait.

C0338.
KRUEGER, EMMY. German Mezzo-Soprano. b. 188? No lexicon listing.

4. H.W.D. Der Weg einer Deutschen Kuenstlerin: Erinnerungen an
   Emmy Krueger. Muenchen: Universitaetsbuchdruckerei Dr. C. Wolf
   & Sohn, 1940. 118, [18], [9] p., 42 illus., poetry.

C0339.
KULLMAN, CHARLES. American Tenor. b. January 13, 1903, New Haven,
Connecticut.

1. BAKER 6; GROVE 6/10; RIEMANN 12 + supp.

2. RC 20/11-12, 21/3-4.

C0340.
KURZ, SELMA. Austrian Soprano. b. November 15, 1874 Bielitz, Silesia;
d. May 10, 1933, Vienna.

1. BAKER 6; EdS 1/6 (Bibliography); GROVE 6/10 (Bibliography);
   RIEMANN 12; SCHMIDL/Supp.

2. ON 26/18; RC 1/7, 13/3; RS 49 (January 1973).

4. Goldmann, Herman. Selma Kurz: der Werdegang einer Saengerin.
   Bielsko [Silesia]: Swiatlo, n.d. [c.1933]. 78 p., 5 illus.

   Author may be related to Cantor Ignanz Goldmann who discovered
   the singer.

   Halban, Dési and Ursula Ebbers. Selma Kurz: die Saengerin und
   ihre Zeit. Stuttgart: Belser Verlag, 1983. 224 p., 130 illus.,
   discography, repertoire, index of names, 50-item bibliography.

C0341.
LABIA, MARIA. Italian Soprano. b. February 14, 1880, Verona; d.
February 10, 1953, Malcesine del Garda.

1. BAKER 6; EdS 1/6 (Bibliography); GROVE 6/10 (Bibliography);
    RIEMANN 12 + Supp.; SCHMIDL + Supp.

2. RNC 3/1.

3. Labia, Maria. Memorie e confessioni. MS signed and dated 24.
    July 1947 Val Di Sogno Sul Garda. 84 p.

    EdS 1/6 lists an autobiography, Guardare indietro: che fatica!
    Trammenti di memorie [Verona, 1950. 145 p.], which I have not
    seen. The MS listed above may be a portion of the publication.

4. SEE: L. Brieger-Wasservogl under EMMY DESTINN (CO165).

5. NOTE: Her sister FAUSTA LABIA (b. April 3, 1870, Verona; d.
    October 6, 1935, Rome) wrote a vocal method: L'arte del
    respiro nello recitazione e nel canto. Roma, 1936.

CO342.
LABLACHE, LUIGI. Italian Bass. b. December 6, 1794, Naples; d.
January 23, 1858, Naples.

1. BAKER 6; EdS 1/6 (Bibliography); GROVE 6/10; MGG 1/8; RIEMANN
    12 + Supp.; SCHMIDL.

2. OPERA 17/9.

3. Lablache, Luigi. Méthode complète de chant. 2 vols. Mayence:
    Les Fils de B. Schott, 1844.

    NOTE: There are several [Boston, Chicago, New York] American
    editions and an Italian translation [Milano]. As in the case
    of Manuel Patricio Garcia (CO231), the pedagogical writings of
    Luigi Lablache have appeared in numerous versions and languages.
    Given the lack of firm evidence, it may be reasonable to date his
    initial attempts at writing to the period 1836-37 when he was
    Singing Master to Queen Victoria in England.

4. Cottrau, Theodore, ed. Onori alla memoria di Luigi Lablache.
    Napoli: Theodore Cottrau, 1858.

    No copy located.

    Widén, Gustaf. Lablache en bild fran sangens guldalder.
    Goeteborg: Wald. Zachrissons Boktryckeri, 1897. xiii, 187 p.,
    40 illus., 49-item bibliography.

CO343.
LANGDON, MICHAEL. English Bass. b. November 12, 1920, Wolverhampton.

1. GROVE 6/10.

2. OPERA 26/12.

3. Langdon, Michael with Richard Fawkes. Notes from a Low Singer.

London, Julia MacRae Books, 1982. 205 p., 30 illus., index.

CO344.
LANZA, MARIO. American Tenor. b. January 31, 1921, Philadelphia, Pennsylvania; d. October 7, 1959, Rome.

1. BAKER 6; RIEMANN 12.

2. ON 26/23; OP 10/2.

4. Bernard, Matt. Mario Lanza. New York: Macfadden-Bartell Corporation, 1971. 224 p.

    Burrows, Michael. Mario Lanza and Max Steiner. Cornwall: Primestyle Limited, n.d. [c.1971]. 44 p., 14 illus., 16-item bibliography, 9-item filmography.

    Callinicos, Constantine and Ray Robinson. The Mario Lanza Story. New York: Coward-McCann, Inc., 1960. 256 p., 15 illus., discography.

    Hausner, Hermann M. Mario Lanza: Tragoedie einer Stimme. Muenchen: Documenten-Verlag, 1962. 135 p., 37 illus., 18-item bibliography.

    Strait, Raymond and Terry Robinson. Lanza: His Tragic Life. Englewood Cliffs: 1980. 181 p., 24 illus., discography, fan clubs, index.

CO345.
LAPPAS, ULYSSES. Greek Tenor. b. 1881, Athens; d. July 26, 1971, Athens. No lexicon listing.

1. KUTSCH 3.

3. Lappas, Ulysses. Basos sampas. Athens: n.p., 1957. 133 p., 31 illus., repertoire.

CO346.
LARSEN-TODSEN, NANNY. Swedish Soprano. b. August 2, 1884, Hagby, Kalmarlaen.

1. BAKER 6; GROVE 6/10; RIEMANN 12 + Supp.

2. ON 21/12; OW 23/6.

CO347.
LAURI-VOLPI, GIACOMO. Italian Tenor. b. December 11, 1892, Lanuvio, near Rome; d. March 17, 1979, Valencia, Spain.

1. BAKER 6; EdS 1/6; GROVE 6/10 (Bibliography); RIEMANN 12 + Supp. (Bibliography); SCHMIDL/Supp.

2. ON 23/10, 44/1; OPERA 12/12; OW 20/5; RC 11/11-12, 12/1-2, 3, 4-5, 20/8, 9, 10; RNC 3/7, 8, 9.

3. Lauri-Volpi, Giacomo. Cristalli viventi. Roma: Atlantica, 1948. 311 p., portrait.

Philosophical, almost mystical book on singing.

Lauri-Volpi, Gaicomo. L'equivoco (così è, e non vi pare). seconda edizione. Milano: Edizioni Corbaccio, 1938. 443 p., 12 illus.

Life and professional career through January 1938.

Lauri-Vopli, Giacomo. A viso aperto. Milano: "Corbaccio" dall' Oglio, editore, 1953. 485 p., 12 illus.

Lauri-Volpi, Giacomo. A viso aperto. Bologna: Bongiovanni Editore, 1982/83. 2 vols. 221 p., 17 illus., 174 notes; 266, [1] p., 14 illus., 163 notes, chronology, list of repertoire, discography by Silvio Serbandini.

Continues L'equivoco through February 1953. The reprint is far superior from a scholarly standpoint.

Lauri-Volpi, Giacomo. Misteri della voce umana. Milano: dall'Oglio, editore, 1957. 366 p.

Pedagogical book on singing.

Lauri-Volpi, Giacomo. Parlando a Maria. Roma: Trevi Editore, 1972. 312, [3] p., 4 illus., index of names.

Maria is María Asunción Aguilar Ros.

Lauri-Volpi, Giacomo. Voci parallele. Roma: Aldo Gerzanti Editore, 1960 [1st edition Milano 1955]. 279 p.

Unique commentary on singers by a famous colleague. Chapters are divided by voice type. There is an MS translation in English by the late George L. Nyklicek. Also listed as A0064

4. Bragaglia, Leonardo. La voce solitaria: cinquanta personaggi per Giacomo Lauri-Volpi con venti lettere autografe inedite di Lauri-Volpi a Bragaglia. Roma: Bulzoni Editore, 1982. 253 p., 42 illus., 15-item bibliography, discography.

Gustarelli, Andrea. Chi è Giacomo Lauri-Volpi. Milano: Edizioni "L'Attuale," 1932. 102 p., 16 illus.

C0348.
LAWRENCE, MARJORIE. Australian Soprano. b. February 17, 1909, Dean's March, near Melbourne; d. January 10, 1979, Little Rock, Arkansas.

1. BAKER 6; GROVE 6/10; RIEMANN 12 + Supp.

2. ON 25/19; 43/20.

3. Lawrence, Marjorie. Interrupted Melody: the Story of My Life.

New York: Appleton-Century-Crofts, Inc., 1949. ix, 307 p.,
16 illus., index.

C0349.
LAWSON, WINIFRED. English Soprano. No lexicon listing.

3. Lawson, Winifred. A Song to Sing-O!. London: Michael Joseph,
    1955. 238 p., 26 illus., index of names.

    Soloist for several seasons with Sadler's Wells Opera Company.

C0350.
LAZARO, HIPOLITO. Spanish Tenor. b. December 13, 1887, Barcelona;
d. May 14, 1974, Madrid.

1. EdS 1/6; SCHMIDL/Supp.

2. RC 15/3-4, 16/3-4, 9-10, 18/11-12.

3. Lázaro, Hipólito. El libro de mi vida. tercera edicion. Madrid:
    Editora Nacional, 1968 [1st edition 1949]. xvi, 691 p., 37 illus.

    Lázaro, Hipólito. Mi método de canto. Barcelona: n.p., n.d.
    [1947]. 177 p., 19 illus., musical exercises, list of theaters.

C0351.
LEAR, EVELYN. American Soprano. b. January 18, 1927, New York City.

1. BAKER 6; GROVE 6/10; RIEMANN 12/Supp.

2. GR 46/8; ON 31/21, 34/22, 38/16, 45/8; OW 7/4, 18/8.

C0352.
LEBLANC, GEORGETTE. French Soprano. b. 1869, Rouen; d. 1948,
Monaco. No lexicon listing.

3. Leblanc, Georgette. Souvenirs (1895-1918). Précédé d'un intro-
    duction par Bernard Grasset. Paris: Editions Bernard Grasset,
    1931. xlii, 344 p.

    Leblanc, Georgette. Souvenirs: My Life with Maeterlinck.
    Translated by Janet Flanner. New York: E.P. Dutton & Co., Inc.,
    1932 [reprint 1976]. 352 p., 25 illus.

    Differs from the previous entry.

    Leblanc, Georgette. La machine a courage: souvenirs. Preface
    by Jean Cocteau. Paris: J.B. Janin, 1947. 230 p., 8 illus., list
    of publications.

C0353.
LEHMANN, LILLI. German Soprano. b. November 24, 1848, Wuerzburg;
d. May 16, 1929, Berlin.

1. BAKER 6; EdS 1/6 (Bibliography); GROVE 6/10 (Bibliography);

MGG 1/8; RIEMANN 12 + Supp. (Bibliography); SCHMIDL + Supp.

2. GR 9/3; ON 29/15; OW 11/11, 20/9; RC 26/7-8, 9-10, 27/2-3.

3. Lehmann, Lilli. How to Sing. Translated by Richard Aldrich.
    New York: The Macmillan Company, 1902. ix, 281 p., portrait,
    anatomical drawings, musical exercises.

    Lehmann, Lilli. Mein Weg. 2 vols. Leipzig: Verlag von S. Hirzel,
    1913 [Edited and translated by Alice Benedict Seligman as My
    Path through Life. New York, 1914. Reprint 1977]. 309; 280 p.,
    41 illus., index, list of repertoire.

    Lehmann, Lilli. Memorandum: ein Don Juan Auffuehungen von 14.
    und 16. August in Salzburg 1906. MS diary signed September 1906,
    Siharfling am Mondsee.

    Lehmann, Lilli. Studie zu Fidelio. Leipzig: Druck und Verlag von
    Breitkopf und Haertel, 1905. 68 p.

    Lehmann, Lilli. Studie zur Norma. MS in a format similar to the
    previous entry. undated. 128 p.

    Lehmann, Lilli. Studie zu Tristan und Isolde. Wittenberg: Herrose
    & Ziemson, G.m.b.H., n.d. [c.1927]. 43 p., portrait.

    SEE: Lilli Lehmann's preface for and translation of Victor Maurel's
         study: Dix ans de carrière 1887-1897. (C0400).

4. Andro, L. [pseud. of Therese Rie]. Lilli Lehmann. Berlin:
    "Harmonie" Verlagsgesellschaft fuer Literatur und Kunst, n.d.
    40 p., portrait.

    Lilli Lehmann. zum Gedaechtnis. Berlin, 1929. 14 p., 3 illus.

    Wagenmann, Josef H. Lilli Lehmanns Geheimnis der Stimmbaender.
    2nd revised edition [1st edition 1905]. Leipzig: A. Felix, 1926.
    131 p.

5. Damrosch, Walter. My Musical Life. New York: Charles Scribner's
    Sons, 1923. ix, 376 p., 19 illus., index.

    Hanslick, Eduard. Musikalisches Skizzenbuch. Berlin: Allge-
    meiner Verein fuer Deutsche Literatur, 1888 [article on Lehmann
    has been translated by Henry Pleasants 3rd: Vienna's Golden
    Years of Music. New York, 1950].

    SEE: autobiography of ANNA EUGENIE SCHOEN-RENE (C0566).

C0354.
LEHMANN, LIZA. English Soprano. b. July 11, 1862, London; d.
September 19, 1918, Pinner, Middlesex.

1. BAKER 6; GROVE 6/10; RIEMANN 12; SCHMIDL.

3. Lehmann, Liza. Practical Hints for Students of Singing. London:
Enoch, n.d. [c.1911].

No copy located.

Lehmann, Liza. The Life of Liza Lehmann by Herself. London: T.
Fisher Unwin, Ltd., 1919 [1st edition New York, 1918. Reprint
1980]. 232 p., 18 illus., index.

CO355.
LEHMANN, LOTTE. German Soprano. b. February 27, 1888, Perleberg;
d. August 26, 1976, Santa Barbara, California.

1. BAKER 6; EdS 1/6 (Bibliography); GROVE 6/10 (Bibliography);
RIEMANN 12 + Supp. (Bibliography).

2. ON 27/7, 32/17, 41/5; OPERA 8/12, 19/2, 27/11; OW 9/2, 14/7;
RNC 4/11, 12, 5/1, 2.

3. Lehmann, Lotte. Anfang und Aufstieg: Lebenserinnerungen. Wien:
Herbert Reichner Verlag, 1937. 237 p., 16 illus.

This work was translated as Wings of Song (London, 1938) and as
Midway in My Song (New York, 1938. Reprint 1970).

Lehmann, Lotte. Eighteen Song Cycles: Studies in Their Interpretation. Forward by Neville Cardus. London: Cassell & Company
Ltd., 1971. xiii, 185 p., index to first lines and titles of the
songs.

Lehmann, Lotte. Five Operas and Richard Strauss. Translated by
Ernst Pawel. New York: The Macmillan Company, 1964. Reprint 1982.
ix, 209 p., 10 illus., index.

"An attempt...to pass on to others the heritage I received from
a great artist."

Lehmann, Lotte. More than Singing: the Interpretation of Songs.
Translated by Frances Holden. New York: Boosey & Hawkes, Inc.,
1945. Reprint 1976. 192 p.

Lehmann, Lotte. My Many Lives. Translated by Frances Holden.
New York: Boosey & Hawkes, Inc., 1948. Reprint 1974. 262 p.,
30 illus.

"I want only to speak of opera roles as I have seen and felt
and lived them."

Lehmann, Lotte. "Twelve Singers and a Conductor," and "Goering,
the Lioness and I." In Opera 66. London: Alan Ross Ltd., 1966.

4. Riemens, Leo. Lotte Lehmann: a Biographical Sketch. London:
The Gramophone Company, n.d. [1960]. 20, [2] p., 3 illus.,
recording details.

Also included: "Some Recollections of Lotte Lehmann," by Alec
Robertson and "Listening to My Old Records," by Lotte Lehmann.
One of a series of pamphlets for "Great Recordings of the
Century."

Wessling, Berndt Wilhelm. Lotte Lehmann...mehr als eine
Saengerin. Salzburg: Residenz Verlag, 1969. 211 p., 74 illus.,
12-item bibliography, list of publications, discography, list
of major roles, index of names.

5. Eustis, Morton Corcoran. Players at Work: Acting According to
    Actors, with a Chapter on the Singing Actor by Lotte Lehmann.
    New York: Theater Arts, 1937. 127 p., illus.

    SEE: Roland Gelatt under PIERRE BERNAC (C0055).

    SEE: memoir of Walter Legge by ELISABETH SCHWARZKOPF (C0576).

C0356.
LEIDER, FRIDA. German Soprano. b. April 18, 1888, Berlin; d. June 3,
1975, Berlin.

1. BAKER 6; EdS 1/6 (Bibliography); GROVE 6/10 (Bibliography);
    RIEMANN 12 + Supp.

2. GR 16/1; ON 31/14; OPERA 26/8; OP 6/3; RC 1/5; RNC 2/10;
    RS 7 (Winter 1957).

3. Leider, Frida. Das war mein Teil: Erinnerungen einer Opern-
    saengerin. Berlin: F.A. Herbig Verlagsbuchhandlung, 1959.
    232 p., 29 illus., index of names.

    Translated by Charles Osborne as Playing My Part (London, 1966.
    Reprint 1978).

    Leider, Frida. Wagnerian Memories. London: The Gramophone
    Company, n.d. [1949]. 24, [2] p., 3 illus., recording
    details.

    Also included: "Some Reminiscences of Frieda Leider," by David
    Harris. One of a series of pamphlets for "Great Recordings of
    the Century."

4. De Schauensee, Max. Some Impressions of Frida Leider. London:
    The Gramophone Company, n.d. [1963]. 24, [2] p., 2 illus.,
    recording details.

    One of a series of pamphlets for "Great Recordings of the
    Century."

5. Fønss, Johannes. Mennseker, musikfolk - og minder: fra kirken til
    teatrene. København: Chr. Erichsens Forlag, 1960.

C0357.
LEMNITZ, TIANA. German Soprano. b. October 26, 1897, Metz.

1. GROVE 6/10; RIEMANN 12 + Supp.

2. ON 31/19, OW 13/10, 23/3; RC 15/2.

C0358.
LENYA, LOTTE. Austrian Mezzo-Soprano. b. October 18, 1898, Vienna;
d. November 27, 1981, New York City.

1. GROVE 6/10; RIEMANN 12/Supp. (birthyear 1900).

2. ON 44/6.

4. Marx, Henry, ed. <u>Kurt Weill und Lotte Leyna: Exhibit sponsored
    by the Library and Museum of the Performing Arts at Lincoln Center
    and Goethe House New York</u>. New York, 1976. unpaginated [84 p.]
    + a folding plate, 78 illus., Weill chronology, Lenya chronology.

C0359.
LIGENDZA, CATARINA. Swedish Soprano. b. October 18, 1937, Stockholm.

1. GROVE 6/10; RIEMANN 12/Supp.

2. ON 38/12; OW 13/10.

C0360.
LIND, JENNY. Swedish Soprano. b. October 6, 1820, Stockholm; d.
November 2, 1887, Malvern Hills, England.

NOTE: There exist four major known collections of 'Lindiana' which
must be consulted by any serious researcher and these are (1) Swanee
Collection of Lindiana which can be accessed through W. Porter Ware;
(2) Leonidas Westervelt Collection at the New York Historical
Society; (3) William Hildebrand Lindiana at the Museum of the City
of New York, and (4) Lindiana Collection at the Musikhistoriska
Museet in Stockholm.

1. BAKER 6 (Bibliography); EdS 1/6 (Bibliography); FETIS 2/5;
    GROVE 6/10 (Bibliography); MGG 1/8 (Bibliography); RIEMANN 12
    (Bibliography) + Supp. (Bibliography); SCHMIDL.

2. MQ 32/4; ON 10/3, 15/11, 22/22.

4. Bayley, Frederic William Naylor. <u>The Souvenir of the Season.
    the Wake of Extacy: a Memoir of Jenny Lind</u>. London: Willoughby
    and Co., 1849. 68 p., 8 illus. including 1 lithograph.

    "Like the Muse, the distinguished artist who illustrated her
    'Memory' has rejected the more REAL, and kept his pencil
    wandering in an IDEAL world."

    Becher, Alfred J. <u>Jenny Lind: eine Skizze ihres Lebens bis zur
    neusten Zeit</u>. zweite vermehrte auflage. Wien: Verlag der Jasper'
    schen Buchhandlung, 1846 [1st edition also 1846]. 48 p.,
    portrait, song.

Same basic information as the original printing with added comments on her appearance in Vienna.

Benet, Laura. Enchanting Jenny Lind. New York: Dodd, Mead & Company, 1940. ix, 452 p., 8 illus., decorations by George Gillett Whitney, 18-item bibliography.

Bullman, Joan. Jenny Lind: a Biography. London: James Barrie, 1956. x, 326 p., 26 illus., 48-item bibliography, appendix of biographical notes.

Bunn, Alfred. The Case of Bunn versus Lind...with a Series of Letters...to Which are added, Notes Explanatory and Critical. London: W.S. Johnson, 1848. 73 p.

Cavanah, Frances. Jenny Lind's America. Philadelphia: Chilton Book Company, 1969. xvi, 227 p., 14 illus., calendar of dates.

A historical novel about her American tour 1850-1852.

Dahlgren, Lotten. Jenny Lind utom scenen foertroliga brev till hennes foermyndare H.M. Munthe: i urval och med kommentarier. Stockholm: Wahlstroem & Widstrand, 1928. 415 p., 41 illus., index of names.

Dorph, Sven. Jenny Linds triumfer genom nya vaerlden och senare levnadsackorder. Uppsala: J.A. Lindblads Forlag, 1918. 439 p., 23 illus.

NOTE: revised edition published later that same year under the title: Jenny Linds triumftag genom nya vaerlden och oevriga levnadsoeden. 464 p., 112 illus. including 2 full-length color portraits of the artist.

Dorph, Sven. Jenny Lindiana tell hundraarsminnet. Uppsala: J.A. Lindblads Forlag, 1919. 351 p., 68 illus.

Elmblad, Sigrid. Jenny Lind en livsstudie. Uppsala: J.A. Lindblads Foerlag, 1920. 192 p., portrait.

Foster, George G. Memoir of Jenny Lind Complied from the Most Authentic Sources. New York: Dewitt & Davenport, 1850. 64 p., portrait.

Headland, Helen. The Swedish Nightingale: a Biography of Jenny Lind. Rock Island: Augustana Book Concern, 1944 [1st edition 1940]. 145, [15] p., 24 illus.

Holland, Henry Scott and William Smith Rockstro. Memoir of Madame Jenny Lind-Goldschmidt: Her Early Art-Life and Dramatic Career 1820-1851. From Original Documents, Letters, MS. Diaries, etc., Collected by Mr. Otto Goldschmidt. 2 vols. London: John Murray, 1891. xx, 438 p., 3 illus.; xiv, 468, 24 p., 6 illus., 3 appendices including music compiled and edited by Otto Gold-schmidt, index.

This is the only extant authorized biography and it covers the
period up to her marriage. Some of Otto Goldschmidt's diaries
are in the New York Public Library.

Holmstrøm, Maria. Jenny Lind som kunstnerinde og menneske.
København: Erslev & Hasselbalchs Forlag, 1915. 284 p., 17 illus.

Horn, Vivi. Pa sangens vingar: Jenny Linds levnadssaga.
Stockholm: Wahlstroem & Widstrand, 1940. 351 p., 34 illus.,
index of names.

Jenny Lind 1820-1920: studier utgigna av Svenska Samfundet foer
Musikforskning. Stockholm: Wahlstroem & Widstrand, 1920. 150 p.,
72 illus., 166-item iconography, 123-item bibliography.

Eight specialists contributed to this comprehensive overview with
Tobias Norlind's iconography and Einar Sundstroem's bilbiography
being extremely important.

Keil, Doris Parkin. The Ploughboy and the Nightingale. Toronto:
Copp Clark Publishing Co., n.d. [c.1958]. x, 304 p., facsimile,
bibliography.

Krohn, Helmi. Jenny Lind. Porvossa: Werner Soederstroem
Osakeyhtioe, 1917. 80 p., 11 illus.

Kyle, Elisabeth [pseud. for Agnes Mary Robinson Dunlop]. The
Swedish Nightingale Jenny Lind. New York: Holt, Rinehart and
Winston, 1964. 224 p., 9 item suggested reading list.

Lindiana: an Interesting Narrative of the Life of Jenny Lind.
Arundex: Sussex, Mitchell & Son, 1847. 52 p., portrait.

Another of the many public realtions' pamphlets, this one
published in anticipation of her visit to London. FETIS 2
lists a number of titles in various languages. The follow-up
to this particular visit is to be found in A Review of the
Performances of Mademoiselle Jenny Lind, during Her Engagement
at Her Majesty's Theater, and Their Influence and Effect upon
our National Drama; with a Notice of Her Life. London:
J. & L. Dickinson, 1847. 36 p., portrait.

Lisei, Cesare. Jenny Lind: note biografiche di Cesare Lisei.
Milano: G. Ricordi & C., n.d. [1888]. 21 p., portrait.

Maude, Mrs. Raymond. The Life of Jenny Lind. London: Cassell
and Company, Ltd., 1926. Reprint 1977. [5], 222 p., 17
illus., index.

Some insights into the singer's "Art and Personality" by her
daughter.

Memoir of Jenny Lind. London: John Ollivier, 1847. 20 p.,
portrait.

Munthe, Curt. Jenny Lind och sangens beateberg. Stockholm: Natur och Kultur, 1960. 205 p., 51 illus., index of names.

Myers, Elisabeth P. Jenny Lind Songbird from Sweden. Champaign: Garrard Publishing Company, 1968. 143 p., 41 illus., index.

Norlind, Tobias. Jenny Lind: en minnesbok till hundraarsdagen. Stockholm: Wahlstroem & Widstrand, 1919. 251 p., 52 illus., 13-item bibliography.

Pergament, Moses. Jenny Lind. Stockholm: P.A. Norstedt & Soeners Foerlag, 1945. 326 p., 219 illus., index of names.

Riiber, Anne Marie. Jenny Lind et navn som aldri dor. Oslo: Lutherstiftelsen, 1945. 328 p., illus.

Rockstro, W.S. Jenny Lind: a Record and Analysis of the 'method' of the Late Madame Jenny Lind-Goldschmidt together with a Selection of Cadenze, Solfeggi, Abellimenti, etc. in illustration of Her Vocal Art. Edited by Otto Goldschmidt. London: Novello and Company, Limited, 1894. 20, xxviii p., portrait.

NOTE: This is taken directly out of the Holland and Rockstro authorized biography.

Rootzén, Kajsa and T. Meyer. Jenny Lind den svenska naektergalen. Stockholm: Lindfors Bokfoerlag AB, 1945. 135 p., 9 illus., list of roles with number and locations of performances, 9-item bibliography.

Rosenberg, Charles G. The Life of Jenny Lind, the Swedish Nightingale: Her Genius, Struggles, and Triumphs. New York: Stringer & Townsend, 1850. 82 p., portrait.

Rosenberg, Charles G. Jenny Lind in America. New York: Stringer & Townsend, 1851. 226 p., portrait.

An account of her first tour to America and Cuba.

Schultz, Gladys Denny. Jenny Lind the Swedish Nightingale. Philadelphia: J.B. Lippincott Company, 1962. 345 p., portrait, index.

Snuffelmann, Genrebild von [pseud. for Adolf Schirmer]. Jenny Lind und die Hamburger, oder ein Staendchen im Jungfernstieg. Hamburg: Wil. Anthes, 1845. 16 p.

Spangberg, Ernest A. The Life of Jenny Lind: a Compilation from Various Sources, in Commemoration of the Centenary of Her Birth. Minneapolis: n.p., 1920. 79 p

Sutter, Otto Ernst, ed. Die "Jenny Lind - Spekulation." den Erinnerungen des Meisters der Reklame Phineas Taylor Barnum nacherzaehlt von Otto Ernst Sutter. Frankfurt am Main: Hauser-Presse, 1927. 55 p., 3 illus.

This is chapter six of Sutter's book printed in an edition of 250 copies for the Frankfurter Bibliophilen-Gesellschaft.

Wagenknecht, Edward. Jenny Lind. Boston: Houghton Mifflin Company, 1931. Reprint 1980. xx, 231 p., 16 illus., 152-item bibliography, index.

"In this book, I have attempted a study of Jenny Lind the woman, in her art life and in her personal life. My aim has been to show her as she was, so as that can be accomplished at this date, without eulogy. The book contains no 'new,' in the sense of hitherto unpublished, material. It contains a good deal of new material, however, in the sense that many volumes of nine-teenth-century reminiscence and biography are for the first time brought to bear upon the study of Jenny Lind."

Ware, W. Porter & Thaddeus C. Lockard, Jr. P.T. Barnum presents Jenny Lind: the American Tour of the Swedish Nightingale. Baton Rouge: Louisiana State University Press, n.d. [c.1980]. xiv, 204 p., 31 illus., 42-item bibliography, index, 4 appendices (letters, contract, financial account of the tour).

Ware, W. Porter & Thaddeus C. Lockard, Jr., eds. The Lost Letters of Jenny Lind Translated from the German and Edited with Commentaries. London: Victor Gollancz Ltd., 1966. 158 p., 9 illus.

Seventy-six letters from a correspondence with Amalia Wichmann 1845-1874.

Willis, Nathaniel Parker. Memoranda of the Life of Jenny Lind. Philadelphia: R.E. Peterson, 1851. 238 p., portrait.

Important resource for the period.

Wilkens, C.A. Jenny Lind: ein Caecilienbild aus der Evangel-ischen Kirche. fuenfte auflage. Guetersloh: Druck und Verlag von C. Bertelsmann, 1915 [1st edition c. 1894]. xix, 241 p.

5. Aldrich, Richard. Musical Discourse from the New York Times. New York: Oxford University Press, 1928. Reprint 1967. 305 p.

Barnum, P.T. Struggles and Triumphs of P.T. Barnum told by Himself. Edited by John G. O'Leary. London: Macgibbon & Kee, 1967. pp. 63-83.

Cairns, C.C. Noble Women. London: T.C. & E.C. Jack, n.d. pp. 248-285, portrait.

Chorley, Henry F. Modern German Music: Recollections and Criticisms. 2 vols. London: Smith, Elder and Co., 1854. 2:351-80.

SEE: autobiography of ISIDOR DANNSTROEM (C0142).

Hoffman, Richard. Some Musical Recollections of Fifty Years.

New York: Charles Scribner's Sons, 1910. viii, 169 p., 24 illus.

SEE: M. Sterling Mackinlay under **MANUEL PATRICIO GARCIA** (C0231).

Miller, Basil William. Ten Singers Who became Famous. Grand Rapids: Zondervan Publishing House, 1954. 87 p.

Riemann, Heinrich. Musikalische Rueckblicke. Berlin: Harmonie verlagsgesellschaft fuer Literatur und Kunst, 1900.

Reinecke, Carl. "Und manche liebe Schatten steigen auf." Gedenk-blaetter an beruehmte Musiker. Leipzig: Verlag von Gebrueder Reinecke, 1900. 164 p., 8 illus.

Stanford, Charles V. Interludes Records and Reflections. New York: E.P. Dutton and Company, 1922. xi, 212 p., 8 illus., index.

Thalberg, Gustave. Artist-profiler och impresario-historier: pikanta inblickar i artistlifvet. Stockholm: Fr. Skoglunds Foerlag, 1915. 288 p., 46 illus.

Speyer, Edward. My Life and Friends. Forward by H.C. Colles. London: Cobden-Sanderson, 1937. xi, 238 p., 8 illus., index of names.

SEE: Edward Wagenknecht under **MARY GARDEN** (C0232).

C0361.
LINDGREN, LYDIA. American Soprano. No lexicon listing.

3. Lindgren, Lydia. My Heart in My Throat: the Story of a Strange Captivity. New York: William Faro Inc., 1931. 716 p., portrait.

    Chicago Opera Company.

C0362.
LINDHOLM, BERIT. Swedish Soprano. b. October 18, 1934, Stockholm.

1. GROVE 6/11; RIEMANN 12/Supp.

2. ON 37/4; OW 12/3, 17/3.

C0363.
LINLEY, ELIZABETH ANN. English Soprano. b. September 5, 1754, Bath; d. June 28, 1792, Bristol.

1. EdS 1/6; GROVE 6/11 (Bibliography); RIEMANN 12.

4. Bor, Margot and Lamond Clelland. Still the Lark: a Biography of Elizabeth Linley. London: Merlin Press, 1962. 185 p., 17 illus., 31-item bibliography, extant music of the Linleys, index.

    Black, Clementina. The Linleys of Bath. revised edition. London: Martin Secker, 1926. xv, 300 p., 12 illus., 18-item bibliography.

C0364.
LITVINNE, FELIA. Russian Soprano. b. 1861, St. Petersburg; d. October 12, 1936, Paris.

1. BAKER 6; GROVE 6/11 (Bibliography); SCHMIDL + Supp.

2. ON 24/10; RC 8/6, 10, 20/6-7, 11-12; RNC 4/5, 6.

3. Litvinne, Félia. Ma vie et mon art (souvenirs). Paris: Librairie Plon, 1933. Reprint 1977. 292 p., 13 illus., list of roles, composers, conductors, and pianists.

    Litvinne, Félia. School of Singing: Exercises and Counsels. Paris: Au Ménestral, n.d. [1924]. iii, 33 p., illus.

4. Quincey, Alain. Félia Litvinne. "Les Trésors de l'Opéra no. 4." Paris: Opéra International, 1979. 63 p., 24 illus., list of roles.

C0365.
LOEFFEL, FELIX. German Bass. b. July 25, 1892, Oberwanzen-Koeniz.

1. RIEMANN 12.

4. Wuergler, Hans and Arthur Loosli, eds. Felix Loeffel: eine Freundesgabe zum siebzigsten Geburtstag. Bern: Francke Verlag, 1962. 109 p., 9 illus., 2 facsimilies.

C0366.
LONDON, GEORGE. American Bass. b. May 30, 1919, Montreal, Canada.

1. BAKER 6 (Bibliography); EdS/Supp.; GROVE 6/11 (Bibliography); RIEMANN 12 + Supp. (Bibliography).

2. ON 17/12, 18/23, 27/13, 22, 36/10, 40/20; OP 2/6; OW 4/8, 12.

3. London, George. "Prima Donnas I have Sung Against." In Opera Annual 6 (1959):116-120.

C0367.
LORENGAR, PILAR. Spanish Soprano. b. January 16, 1928, Saragossa.

1. EdS/Supp.; GROVE 6/11; RIEMANN 12/Supp.

2. ON 31/14; OW 13/3.

C0368.
LORENZ, MAX. German Tenor. b. May 17, 1901, Duesseldorf; d. January 11, 1975, Salzburg.

1. BAKER 6; EdS 1/6 (Bibliography); GROVE 6/11 (Bibliography); RIEMANN 12 + Supp.

2. OW 20/4.

4. Herrmann, Walter. Max Lorenz. Wien: Oesterreichischer Bundes-

verlag fuer Unterricht, Wissenschaft und Kunst, 1976. 48 p.,
31 illus., discography, 17-item bibliography.

C0369.
de LOS ANGELES, VICTORIA. Spanish Soprano. b. November 1, 1923,
Barcelona.

1. BAKER 6 (under Angeles): EdS 1/6 (under Los Angeles with Bibliog-
    raphy); GROVE 6/11 (under Los Angeles with Bibliography); RIEMANN
    12 + Supp. (under Los Angeles with Bibliography).

2. ON 33/5; OPERA 8/4; OW 4/12.

4. Fernández-Cid, Antonio. <u>Victoria de los Angeles</u>. Madrid: Aldus,
    1970. 269 p., numerous illus., repertoire, discography, index.

    Gavoty, Bernard. <u>Victoria de los Angeles</u>. Translated by F.E.
    Richardson. Geneva: René Kister, n.d. [c.1956]. 32 p., 18
    portraits by Roger Hauert, 4 candid shots and 1 facsimilie, list
    of recordings.

    Llopis, Artur. <u>Victòria dels Àngels</u>. Barcelona: Editorial
    Alcides, S.A., 1963. 79 p., 14 illus.

    Roberts, Peter. <u>Victoria de los Angeles</u>. London: Weidenfeld &
    Nicolson, 1982. vii, 184 p., 59 illus., discography, index.

C0370.
LUBIN, GERMAINE. French Soprano. b. February 1, 1890, Paris; d.
October 27, 1979, Paris.

1. EdS 1/6; GROVE 6/11 (Bibliography); RIEMANN 12 + Supp.

2. ON 30/12, 44/18; RS 19 (July 1965).

4. Casanova, Nicole. <u>Isolde 39: Germaine Lubin</u>. Paris: Flam-
    marion, 1974. 251 p., 16 illus., discography by G. Mannoni.

C0371.
LUCCA, PAULINE. Austrian Soprano. b. April 25, 1841, Vienna; d.
February 28, 1908, Vienna.

1. BAKER 6; EdS 1/6 (Bibliography); FETIS 2/Supp.; GROVE 6/11
    (Bibliography); MGG 1/8 (Bibliography); RIEMANN 12; SCHMIDL.

4. <u>Bellicose Adventures of a Peaceable Prima Donna</u>. New York, 1872.

    Published for her American tour. No copy located.

    Jansen-Mara, Anna and Dorothea Weisse-Zehrer. <u>Die Wiener Nachti-
    gall: der Lebensweg der Pauline Lucca</u>. Berlin: Otto Petters
    Verlag, n.d [1935]. 216 p., 18 illus.

    Waldstein, Max. <u>Pauline Lucca</u>. Chemnitz: B. Richards Verlag,

C0372.
LUCCIONI, JOSE. French Tenor. b. October 14, 1903, Bastia, Corsica; d. October 6, 1979, Marseille. No lexicon listing.

1. KUTSCH 3.

4. Mancini, Roland. José Luccioni. "Les Cahiers d'Opéra No. 5."
   Paris: Sodal, 1966. Reprint 1978 in the series, "Les Tresors
   de l'Opéra No. 1." 32 p., 31 illus., discography.

C0373.
LUDWIG, CHRISTA. German Mezzo-Soprano. b. March 16, 1928, Berlin.

1. BAKER 6; EdS/Supp.; GROVE 6/11; MGG 1/16; RIEMANN 12 + Supp.
   (Bibliography).

2. ON 31/8, 38/19; OPERA 24/3; OW 1/8, 9/6, 20/9.

4. Lorenz, Paul. Christa Ludwig. Walter Berry. Wien: Bergland
   Verlag, 1968. 127 p., 86 illus.

C0374.
LYNN, OLGA. English Soprano. No lexicon listing.

3. Lynn, Olga. Oggie: the Memoirs of Olga Lynn. London: Weiden-
   feld and Nicolson, 1955. xvi, 160 p., 19 illus., index.

   "I never really followed the normal career of a professional
   singer..." Note material on Melba and Raimund von zur Muehlen.

C0375.
MacNEIL, CORNELL. American Baritone. b. September 24, 1922, Minneapolis, Minnesota.

1. BAKER 6; GROVE 6/11; RIEMANN 12/Supp.

2. ON 33/7, 39/19.

C0376.
MADEIRA, JEAN. American Mezzo-Soprano. b. November 14, 1918,
Centralia, Illinois; d. July 10, 1972, Providence, Rhode Island.

1. BAKER 6; GROVE 6/11; RIEMANN 12 + Supp.

2. ON 25/20; OW 1/9.

C0377.
MAINVILLE-FODOR, JOSEPHINE. SEE: FODOR MAINVILLE (C0208).

C0378.
MAILBRAN, MARIA FELICITA. Spanish Mezzo-Soprano. b. March 24, 1808,
Paris; d. September 23, 1836, Manchester, England.

1. BAKER 6 (Bibliography); EdS 1/7 (Bibliography); FETIS 2/5 +
   Supp.; GROVE 6/11 (Bibliography); MGG 1/4 (under Garcia with

Bibliography); RIEMANN 12; SCHMIDL + Supp. (under Malibran-Garcia).

2. OW 22/5.

4. Barbieri, Gaetano. Notizie biografiche de M.F. Malibran. Milano: Ant. Fort. Stella e Figli, 1836. 54 p., portrait.

NOTE: The same title, i.e. Cenni biografici, as the first known publication on Malibran (Venezia, 1835) appears on page five of Barbieri.

Bertrand, Jules. La Malibran: anecdotes. Paris: Librairie du Petit Journal, 1864. 12 p., portrait.

Bielli, Domenico. Maria Malibran nel centenario della sua morte (23 sett. 1836 -- 23 sett. 1936). Casalbordino: Casa Tip. Ed. Comm. N. De Arcangelis, 1936. 46 p., portrait.

Initial publication of a proposed series titled: "I grandi maestri e i grandi artisti del teatro lirico."

Buerkli, Johann Georg. Zuege aus dem Leben der beruehmten saengerin Maria Malibran-Garcia. Achtundzwanzigstes neujahrs-stueck der Allgemeinen Musik-Gesellschaft in Zuerich 1840. Zuerich: gedruckt bei Orell, Fuessli und Compagnie, 1840. 16 p., portrait.

Bushnell, Howard. Maria Malibran: a Biography of the Singer. Forward by Elaine Brody. University Park: The Pennsylvania State University, 1979. xix, 264, [2] p., 36 illus., career chronology, operatic repertoire, 224-item bibliography, index.

This definitive study is a marvelous and all too rare example of the scholarship needed in this area. Excellent bibliography.

Campetti, Placido. In morte della Malibran. Lucca Tipografia, 1837. 13 p.

Crump, Phyllis Eirene. "Musset and Malibran: an Episode in the Literary Career of A6fred de Musset." In A Miscellaneous of Studies in Romance Languages and Literatures presented to Leon E. Kastner. Cambridge, 1932. pp. 162-171.

de Bradi, Lorenzi. La brève et marveilleuse vie de la Malibran. Paris: Editions Julles Tallandier, 1936. 253 p., portrait.

Desternes, Suzanne and Henriette Chandet. La Malibran et Pauline Viardot avec la collaboration d'Alice Viardot. Paris: Librairie Artheme Fayard, 1969. 275 p., 29 illus., 12-item bibliography.

Flament, Albert. L'enchanteresse errante: la Malibran. Paris: Ernest Flammarion, Editeur, 1937. 286 p.

Flament, Albert. Une étoile en 1830: la Malibran. Paris:

Editions Pierre Lafitte, 1928. 126 p.

Covers the period from 1827 when she left Eugene Malibran.

Heron-Allen, Edward. A Contribution towards an Accurate Biog-
raphy of Charles Auguste de Bériot and Maria Felicita Malibran-
Garcia: Extracted from the Correspondence of the Former.
London: 125 copies reprinted from The Violin Times for the
author by F.W. Wakeham, 1894. 24 p. + facsimile of a letter of
C. de Beriot [unbound].

Each copy is numbered and initialed by Heron-Allen.

Husk, W.H. Templeton and Malibran: Reminiscences of These
Renowned Singers, with Original Letters and Anecdotes. London:
William Reeves, 1880. xii, 50 p., 3 portraits.

Kruse, L. Erinnerungen aus dem leben einer kreolin. 4 bde.
Leipzig, 1837.

Mentioned in Heinrich Stuemke's biography of Henriette Sontag.
No copy located.

Lanquine, Clément. La Malibran. "Les écrits et la vie anecdotique
et pittoresque des grands artistes." Paris: Louis-Michaud, n.d.
[c.1913]. 192 p., 33 illus.

Larinoff, P. and F. Pestellini. Maria Malibran e i suoi tempi.
terza edizione. Firenze: Casa Editrice Marzocco, 1949. 253 p.,
8 illus., 31-item bibliography.

Legouvé, Ernest. Etudes et souvenirs de théâtre -- les initia-
teurs -- Maria Malibran. Paris: Hetzel, 1880. 48 p.

This was reprinted in 1888 in the first volume (pp. 234-277) of
Legouve's reminiscences: Soixante ans de souvenirs.

Madama Maria Malibran e il suo secolo. Lucca: Tipografia Pas-
quinelli, 1836.

Mentioned in FETIS 2/5. No copy located.

Malherbe, Henry [pseud. of Henry Croisilles]. La passion de la
Malibran. Paris: Editions Albin Michel, 1937. 255 p.

Historical novel based upon material supplied by Mme. Jeanne
de Beriot-Wettnall.

Merlin, Comtesse Maria de los Mercedes de Jaruco. Memoirs and
Letters of Madame Malibran with Notices of the Progress of the
Musical Drama in England. 2 vols. Philadelphia: Carey and Hart,
1840. xiii, 13-240 p., portrait; v, 13-226 p.

The Comtesse Merlin (1788-1853) was a talented amateur singer
and a friend of Malibran. The original of this work was pub-

lished by Ladvocat in Paris in 1838 as <u>Loisirs d'un femme de monde</u> with a simultaneous release in Bruxelles by Ad. Wahlen & Cie. Georg Lotz published his translation in Leipzig in 1839 as <u>Maria Malibran als Weib und Kuenstlerin, nebst Character-zuegen und Anecdoten aus ihren Leben</u>. There also exists a London edition dated 1844.

Minarell, Camell. <u>Per la malibran</u>. Bulogna: n.p., 1836. 12 p.

6 pages of poetical tributes in Bolognese dialect.

Myers, Henry. <u>The Signora</u>. New York: Crown Publishers, Inc., 1956. 312 p.

Historical novel. "...I inferred what she must have been like...working only from hint and hearsay."

Nathan, Isaac. <u>The Life of Madame Maria Malibran de Bériot: interspersed with Original Anecdotes and Critical Remarks on Her Musical Powers</u>. London: Joseph Thomas, 1836. ii, 72 p.

Parkinson, Reverend Richard. <u>A Sermon Preached on the Second Day of October, 1836: being the Day after the Public Funeral of the Late Madame Malibran de Beriot in the Collegiate Church of Manchester</u>. Manchester: T. Sowler, 1836. 23 p., appendix (Statement of the Manchester Music Festival Committee).

Pougin, Arthur. <u>Marie Malibran histoire d'un cantatrice</u>. Paris: Plon-Nourrit et Cie, 1911. 284 p., portrait, lists of repertoire and publications, 14-item bibliography including laudatory odes, etc.

NOTE: There is an English translation of the above by L.A.M., <u>Madame Malibran: the Story of a Great Singer</u>. London: Eveleigh Nash, 1911. 324 p., 2 portraits, repertoire, list of compositions, 16-item bibliography, representative contract, tomb, statement regarding her death and burial.

Reparaz, Carmen de. <u>Maria Malibrán, 1808-1836: estudio bio-gráfico</u>. Madrid: Servicio de Publicaciones del Ministerio de Educacion y Ciencia, n.d. [c.1976]. 269 p., 110 illus., notes (which include biographical references), genealogical table, list of works composed for Malibran, index of names, 116-item bibliography.

Teneo, Martial. "La Malibran, d'après des documents inédits." In <u>Recueil de la société internationale de musique</u> (1905): 437-482.

Weatherson, Alexander. "Lament of a Dead Nightengale: the Cantata 'In Morte de M.F. Malibran de Beriot'." In <u>The Donizetti Society Journal</u> 5 (1984):155-168.

Limited membership edition of 1000 copies. There is an article on the Italian baritone, **GIORGIO RONCONI**, in the same issue.

5. Bunn, Alfred. The Stage: both Before and Behind the Curtain, from "Observations taken on the Spot." 3 vols. London: Richard Bentley, 1840.

   SEE: Louis Heriette de la Tour under MANUEL PATRICIO GARCIA (C0231).

   SEE: autobiography of LOUISE HERIETTE-VIARDOT (C0281).

   SEE: M. Sterling Mackinlay under MANUEL PATRICIO GARCIA (C0231).

   SEE: Gladys Malvern under MANUEL PATRICIO GARCIA (C0231).

   SEE: autobiography of ANNA EUGENIE SCHOEN-RENE (C0566).

   Trebbe, Oreste. Nella vecchia Bologna: cronache e ricordi. Bologna: N. Zanichelli, 1924. xiii, 229 p., illus.

C0379.
MALIPONTE, ADRIANA. Italian Soprano. b. December 26, 1942, Brescia.

1. GROVE 6/11.

2. ON 36/4, 45/14; OW 22/2.

C0380.
MANCINI, GIAMBATISTA. Italian Castrato Soprano. b. January 1, 1714, Ascoli, near Piacenza; d. January 4, 1800, Vienna.

1. EdS 1/7 (Bibliography); GROVE 6/11 (Bibliography); MGG 1/8 (Bibliography); RIEMANN 12 + Supp. (Bibliography); SCHMIDL + Supp. (Bibliography).

3. Mancini, Giambatista. Pensieri e riflessioni pratiche sopra il canto figurato. Vienna: Nella Stamparia Di Ghelen, 1774. iv, 188, i p.

   Translated by Pietro Buzzi as: Practical Reflections on the Figurative Art of Singing. Boston: The Gorham Press, 1912. Also by E.V. Foreman in 1967 (see B0046).

5. Della Corte, Andrea, ed. Canto e bel canto. Torino: G.B. Paravia, 1933. 274 p.

C0381.
MARA, GERTRUDE ELISABETH. German Soprano. b. February 23, 1749, Kassel; d. January 20, 1833, Reval, Russia.

1. BAKER 6 (Bibliography); EdS 1/7 (Bibliography); FETIS 2/5; GROVE 6/11 (Bibliography); MGG 1/8 (Bibliography); RIEMANN 12 (Bibliography) + Supp.; SCHMIDL + Supp.

3. Mara, Gertrude Elisabeth. Eine Selbstbiographie der Saengerin Gertrude Elisabeth Mara. Leipzig: Allgemeine Musikalische

Zeitung X/32-39, 1875. 25 p.

Printed with corrections and additions by Otto von Riesemann from a handwritten MS left by the singer. As recently as 1929 this MS was in the Reval Stadtarchiv. Present whereabouts unknown. Covers the period from her birth to 1793.

4. Buerkli, Johann Georg. Biographie der Saengerin Mara, geborne Gertrude Elisabeth Schmaehling. Dreiundzwanzigstes Neujarh-stueck der Allgemeinen Musik-Gesellschaft in Zuerich, 1835. 12 p., portrait.

   Grosheim, Georg E. Das Leben der Kuenstlerin Mara. Cassel: in der Luckhardt'schen Hofbuchhandlung, 1823. Reprint in an edition of 250 by Horst Hamecher, Kassel, 1972. 72 p.

   Kaulitz-Niedeck, R. Die Mara: das Leben einer beruehmten Saengerin. Heilbronn: Eugen Salzer, 1929. 236 p., 8 illus., index of names, 102-item bibliography.

   Niggli, A. Gertrude Elisabeth Mara: eine Deutsche Kuenstlerin des 18. Jahrhunderts. Leipzig: Bretikopf & Haertel, 1881. 45 p., 12-item bibliography.

   Scherer, Carl. "Gertrude Elisabeth Schmaeling und ihre Bezei-hungen zu Rudolf Erich Raspe und Carl Matthaei." In Viertel-jahrsschrift fuer Musikwissenschaft 9 (1893):99-127.

5. SEE: John R. Parker under ELIZABETH BILLINGTON (C0058).

   SEE: Quarterly Musical Magazine and Review under ELIZABETH BILLINGTON (C0058).

   Polko, Elise. Vom Gesang: musikalische Winke und Lebensbilder. Leipzig: Verlag von Johan Ambrosius Barth, 1876. 349 p., portrait.

   Rochlitz, Friedrich. Fuer Freunde der Tonkunst. 4 vols. dritte auflage. Leipzig: Carl Cnobloch, 1868 [1st edition 1824]. vol. 1. pp. 30-69.

   Sternberg, A. von. Beruehmten Deutschen Frauen des achtzehnten Jahrhunderts. Leipzig: F.A. Brockhaus, 1848. part 1, pp. 203-290.

C0382.
MARCHESI, BLANCHE. French Soprano. b. April 4, 1863, Paris; d. December 15, 1940, London.

1. BAKER 6; GROVE 6/11; RIEMANN 12 + Supp.

2. GR 17/1; ON 37/19; RC 5/12.

3. Marchesi, Blanche. Singer's Pilgrimage. Boston: Small, Maynard and Company, 1923. Reprint 1978 with discography by W.A. Moran. 304 p., 16 illus., index.

Marchesi, Blanche. <u>The Singer's Catechism and Creed</u>. London: J.M. Dent & Sons, 1932. xxvi, 168 p., illus.

5. SEE: autobiography of **MARIA JERITZA** (C0309).

O'Connor, T.P., ed. <u>In the Days of My Youth</u>. London: C. Arthur Pearson, Limited. 1901. ix, 318 p., 16 illus.

The material on Marchesi was written by herself.

C0383.
MARCHESI, LUIGI. Italian Castrato Soprano. b. August 8, 1754, Milan: d. December 14, 1829, Inzago.

1. BAKER 6 (Bibliography); EdS 1/7 (Bibliography); FETIS 2/5; GROVE 6/11 (Bibliography); RIEMANN 12 + Supp.; SCHMIDL + Supp.

4. <u>Lettera d'un filarmonico imparziale, ossia parallelo fra i due celebri personaggi signora Luigia Todi e signor Luigi Marchesi</u>. Venezia: n.p., 1791. 28. febbraio. 30 p.

<u>Lodi caratteristiche del celebre cantore signor Luigi Marchesi</u>. Siena: Nella stamperia de Vincenzo Pazzini Carli e figli, 1781. x p.

C0384.
MARCHESI, MATHILDE de CASTRONE. German Mezzo-Soprano. b. March 24, 24, 1821, Frankfurt/M.; d. November 17, 1913, London.

1. BAKER 6; EdS 1/7; GROVE 6/11; MGG 1/8; RIEMANN 12 + Supp. (Bibliography); SCHMIDL.

2. ON 37/19; RNC 1/6.

3. Marchesi, Mathilde. <u>Aus meinem Leben</u>. Duesseldorf: Felix Hagel, n.d. [1888]. 246 p., portrait, musical examples.

Covers the period up to 1887. There exists an MS translation in English by the late George L. Nyklicek.

Marchesi, Mathilde. <u>Erinnerungen aus meinem Leben</u>. Wien: Verlag von Carl Gerold's Sohn, 1877. vi, 104 p., portrait.

Marchesi, Mathilde. <u>Marchesi and Music: Passages from the Life of a Famous Singing-Teacher</u>. New York: Harper & Brothers Publishers, 1897. Reprint 1978. xiv, 301 p., 7 illus.

An expansion of her 1877 memoirs. Prominent mention of Garcia, Lind, Krauss, Patti, Melba, Eames, and Sanderson.

Marchesi, Mathilde. <u>Ten Singing Lessons</u>. Preface by Nellie Melba. New York: Harper & Brothers, 1901. xx, 198 p., portrait.

Teacher of Calvé, Eames, Gerster, Melba, and Murska!

Marchesi, Mathilde. The Marchesi School: a Theoretical and Practical Method of Singing. New York: G. Schirmer, n.d. [c.1903]. xviii, 108 p.

Reprint as: Theoretical and Practical Vocal Method. Introduction by Philip L. Miller. New York: Dover Publications, 1970.

CO385.
MARCHISIO, BARBARA. Italian Mezzo-Soprano. b. December 6, 1833, Turin; d. April 19, 1919, Venice.

1. EdS 1/7 (Bibliography); GROVE 6/11 (Bibliography); SCHMIDL (Bibliography).

3. Marchisio, Barbara. Solfeggi per mezzo-soprano della scuola classica nepolitana, scelti, ordinati e trascritti con accompagnamento di pianoforte. Roma: G. Ricordi e Cie, n.d.

No copy located.

4. Marchisio, E. Gorin. Le sorelle Marchisio: ricordi. Milano: Amici del Museo Teatrale alla Scala, 1930.

No copy located.

CO386.
MARCHISIO, CARLOTTA. Italian Soprano. b. December 8, 1835, Turin; d. June 28, 1872, Turin.

1. EdS 1/7 (Bibliography); GROVE 6/11 (Bibliography); SCHMIDL (Bibliography).

4. Marchisio, E. Gorin. Le sorelle Marchisio: ricordi. Milano: Amici del Museo Teatrale alla Scala, 1930.

No copy located.

CO387.
MARCOUX, VANNI. French Baritone. b. June 12, 1877, Turin; d. October 21, 1962, Paris.

1. BAKER 6; EdS 1/7.

2. OPERA 14/3; RS 29-30 (January-April 1968).

CO388.
MARDONES, JOSE. Spanish Bass. b. 1869, Fontecha; d. May 4, 1932, Madrid.

1. EdS 1/7 (Bibliography).

4. del Val, Venancio. Alvaveses celebres: José Mardones el mejor bajo-cantante del mundo. n.p.: Diputación Foral De Alava Consejo De Cultura, n.d. [c.1972]. 57, [4] p., 5 illus.

C0389.
MARIO [Count Giovanni Matteo de Candia]. Italian Tenor. b. October 17, 1810, Cagliari, Sardinia; d. December 11, 1883, Rome.

1. BAKER 6; EdS 1/7 (Bibliography); FETIS 2/5 + Supp. (Bibliography); GROVE 6/11 (Bibliography); MGG 1/8 (also consult article on Grisi); RIEMANN 12 + Supp. (Bibliography); SCHMIDL + Supp. (Bibliography).

2. ON 18/20.

4. Gautier, Judith. Le roman d'un grand chanteur (Mario de Candida) d'aprés les "souvenirs" de sa fille madame Cecilia Pearse. Paris: Bibliothéque Charpentier, 1912. 274 p.

    Pearse, Mrs. Godfrey [Cecilia Maria de Candia] and Frank Hird. The Romance of a Great Singer: a Memoir of Mario. London: Smith, Elder & Co., 1910. Reprint 1977. x, 309 p., 9 illus., list of London operas, index of names.

    Mario married Grisi in 1844. Together with Tamburini and Lablache they formed one of the greatest operatic quartets of all time.

5. Beale, Thomas Willert. The Light of Other Days seen through the Wrong End of an Opera Glass. London: R. Bentley and Son, 1890.

    Engel, Louis. From Mozart to Mario: Reminiscences of Half a Century. 2 vols. London: Richard Bentley and Son, 1886.

C0390.
MARTIN, RICCARDO. American Tenor. b. November 18, 1874, Hopkinsville, Kentucky; d. August 11, 1952, New York City.

1. BAKER 6.

2. ON 17/6; RC 26/1-2.

C0391.
MARTINELLI, GIOVANNI. Italian Tenor. b. October 22, 1885, Montagnana, near Venice; d. February 2, 1969, New York City.

1. BAKER 6; EdS 1/7 (Bibliography); GROVE 6/11 (Bibliography); RIEMANN 12 + Supp. (Bibliography); SCHMIDL.

2. GR 46/11; ON 28/2, 33/21; OPERA 13/5, 20/4; OW 10/7; RC 5/8, 10, 7/6-7, 13/11-12, 25/7-12, 26/9-10; RS 53 (January 1974).

C0392.
MASINI, ANGELO. Italian Tenor. b. November 28, 1844, Terra del Sole, Forli; d. September 26, 1926, Forli.

1. EdS 1/7; GROVE 6/11; RIEMANN 12; SCHMIDL.

4. Angelo Masini, il tenore angelico Forlí: Comitato cittadino per le onoranze ad Angelo Masini nel quarantesimo della morte, 1966.

95 p., illus., repertoire, bibliography, index.

Atti del convengo su Angelo Masini, ottobre 1976. Forlí: Comune di Forli, 1977. 57 p., illus., bibliography.

Montanelli, Archim. Angelo Masini: note biografiche. Forli, 1882.

Rivalta, C. Il tenore Angelo Masini e Faenza. Faenza, 1929.

No copy located of either of the above titles.

C0393.
MASINI, GALLIANO. Italian Tenor. b. February 7, 1896, Livorno. No lexicon listing.

4. Calvetti, Mauro. Galliano Masini. Livorno: Tipografia O. Debatte & F., 1980. 122 p., 36 illus., list of repertoire, films, discography, list of theaters.

C0394.
MASON, EDITH. American Soprano. b. March 22, 1893, St. Louis, Missouri; d. November 26, 1973, San Diego, California.

1. GROVE 6/11.

2. ON 31/21; RC 10/4.

C0395.
MASSARDI, ROMARINA. Uruguayan Soprano. No lexicon listing.

4. Massardi, Alba Luz, ed. Una artista lírica: anécdotas -- descripción de paises teatros -- ciudades -- costumbres la enseñanza del canto -- meditaciones y vida de Rina Massardi. Montevideo: Curbelo & Cia, 1957. 99 p., 121 illus.

C0396.
MASTILOVIC, DANICA. Yugoslavian Soprano. b. November 7, 1933, Negotin.

1. GROVE 6/11; RIEMANN 12/Supp.

2. OW 13/3, 17/8.

C0397.
MATHIS, EDITH. Swiss Soprano. b. February 11, 1938, Lucerne.

1. BAKER 6; GROVE 6/11; RIEMANN 12/Supp.

2. OW 15/6.

C0398.
MATZENAUER, MARGARITE. Hungarian Soprano. b. June 1, 1881, Temesvar; d. May 19, 1963, Van Nuys, California.

1. BAKER 6; EdS 1/7; GROVE 6/11 (Bibliography); RIEMANN 12 + Supp.

2. RC 23/1-2.

C0399.
MAUPIN. French Mezzo-Soprano. b. 1670; d. 1707, Provence.

1. EdS 1/7 (Bibliography); GROVE 6/11 (Bibliography); SCHMIDL/Supp.

4. Gautier, Théophile. Mademoiselle de Maupin, double amour.
   Paris, n.d. [c.1835].

   Letainturier-Fradin, G.-J. and A.P. Letainturier-Fradin. La Maupin
   (1670-1707): sa vie, ses duels, ses adventures. Paris, 1904.

   No copy seen of either of the above two titles.

C0400.
MAUREL, VICTOR. French Baritone. b. June 17, 1848, Marseilles; d.
October 22, 1923, New York City.

1. BAKER 6 (Bibliography); EdS 1/7 (Bibliography); GROVE 6/11 (Bibliography); MGG 1/8; RIEMANN 12; SCHMIDL.

2. MQ 12/4; ON 28/19; OPERA 6/5.

3. Maurel, Victor. A propos de la mise en scène de Don Juan:
   réflexions et souvenirs. Paris: P. Dupont, 1896. viii, 81 p.

   Maurel, Victor. A propos de la mise en scène du drame lyrique
   Otello de Verdi: etude précédée d'aperçus sur le théâtre chanté en
   1887. Roma: Tipografia Editrice Romana, 1888. 183 p.

   Maurel, Victor. Dix ans de carrière 1887-1897. Paris: Imprimerie
   Paul Dupont, 1897. Reprint 1977. xv, 421 p., illus.

   Translated by Lilli Lehmann-Kalisch as: Zehn Jahre aus meinem
   Kuenstlerleben 1887-1897. Berlin: Raabe & Plothow, Musikverlag,
   1899. iii, 284 p., 4 illus.

   The first Iago and the first Falstaff!

   Maurel, Victor. Le chant rénové par le science. Paris: A.
   Quinzard & Cie, 1892. 71 p.

   Maurel, Victor. Un probleme d'art. Paris: Tresse & Stock, 1893.
   vii, 314 p.

4. Maurel, Berty. Victor Maurel - ses idées - son art. Paris: n.p.,
   n.d. 80 p., illus.

5. Garceau, Edouard. The Little Doustes. Translated by Vera A.
   Chappell. London: Frederich Muller Ltd., n.d. [1935]. 307 p.,
   9 illus., index.

   SEE: Alexis Wicart under **LUCIEN MURATORE** (C0437). "Un bel exemple
   la vie artistique de Victor Maurel et ses méthodes." A

chapter in volume 2 by Berty Maurel, pp. 275-300. 6 illus.

C0401.
MAYNOR, DOROTHY. American Soprano. b. September 3, 1910, Norfolk, Virginia.

1. BAKER 6; GROVE 6/11; RIEMANN 12 + Supp.

2. ON 31/4.

C0402.
MAYR, RICHARD. Austrian Bass. b. November 18, 1877, Herndorf, near Salzburg; d. December 1, 1935, Vienna.

1. BAKER 6; EdS 1/7 (Bibliography); GROVE 6/11 (Bibliography); RIEMANN 12 + Supp. (Bibliography).

4. Holz, Herbert Johannes. Richard Mayr. Wien: Literarische Anstalt, 1923. 33 p., illus.

   Kunz, Otto. Richard Mayr: Weihe, Herz und Humor im Bass-schluessel. Wien: "Das Bergland-Buch," 1933. 206 p., 15 illus., list of roles, honors, index.

C0403.
McCORMACK, JOHN. Irish Tenor. b. June 14, 1884, Athlone; d. September 16, 1945, Glena, Booterstown.

1. BAKER 6 (Bibliography); EdS 1/6; GROVE 6/11; RIEMANN 12 + Supp.

2. GR 2/5, 11/5, 17/3, 24/7, 8, 11, 12, 28/8; ON 25/4; OPERA 30/8; OW 11/10; RC 11/1, 8.

3. McCormack, John. John McCormack: His Own Life Story. Trans-scribed by Pierre V.R. Key. Boston: Small, Maynard & Company, 1918. Reprint 1973 edited and with an introduction by John Scarry. 433 p., 22 illus.

4. Foxall, Raymond. John McCormack. New York: Alba House, 1963. 186 p., 13 illus., index.

   Hume, Ruth and Paul Hume. The King of Song: the Story of John McCormack. New York: Hawthorn Books, Inc., 1964. 185 p., 20 illus., currently available recordings, index.

   Ledbetter, Gordon T. The Great Irish Tenor. London: Gerald Duckworth & Co., Ltd., 1977. 160 p., 124 illus., 10-item biblio-graphy, index.

   McCormack, Lily. I Hear You Calling Me. Milwaukee: The Bruce Publishing Company, 1949. Reprint 1975. 201 p., 29 illus., discography by Philip F. Roden.

   McDermott Roe, Leonard F.X. John McCormack Complete Discography. London: Charles Jackson, 1956. 93, [17] p., 27 illus, honors, speeches, dealers.

This was published in a revised edition: <u>The John McCormack</u>
<u>Discography</u>. Bolton, Lancashire: The Oakwood Press, 1971.

Shawe-Taylor, Desmond. <u>John McCormack and Classical Song</u>.
London: The Gramophone Company, n.d. [1962]. 12, [2] p.,
2 illus., recording details.

One of a series of pamphlets for "Great Recordings of the
Century."

Shawe-Taylor, Desmond. <u>John McCormack and Popular Song</u>.
London: The Gramophone Company, n.d. [1962]. 16, [2] p.,
2 illus., recording details.

One of a series of pamphlets for "Great Recordings of the
Century."

Strong, L.A.G. <u>John McCormack</u>. London: Peter Nevill Limited,
1949. x, 309 p., 20 illus., list of recordings made by the 112
artists mentioned, discography 1907-1939.

5. Beddington, Frances Ethel. <u>All That I Have Met</u>. London: Cassell,
1929. xii, 286 p., illus.

SEE: Merle Armitage under **MARY GARDEN** (C0232).

SEE: autobiography of **ROLAND FOSTER** (C0214).

Senan, Father, ed. "John McCormack 1884-1945: a Symposium of
Tributes." In <u>The Capuchin Annual 1946-47</u>:215-290, 49 illus.

C0404.
McCRACKEN, JAMES. American Tenor. b. December 11, 1926, Gary,
Indiana.

1. GROVE 6/11; RIEMANN/Supp.

2. ON 27/20, 30/4, 35/18, 42/11; OPERA 18/1; OW 16/9.

3. McCracken, James and Sandra Warfield. <u>A Star in the Family: an</u>
<u>Autobiography in Diary Form</u>. Edited by Robert Daley. New York:
Coward McCann & Geoghegan, Inc., 1970. 388 p., 33 illus.

5. SEE: Harvey E. Phillips under **MARILYN HORNE** (C0293).

C0405.
McDANIEL, BARRY. American Baritone. b. October 10, 1930, Topeka,
Kansas.

1. GROVE 6/11; RIEMANN/Supp.

2. ON 36/10; OW 7/7, 15/2.

C0406.
McINTRYE, DONALD. New Zealand Baritone. b. October 22, 1934,
Auckland.

1. GROVE 6/11; RIEMANN 12/Supp.

2. OPERA 26/6; OW 20/9.

C0407.
MEI-FIGNER, MEDEA. SEE: FIGNER-MEI, MEDEA (C0201).

C0408.
MELBA, NELLIE. Australian Soprano. b. May 19, 1859, Burnley, near
Richmond; d. February 23, 1931, Sidney.

1. BAKER 6; EdS 1/7; GROVE 6/12; MGG 1/9; RIEMANN 12 (Bibliography)
    + Supp. (Bibliography); SCHMIDL.

2. GR 1/10, 2/6, 9/7, 8; ON 25/16, 26/10; OPERA 6/2, 21/12; OW 6/7,
    23/2; RC 4/12.

3. Melba, Nellie. <u>Melodies and Memories</u>. New York: George H. Doran
    Company, 1926. Reprint 1970; 1971; 1980. 339 p., 20 illus., index.

    John Hetherington claims this was ghost written. SEE: Nichols,
    Beverley: <u>All I could ever be: Some Recollections</u>. London:
    Jonathan Cape, 1949. pp. 63-64. These recollections were pub-
    lished initially as a series in <u>Liberty Magazine</u>.

    The singer is alleged to have written a vocal methods' book in
    1926, but I have not been able to trace a copy.

4. Casey, Maie. <u>Melba Revisited</u>. Melbourne: privately printed for
    the author, 1975. 30 p., illus.

    Colson, Percy. <u>Melba: an Unconventional Biography</u>. London:
    Grayson & Grayson, 1932. xv, 279 p., 16 illus., "Melba on the
    science of singing," "Melba's advice on the selection of music
    as a profession," list of roles, index.

    "Great singers are, generally speaking, not particularly inter-
    esting people. They are, as a rule, entirely concentrated on
    themselves and their voices, and the careful lives they are
    obliged to lead in order to preserve those voices, combined with
    the strenuous work which their career entails, leaves them but
    little time for anything else. Melba, however, appears to me
    to offer an exception to the general rule."

    Hetherington, John. <u>Melba: a Biography</u>. London: Faber & Faber,
    1967. 312 p., 29 illus., 109-item bibliography, index.

    Hutton, Geoffrey William. <u>Melba</u>. Melbourne: Oxford University
    Press, 1962. 30 p., 8 illus.

    Murphy, Agnes G. <u>Melba: a Biography with Chapters by Madame Melba</u>

on the Selection of Music as a Profession, & on the Science of
Singing. New York: Doubleday, Page & Co., 1909. Reprint 1977.
xiv, 348 p., 36 illus., list of roles, index.

Shawe-Taylor, Desmond. Nellie Melba (1861-1931): a Biographical
and Critical Sketch. London: The Gramophone Company, n.d.
[1961]. 16, [2] p., 3 illus., recording details.

One of a series of pamphlets for "Great Recordings of the
Century."

Wechsberg, Joseph. Red Plush and Black Velvet: the Story of
Melba and Her Times. Boston: Little, Brown and Company, 1961.
372 p., 19 illus., 9-item bibliography.

5. SEE: autobiography of **ROLAND FOSTER** (C0214).

    SEE: autobiography of **OLGA LYNN** (C0374).

    SEE: T.P. O'Connor under **BLANCHE MARCHESI** (C0382).

    Nicols, Beverly. 25: being a Young Man's Candid Recollections of
    His Elders and Betters. New York: George H. Doran Company, 1926.

    Ronald, Landon. Variations on a Personal Theme. London: Hodder
    and Stroughton Ltd., 1922. 177 p., 20 illus.

C0409.
MELCHOIR, LAURITZ. Danish Tenor. b. March 20, 1890, Copenhagen;
d. March 18, 1973, Santa Monica, California.

1. BAKER 6; EdS 1/7 (Bibliography); GROVE 6/12 (Bibliography);
    RIEMANN 12.

2. GR 16/8; ON 10/13, 28/12, 34/22; OW 14/5, 22/1; RNC 3/12,
    4/1, 2.

4. Hansen, Hans. Lauritz Melchoir: a Discography. 2nd revised
    edition. Copenhagen: Nationaldiskoteket, 1965. 44 p.

    Naully, Jana. Lauritz Melchoir. København: Steen Hasselbalchs
    Forlag, 1969. 223 p., 25 illus.

C0410.
MELLISH, MARY. American Soprano. b. 1890. No lexicon listing.

3. Mellish, Mary. Sometimes I Reminisce: Autobiography. New York:
    G.P. Putnam's Sons, 1941. 336 p

    Sang small roles at the Met 1918-1923 under the stage name of
    FLANNERY.

C0411.
MENGOZZI, BERNARDO. Italian Tenor. b. 1758, Florence; d. March ?,
1800, Paris.

1. EdS 1/7; RIEMANN 12; SCHMIDL + Supp.

3. Mengozzi, Bernardo. Autobiografia.

    This autographed MS was at one time in the Musikhist. Museum von
    Wilhelm Heyer in Cologne. It was possibly auctioned by Otto
    Haas for the antiquarian firm of K.E. Henrici and L. Liepmanns-
    sohn during the period December 1926-February 1928. Present
    whereabouts unknown.

    Langlé, Honoré, ed. Méthode de chant du conservatoire du musique
    contenant les principes du chant des exercises pour la voix.
    Paris: n.p., 1802.

    RIEMANN 12 states that this is essentially Mengozzi's work,
    and the 1st Italian edition [Firenze: Giglio, 1807] lists
    Mengozzi as the author.

C0412.
MERRILL, ROBERT. American Baritone. b. June 4, 1917, Brooklyn, New
York.

1. BAKER 6; GROVE 6/12 (Bibliography); RIEMANN 12/Supp.

2. GR 32/2, 41/5; ON 30/17, 35/11; OW 3/1.

3. Merrill, Robert. Between Acts: an Irreverent Look at Opera and
    Other Madness. New York: McGraw-Hill Book Company, 1976. 240 p.,
    28 illus.

    Merrill, Robert and Sandford Dody. Once More from the Beginning.
    New York: The Macmillan Company, 1965. 286 p., 38 illus., index.

C0413.
MESSCHAERT, JOHANNES MARTINUS. Dutch Baritone. b. August 22, 1857,
Hoorn; d. September 9, 1922, Zuerich.

1. BAKER 6; GROVE 6/12; MGG 1/9 (Bibliography); RIEMANN 12 +
    Supp. (Bibliography); SCHMIDL/Supp.

4. Canneman, M.C., ed. Inventaris von gedenkstukken met betrekking
    tot de zanger Johannes Martinus Messchaert. Hoorn, 1968.

    No copy located.

    Martienssen-Lohmann, Franziska. De kunst van het zingen: getoetst
    aan Johannes Messchaert. 's-Gravenhage: N.V. Uitg. W.P. van
    van Stockum & Zn., 1947. 59 p., 6 illus.

    Martienssen-Lohmann, Franziska. Die echte Gesangskunst dargestellt
    an Johannes Messchaert. Berlin: B. Behr, 1920 [1st edition
    1914]. 103, [1] p., illus.

    Martienssen-Lohmann, Franziska. Johannes Messchaert, eine Gesangs-
    stunde: allgemeine Ratschlaege nebst gesangtechnischen Analysen von

einigen Schubert-Liedern. Berlin: B. Schott, 1927. 16, [11] p. illus.

C0414.
MEYER, KERSTIN. Swedish Mezzo-Soprano. b. April 3, 1928, Stockholm.

1. EdS/Supp.; GROVE 6/12; RIEMANN 12/Supp.

2. ON 26/17; OPERA 24/10; OW 17/5.

C0415.
LA MIGNATA. SEE: MUSI, MARIA MADDALENA (C0438).

C0416.
MIKSCH, JOHANN ALOYS. German Baritone. b. July 19, 1765, Georgental, Bohemia; d. September 24, 1845, Dresden.

1. BAKER 6; RIEMANN 12; SCHMIDL.

4. Kohut, Adolph. Johannes Miksch, der groesste deutsche Singemeister meister und sein Gesangssystem. Leipzig-Reudnitz: Carl Ruehles Musik-Verlag, 1890. 44 p.

C0417.
MILANOV, ZINKA. Yugoslavian Soprano. b. May 17, 1906, Zagreb.

1. BAKER 6; EdS 1/7 (Bibliography); GROVE 6/12 (Bibliography); RIEMANN 12 + Supp.

2. ON 22/12, 29/24, 41/22.

C0418.
von MILDE, HANS FEODOR. Austrian Baritone. b. April 13, 1821, Petronell, near Vienna; d. December 10, 1899, Weimar.

1. BAKER 6; MGG 1/9 (Bibliography); RIEMANN 12 (Bibliography); SCHMIDL/Supp.

4. von Milde, Franz. Ein ideales Kuenstlerpaar Rosa und Feodor von Milde: ihre Kunst und ihre Zeit. band 1. Leipzig: Druck und Verlag von Breitkopf & Haertel, 1918. 324 p., 13 illus.

   von Milde, Natalie. Briefe in Poesie und Prosa von Peter Cornelius an Feodor und Rosa von Milde. Weimar: Hermann Boehlaus Nachfolger, 1901. 127 p., 4 illus.

C0419.
von MILDE, ROSA AGATHE. Austrian Soprano. b. June 25, 1827, Weimar; d. January 26, 1906, Weimar

1. BAKER 6; MGG 1/9 (Bibliography); RIEMANN 12 (Bibliography); SCHMIDL/Supp.

4. von Milde, Franz. Ein ideales Kuenstlerpaar Rosa und Feodor von Milde: ihre Kunst und ihre Zeit. band 1. Leipzig: Druck und

Verlag von Breitkopf & Haertel, 1918. 324 p., 13:illus.

von Milde, Natalie. Briefe in Poesie und Prosa von Peter Cornelius an Feodor und Rosa von Milde. Weimar: Hermann Boehlaus Nachfolger, 1901. 127 p., 4 illus.

C0420.
MILESI, PIETRO. Italian Bass. b. 1832, Bergamo; d. April 8, 1897, Bergamo.

1. SCHMIDL.

4. Fanelli, F. Memoria biografica di Pietro Milesi. Bologna: n.p., 1892. 28 p.

C0421.
MILNES, SHERRILL. American Baritone. b. January 10, 1935, Downers Grove, Illinois.

1. GROVE 6/12 (Bibliography); RIEMANN 12/Supp.

2. ON 36/2, 39/18, 41/9; OPERA 31/6; OW 14/7, 23/8-9.

5. Blackwood, Alan. The Performing World of the Singer, with a Profile of Sherrill Milnes. Morristown: Silver Burdett Company, 1981. 113 p., illus.

C0422.
MINGOTTI, REGINA. Austrian Soprano. February 16, 1722, Naples; d. October 1, 1808, Neuberg an der Donau.

1. EdS 1/7 (Bibliography); Fetis 2/6; GROVE 6/12 (Bibliography); RIEMANN 12; SCHMIDL + Supp.

3. Mingotti, Regina. An Appeal to the Publick. London: privately printed, n.d. [c.1757]. 13 p.

Mingotti, Regina. A Second Appeal to the Publick. London: privately printed, n.d. [c.1757]. 11 p.

A personal defense resulting from a disagreement with her management.

4. Mueller, Erich H. Angelo und Pietro Mingotti: ein Beitrag zur Geschichte der Oper im XVIII. Jahrhundert. Dresden: Richard Bertling, 1917. xvii, 141, CCCX p., portrait of Regina + 20 illus., 89 + 5 item bibliography, index.

Edition of 300 copies.

C0423.
MINTON, YVONNE. Australian Mezzo-Soprano. b. December 4, 1938, Sydney.

1. GROVE 6/12.

2. OPERA 28/9, 37/23; OW 19/6.

CO424.
MIRATE, RAFFAELE. Italian Tenor. b. September 3, 1815, Naples; d.
November ?, 1885 Sorrento.

1. EdS 1/7 (Bibliography); SCHMIDL + Supp.

3. Mirate, Raffaele. Memorie.

    An MS of his autobiography is in the Museo del Conservatorio
    di Santo Pietro a Majella in Naples.

CO425.
MIURA, TAMAKI. Japanese Soprano. b. 1884, Tokyo; d. May 26, 1946,
Tokyo. No lexicon listing.

1. KUTSCH 3.

4. Setouchi, Harumi. Madame Butterfly. Tokyo: Toyo Publications,
    1969 [1st edition 1944]. 250 p., 7 prints.

    The first internationally recognized Japanese soprano.

CO426.
MOEDL, MARTHA. German Soprano. b. March 22, 1912, Nuernberg.

1. GROVE 6/12 (Bibliography); MGG 1/16 (Bibliography); RIEMANN 12
    + Supp.

2. OW 5/1, 9/8, 14/2, 23/3.

4. Schaefer, Walter Erich. Martha Moedl. Velber bei Hannover:
    Friedrich Verlag, 1967. 99 p., 43 illus., list of engagements
    with roles, festival appearances, discography.

CO427.
MOFFO, ANNA. American Soprano. b. June 27, 1932, Wayne, Pennsylvania.

1. BAKER 6; EdS/Supp.; GROVE 6/12; RIEMANN 12/Supp.

2. GR 41/11; ON 25/17, 31/2, 34/24; OW 10/1.

CO428.
MOJICA, JOSE. Mexican Tenor. b. April 4, 1896, Mexico City. No
lexicon listing.

1. KUTSCH 3.

3. Mojica, José. I, a Sinner. Translated by Fanchon Royer. Chicago:
    Franciscan Herald Press, 1963. 393.p., 82 illus.

    Probable first edition: Yo pecador.... México: Editorial Jus.,
    1956. 662 p., 115 illus.

Mjoica, Fray José G. Mi guia y mi estrella. Chicago: Franciscan Herald Press, 1975. 99 p., 25 illus.

Extends previous title up to his death.

4. Spota, Luis. José Mjoica: hombre, artista y fraile. México, D.F.: Prometio, 1944. 138 p., 8 illus.

C0429.
MOLL, KURT. German Bass. b. April 11, 1938, Buir.

1. GROVE 6/12.

2. ON 47/13; OW 20/11.

C0430.
MONGELLI, ANDREA. Italian Bass. b. December 16, 1901, Bari; d. February 12, 1970, Rome. No lexicon listing.

1. KUTSCH 3.

4. Giovine, Alfredo. Andrea Mongelli, basso Barese: cenni biografici, elenco di rapprasentazioni e iconografia. Bari: n.p., 1970. 19 p., 27 illus., list of operatic appearances.

C0431.
MOORE, GRACE. American Soprano. b. December 5, 1898, Slabtown, Tennessee; d. January 27, 1947, Copenhagen, Denmark.

1. BAKER 6; EdS 1/7 (Bibliography); GROVE 6/12 (Bibliography -- note birthplace and date discrepancy); RIEMANN 12 + Supp.

2. GR 13/8; ON 21/19.

3. Moore, Grace. You're Only Human Once. Garden City: Doubleday, Doran & Co., Inc., 1944. Reprint 1977. 275 p.

4. Farrar, Rowena Rutherford. Grace Moore and Her Many Worlds. East Brunswick: Cornwall Books, 1981. 305 p., illus., Metropolitan Opera appearances, bibliography, discography, index.

C0432.
MORENA, BERTA. German Soprano. b. January 27, 1878, Mannheim; d. October 7, 1952, Rottlach-Eggern, Tegernsee.

1. BAKER 6; GROVE 6/12; RIEMANN 12.

4. Berta Morena und ihre Kunst. Muenchen: Hugo Schmidt Verlag, 1919. unpaginated [14, 34, 28 p.], 34 portraits, list of portraits.

    Edition of 500 copies. Certainly one of the most magnificent examples of this type ever published. Beautiful plates.

C0433.
MOSER, EDDA. Austrian Soprano. b. October 27, 1941, Berlin.

1. GROVE 6/12; RIEMANN 12/Supp.

2. OW 10/7, 12/8, 14/6, 20/4.

C0434.
MOULTON, LILLI. SEE: de HEGERMANN-LINDENCRONE, L. (C0275).

C0435.
MUEHLMANN, ADOLF. No lexicon listing.

3. Muehlmann, Adolf. A grobber Koll: der Wiedergang eines Opera-
   saengers. Erinnerungen. Chicago: Gutenberg Press, 1932. 323 p.,
   12 illus.

C0436.
MUELLER, MARIA. Czechoslovakian Soprano. b. January 29, 1898,
Litomerice; d. March 13, 1958, Bayreuth, Germany.

1. BAKER 6; EdS 1/7 (Bibliography); GROVE 6/12; RIEMANN 12 + Supp.
   (Bibliography).

2. OW 20/7.

C0437.
MURATORE, LUCIEN. French Tenor. b. August 29, 1876, Marseilles;
d. July 16, 1954, Paris.

1. BAKER 6; EdS 1/7 (Bibliography); GROVE 6/ 12 (Bibliography);
   RIEMANN 12/Supp.; SCHMIDL.

2. GR 32/5; OPERA 5/11.

5. Wicart, Alexis. Le chanteur. 2 vols. Paris: Philippe Ortiz,
   1931. "Preparation d'un role lyrique." In vol. 2, pp. 255-274,
   4 illus.

C0438.
MUSI, MARIA MADDALENA. Italian Soprano. b. June 18, 1669, Bologna;
d. May 2, 1751, Bologna?

1. SCHMIDL + Supp. (Bibliography).

4. Cosentino, Giuseppe. La Mignatta: Maria Maddelena Musi cantatrice Bolognese famosa 1669-1751. Bologna: Nicola Zanichelli,
   1930. ix, 202 p., 5 illus.

C0439.
MUZIO, CLAUDIA. Italian Soprano. b. February 7, 1889, Pavia; d. May
24, 1936, Rome.

1. BAKER 6; EdS 1/7 (Bibliography); GROVE 6/13; RIEMANN 12/Supp.
   (Bibliography); SCHMIDL/Supp.

2. ON 24/24; RC 17/9-10, 11.

4. Barnes Jr., Harold M. Claudia Muzio: a Biographical Sketch and Discography. revised edition. Junction: Texas, privately printed, 1947 [1st edition Princeton, 1941]. 18 p.

   Barnes Jr., Harold M. Claudia Muzio (1889-1936): a Biographical Sketch. London: The Gramophone Company, n.d. [1958]. 12, [2] p., 2 illus., recording details.

   One of a series of pamphlets for "Great Recordings of the Century."

C0440.
NAUDIN, EMILIO. French Tenor. b. October 23, 1823, Parma; d. May 5, 1890, Boulogne-sur-Mer.

1. BAKER 6 (Bibliography); EdS 1/7; SCHMIDL.

4. SEE: Mario Ferrarini under ITALO CAMPANINI (C0093).

C0441.
NERI, GIULIO. Italian Bass. b. April 21, 1909, Torrita di Siena; d. April 21, 1958, Rome.

1. RIEMANN/Supp.

4. Clerico, Cesare. Giulio Neri: una vita nella voce. Torino: Edizioni Musicali Scomegna, 1981. 81 p., 24 illus., chronology, repertoire, 11-item bibliography, index of names.

C0442.
NEUMANN, ANGELO. Austrian Tenor. b. August 18, 1838, Vienna; d. December 20, 1910, Prague.

1. BAKER 6; EdS 1/7 (Bibliography); RIEMANN 12 + Supp. (Bibliography); SCHMIDL.

3. Neumann, Angelo. Erinnerungen an Richard Wagner. fuenfte auflage. Leipzig: Verlag von L. Staackmann, 1907. 341 p. + facsimilies and 3 plates, 6 illus.

   The 4th edition of this work was translated by E. Levermore as: Personal Recollections of Wagner. New York, 1906. Reprint 1976.

C0443.
NEVADA, EMMA. American Soprano. b. February 7, 1859, Nevada City, California; d. June 20, 1940, Liverpool, England.

1. BAKER 6 (Bibliography); GROVE 6/12 (Bibliography); SCHMIDL.

2. ON 37/21.

C0444.
NEZHDANOVA, ANTONIA. Russian Soprano. b. June 16, 1873, Krivaya, near Odessa; d. June 26, 1950, Moscow.

1. BAKER 6; GROVE 6/12 (Bibliography).

2. OPERA 21/8; RC 24/1-2, 26/5-6.

3. Nezhdanova, Antonia. <u>Antonina Vasil'evna Nezdanova: materialy i</u>
    <u>issledovaniia</u>. Moskova: Iskusstvo, 1967. 544 p., 80 p. of illus.,
    list of names with biographical notes, chronological survey of
    career, list of roles, index.

CO445.
NICULESCU-BASU, GEORGE. Romanian Bass. No lexicon listing.

3. Niculescu-Basu, George. <u>Amintirile: unui artist de operă</u>.
    București: Editura Muzicală, 1962. 566 p., 38 illus.

    Niculescu-Basu, George. <u>Cum am cîntat eu ....</u> București: Editura
    Muzicală, 1961. 261 p., 15 illus.

CO446.
NIEMANN, ALBERT. German Tenor. b. January 15, 1831, Erxleben, near
Magdeburg; d. January 13, 1917, Berlin.

1. BAKER 6; EdS 1/7 (Bibliography); FETIS 2/Supp.; GROVE 6/13 (Bib-
    liography); MGG 1/9 (Bibliography); RIEMANN 12 + Supp. (Bibliog-
    raphy); SCHMIDL.

4. Altmann, Wilhelm. <u>Richard Wagner und Albert Niemann: ein Gedenk-</u>
    <u>buch mit bisher unveroeffentlichten Briefen, besonders Wagners,</u>
    <u>Bildern und einem Faksimilie</u>. Berlin: Verlag von Georg Stilke,
    1924. 264 p., 15 illus., index of names.

    Sternfeld, Richard. <u>Albert Niemann</u>. Berlin: Schuster & Loeffler,
    n.d. [c.1904]. 91 p., 6 illus., facsimilie.

    Wagner, Karlheinz. <u>Albert Niemann als Wagner-Darsteller: eine</u>
    <u>Studie zur durchsetzung des musikdramatischen Darstellungsstils</u>.
    Muenchen: university dissertation, 1954. iv, 110, vii p., 95-item
    bibliography.

CO447.
NILSSON, BIRGIT. Swedish Soprano. b. May 17, 1918, near Karup.

1. BAKER 6; EdS/Supp.; GROVE 6/13 (Bibliography); MGG 1/16;
    RIEMANN 12 + Supp. (Bibliography).

2. GR 47/8; ON 28/21, 35/3, 39/15, 44/13; OPERA 11/9; OP 6/1;
    OW 4/7, 17/2.

3. Nilsson, Birgit. <u>My Memoirs in Pictures</u>. Translated by Thomas
    Teal. Garden City: Doubleday & Company, Inc., 1981 [1st edition
    Stockholm, 1977]. 127 p., 273 illus., index.

CO448.
NILSSON, KRISTINA. Swedish Soprano. b. August 20, 1843, Sjoeabol,
near Vexioe; d. November 22, 1921, Stockholm.

1. BAKER 6; EdS 1/7 (Bibliography); GROVE 6/13 (Bibliography);
   MGG 1/9 (Bibliography); RIEMANN 12 + Supp. (Bibliography);
   SCHMIDL + Supp.

2. ON 8/2.

4. Carlsson, Beyron. Kristina Nilsson grevinna de casa miranda:
   minnen och upplevelser upptecknade av Beyron Carlsson. Stockholm:
   Ahlen & Akerlunds foerlag, 1928 [1st edition 1921]. 464 p.,
   107 illus.

   de Charnacé, Guy. Christina Nilsson. Paris: Henri Plon,
   Imprimeur-Editeur, 1869. 28 p., portrait.

   Franzén, Nils Olof. Christina Nilsson en svensk saga. Stockholm:
   Albert Bonniers Foerlag, 1976. 271 p., illus., bibliography,
   index.

   Headland, Helen. Christina Nilsson: the Songbird of the North.
   Rock Island: Augustana Book Concern, 1943. 173 p., 15 illus.,
   5 facsimilies.

   Lawson, Evald Benjamin. Christina Nilsson's Visit to Brockton,
   Mass., in November, 1870.... Rock Island: n.p., 1934. 16 p.,1
   illus.

   Memoir of Madamoiselle Christine Nilsson. London: n.p., 1869.
   60 p., portrait.

   Norlind, Tobias. Kristina Nilsson, grevinna de casa miranda:
   sangerskan och konstnaerinnan. Stockholm: Ahlen & Akerlunds
   Foerlag, 1923. 300 p., 78 illus., bibliography, index of names.

5. SEE: Louis Engel under MARIO (C0389).

   SEE: Gustav Thalberg under JENNY LIND (C0360).

C0449.
NOORDEWIER-REDDINGIUS, AALTJE. Dutch Soprano. b. September 1, 1868,
Deurne; d. April 6, 1949, Hilversum.

1. RIEMANN 12 + Supp. (Bibliography).

4. Schouwman, Hans. Aaltje Noordewier-Reddingius en haar zangkunst.
   Den Haag: Servire, 1958. 119 p., 7 illus., index of names.

C0450.
NORDICA, LILLIAN. American Soprano. b. December 12, 1857,
Farmington, Maine; d. May 10, 1914, Batavia, Java.

1. BAKER 6; EdS 1/7 (Bibliography); GROVE 6/13; RIEMANN 12 + Supp.
   (Bibliography); SCHMIDL.

2. GR 4/4, 14/12; ON 16/11, 28/24, 46/1; OPERA 22/12; RC 6/9.

4. Armstrong, William, ed. <u>Lillian Nordica's Hints to Singers</u>
   <u>together with an Account of Lillian Nordica's Training for the</u>
   <u>Opera, as told in the Letters of the Singer and Her Mother, Amanda</u>
   <u>Allen Norton</u>. New York: E.P. Dutton and Company, 1923. xix, 167
   p., 8 illus.

   Glackens, Ira. <u>Yankee Diva: Lillian Nordica and the Golden Days</u>
   <u>of Opera</u>. New York: Coleridge Press, 1963. xiv, 366 p., 54
   illus., 42-item bibliography, repertoire list, discography,
   reprint of <u>Hints to Singers</u>, index.

5. Benoist, Andre. <u>The Accompanist: an Autobiography of Andre</u>
   <u>Benoist</u>. Edited by John Anthony Maltese. Neptune [New Jersey]:
   Paganiniana Publications, Inc., 1978. 384 p., aprox. 200 illus.,
   discography, index.

   SEE: Walter Damrosch under **LILLI LEHMANN** (C0353).

C0451.
NOURRIT, ADOLPHE. French Tenor. b. March 3, 1902, Montpellier; d.
March 8, 1839, Naples.

1. BAKER 6; EdS 1/7 (Bibliography); GROVE 6/13; MGG 1/9; RIEMANN
   12 (Bibliography) + Supp. (Bibliography); SCHMIDL + Supp.

2. MQ 25/1; ON 27/18.

4. de Monvel, Etienne Boutet. <u>Un artiste d'autrefois, Adolphe</u>
   <u>Nourrit: sa vie et sa correspondance</u>. Paris: Plon-Nourri et cie,
   Imprimeurs-Editeurs, 1903. 319 p., 2 portraits.

   Quicherat, Louis. <u>Adolphe Nourrit: sa vie et son talent, son</u>
   <u>charactère sa correspondance</u>. 3 vols. Paris: Librairie de L.
   Hachette et cie, 1867. x, 526 p., portrait; 546 p.; 445 p.,
   list of roles.

5. Halévy, Fromantel. <u>Derniers souvenirs et portraits</u>. Paris:
   Michel Lévy Frères, Libraires Editeurs, 1863. pp. 123-203.

   SEE: Ernest Legouvé under **MARIA MALIBRAN** (C0378).

C0452.
NOVELLO, CLARA ANASTASIA. English Soprano. b. June 10, 1818, London;
d. March 12, 1908, Rome.

1. BAKER 6; EdS 1/7 (Bibliography); GROVE 6/13 (Bibliography);
   RIEMANN 12/Supp. (Bibliography); SCHMIDL.

3. Novello, Clara Anastasia. <u>Clara Novello's Reminiscences</u>. Compiled
   by Contessa Valeria Gigliucci [daughter]. London: Edward Arnold,
   1910. 216 p., 3 illus.

   Mackenzie-Grieve, Averil. <u>Clara Novello 1818-1908</u>. London:
   Geoffrey Bles, 1955. Reprint 1980. xiv, 338 p., 10 illus.,
   65-item bibliography, index.

C0453.
NOVOTNA, JARMILA. Czechoslovakian Soprano. b. September 23, 1903, Prague.

1. BAKER 6; GROVE 6/13 (birthyear of 1907); RIEMANN 12 + Supp.

2. ON 39/13; RC 25/5-6, 27/7-8.

C0454.
OBRAZTSOVA, ELENA. Russian Mezzo-Soprano. b. July 7, 1937, Lenningrad.

1. BAKER 6; GROVE 6/13 (Bibliography).

2. ON 42/3; OW 22/7.

C0455.
OEDMANN, ARVID. Swedish Tenor. b. April 3, 1859, Karlstad; d. July 15, 1914, Stockholm. No lexicon listing.

4. Hard-Oedmann, Alma. Arvid Oedmann: minnesblad. Stockholm: Hugo Gebers Foerlag, 1915. [6], 255 p., 25 illus.

C0456.
OLIVERO, MAGDA. Italian Soprano. b. March 25, 1912, Saluzzo, near Turin.

1. BAKER 6; EdS 1/7; GROVE 6/13 (Bibliography -- birthyear 1916 or 1917); RIEMANN 12/Supp. (Bibliography).

2. ON 34/5, 42/6; OP 10/7.

4. Quattrocchi, Vincenzo. Magda Olivero: una voce per tre generazioni. Torino: Italgrafica, 1984. xxii, 286, [1] p., 105 illus., chronology, discography by Gilberto Starone, radio and TV appearances, 143-item bibliography, index of names,

C0457.
ONEGIN, SIGRID. German Mezzo-Soprano. b. June 1, 1889, Stockholm; d. June 16, 1943, Magliaso, Switzerland.

1. BAKER 6; EdS 1/7; GROVE 6/13; RIEMANN 12.

2. OW 10/11, 21/8-9; RC 5/10, 12, 12/8-9.

4. Penzoldt, Fritz. Sigrid Onégin. Magdeburg: Karl Josef Sander Verlag, 1939. 326 p., illus.

   The 2nd edition was published as: Alt-Rhapsodie: Sigrid Onégin - Leben und Werk. Neustadt an der Aisch: Verlag Degewer & Co., 242 p., 29 illus., list of roles, discography.

C0458.
ONOFREI, DIMITRI. Romanian Tenor. b. August 8, 1897? No lexicon listing.

4. Onofrei, Constantin and Grigore Constantinescu. <u>Dinitri Onofrei</u>. Bucuresti: Editura Muzicala, 1970. 151 p., discography, reper- toire.

C0459.
ORELIO, JOSEPH M. Dutch Baritone. b. 1854, s'Hertogenbosch; d. October 1925, Zandvoort. No lexicon listing.

1. KUTSCH 3.

3. Orelio, Joseph M. <u>M'n gedenkschriften voor 't nederlandsche volk opgeschreven...naar aanleiding van m'n 40-jubileum als concert- en operazanger (1876-1916)</u>. Amsterdam: Scheltens & Giltay, 1916. ix, 10-192 p., 23 illus.

C0460.
ORGENI, AGLAJA. Hungarian Soprano. b. December 17, 1841, Roma Szombat; d. March 15, 1926, Vienna.

1. BAKER 6; GROVE 6/13 (Bibliography); RIEMANN 12.

4. Brand, Erna. <u>Aglaja Orgeni: das Leben einer grossen Saengerin nach Briefen, Zeitquellen und Ueberlieferung</u>. Muenchen: C.H. Beck'sche Verlagsbuchhandlung, 1931. xi, 253 p., 18 letters from Pauline Viardot-Garcia.

5. SEE: autobiography of **EMI de BIDOLI** (C0148).

C0461.
OTS, GEORG KARLOVICH. Russian Baritone. b. March 21, 1920, Petrograd; d. 1975, Moscow.

1. GROVE 6/14 (Bibliography).

4. Toñson, Helga. <u>Georg Ots</u>. Tallinn: Eesti Raamat, 1975. 39 + 23 p., 47 illus., list of roles.

C0462.
PACCHIEROTTI, GASPARO. Italian Castrato Soprano. b. May 1740, Fabriano, near Ancona; d. October 28, 1821, Padua.

1. BAKER 6; EdS 1/7 (Bibliography); GROVE 6/14 (Bibliography); RIEMANN 12 (Bibliography).

4. Calegari, Antonio. <u>Modi generali del canto premessi alle maniere parziali onde adornare o rifiorire le nude o semplici melodie o cantilene giusta il metodo di Gasparo Pacchiarotti</u>. Milano, 1836.

No copy located.

Pacchierotti, Giuseppe Cecchini [adopted son]. <u>Ai cultori ed amatori della musica vocale cenni biografici intorno a Gaspare Pacchierotti dettati da Giuseppe Cecchini Pacchierotti</u>. Padova: coi Tipi del Seminario, 1844. 16 p.

Sassi, Romualdo. Un celebre musico fabrianese Gaspare Pacchierotti. Fabriano: Stab. di art. grafiche "Gentile," n.d.
[1935]. 51 p., portrait.

The Library of Congress copy has two portraits.

C0463.
PACCINI, REGINA. Spanish Soprano. b. January 6, 1871, Lisbon; d.
September 18, 1965, Buenos Aires.

1. EdS 1/7.

3. An MS autobiography exists. This material along with that of
   Lilli Lehmann (among others) should be published.

C0464.
PAGLIUGHI, LINA. Italian Soprano. b. May 27, 1911, New York City;
d. October 2, 1980, Rubicone.

1. EdS 1/7; GROVE 6/14; RIEMANN 12/Supp.

2. GR 21/2; ON 44/11; RC 21/5-6.

4. Cernaz, Bruno. Lina Pagliughi ricordi. Savignano: L'Associazione
   Amici della Musica "Lina Pagliughi," 1982. 83 p., 69 illus., discography, 9 item, bibliography.

5. Lengyel, Cornel, ed. History of Musicians in San Francisco: Fifty
   Local Prodigies 1906-1940. San Francisco: WPA #10377, 1940. 203
   p., 13 illus., bibliography.

C0465.
PALLO, IMRE. Hungarian Baritone. b. October 23, 1892, Matisfalva.

1. GROVE 6/14.

4. Németh, Amadé. Palló Imre. Budapest: Zenemuekiadó, 1970. 54,
   [22] p., 30 illus., list of roles, 2 LP records.

C0466.
PALMER, BESSIE. English Mezzo-Soprano. b. August 9, 1831, London;
d. September 1, 1910, London? No lexicon listing.

3. Palmer, Bessie. Musical Recollections. London: The Walter Scott
   Publishing Co., Ltd., 1904. vi, 314 p., 32 illus., index of names.

C0467.
PALSON-WETTERGREN, GERTRUD. Swedish Mezzo-Soprano. b. February 17,
1897, Esloev.

1. RIEMANN 12/Supp.

3. Palson-Wettergren, Gertrud. Mitt oedes stjaerna. Stockholm:
   Raben & Sjoegren, 1964. 293 p., 33 illus., index of names.

C0468.
PANZÉRA, CHARLES. French Baritone. b. February 16, 1896, Hyeres; d.
June 6, 1976, Paris.

1. BAKER 6; GROVE 6/14 (birthplace discrepancy); RIEMANN 12 (birth-
    place discrepency).

3. Panzéra, Charles. L'amour de chanteur. Paris: H. Lemoine, 1957.
    126 p.

    Panzéra, Charles. L'art de chanteur. Preface by Arthur Honneger.
    Paris: Editions littéraires de France, 1945. 120 p., illus.

    Panzéra, Charles. L'art vocal: 30 lecons de chant. Paris:
    Librairie théatrale, 1959. 122 p., Illus.

    Panzéra, Charles. Votre voix: directives générales. Paris:
    Edition musicales transatlantiques, 1967. 32 p.

4. Fabre, Michel. Souvenirs de Magdeleine et Charles Panzera. Pau:
    M. Fabre, 1972. 19 p., illus.

C0469.
PARETO, GRAZIELLA. Spanish Soprano. b. March 6, 1889, Barcelona;
d. September 1, 1973, Rome.

1. EdS 1/7; GROVE 6/14 (Bibliography).

2. OPERA 17/4; RC 17/4.

C0470.
PASKALIS, KOSTAS. Greek Baritone. b. September 1, 1929, Levadia,
Boestia.

1. GROVE 6/14; RIEMANN 12/Supp.

2. OW 9/3, 15/6.

C0471.
PASTA, GIUDITTA. Italian Soprano. b. October 28, 1797, Saronno, near
Milan; d. April 1, 1865, her villa on Lake Como.

1. BAKER 6; EdS 1/7 (Bibliography); GROVE 6/14; MGG 1/10 (Bibliog-
    raphy); RIEMANN 12 + Supp. (Bibliography includes a reference
    to over 500 personal letters written to Pasta now in the
    possession of the New York Public Library); SCHMIDL + Supp.

2. ON 27/21, 40/16, 46/12; OPERA 29/9.

4. Alberti, Celso. Giuditta Pasta al Carcano: poema eriocomico.
    Milano: G. Pirotta, 1829. 32 p.

    Giulini, Maria Ferranti: Giuditta Pasta e i suoi tempi: memorie
    e lettere. Milano: Ettore, Sormani, 1935. 221 p., 21 illus.

Giuditta Pasta a Como: sermone. Como: Presso i Figli di C.A.
Ostinelli stampatori provinciali, 1832. unpaginated, [9] p.

Marchetti, Giovanni. A Giuditta Pasta: ode. Bologna: Alla Volpe,
1934. 8 p.

5. SEE: Alfred Bunn under **MARIA MALIBRAN** (C0378).

C0472.
PATAKY, KALMAN. Hungraian Tenor. b. November 14, 1896, Alsolendva;
d. March 3, 1964, Los Angeles, California.

1. GROVE 6/14 (Bibliography); RIEMANN 12.

4. Somogyi, Vilmos and Imre Molnár. Pataky Kálmán. Budapest:
Zenemuekiadó, 1968. 71, [20] p., 26 illus., list of roles,
2 LP records.

C0473.
PATTI, ADELINA. Italian Soprano. b. February 10, 1843, Madrid; d.
September 27, 1919, Craig-y-Nos Castle, near Brecon.

1. BAKER 6; EdS 1/7 (Bibliography); FETIS 2/Supp.; GROVE 6/14 (Bibliography); MGG 1/10 (Bibliography); RIEMANN 12 (Bibliography)
+ Supp.; SCHMIDL.

2. GR 12/5, 20/9; ON 7/17, 10/18, 12/13, 23, 24, 18/4, 22/2, 28/15;
RC 10/8-9.

3. SCHMIDL mentions an autobiography which I have not been able to
verify: "Pubblico inoltre, in inglese, le sue memorie My Reminiscences (1909)."

The Library of Congress owns a substantial collection of Patti
materials and memorabilia.

4. Cabezas, Jaun Antonio. Adelina Patti (la cantante de la voz de
oro). Madrid: Cuesta de Santo Domingo, n.d. [1956]. 96 p.,
8 illus.

Castán Palomar, Fernando. Adelina Patti: su vida. Madrid:
General Ediciones, 1947. 202 p.

Dalmazzo, G.M. Adelina Patti's Life and Her Appearances at the
Royal Italian Opera, Covent Garden, with Particular Documents.
London: Cooper Bros. and Attwood, 1877. 48 p., portrait.

de Charnacé, Guy. Adelina Patti. Paris: Henri Plon, Imprimeur-
Editeur, 1868. 28 p., portrait.

de Grave, Théodore. Biographie d'Adelina Patti. Paris: Librairie
de Castel, 1865. 36 p.

Hernández Girbal, F. Adelina Patti: la reina del canto. Madrid:
Ediciones Lira, 1979. 9-446, [1], [30] p., 34 illus.,

chronology, 76-item bibliography.

The autobiography mentioned in SCHMIDL is also listed in Hernandez Girbal's bibliography. Is this another case of perpetuating mis-information?

Hills, Lucius Berry. <u>When Patti sang: a Souvenir Poem</u>. Atlanta: Chas. P. Byrd, 1894. 12 p., 6 illus.

In memory of a concert performed on January 11, 1894.

Klein, Herman. <u>The Reign of Patti</u>. New York: The Century Co., 1920. Reprint 1977 with discography by W.R. Moran. Reprint 1978. ix, 470 p., 40 illus., 30 reviews, index.

The author was originally asked by Patti to assist her with her autobiography. This may offer a clue as to the SCHMIDL entry.

Klein, Herman. <u>The Bel Canto with Particular Reference to the singing of Mozart</u>. London: Oxford University Press, 1923. 53 p.

Thought by some to be a summation of Patti's vocal method. However, Klein was a student of Garcia for four years, and the pedagogical suggestions all agree with Garcia's methodology.

Lauw, Louisa. <u>Fourteen Years with Adelina Patti</u>. Translated by Clare Brune. London: Remington & Co., Publishers, 1884. 199 p.

There is an abridged version translated by Jeremiah Loder: New York, Norman L. Monro, Publisher, 1884. Reprint 1977. 91 p.

Mortier, Michel. <u>Biographical Sketch of Madame Adelina Patti</u>. New York: H.A. Rost, 1882. 14 p.

The same pamphlet was also published by Steinway & Sons and was used at her concerts during this unsuccessful tour. 16 p., portrait. Another version 7 p., portrait.

Vacano, Emile Mario. <u>Der Roman der Adelina Patti...nach spanischen, englischen und muendlichen Quellen</u>. Wien: Verlag von Klíč & Spitzer, 1875. 84 p., 8 portrait sketches.

One of the earliest of the popular novels about famous singers.

5. SEE: Richard Aldrich under **JENNY LIND** (C0360).

SEE: Louis Engel under **MARIO** (C0389).

Hanslick, Eduard. <u>Musikalische Stationen</u>. Berlin: Allgemeiner Verein fuer Deutsche Literatur, 1885. pp. 13-44.

SEE: autobiography of **BLANCHE MARCHESI** (C0382).

SEE: T.P. O'Connor under **BLANCHE MARCHESI** (C0382).

SEE: Heinrich Riemann under **JENNY LIND** (C0360).

SEE: Gustav Thalberg under **JENNY LIND** (C0360).

C0474.
PATTIERA, TINO. Austrian Tenor. b. June 27, 1890, Cavtat, near
Ragusa; d. April 24, 1966, Cavtat, near Ragusa.

1. RIEMANN 12 + Supp.

2. OW 19/11; RC 17/12, 18/11-12.

C0475.
PATZAK, JULIUS. Austrian Tenor. b. April 9, 1898, Vienna; d. January
26, 1974, Rottach-Egern, Baveria.

1. BAKER 6; GROVE 6/14; MGG 1/16 (Bibliography); RIEMANN 12 + Supp.
    (Bibliography).

2. OPERA 5/7; RC 19/9-10.

C0476.
PAULY, ROSA. Hungarian Soprano. b. March 15, 1894, Eperjes; d.
December 14, 1975, Kfar Shmaryahn, near Tel-Aviv, Israel.

1. BAKER 6; EdS 1/7 (Bibliography); GROVE 6/14 (Bibliography);
    RIEMANN 12 + Supp.

2. ON 35/18; RC 8/11-12.

C0477.
PAVAROTTI, LUCIANO. Italian Tenor. b. October 12, 1935, Modena.

1. GROVE 6/14; RIEMANN 12/Supp.

2. GR 49/12; ON 33/8, 37/9, 41/4, 5, 47/3; OPERA 32/2; OW 14/6.

3. Pavarotti, Luciano & William Wright. Pavarotti: My Own Story.
    Garden City: Doubleday & Company, Inc., 1981. xviii, 316 p.,
    49 illus., appendix of first performances "(and significant
    subsequent performances)," discography, index.

4. Gatti, Gian Carlo and Giuseppe Cherpelli, eds. Luciano Pavarotti:
    vent'anni di teatro. Modena: Cooperativa Tipografi, 1981. 92 p.,
    illus., chronology, discography, television appearances.

C0478.
PEARS, PETER. English Tenor. b. June 22, 1910, Farnham.

1. BAKER 6; GROVE 6/14 (Bibliography); MGG 1/16 (Bibliography);
    RIEMANN 12 + Supp.

2. GR 32/10, 46/4; ON 34/11; OPERA 2/6.

C0479.

PEERCE, JAN. American Tenor. b. June 3, 1904, New York City.

1. BAKER 6; GROVE 6/14 (Bibliography); RIEMANN 12 + Supp.

3. Peerce, Jan and Alan Levy. <u>The Bluebird of Happiness: the Memoirs</u>
   <u>of Jan Peerce</u>. New York: Harper & Row, Publishers, 1976. 325 p.,
   17 illus., index.

C0480.
PELISSIER, MARIE. French Soprano. b. 1707?, Paris; d. March 21,
1749, Paris.

1. EdS 1/7 (Bibliography); FETIS 2/Supp.; GROVE 6/14; MGG 1/10
   (1759 listed as year of death); SCHMIDL.

4. <u>Mémoirs-anecdotes pour servir à l'histoire de M. Duliz, et la</u>
   <u>suite de ses aventures après la catastrophe de Mlle Pélissier,</u>
   <u>actrice de l'opéra</u>. Paris, 1739.

   Duliz was her lover, and she had to seek asylum in London in 1734
   as the result of a lawsuit brought by him. No copy located.

5. Jullien, Adolphe. <u>Amours d'opéra au XVIIIe siecle</u>. Paris: H.
   Daragon, Editeur, 1908. pp. 59-88, portrait.

C0481.
PERALTA, ANGELA. Mexican Soprano. b. July 6, 1845, Puebla; d.
August 30, 1883, Matzatlán.

1. GROVE 6/14; RIEMANN/Supp. (Bibliography); SCHMIDL/Supp.

4. Cuenca, Agustin, F. <u>Angela Peralta de castera: rasgos biogra-</u>
   <u>ficos</u>. Mexico: Valle Hermanos, impresores, 1873. 50 p.

   de Maria y Campos, Armando. <u>Angela Peralta, el ruiseñor</u>
   <u>mexicano</u>. Mexico: Ediciones Xochitl, 1944. 185 p., 5 illus.,
   list of roles.

C0482.
PERSIANI, FANNY. Italian Soprano. b. October 4, 1812, Rome; d. May
3, 1867, Neuilly-sur-Siene.

1. BAKER 6 (Bibliography); RIEMANN 12 (Bibliography) + Supp.;
   SCHMIDL (under Tacchinardi-Persiani).

4. Chandesaignes. <u>Madame Persiani</u>. Paris, 1839.

   No copy located.

C0483.
PERTILE, AURELIANO. Italian Tenor. b. November 9, 1885, Montagnara;
d. January 11, 1952, Milan.

1. BAKER 6; GROVE 6/14 (Bibliography); RIEMANN 12/Supp.; SCHMIDL
   + Supp.

2. GR 30/1; OW 6/8; RC 7/11, 12, 8/1, 10/12; RNC 5/6.

4. Silvestrini, Domenico. I tenori celebri: Aureliano Pertile e il
    suo metodo di canto. Bologna: Tipografia Aldina Editrice, 1932.
    192 p.

C0484.
PETERS, ROBERTA. American Soprano. b. May 4, 1930, New York City.

1. BAKER 6; EdS/Supp.; GROVE 6/14; RIEMANN/Supp.

2. ON 21/11, 29/9, 40/6.

3. Peters, Roberta and Louis Biancolli. A Debut at the Met. New
    York: Meredith Press, 1967. ix, 86 p.

    A brief chronical of events prior to her unexpected debut in
    1950.

C0485.
PETROV, IVAN IVANOVICH. Russian Bass. b. February 29, 1920, Irkutsk.

1. BAKER 6 (Bibliography); EdS/Supp. (Bibliography); GROVE 6/14
    (Bibliography); RIEMANN 12/Supp.

2. OP 3/10, 9/10.

C0486.
PETROV, OSSIP. Russian Bass. b. November 15, 1806, Elizavetgrad;
d. March 11, 1878, St. Petersburg.

1. BAKER 6 (Bibliography); EdS 1/8; GROVE 6/14 (Bibliography); MGG
    1/10; RIEMANN 12 + Supp. (Bibliography); SCHMIDL.

C0487.
PHILLIPPS, ADELAIDE. English Mezzo-Soprano. b. October 26, 1833,
Stratford-on-Avon; d. October 3, 1882, Karlsbad, Czechoslovakia.

1. BAKER 6 (Bibliography).

4. Waterston, R.C. Adelaide Phillipps: a Record. Boston: A.
    Williams and Company, 1883. 170 p., 2 illus.

    In Europe she sang under the name of **SIGNORINA FILIPPI.**

C0488.
PHILLIPS, HENRY. English Bass. b. August 13, 1801, Bristol; d.
November 8, 1876, London.

1. GROVE 6/14 (Bibliography).

3. Phillips, Henry. Hints on Declamation. London. 1848.

    No copy located.

Phillips, Henry. <u>Musical and Personal Recollections during Half a Century</u>. 2 vols. London: Charles J. Skeet, 1864. 316 p., portrait; 325 p.

C0489.
PICCAVER, ALFRED. English Tenor. b. February 25, 1884, Long Sutton, Lincolnshire; d. September 23, 1958, Vienna.

1. EdS 1/8 (Bibliography); GROVE 6/14.

2. GR 11/1, 16/11; OPERA 9/12; OW 7/1; RC 22/5, 6, 7.

C0490.
PICCHI, MIRTO. Italian Tenor. b. March 15, 1915, Signa, near Florence; d. September 25, 1980, Florence.

1. SCHMIDL/Supp.

3. Picchi, Mirto. <u>E lucevan le stelle</u>. Preface by Luigi Baldacci. Bologna: Edizioni Bongiovanni, 1981. 109 p., 17 illus., index of names.

C0491.
PICCOLOMINI, MARIETTA. Italian Soprano. b. March 15, 1834, Siena; d. December 23, 1899, Poggio Imperiale, near Florence.

1. EdS 1/8 (Bibliography); GROVE 6/14 (Bibliography); SCHMIDL + Supp.

4. Piccolomini, F.C. <u>Giuseppe Verdi e Marietta Piccolomini: ricordanze d'amicizia</u>. Siena: Tipografia Sociale, 1913.

No copy located.

C0492.
PILARCZYK, HELGA Katharina. German Soprano. b. March 12, 1925, Schoeningen, near Braunschweig.

1. BAKER 6; EdS/Supp.; GROVE 6/14; MGG 1/16 (Bibliography); RIEMANN 12 + Supp.

2. OPERA 13/9 [reprinted in OW, Vol. 5].

C0493.
PILOU, JEANNETTE. Greek Soprano. b. 1931, Alexandria.

1. GROVE 6/14.

2. ON 32/11; OW 8/3.

C0494.
PINZA, EZIO. Italian Bass. b. May 18, 1892, Rome; d. May 9, 1957, Stamford, Connecticut.

1. BAKER 6; EdS 1/8 (Bibliography); GROVE 6/14; RIEMANN 12 + Supp.

(Bibliography).

2. GR 14/4, 35/3; ON 10/22; OPERA 8/7; OW 9/12; RC 3/1, 26/3-4, 5-6; RNC 1/11, 12.

3. Pinza, Ezio and Robert Magidoff. Ezio Pinza, an Autobiography. New York: Reinhart & Company, Inc., 1958. Reprint 1977. xi, 307 p., 39 illus., repertoire list, index.

5. Sargeant, Winthrop. Geniuses, Goddesses and People. New York: E.P. Dutton & Company, 1949. 317 p.

C0495.
PIRKER, MARIANNE. German Soprano. b. January 27, 1717, Eschaneu bei Heilbronn; d. November 10, 1782, Eschaneu bei Heilbronn.

1. FETIS 2/7; RIEMANN 12 (Bibliography).

4. Erdmann, Gabriele. Marianne Pyrker: das Lebenslied einer Saengerin. Wuerttemberg: Karl Rohm Verlag, 1950. 300 p.

C0496.
PISARONI, BENEDETTA ROSAMONDA. Italian Soprano. b. May 16, 1793, Piacenza; d. August 6, 1872, Piacenza.

1. EdS 1/8 (Bibliography); FETIS 2/6; GROVE 6/14; RIEMANN 12; SCHMIDL.

4. Pavesi, C. Benedetta Rosamonda Pisaroni. Piacenza: Marchesetti a C., 1872.

   No copy located.

C0497.
PLANCON, POL HENRI. French Bass. b. June 12, 1851, Fumay; d. August 12, 1914, Paris.

1. BAKER 6; EdS 1/8; GROVE 6/14.

2. ON 30/15; RC 8/7-8, 10, 10/12, 12/7.

C0498.
PLISHKA, PAUL. American Bass. b. August 28, 1941, Old Forge, Pennsylvania.

1. BAKER 6; GROVE 6/15.

2. ON 33/25, 41/11.

C0499.
PONCHARD, LOUIS-ANTOINE. French Tenor. b. August 31, 1787, Paris; d. January 6, 1866, Paris.

1. EdS 1/8; SCHMIDL/Supp.

4. Méreaux, Amédée. Ponchard. Paris: Heugel et cie., 1866. 31 p.

C0500.
PONS, LILY. French Soprano. b. April 12, 1898, Draguignan; d.
February 13, 1976, Dallas, Texas.

1. BAKER 6; EdS 1/8; GROVE 6/15 (Bibliography); RIEMANN 12 + Supp.
    (Bibliography).

2. GR 11/12; ON 9/22, 20/10, 37/14, 40/19; RC 13/11-12.

5. SEE: Caro Canaille under **MARY GARDEN** (C0232).

C0501.
PONSELLE, ROSA. American Soprano. b. January 22, 1897, Meridien,
Connecticut; d. May 25, 1981, Baltimore, Maryland.

1. BAKER 6, EdS 1/8 (Bibliography); GROVE 6/15 (Bibliography);
    RIEMANN 12/Supp.

2. GR 6/12, 7/2; ON 21/7, 41/18, 46/1; OPERA 3/2, 27/3, 28/1, 32/8;
    OW 8/9; RC 5/4, 5, 12.

3. Ponselle, Rosa and James A. Drake. Ponselle: a Singer's Life.
    Forward by Luciano Pavarotti. Garden City: Doubleday & Company,
    Inc., 1982. xxv, 328 p., 49 illus., discography by Bill Park,
    radio broadcasts, index.

5. SEE: Merle Armitage under **MARY GARDEN** (C0232).

    SEE: memoir of Walter Legge by **ELISABETH SCHWARZKOPF** (C0576).

C0502.
POPOVICI-BAYREUTH, DIMITRIE. Romanian Baritone. No lexicon listing.

4. Sbârcea, George. Dimitrie Popovici-Bayreuth. "cîntăretul pribeag"
    1860-1927. Bucureşti: Editura Muzicală, 1965. 216, [6] p.,
    45 illus., notes, list of roles.

C0503.
POPP, LUCIA. Austrian Soprano. b. November 12, 1939, Bratislava.

1. GROVE 6/15; RIEMANN 12/Supp.

2. ON 31/24; OPERA 33/2; OW 13/4, 16/8, 21/10.

C0504.
POULTIER, PLACIDE ALEXANDRE GUILLAUME. French Tenor. b. May 27,
1814, Villequier; d. ?

1. FETIS 2/Supp.

2. Spalikowski, Edmond. Quelques souvenirs sur le chanteur Poultier.
    Rouen: Imprimerie Lainé, 1938. 12 p.

C0505.
PREGI, MARCELLA. Swiss Soprano. No lexicon listing.

4. Koner, Anna, ed. <u>Die Frau in Musikberuf: vom Leben und Schaffen
   Zuericher Musikerinnen</u>. Zuerich: Jean Frey A.-G., 1928. pp. 5-15.
   "Wie ich Saengerin wurde."

C0506.
PREY, HERMANN. German Baritone. b. July 11, 1928 Berlin.

1. BAKER 6; GROVE 6/15; RIEMANN 12 + Supp.

2. ON 29/8; OW 4/2, 20/6.

3. Prey, Hermann and Robert D. Abraham. <u>Premierenfieber</u>. Muenchen:
   Kindler Verlag GmbH, 1981. 371 p., 59 illus., discography, index
   of names.

C0507.
PRICE, LEONTYNE. American Soprano. b. February 10, 1927, Laurel,
Mississippi.

1. BAKER 6; EdS/Supp.; GROVE 6/15 (Bibliography); MGG 1/16 (Bibliography); RIEMANN 12/Supp.

2. GR 49/3; ON 25/13, 28/20, 40/17, 43/16, 46/10; OP 8/2-3; OW 12/5.

4. Lyon, Hugh Lee. <u>Leontyne Price: Highlights of a Prima Donna</u>.
   New York: Vantage Press, 1973. 218 p., 20 illus., principal
   events, opera debuts, discography, honors and memberships.
   pp. 192-210 "Other Black Singers at the Metropolitan Opera
   House."

5. Chotzinoff, Samuel. <u>A Little Nightmusic: Intimate Conversations
   with [7 artists]</u>.... New York: Harper & Row, 1964. 150 p.

   SEE: Charlemae Rollins under **MARIAN ANDERSON** (C0017).

C0508.
RAAFF, ANTON. German Tenor. b. May 6, 1714, Holzem, near Bonn; d. May
27, 1797 Munich.

1. BAKER 6; EdS 1/8 (Bibliography); FETIS 2/7; GROVE 6/15 (Bibliography); MGG 1/10 (Bibliography); RIEMANN 12 + Supp. (Bibliography); SCHMIDL.

4. Freiberger, Heinz. <u>Anton Raaff (1714-1797): sein Leben und Wirken
   als Beitrag zur Musikgeschichte des 18. Jahrhunderts</u>. Bonn: University Dissertation, 1929. vii, 83 p., illus., bibliography.

C0509.
RADAMSKY, SERGI. Russian Tenor. No lexicon listing.

3. Radamsky, Sergi. <u>Der verfolgte Tenor: mein Saengerleben zwischen
   Moskau and Hollywood</u>. Translated by Horst Leuchtmann. Muenchen:
   R. Piper & Co. Verlag, 1972. 276 p., 28 illus.

C0510.

RAIMONDI, GIANNI. Italian Tenor. b. April 17, 1923, Bologna.

1. BAKER 6; EdS/Supp.; GROVE 6/15 (Bibliography); RIEMANN 12/Supp.

2. GR 50/12; ON 31/15; OW 13/6, 23/1.

C0511.
RAIMONDI, RUGGERO. Italian Bass. b. October 3, 1941, Bologna.

1. GROVE 6/15; RIEMANN 12/Supp.

2. GR 51/1.

4. Segalini, Sergio. <u>Ruggero Raimondi</u>. Paris: Librairie Arthème Fayard, 1981. 95 p., 80 illus., selective chronology, discography.

C0512.
RAISA, ROSA. Polish Soprano. b. May 30, 1893, Bialystok; d. September 28, 1963, Los Angeles, California.

1. BAKER 6; EdS 1/8 (Bibliography); GROVE 6/15 (Bibliography); RIEMANN/Supp.

2. ON 25/17; OPERA 14/12.

C0513.
RALF, OSCAR GEORG. Swedish Tenor. b. October 3, 1881, Malmoe; d. April 3, 1964, Kalmar.

1. GROVE 6/15.

3. Ralf, Oscar Georg. <u>Tenoren han gar i ringen</u>. Stockholm: Albert Bonniers Foerlag, 1953. 214 p., 52 illus.

   His brother, Torsten (b. January 2, 1901, Malmoe; d. April 27, 1954, Stockholm), also a tenor, sang at the Metropolitan Opera 1945-1948. SEE: RIEMANN 12 + Supp.; OW 23/4.

C0514.
RASKIN, JUDITH. American Soprano. b. June 21, 1928, New York City.

1. BAKER 6; GROVE 6/15.

2. ON 30/2, 11, 33/17.

C0515.
REDDISH, META. American Soprano. b. 1890?, Wyoming, New York; d. ? No lexicon listing.

4. Reddish, Claude. <u>A Chronicle of Memories</u>. Miami: privately printed for the author, 1950. 253 p., 14 illus.

C0516.
REDONDO, MARCOS. Spanish Baritone. b. 1893. No lexicon listing.

4. Marcos Redondo un hombre que se va. Barcelona: Editorial Planeta,
   S.A., 1973. 312 p., 49 illus.

C0517.
REEVES, JOHN SIMS. English Tenor. b. September 26, 1818, Shooter's
Hill, Kent; d. October 25, 1900, Worthing.

1. BAKER 6 (Bibliography); EdS 1/8 (Bibliography); GROVE 6/15;
   SCHMIDL.

2. GR 4/7.

3. Reeves, John Sims. My Jubilee or Fifty Years of Artistic Life.
   London: The London Music Publishing Company, Limited, 1889.
   viii, 280 p., 6 illus., index.

   Reeves, John Sims. The Art of Singing. London: Chappell & Co.,
   Ltd., 1900. 46 p., illus.

   Reeves, John Sims. The Life of Sims Reeves by Himself. London:
   Simpkin Marshall & Co., 1888. 279 p., portrait.

4. Edwards, H. Sutherland. The Life and Artistic Career of Sims
   Reeves. London: Tinsley Bros., 1881. 80 p., portrait.

   Pearce, Charles E. Sims Reeves: Fifty Years of Music in England.
   London: Stanley Paul & Co., Ltd., 1924. Reprint 1980. 315 p., 16
   illus., index of names.

   Corrects much of the inaccurate material found in the singer's
   own writings.

C0518.
REISSENBERGER-UMLING, ADELE. German Soprano. b. September 26, 1882,
Kelling; d. April 14, 1933, Hermannstadt. No lexicon listing.

4. Reissenberger, Albert, ed. Adele Reissenberger-Umling: Konzert-
   und Oratoriensaengerin, Gesangspaedagogin. Hermannstadt-Sibiu:
   privately printed, 1934. 136 p., 13 illus.

C0519.
RENAUD, MAURICE. French Baritone. b. July 24, 1861, Bordeaux; d.
October 16, 1933, Paris.

1. BAKER 6; EdS 1/8; GROVE 6/15 (Bibliography); SCHMIDL.

2. RC 11/4-5, 7, 12/1-2.

C0520.
RESNIK, REGINA. American Mezzo-Soprano. b. August 30, 1922, New York
City.

1. BAKER 6; GROVE 6/15 (Bibliography); RIEMANN 12/Supp.

2. ON 26/16, 28/20, 31/7; OPERA 14/1, 16/3; OW 3/3.

C0521.
RETHBERG, ELISABETH. German Soprano. b. September 22, 1894,
Schwarzenberg; d. June 6, 1976, Yorktown Heights, New York.

1. BAKER 6; EdS 1/8 (Bibliography); GROVE 6/15 (Bibliography); MGG
    1/11, 1/16 (Bibliography); RIEMANN 12 + Supp.; SCHMIDL/Supp.

2. GR 13/8; ON 28/14, 41/3; OW 9/7; RC 3/2, 4, 4/11, 5/1, 8/1.

4. Henschel, Horst and Ehrhard Friedrich. Elisabeth Rethberg: ihr
    Leben und Kuenstlertum. Schwarzenberg/Sa.: Verlag: Staedtischer
    Geschichtsverein, 1928. Reprint 1977. 119, [1] p., 19 illus.

C0522.
RICCIARELLI, KATIA. Italian Soprano. b. January 16, 1946, Rovigo.

1. GROVE 6/15.

2. ON 44/14; OW 14/6.

C0523.
RIDDERBUSCH, KARL. German Bass. b. May 29, 1932, Recklinghausen.

1. GROVE 6/15; RIEMANN 12/Supp.

2. OW 9/10, 15/4.

C0524.
RIDER-KELSEY, CORRINE. American Soprano. b. February 24, 1877, near
Batavia, New York; d. July 10, 1947, Toledo, Ohio.

1. BAKER 6.

4. Reed, Lynnel. Be Not Afraid: Biography of Madame Rider-Kelsey.
    New York: Vantage Press, 1955. 168 p., portrait.

5. David, Elizabeth Harbison. I Played Their Accompaniments. New
    York: D. Appleton-Century Company, 1940. vi, 246 p., 14 illus.,
    index.

    Important material on Rider-Kelsey and Schumann-Heink.

C0525.
ROBESON, PAUL. American Bass. b. April 9, 1898, Princeton, New
Jersey; d. January 23, 1976, Philadelphia, Pennsylvania.

1. BAKER 6; EdS 1/8(Bibliography); GROVE 6/16; RIEMANN 12/Supp.
    (Bibliography).

2. GR 6/4.

3. Robeson, Paul. Forge Negro-Labor Unity for Peace and Jobs. New
    York: Harlem Trade Union Council, 1950. 15 p.

    Robeson, Paul. Here I Stand. London: Dennis Dobson, 1958. 128 p.

4. Davis, Lenwood G. A Paul Robeson Research Guide: a Selected, Annotated Bibliography. Westport: Greenwood Press, 1982. xxv, 879 p., portrait, discography, filmography, list of perform- ances, monuments and memorials, manuscript materials, index.

Days with Paul Robeson. Berlin: Der Deutsche Friedensrat, 1961. 36 p., 38 illus.

A record of his October 1960 visit to the DDR.

Dent, Roberta Yancy, ed. Paul Robeson: Tributes, Selected Writings. New York: Paul Robeson Archives, 1976. 112 p., illus.

Foner, Philip S., ed. Paul Robeson Speaks: Writings, Speeches, Interviews, 1918-1974. Larchmont: Brunner/Mazel Publishers, 1978. xvii, 623 p., illus., bibliography, index.

Gilliam, Dorothy Butler. Paul Robeson: All-American. New York: New Republic Book Company, 1976. 216 p., illus., bibliography, index.

Graham, Shirley. Paul Robeson Citizen of the World. New York: Julian Messner, Inc., 1946. Reprint 1971. viii, 264 p., 17 illus., 13-item bibliography, index.

Greenfield, Eloise. Paul Robeson. New York: Thomas Y. Crowell, 1975. 32 p., illus.

Hamilton, Virginia. Paul Robeson: the Life and Times of a Free Black Man. New York: Harper & Row, 1974. xvi, 217 p., illus., bibliography, index.

Hoyt, Edwin P. Paul Robeson: the American Othello. New York: The World Publishing Company, 1967. ix, 228 p.

Nazel, Joseph. Paul Robeson: Biography of a Proud Man. Los Angeles: Holloway House, 1980. 216 p., bibliography.

Paul Robeson: the Great Forerunner. New York: Dodd, Mead, 1978. x, 383 p., illus., bibliography, index.

Compiled by the editors of Freedomways magazine and based upon a special issue published in 1971.

Robeson, Eslanda Goode. Paul Robeson, Negro. New York: Harper & Brothers, 1930. 178 p., 15 illus.

Robeson, Susan. The Whole World in His Hands: a Pictorial Biog- raphy of Paul Robeson. Secaucus [New Jersey]: Citadel Press, 1981. 254 p., numerous illustrations, notes.

Susan is the artist's granddaughter.

Salute to Paul Robeson Journal. New York: n.p., 1973. 48 p.

Biographical souvenir journal prepared for the Carnegie Hall celebration of Robeson's 75th birthday.

Schlosser, Anatole I. Paul Robeson: His Career in the Theater, in
Motion Pictures, and on the Concert Stage. New York University
Dissertation, 1970. viii, 480 p.

Seton, Marie. Paul Robeson. London: Dennis Dobson, 1958. 254 p.,
13 illus., index.

Wright, Charles H. Robeson: Labor's Forgotten Champion. Detroit:
Balamp Publishing, 1975. vii, 171 p., illus., bibliography, index.

5. SEE: Arnold Dobrin under MARIAN ANDERSON (C0017).

    SEE: Ben Albert Richardson under MARIAN ANDERSON (C0017).

    SEE: Charlemae Rollins under MARIAN ANDERSON (C0017).

    Miers, Earl Schenck. Big Ben, a Novel. Philadelphia: The West-
    minster Press, 1942. xiii, 238 p., illus.

C0526.
ROBIN, MADO. French Soprano. b. December 29. 1918, Yseures-sur-
Creuse, near Tours; d. December 10, 1960, Paris.

1. RIEMANN 12/Supp.

2. RC 19/9-10.

4. Jacqueton, Henry. Biographical Notes and Sketches on Mado Robin.
    Paris: Decca, 1952. 6 p.

    There is an MS translation by Robert Parylak (New York, 1965).

    Jacqueton, Henry. Mado Robin. Paris: Sodal, 1966. 32 p., 20
    illus., discography.

C0527.
ROESLER, ENDRE. Hungraian Tenor. b. November 24, 1904, Budapest;
d. December 13, 1963, Budapest.

1. GROVE 6/16.

4. Várnai, Péter. Roesler Endre. Budapest: Zenemuekiadó, 1969.
    80 p., 35 illus., list of roles, 2 LP records.

C0528.
ROGER, GUSTAVE-HIPPOLYTE. French Tenor. December 17, 1815, La
Chapelle St.-Denis, near Paris; d. September 12, 1879, Paris.

1. BAKER 6; EdS 1/8 (Bibliography); FETIS 2/7 + Supp. (Bibliography);
    GROVE 6/16 (Bibliography).

3. Roger, Gustave-Hippolyte. Le carnet d'un ténor. deuxieme édition.

Paris: Paul Ollendorff, Editeur, 1880. xxviii, x, 348 p., portrait.

4. <u>Les grands et les petits hommes du jour: portraits et scènes d'intérieur de nos contemporains. roger.</u> Paris: Poujaud de Laroche, Editeur, n.d. 16 p., portrait.

C0529.
ROGERS, CLARA KATHLEEN. English Soprano. b. January 14, 1844, Cheltenham; d. March 8, 1831, Boston.

1. BAKER 6.

3. Rogers, Clara Kathleen. <u>Clearcut Speech in Song</u>. Boston: Oliver Ditson Company, 1927. 102 p., illus., bibliography.

A large collection of memorabilia was given to Harvard College in 1930.

Rogers, Clara Kathleen. <u>English Diction for Singers and Speakers</u>. Boston: privately printed, 1912. ix, 105 p.

Rogers, Clara Kathleen. <u>Memories of a Musical Career</u>. Boston: Little, Brown, and Company, 1919. xvi, 503 p., 10 illus., index.

NOTE: 500 copies of this were privately printed at the Plimpton Press in 1932 as a Memorial Edition.

Rogers, Clara Kathleen. <u>The Philosophy of Singing</u>. New York: Harper, 1893. xv, 218 p., illus.

Rogers, Clara Kathleen. <u>The Story of Two Lives: Home, Friends, and Travels</u>. Norwood: privately printed, 1932. xvii, 348 p., 19 illus., index.

500 copies privately printed at the Plimpton Press in 1932 as a "Sequence" to the previous entry. Memorial Edition. "printed from type and type distributed." The book was written before her death.

Rogers, Clara Kathleen. <u>My Voice and I or the Relation of the Singer to the Song</u>. Chicago: A.C. McClurg & Co., 1910. xiv, 265 p., portrait.

NOTE: She published Two other books on singing, neither of which I have seen: <u>The Voice in Speech</u>; <u>Your Voice and You (What the Singer should do): a Practical Application of Psychology to Singing</u>. Boston: Oliver Ditson Co., n.d. [c.1925].

C0530.
ROSENBLATT, YOSSELE. Hungarian Cantor. b. 1882; d. June 18, 1933, Jerusalem. No lexicon listing.

4. Rosenblatt, Samuel. <u>Yossele Rosenblatt: the Story of His Life as told by his Son</u>. New York: Farrar, Straus and Young, 1954. ix, 372 p., glossary, discography.

C0531.
ROSSI-LEMENI, NICOLA. Italian Bass. b. November 6, 1920, Istanbul.

1. BAKER 6; EdS 1/8; GROVE 6/16 (Bibliography); RIEMANN 12 + Supp.

2. ON 18/4.

3. Rossi-Lemeni, Nicola. Oltrè l'angoscia. Rome: privately printed,
   1972. 55 p.

   Edition of 600 copies.

C0532.
ROSWAENGE, HELGE. Danish Tenor. b. August 29, 1897, Copenhagen; d.
June 19, 1972, Munich.

1. BAKER 6; GROVE 6/16; RIEMANN 12 + Supp. (Bibliography).

2. ON 31/19; OW 13/8, 21/1; RC 23/5-6, 25/5-6, 26/9-10.

3. Roswaenge, Helge. Leitfaden fuer Gesangsbeflissene: eine heitere
   Plauderei ueber ernste Dinge. Meunchen: Bei Obpacher, 1964. 51,
   [1] p., 9 illus.

   This was translated by James Dennis as: Guidelines for Aspiring
   Singers. Ipswich: Calver Press, n.d. 32 p., illus.

   NOTE: There is also an MS translation in English by the late
   George L. Nyklicek.

   Roswaenge, Helge. Mach es besser mein Sohn: ein Tenor erzaehlt
   aus seinem Leben. zweite auflage. Leipzig: Koehler & Amelang,
   1963. 234 p., 44 illus.

   Roswaenge, Helge. Skratta pajazzo. Stockholm: Mendens Foerlags
   Aktiebolag, 1945. 332 p., 27 illus.

   The German edition, Lache Bajazzo; ernstes und heiteres aus meinem
   Leben. Muenchen, 1953, is perhaps better known. There is an MS
   translation in English by the late George L. Nyklicek.

4. Tassie, Franz. Helge Rosvaenge. Augsburg: Schroff-Druck Verlags-
   gellschaft mbH, 1975. 216 p., 60 illus., complete list of roles
   including theater and year, discography.

C0533.
ROTHENBERGER, ANNELIESE. German Soprano. b. June 19, 1924, Mannheim.

1. BAKER 6; GROVE 6/16; RIEMANN 12 + Supp.

2. ON 25/11; OW 4/9, 6/5.

3. Rothenberger, Anneliese. Melodie meines Lebens: Selbsterlebtes,
   Selbsterzaehltes. Muenchen: Lichtenberg Verlag, 1972. 192 p.,
   19 illus., discography, list of roles, important dates' register.

4. von Lewinski, Wolf-Eberhard. Anneliese Rothenberger. Velber:
    Friedrich Verlag, 1968. 104 p., 43 illus., discography, reper-
    toire list.

C0534.
RUBINI, GIOVANNI BATTISTA. Italian Tenor. b. April 7, 1794, Romano,
near Bergamo; d. March 3, 1854, Romano.

1. BAKER 6; EdS 1/8 (Bibliography); FETIS 2/7 + Supp.; GROVE 6/16
    (Bibliography); MGG 1/11; RIEMANN 12; SCHMIDL + Supp.

2. ON 33/14, 46/12, 47/2; OPERA 30/4.

3. Rubini, Giovanni Battista. 12 lezioni de canto moderno per tenore
    o soprano. Milano: G. Ricordi, n.d.

    No copy located.

4. Gara, Eugenio. Giovan Battista Rubini nel centenario della morte
    (7 aprile 1794 - 3 marzo 1854). Bergamo: Industrie Grafiche
    Cattaneo, 1968. 35 p.

    Locatelli, Agostino. Cenni biografici sulla straordinaria carriera
    teatrale percorsa da Gio. Battista Rubini da Romano: cantante di
    camera. Milano: F. Colombo, 1844. 88 p.

    Traini, Carlo. Il cigno di romano: Giovan Battista Rubini, re dei
    tenori. Bergamo: Tipografia Scuole Professionale Orfanotrofio M.,
    1954. 204 p., 12 illus.

5. SEE: Alexander Weatherson under **GIUDITTA GRISI** (C0257).

C0535.
RUFFO, TITTA. Italian Baritone. b. June 9, 1877, Pisa; d. July 5,
1953, Florence.

1. BAKER 6; EdS 1/8 (Bibliography); GROVE 6/16; RIEMANN 12 + Supp.

2. GR 6/5, 6; ON 31/24; RC 2/5, 6/6.

3. Ruffo, Titta. La mia parabola: memorie. seconda edizione. Milano:
    Fratelli Treves Editori, 1937. Reprint 1977 with discography by
    W.R. Moran. 371 p., 18 illus.

    Ruffo, Titta. La mia parabola: memorie. "a cura del figlio Ruffo
    Titta, Jr.". Roma: Staderini, 1977. xviii, 444 p., illus., notes,
    chronology of performances, repertoire, discography, bibliography,
    index.

    Several MS translations in English of the original exist. BAKER 5
    mentions a sequel in MS which has not been published.

4. Arnosi, Eduardo. Titta Ruffo, el titán de los barítonos. Buenos
    Aires: Ayer y Hoy de la Opera, 1977. 30 p., illus.

Barrenechea, Mariano Antonio. <u>Titta Ruffo: notas de psicológia artística</u>. Buenos Aires: Edicion de la revista <u>Música</u>, 1911. 137 p., 2 illus.

Reprinted in <u>Historia estetica de la musica</u>. tercera edicion. Buenos Aires: Editorial Claridad, 1963 [1st edition 1941] .

<u>Biografiá i juicio crítico de Titta Ruffo</u>. Madrid: P. Pérez de Velasco, 1912. 71 p.

Contreras, Vicente. <u>Titta Ruffo y su arte</u>. Madrid: Castro y Compania, 1910. 148 p., index.

Text in Italian and Spanish.

Farkas, Andrew, ed. <u>Titta Ruffo, an Anthology</u>. Forward by Tito Gobbi. Westport: Greenwood Press, 1984. xii, 289 p., 24 illus., chronology, repretoire, theaters, discography by William R. Moran, 94-item bibliography, index of names.

Fifteen colleagues undertake a chapter each.

5. SEE: autobiography of **GEORGE CUNELLI** (C0135).

Pérez Lugín, Alejandro. <u>De Titta Ruffo a la fons pasando machaquito: notas de un reporter</u>. Madrid: n.p., 1912. 227 p., numerous illus.

SEE: memoir of Walter Legge by **ELISABETH SCHWARZKOPF** (C0576).

C0536.
RUSS, GIANNINA. Italian Soprano. b. 1878, Lodi; d. February 28, 1951, Milan.

1. EdS 1/8; SCHMIDL (under Russ-Ceri).

2. RC 27/4-5, 11-12.

C0537.
RUSSELL, HENRY. English Baritone. b. December 24, 1812, Sheerness; d. December 8, 1900, London.

1. BAKER 6; GROVE 6/16 (Bibliography); SCHMIDL/Supp.

3. Russell, Henry. <u>Cheer! Boys, Cheer: Memories of Men & Music</u>. London: John Macqueen, 1895. 276 p., portrait.

He is thought to have written a book on singing, <u>L'amico dei cantanti</u>, but I have been unable to trace a copy.

4. Stephens, J.A. <u>Henry Russell in America: Chutzpah and Huzzah</u>. Urbana: University of Illinois Dissertation, 1975.

C0538.
RYSANEK, LEONIE. Austrian Soprano. b. November 14, 1926, Vienna.

1. BAKER 6; EdS/Supp.; GROVE 6/16 (Bibliography); RIEMANN 12 (under Rysanek-Grossmann); RIEMANN 12/Supp. (Bibliography).

2. ON 27/13, 29/17, 35/12, 41/14, 42/19, 44/13, 46/5; OW 3/12, 13/1, 15/8.

C0539.
SADKO, KONSTANTIN. Russian Tenor. No lexicon listing.

3. Sadko, Konstantin. Das Leben ist koestlich: eine fahrender Saenger erzaehlt. Tuebingen: Katzmann-Verlag, 1951. 340 p., portrait.

C0540.
SAINT-HUBERTY, ANTOINETTE. French Soprano. b. December 15, 1756, Strasbourg; d. July 22, 1812, London.

1. EdS 1/8 (Bibliography); FETIS 2/7; GROVE 6/16 (Bibliography); RIEMANN 12 + Supp.; SCHMIDL.

4. de Goncourt, Edmond. Madame Saint-Huberty d'après sa corres- pondance et ses papiers de famille. Paris: Bibliothèque Charpentier, 1900. Reprint 1969. viii, 319 p.

5. SEE: H. Noel Williams under **SOPHIE ARNOULD** (C0020).

C0541.
SALAZAR, MELICO [Manuel]. Costa Rican Tenor. b. January 3, 1887, San José; d. August 6, 1950, San José. No lexicon listing.

1. KUTSCH 3.

4. Mendez, Manuel Segura. Melico. San José: Editorial Costa Rica, 1965. 172, [1], [20] p., 21 illus., list of roles.

C0542.
SALICOLA, MARGHERITA. Italian Soprano. b. 1660, Bologna; d. 1717, Bologna.

1. MENDEL 1/9 (Bibliography); SCHMIDL (Bibliography).

4. Ademollo, Alessandro. "Le cantanti italiane celebri del secolo decimottavo: Margherita Salicola." In Nuova antologia 22 (1889): 526-553.

C0543.
SAMMARCO, GIUSEPPE MARIO. Italian Baritone. b. December 13, 1868, Palermo; d. January 24, 1930, Milan.

1. BAKER 6; EdS 1/8 (Bibliography); GROVE 6/16 (Bibliography); SCHMIDL + Supp.

2. GR 29/5.

C0544.
SANDERSON, SIBYL. American Soprano. b. December 7, 1865, Sacramento,

California; d. May 15, 1903, Paris.

1. BAKER 6; GROVE 6/16; SCHMIDL.

2. ON 40/7, 42/12.

CO545.
SANDOR, ERZSI. Hungarian Soprano. b. 1885, Kolosvár; d. 1962, Budapest. No lexicon listing.

1. KUTSCH 3.

4. Balassa, Imre. Sándor Erzsi. Budapest: Zenemuekiadó, 1968. 96 p., 23 illus., list of roles, 2 LP records.

CO546.
SANTLEY, CHARLES. English Baritone. b. February 28, 1834, Liverpool; d. September 22, 1922, Hove, near London.

1. BAKER 6; EdS 1/8 (Bibliography); FETIS 2/Supp.; GROVE 6/16; SCHMIDL.

3. Santley, Charles. Reminiscences of My Life. London: Isaac Pitman & Sons, Ltd., 1909. Reprint 1977 with discography by W.R. Moran. xiv, 319 p., 14 illus., index.

   Santley, Charles. Student and Singer: the Reminiscences of Charles Santley. new edition. London: Edward Arnold, 1893 [1st edition New York, 1892]. xvii, 358 p., portrait.

   Santley, Charles. The Art of Singing and Vocal Declamation. New York: The Macmillan Company, 1908. xvi, 143 p.

   Includes reminiscences.

4. Levien, John Mewburn. Sir Charles Santley. London: Novello & Company, Ltd., n.d. [c.1927]. 27 p., 3 illus.

5. SEE: M. Sterling Mackinlay under **MANUEL PATRICIO GARCIA** (CO231).

CO547.
SAYAO, BIDU. Brazilian Soprano. b. May 11, 1902, Niteroi, near Rio de Janeiro.

1. BAKER 6; EdS 1/8 (Bibliography); GROVE 6/16 (Bibliography); RIEMANN 12 + Supp.

2. ON 29/8, 41/17; RC 13/6; 16/2; RNC 2/11.

CO548.
SCHAETZLER, FRITZ. German Baritone. b. ? Nuernberg. No lexicon listing.

4. Schaetzler, Ernst. Nun erst Recht! Ein Schwerverwundeter geht zur

Buehne: Lebensbericht von Ernst Schaetzler. Berlin: Deutschen Verlag, 1943. 179 p., 36 illus.

A wartime morale builder.

CO549.
SCHEBEST, AGNESE. Austrian Mezzo-Soprano. b. February 10, 1813, Vienna; d. December 22, 1869, Stuttgart.

1. BAKER 6.

3. Schebest, Agnese. Aus dem Leben einer Kuenstlerin. Stuttgart: Verlag von Ebner & Seubert, 1857. viii, 304 p., portrait.

4. Heusler, Irma. Agnese Schebest, ein Kuenstlerleben: zum hundert-sten Todestag. n.p.: privately printed, 1970. 73 p., 23 illus.

CO550.
SCHEIDEMANTEL KARL. German Baritone. b. January 21, 1859, Weimar; d. June 26, 1923, Weimar.

1. BAKER 6; EdS 1/8 (Bibliography); GROVE 6/16 (Bibliography); MGG 1/11; RIEMANN 12 (Bibliography); SCHMIDL.

2. RC 5/11.

3. Scheidemantel, Karl. Stimmbildung. dritte unveraenderte auflage. Leipzig: Druck und Verlag Breitkopf & Haertel, 1910 [1st edition c.1908]. 85 p., musical examples.

4. Trede, Paul. Karl Scheidemantel. Dresden-Blasewitz, C. Reissner, 1911. 79 p., illus.

CO551.
SCHELBLE, JOHANN NEPOMUK. German Baritone. b. May 16, 1789, Huefingen; d. August 6, 1837, Huefingen.

1. BAKER 6; MGG 1/11 (Bibliography); RIEMANN 12 + Supp. (Bibliog-raphy).

4. Bormann, Oskar. Johann Nepomuk Schelble 1789-1837: sein Leben, sein Wirken und seine Werke. Ein Beitrag zur Musikgeschichte in Frankfurt am Main. Frankfurt/M.: university dissertation, 1926. 145 p.

CO552.
SCHIAVAZZI, PIETRO. Italian Tenor. b. March 14, 1875, Cagliari, Sardinia; d. May 25, 1949, Rome.

1. EdS 1/8 (Bibliography); SCHMIDL + Supp.

2. RNC 5/1.

3. Schiavazzi, Pietro. Pietro Schiavazzi racconta! Roma, 1936.

Although mentioned by several authors, no copy has surfaced.

C0553.
SCHICK, MARGARETE LUISE. German Soprano. b. April 26, 1773, Mainz;
d. April 29, 1809, Berlin.

1. BAKER 6; GROVE 6/16 (Bibliography); RIEMANN 12 + Supp.

4. Levezow, Konrad. Leben und Kunst der Frau Margarete Luise Schick,
    gebornen Hamel, Koenigl. Preuss. Kammersaengerin mitgliedes des
    Nationaltheaters zu Berlin. Berlin: Duncker und Humblot, 1809.
    75 p., portrait.

C0554.
SCHIØTZ, AKSEL. Danish Tenor. b. September 1, 1906, Roskilde; d.
April 19, 1975, Copenhagen.

1. BAKER 6; GROVE 6/16.

3. Schiøtz, Gerd and Aksel Schiøtz. Kunst og kamp. København:
    Westermann, 1951. 238 p., 76 illus., discography.

    Schiøtz, Aksel. The Singer and His Art. Preface by Gerald Moore.
    New York: Harper & Row, Publishers, 1970. xix, 215 p., recommended
    listening, discography, 40-item bibliography, index.

4. Rosenberg, Herbert. Aksel Schiøtz: a Discography. Copenhagen:
    Nationaldiskoteket, 1966. 48 p., index.

C0555.
SCHIPA, TITO. Italian Tenor. b. January 2, 1889, Lecce; d. December
16, 1965, New York City.

1. BAKER 6; EdS 1/8 (Bibliography); GROVE 6/16; RIEMANN 12 + Supp.
    (Bibliography); SCHMIDL + Supp.

2. GR 5/12; RC 13/4-5.

3. Schipa, Tito. Si confessa. Roma: Pubblimusica, 1961. 107 p.,
    discography by Raffaele Vegeto.

4. Celletti, Rodolfo. Tito Schipa: a Biographical and Critical
    Sketch. London: The Gramophone Company, n.d. [1961]. 16, [2]
    p., 2 illus., recording details.

    One of a series of pamphlets for "Great Recordings of the
    Century."

    D'Andrea, Renzo. Tito Schipa nella vita, nell'arte, nel suo
    tempo. Fasano di Puglia: privately printed, 1981. 246 p., 49
    illus., discography by Daniele Rubboli.

C0556.
SCHLOSS, SOPHIE. German Mezzo-Soprano. b. December 12, 1822, Cologne;
d. May ?, 1903, Cologne.

1. SCHMIDL.

4. Tank, Ulrich. Die geschwister Schloss: Studien zur Biographie der
    Koelner Altistin Sophie Schloss (1822-1903) und zur Geschichte des
    Musikalienverlages ihres Bruders Michael (1823-1891). Koeln: A.
    Volk-Verlag, 1976. 97 p., bibliographic references.

CO557.
SCHLUSNUS, HEINRICH. German Baritone. b. August 6, 1888, Braubach;
d. June 18, 1952, Frankfurt/M.

1. BAKER 6; GROVE 6/16 (Bibliography); MGG 1/16 (Bibliography);
    RIEMANN 12 + Supp (Bibliography).

2. GR 17/5; OW 13/6; RNC 3/4, 5, 6, 9, 11; RS 13 (Summer 1959),
    14 (Autumn 1959), 15-16 (Spring 1960).

3. Schlusnus, Heinrich. Plauderein um Heinrich Schlusnus. Berlin:
    Selbstverlag, 1935. 48 p., 39 illus.

4. von Nasso, Eckart and Annemay Schlusnus. Heinrich Schlusnus.
    Mensch und Saenger. Hamburg: Wolfgang Krueger Verlag, 1957.
    335 p., 23 illus.

    SEE: Mueller and Mertz under **KARL ERB** (CO184).

CO558.
SCHMEDES, ERIK. Danish Tenor. b. August 27, 1868, Gentofte, near
Copenhagen; d. March 21, 1931, Vienna.

1. BAKER 6; EdS 1/8 (Bibliography); GROVE 6/16 (Bibliography);
    RIEMANN 12 + Supp.; SCHMIDL.

2. OPERA 4/1; RC 27/1-2.

CO559.
SCHMIDT, JOSEPH. Romanian Tenor. b. March 4, 1904 Bavideni, Bukovina;
d. November 16, 1942, Zurich.

1. BAKER 6; RIEMANN 12/Supp.

2. RNC 2/4, 12.

4. Ney-Nowotny, Karl and Gertrude Ney-Nowotny. Joseph Schmidt: das
    Leben und Sterben eines Unvergesslichen. Wien: Europaeischer
    Verlag, 1962. 190 p., 50 illus.

    Takes great exception to Carl Ritter's biography.

    Ritter, Carl [pseud. for Carl Rosenfelder]. Ein Lied geht um die
    Welt: ein Joseph Schmidt-Buch. Rottenburg ob der Tauber: Verlag J.
    P. Peter, Gebr. Holstein, 1961. 221 p., 7 illus., discography.

CO560.
SCHNEIDER, HORTENSE. French Soprano. b. April 30, 1833, Bordeaux;

d. May 6, 1920, Paris.

1. EdS 1/8; GROVE 6/16 (Bibliography); MGG 1/11; RIEMANN 12/Supp.
   (Bibliography).

4. Rouff, Marcel and Therese Casevitz. La vie de fête sous le second
   empire Hortense Schneider. Paris: Editions Jules Tallandier,
   1931. 221 p.

5. Loliée, Frederic. The Gilded Beauties of the Second Empire.
   Translated and edited by Bryan O'Donnell. London: John Long,
   Limited, 1909. xvi, 330 p., 42 illus., index.

C0561.
SCHNORR von CAROLSFELD, LUDWIG. German Tenor. b. July 2, 1836,
Munich; d. July 21, 1865, Dresden.

1. BAKER 6; EdS 1/8 (Bibliography); GROVE 6/16 (Bibliography); MGG
   1/11 (Bibliography); RIEMANN 12 + Supp. (Bibliography); SCHMIDL.

4. Garrigues, C.H.N. De første fortolkere af Richard Wagners
   "Tristan" og "Isolde" aegteparret Ludwig og Malvina Schnorr von
   Carolsfeld. København: I komission hos V. Tryde, 1914. 15 p.,
   illus.

   Garrigues, C.H.N. Ein ideales Saengerpaar Ludwig Schnorr von
   Carolsfeld und Malvina Schnorr von Carolsfeld geborene Garrigues:
   zwei in einander verwobene Lebensbilder, nach eigenen und zeit-
   genoessischen Briefen, Tagebuchblaettern, Lebenserinnerungen und
   Berichten geschildert. Kopenhagen: Levin & Munksgaard, 1937.
   493 p., 32 illus., 58-item bibliography, register of names.

5. Schure, Edouard. Souvenirs sur Richard Wagner: la premiere de
   Tristan et Iseult. Paris: Perrin et cie, 1900.

   No copy located.

   Wagner, Richard. Gesammelte Schriften und Dichtungen. vol. 3.
   Edited by Wolfgang Golter. Berlin: Deutsches Verlagshaus Bong &
   Co. pp. 177-194, "Meine erinnerungen an Ludwig Schnorr von
   Carolsfeld."

C0562.
SCHNORR von CAROLSFELD, MALVINA. French Soprano. b. December 7, 1832,
Copenhagen; d. February 8, 1904, Karlsruhe.

1. BAKER 6; EdS 1/8 (Bibliography); GROVE 6/16 (Bibliography); MGG
   1/11 (Bibliography); RIEMANN 12 + Supp. (Bibliography); SCHMIDL.

4. Garrigues, C.H.N. De første fortolkere af Richard Wagners
   "Tristan" og "Isolde" aegteparret Ludwig of Malvina Schnorr von
   Carolsfeld. København: I komission hos V. Tryde, 1914. 15 p.,
   illus.

   Garrigues, C.H.N. Ein ideales Saengerpaar Ludwig Schnorr von

Carolsfeld and Malvina Schnorr von Carolsfeld geborene Garrigues:
zwei in einander verwobene Lebensbilder, nach eigenen und zeit-
genoessischen Breifen, Tagebuchblaettern, Lebenserinnerungen und
Berichten geschildert. Kopenhagen: Levin & Munksgaard, 1937.
493 p., 32 illus., 58-item bibliography, register of names.

5. Schuré, Edouard. Souvenirs sur Richard Wagner: la premiere de
Tristan et Iseult. Paris: Perrin et cie, 1900.

No copy located.

C0563.
SCHOCK, RUDOLF JOHANN. German Tenor. b. September 4, 1915, Duisburg.

1. RIEMANN 12.

4. Herzfeld, Friedrich. Rudolf Schock. Berlin: Rembrandt Verlag,
1962. 61 p., 32 illus.

C0564.
SCHOEFFLER, PAUL. German Bass. b. July 15, 1897, Dresden; d. November
22, 1977, Amersham, England.

1. BAKER 6; EdS 1/8 (Bibliography); GROVE 6/16 (Bibliography. birth
month discrepency); RIEMANN 12.

2. ON 28/18.

4. Christian, Hans. Paul Schoeffler: versuch einer Wuerdigung. Wien:
Oesterreichischer Bundesverlag fuer Unterricht, Wissenschaft und
Kunst, 1967. 40 p., 9 illus., list of roles, discography.

C0565.
SCHOENE, LOTTE. Austrian Soprano. b. December 15, 1891, Vienna; d.
December 23, 1977, Paris.

1. GROVE 6/16.

2. RC 20/4; RNC 5/9, 10.

C0566.
SCHOEN-RENE, ANNA EUGENIE. German Soprano. b. January 12, 1864,
Coblenz; d. November 13, 1942, New York City.

1. BAKER 6.

3. Schoen-Rene, Anna Eugénie. America's Musical Inheritance:
Memories and Reminiscences. New York: G.P. Putnam's Sons, 1941.
xi, 244 p., 18 illus., index.

The teacher of RISE STEVENS (C0617) and JULIUS HUEHN (C0296)
among others. This title is also listed as B130 because of the
breadth of its contents. A student of Pauline Viardot-Garcia,
she was a noted singer in her own right prior to teaching.

C0567.
SCHORR, FRIEDRICH. Hungarian Baritone. b. September 2, 1888,
Nagyvarad; d. August 14, 1953, Farmington, Connecticut.

1. BAKER 6; EdS 1/8; GROVE 6/16 (Bibliography); RIEMANN 12.

2. GR 31/5; ON 7/19, 9/7; OPERA 4/11, 16/5; RC 19/11-12, 20/3;
   RS 8 (Spring 1958).

C0568.
von SCHOULTZ, JOHANNA. No lexicon listing.

4. Andersson, Otto Emanuel. Johanna von Schoultz: i sol och skugga.
   Abo: Foerlaget Bro, 1939. 216 p., 40 illus., index of names.

C0569.
SCHREIER, PETER. German Tenor. b. July 29, 1935, Meissen.

1. GROVE 6/16 (Bibliography); MGG 1/16 (Bibliography); RIEMANN 12/
   Supp. (Bibliography).

2. ON 32/10; OW 7/5, 14/11, 18/5.

4. Schmiedel, Gottfried. Peter Schreier. Leipzig: Deutscher Verlag
   fuer Musik, 1976. 73 p., illus., discography.

   Schmiedel, Gottfried. Peter Schreier: eine Bildbiographie.
   Berlin: Henschelverlag, 1979. 174 p., 124 illus., career highlights, repertoire list, list of accompanists and conductors,
   discography.

C0570.
SCHROEDER-DEVRIENT, WILHELMINE. German Soprano. b. December 6, 1804,
Hamburg; d. January 26, 1860, Coburg.

1. BAKER 6; EdS 1/8 (Bibliography); FETIS 2/7 + Supp.; GROVE 6/16
   (Bibliography); MGG 1/12 (Bibliography); RIEMANN 12 + Supp.
   (Bibliography); SCHMIDL.

2. ON 24/18.

4. Bab, Julius. Die Devrients: Geschichte einer Deutschen Theater-
   Familie. Berlin: Verlag von Georg Stilke, 1932. vii, 360 p.,
   57 illus., genealogy.

   Baudissin, Eva, Graefin von. Wilhelmine Schroeder-Devrient: der
   Schicksalweg einer grossen Kuenstlerin. Berlin: Drei Masken
   Verlag, 1937. 267 p., 16 illus.

   Bonnacci, Giuliano. Guglielmina Schroeder-Devrient e Gaspare
   Spontini. Roma: n.p., 1903. 32 p.

   von Gluemer, Claire. Erinnerungen an Wilhelmine Schroeder-
   Devrient. Leipzig: Verlag von Joh. Ambr. Barth, 1862. vi, 277 p.,
   portrait, facsimilie, list of 70 roles.

The singer requested that this be written, and it is based in part upon her own uncompleted autobiography.

Hagemann, Carl. Wilhelmine Schroeder-Devrient. Berlin: Schuster & Loeffler, n.d. [c.1904]. 85 p., 8 illus.

Kohler, Eugen. Aus den Memorien einer Saengerin nach Wilhelmine Schroeder-Devrient-Dumas. Berlin: Privatdruck im Lilien Verlag, 1929 [Originally published in 2 parts, 1868/1875, by Reginald Chesterfield in Boston].

Listed only because the title has engendered so much misunderstanding. This is actually a famous piece of erotica in its 13th known edition and has absolutely nothing to do with the singer. Philip K. Roggis traces some of the history of this work in his introduction to: Pauline: Memories of a Singer. Los Angeles: Holloway House Publishing Co., 1967.

Richter, Hermann. Das wilde Herz: Lebensroman der Wilhelmine Schroeder-Devrient. Leipzig: Koehler & Amelang, c.1927. 232, [1] p.

Rie-Andro, Theodore. Vox Humana: das Leben einer Saengerin. Ebenhausen: Wilhelm Langeweische-Brandt, 1928. 159 p.

Basically a novel based upon von Gluemer's reminiscences.

von Wolzogen, Alfred Freiherrn. Wilhelmine Schroeder-Devrient: ein Beitrag zur Geschichte des Musikalischen dramas. Leipzig: F.A. Brockhaus, 1863. xii, 351 p.

The expansion of an earlier biographical article. His sources are mentioned in the initial chapter.

5. SEE: autobiography of ELISA ASZTALOS (C0022).

   SEE: Alfred Bunn under MARIA MALIBRAN (C0378).

   Hagemann, Carl. "Wilhelmine Schreoder-Devrient zu ihrem hundertsten Geburtstage am 6. Dezember 1904." In Die Musik 4/5 (1904-5): 307-313. 3 illus., facsimile.

   SEE: Carl Reinecke under JENNY LIND (C0360).

   Schuré, Edouard. Précurseurs et revoltés. Paris, 1904.

   Wagner, Richard. My Life. New York: Tudor Publishing Co., 1936 [1st edition 1911].

C0571.
SCHROETER, CARONA. German Soprano. b. January 14, 1751, Guben; d. August 23, 1802, Ilmenau.

1. BAKER 6; EdS 1/8; FETIS 2/7; GROVE 6/16 (Bibliography); MGG 1/12 (Bibliography); RIEMANN 12; SCHMIDL.

3. Schroeter, Carona. MGG 1/12 mentions an MS autobiography given to
    Goethe in 1778. Present whereabouts unknown.

4. Duentzer, Heinrich. Charlotte von Stein und Carona Schroeter: eine
    Vertheidigung. Stuttgart: J.G. Cotta, 1876. Reprint Illmenau 1902.
    viii, 301 p.

    Stuemcke, Heinrich. Carona Schroeter. zweite auflage. Bielefeld:
    Verlag von Velhagen und Klasing, 1926. xi, 172 p., 9 illus.

5. Keil, Robert. Vor hundert Jahren: Mittheilungen ueber Weimar,
    Goethe und Carona Schroeter aus dem Tagen der Genie-Periode. Fest-
    gabe zur Saekularfeier von Goethes entritt in Weimar (7. November
    1775). 2 vols. Leipzig: Veit und Comp., 1875.

    The second volume is titled: Carona Schroeter: eine Lebensskizze
    mit Beitraegen zur Geschichte der Genie-Periode.

    Pasig, Paul. Goethe und Ilmenau mit einer Beigabe: Goethe und
    Carona Schroeter. zweite durchweg ergaenzte auflage. Weimar:
    Verlag von Huschke's Hofbuchhandlung, 1902. pp. 17-27.

C0572.
SCHUETZENDORF, LEO. German Baritone. b. May 7, 1886, Cologne; d.
December 18, 1931, Berlin.

1. BAKER 6; GROVE 6/17.

2. RC 16/9-10, 17/4, 18/11-12.

4. Schuetzendorf, Eugene. Kuenstlerblut: Leo Schuetzendorf und
    seine Brueder. Berlin: Deutsche Buchvertriebs- und Verlags-
    Gesellschaft, 1943. 352 p., 9 illus.

    All 4 brothers were operatic baritones!

C0573.
SCHUMANN, ELISABETH. German Soprano. b. June 13, 1885
Merseburg; d. April 23, 1952 New York City.

1. BAKER 6; EdS 1/8 (Bibliography); GROVE 6/16; MGG 1/12; RIEMANN
    12 + Supp. (Bibliography).

2. GR 30/1; ON 9/21, 27/7; OPERA 3/6, 24/8-9, 11, 25/1; RC 7/10.

3. Schumann, Elisabeth. German Song. London: Max Parrish & Co.
    Limited, 1948. Reprint 1979. 72 p., 45 illus., index.

4. Puritz, Elizabeth. The Teaching of Elisabeth Schumann. London:
    Methuen & Co., Ltd., 1956. 136 p., 7 illus.

    NOTE: GROVE 6/16 mentions a biography in preparation by G. Puritz.
    Elizabeth is the singer's daughter. Could this author be a
    grandchild?

Shawe-Taylor, Desmond. <u>Elisabeth Schumann and the Songs of Schubert</u>. London: The Gramophone Company, n.d. [1962]. 20, [2] p., 2 illus., recording details.

One of a series of pamphlets for "Great Recordings of the Century."

Shawe-Taylor, Desmond. <u>Elisabeth Schumann (1888-1952)</u>. London: The Gramophone Company, n.d. [1958]. 12, [2] p., 2 illus., recording details.

One of series of pamphlets for "Great Recordings of the Century," this one devoted to the songs of Hugo Wolf and Richard Strauss.

C0574.
SCHUMANN-HEINK, ERNESTINE. Austrian Mezzo-Soprano. b. June 15, 1861, Lieben, near Prague; d. November 17, 1936, Hollywood, California.

1. BAKER 6 (Bibliography); EdS 1/8 (Bibliography); GROVE 6/18; MGG 1/12; RIEMANN 12 + Supp. (Bibliography); SCHMIDL + Supp.

2. OPERA 18/11; RC 17/5-6, 7; 20/6-7; 25/3-4; RNC 2/8, 9.

4. Lawton, Mary. <u>Schumann-Heink: the Last of the Titans</u>. New York: The Macmillan Company, 1929. Reprint 1977 with discography by W.R. Moran. ix, 390 p., 58 illus.

   Mayfield, John S. <u>A Conversation in 1026</u>. Austin: privately printed, 1925. 20 p.

   Limited to 199 numbered copies.

5. SEE: Elizabeth Harbison David under **CORINNE RIDER-KELSEY** (C0524).

C0575.
SCHWARZ, JOSEPH. German Baritone. b. October 10, 1880, Riga; d. November 10, 1926, Berlin.

1. GROVE 6/17.

2. OW 11/6; RC 26/9-10.

C0576.
SCHWARZKOPF, ELISABETH. German Soprano. b. December 9, 1915, Jarotschin, near Poznan.

1. BAKER 6; EdS 1/8 (Bibliography); GRCVE 6/17 (Bibliography); MGG 1/16; RIEMANN 12 + Supp.

2. GR 54/5, 6; ON 24/23, 29/6, 39/22, 41/11, 46/3; OPERA 4/7, 27/4; OP 2/1; OW 4/10; RNC 1/9.

3. Schwarzkopf, Elisabeth. <u>On and Off the Record: a Memoir of Walter</u>

Legge. Introduction by Herbert von Karajan. New York: Charles Scribner's Sons, 1982. xi, 292 p., 43 illus., selected discography by Alan Sanders, index of names.

4. **Elisabeth Schwarzkopf**. Paris: L'Avant Scène Opéra, 1983. 146 p., numerous illus., 55-item bibliography, discography by Georges Voisin.

Articles by sixteen colleagues and the singer herself.

Gavoty, Bernard. **Elisabeth Schwarzkopf**. Geneva: Rene Kister, 195? 31 p., 20 illus., discography.

Segalini, Sergio. **Elisabeth Schwarzkopf**. Paris: Librairie Arthème Fayard, 1983. 156 p., 178 illus., chronology of performances, discography.

C0577.
SCIUTTI, GRAZIELLA. Italian Soprano. b. April 17, 1932, Turin.

1. BAKER 6; EdS/Supp.; GROVE 6/17 (Bibliography); RIEMANN 12 + Supp.

2. OW 19/1.

C0578.
SCOTTI, ANTONIO. Italian Baritone. b. January 25, 1866, Naples; d. February 26, 1936, Naples.

1. BAKER 6; EdS 1/8; GROVE 6/17 (Bibliography); RIEMANN 12; SCHMIDL + Supp.

2. GR 17/1; ON 26/21; OPERA 27/12.

5. SEE: Otto Hermann Kahn under **MARY GARDEN** (C0232).

C0579.
SCOTTO, RENATA. Italian Soprano. b. February 24, 1934, Savona.

1. BAKER 6; EdS/Supp.; GROVE 6/17; RIEMANN 12/Supp.

2. ON 30/9, 37/24, 42/8, 44/17, 46/5; OPERA 22/3; OW 11/1, 14/5, 23/8-9.

3. Scotto, Renata and Octavio Roca. Scotto: More than a Diva. Forward by Placido Domingo. Garden City: Doubleday & Company, Inc., 1984. xiii, 245 p., 47 illus., discography, select list of performances on videotape, index.

4. Bonafini, Umberto. Perché sona Renato Scotto. Mantova: C.I.T.E. M., 1976. 209 p., illus., discography, index.

C0580.
SEEFRIED, IRMGARD. German Soprano. b. October 9, 1919, Koengetried, Bavaria.

1. BAKER 6; EdS 1/8 (Bibliography); GROVE 6/17 (Bibliography); RIEMANN
   12 + Supp.

2. OPERA 17/8; OW 2/3.

4. Fassbind, Franz. Wolfgang Schneiderhan - Irmgard Seefried: eine
   Kuenstler- und Lebensgemeinschaft. Bern: Alfred Scherz Verlag,
   1960. 308 p., 27 illus., index of names, discography.

CO581.
SEINEMEYER, META. German Soprano. b. September 5, 1895, Berlin; d.
August 19, 1929, Dresden.

1. BAKER 6; GROVE 6/17.

2. GR 7/5; RC 14/7-8, 21/3-4.

CO582.
SEMBRICH, MARCELLA. Polish Soprano. b. February 15, 1858,
Wisniewcyzyk, Galicia; d. January 11, 1935, New York City.

1. BAKER 6; EdS 1/8 (Bibliography); GROVE 6/17; MGG 1/12; RIEMANN
   12 + Supp. (Bibliography); SCHMIDL.

2. ON 8/14, 20/10, 32/16, 47/2; OW 10/8; RC 4/7, 9, 11, 18/5-6,
   20/6-7.

4. An Outline of the Life and Career of Madame Marcella Sembrich.
   New York: The Sembrich Memorial Association, Inc., 1955 [1st
   edition 1940]. 28 p., 41 illus.

   Armin, George [pseud. for George Hermann]. Marcella Sembrich und
   Herr Professor Julius Hey: eine Antwort an die Streitfrage: "Was
   ist Koloratur?" Nebst ein Epilog an den "Kunstgesang". Leipzig:
   privately printed, 1898. 16 p.

   Hutcheson, Ernest. Marcella Sembrich: a Tribute to a surpassing
   Musician and Interpreter of Song. New York: Julliard School,
   1935. 5 p.

   Owen, H. Goddard. A Recollection of Marcella Sembrich. New York:
   The Marcella Sembrich Memorial Association, Inc., 1950. Reprint
   1982 with introduction by Philip L. Miller. 79 p., 79 illus.

5. Brown, William Earl. Vocal Wisdom: Maxims of Giovanni Battista
   Lamperti. Enlarged edition edited by Lillian Strongin. New York:
   Arno Press, Inc., 1957. [vi], 146 p.

   Lamperti, who was Sembrich's teacher, wrote Two books on singing:
   Guida teorica-practica-elementare per lo studio del canto.
   Milano: T. di G. Ricordi, 1864. Translated by J.C. Griffith as:
   A Treatise on the Art of Singing. New York: E. Schuberth & Co.,
   c.1871.
   L'arte del canto in ordine alle tradizioni classiche ed parti-
   colare esperienza. Milano: G. Ricordi, 1883.

C0583.
SENESINO, FRANCESCO. Italian Castrato Mezzo-Soprano. b. c.1680,
Siena; d. c.1750, Siena?

1. BAKER 6; FETIS 2/1 (under Bernardi); GROVE 6/7; MGG 1/12; RIEMANN
    12 (under Bernardi); SCHMIDL + Supp. (under Bernardi).

C0584.
SHALIAPIN or **SHALYAPIN.** SEE: C0112.

C0585.
SHERIDAN, MARGARET. Irish Soprano. b. October 15, 1889, Castlebar,
County Mayo; d. April 16, 1958, Dublin.

1. EdS 1/8; GROVE 6/17 (Bibliography).

5. Herbert-Caesari, E. The Alchemy of the Voice. London: Robert
    Hale, 1965. pp. 226-236.

C0586.
SHIRLEY, GEORGE. American Tenor. b. April 18, 1934, Indianapolis,
Indiana.

1. GROVE 6/17; RIEMANN 12.

2. ON 35/14; OPERA 22/10.

C0587.
SHIRLEY-QUIRK, JOHN. English Baritone. b. August 2, 1931, Liverpool.

1. BAKER 6; GROVE 6/17; RIEMANN 12.

2. GR 49/8.

C0588.
SHUARD, AMY. English Soprano. b. July 19, 1924, London; d. April 18,
1975, London.

1. EdS/Supp.; GROVE 6/17; RIEMANN 12/Supp.

2. OPERA 11/4, 26/6.

C0589.
SIBONI, GIUSEPPE. Italian Tenor. b. January 27, 1780, Forli; d.
March 28, 1839, Copenhagen.

1. GROVE 6/17; MGG 1/12 (Bibliography); SCHMIDL.

4. Ingerslev-Jensen, P. 'Giuseppe Siboni: selvbiografiske notater
    1780-1818'. Copenhagen: Det Kongleige Danske Musik-konserva-
    torium: Aarsberetning for 1961, 1962.

    No copy located.

    Monti, Attilio. Giuseppe Siboni: tenore e musicista forlevese.

Forli: Stabilimento tipografico romagnolo, 1922. 23, [1] p.,
11 illus.

C0590.
SIEMS, MARGARETHE. German Soprano. b. December 30, 1879, Breslau;
d. April 13, 1952, Dresden.

1. GROVE 6/17; RIEMANN 12/Supp.

2. RNC 2/12.

C0591.
SIEPI, CESARE. Italian Bass. b. February 10, 1923, Milan.

1. BAKER 6; EdS 1/8; GROVE 6/17 (Bibliography); MGG 1/16 (Bibliog-
    raphy); RIEMANN 12 + Supp.

2. ON 22/6, 28/7; OPERA 13/2; OP 6/6; OW 3/9, 16/8.

C0592.
SILJA, ANJA. German Soprano. b. April 17, 1940, Berlin.

1. GROVE 6/17; RIEMANN 12/Supp.

2. ON 32/3; OPERA 20/3; OW 5/8, 16/1.

4. Heinzelmann, Josef. <u>Anja Silja</u>. Berlin: Rembrandt Verlag, 1965.
    61 p., 28 illus.

C0593.
SILLS, BEVERLY. American Soprano. b. May 25, 1929, Brooklyn, New
York.

1. BAKER 6; GROVE 6/17 (Bibliography); RIEMANN 12/Supp.

2. ON 31/16, 35/2, 39/21, 40/14, 45/4; OPERA 21/12; OP 10/4.

3. Sills, Beverly. <u>Bubbles: a Self Portrait</u>. New York: Bobbs-
    Merrill, 1976. 240 p., 171 illus., index.

    Sills, Beverly. <u>Bubbles: an Encore</u>. New York: Grosset & Dunlap,
    1981. 280 p., numerous illus., index.

C0594.
SIMANDY, JOSZEF. Romanian Tenor. b. 1916, Budapest. No lexicon
listing.

1. KUTSCH 3.

3. Simándy, Jószef and László Dalos. <u>Bánk bán elmondja...</u> Budapest:
    Zenemuekiadó, 1983. 307 p., 53 illus.

C0595.
SIMIONATO, GIULETTA. Italian Mezzo-Soprano. b. December 15, 1910,
Forli.

1. BAKER 6; EdS 1/8 (Bibliography); GROVE 6/17; RIEMANN 12.

2. ON 24/17, 42/17; OPERA 15/2; OW 5/4.

C0596.
SINGHER, MARTIAL. French Baritone. August 14, 1904, Oloron-Sainte-Marie, Basses-Pyrénées.

1. BAKER 6; EdS 1/8 (Bibliography); GROVE 6/17 (Bibliography); RIEMANN 12 + Supp.

2. ON 25/24.

3. Singher, Martial. An Interpretive Guide to Operatic Arias: a Handbook for Singers, Coaches, Teachers, and Students. University Park: The Pennsylvania State University Press, 1983. 368 p.

C0597.
SKOUGAARD, LORENTZ SEVERIN. Norwegian Baritone. No lexicon listing.

4. Clark, Alfred Corning, ed. Skougaard, Lorentz Severin: a Sketch Mainly Autobiographic. New York: G.P Putnam's Sons, printed for private distribution, 1885. 248 p., portrait.

    He studied under Meyerbeer and became the first internationally recognized Norwegian opera singer.

C0598.
SLADEN, VICTORIA. English Soprano. b. May 24, 1910, London. No lexicon listing.

1. KUTSCH 3.

3. Sladen, Victoria. Singing My Way. London: Rockliff Publishing Corporation Ltd., 1951. x, 117 p., 14 illus., index.

C0599.
SLEZAK, LEO. Austrian Tenor. b. August 18, 1873, Maehrisch-Schoenberg, Moravia; d. June 1, 1946, Egern am Tegernsee.

1. BAKER 6; EdS 1/9 (Bibliography); GROVE 6/17; MGG 1/12; RIEMANN 12 + Supp. (Bibliography); SCHMIDL.

2. ON 24/5; OW 10/10; RC 15/9-10.

3. Slezak, Leo. Der Wortbruch. Berlin: Ernst Rowohlt Verlag, 1927. 283 p., illus.

    Slezak, Leo. Meine saemtliche Werke. Berlin: Ernst Rowohlt Verlag, 1923. 263 p., 15 illus.

    The English version was published as: Song of Motley. London: W. Hodge, 1938. Reprint 1977. 263 p., 15 illus. This includes a translation of Der wortbruch.

Slezak, Leo. <u>Mein Lebensmaerchen</u>. Muenchen: R. Piper & Co.,
Verlag, 1948. 240 p., portrait + 42 illus. by Franziska Bilek.

Released posthumously by his daughter, Margarete.

Slezak, Leo. <u>Ruckfall</u>. Hamburg: Rowohlt Verlag, 1940. 226 p.,
illus.

4. Klinenberger, Ludwig. <u>Leo Slezak: ein Beitrag zur Geschichte der
dramatischen Gesangskunst</u>. Wien: Verlag Paul Knepler, 1910. 23 p.

   Leitenberger, Friedrich Alfons and Lothar Ring. <u>Der goettliche
Leo: ein Volksbuch ueber Leo Slezak</u>. Wien: Verlag Kurt Klebert,
1948. 64 p., 5 illus.

   Slezak, Margarete. <u>Der Apfel faellt nicht weit vom Stamm</u>.
Muenchen: R. Piper & Co., Verlag, 1953. 233 p., 45 illus.

   Slezak, Walter, ed. <u>Mein lieber Bub: Briefe eines besorgten
Vaters</u>. Muenchen: R. Piper & Co., Verlag, 1966. 323 p., 27
illus.

   Slezak, Walter. <u>What Time's the Next Swan?</u> Garden City: Doubleday
& Company, Inc., 1962. 227 p., 33 illus.

5. Morgan, Paul. <u>Prominententeich: Abenteuer und Erlebnisse mit
Stars, Sternchen und allerlei Gelechter...</u>. Berlin: Amonestra-
Verlag, 1934. 251 p., illus.

C0600.
SLOBODSKAYA, ODA. Russian Soprano. b. December 12, 1888, Vilna; d.
July 29, 1970, London.

1. BAKER 6; GROVE 6/17 (Bibliography); RIEMANN 12 + Supp.

2. OPERA 2/5; RS 35 (July 1969).

3. Slobodskaya, Oda. "Reminiscences of Oda Slobodskaya as told to
Grenville Eves." In <u>Recorded Sound</u> 35 (1969). discography by
Harold Barnes and Sylvia Junge.

4. Leonard, Maurice. <u>Slobodskaya: a Biography of Oda Slobodskaya</u>.
London: Victor Gollancz Ltd., 1979. 142 p., 13 illus., discography, index.

C0601.
SOBINOV, LEONID. Russian Tenor. b. June 7, 1872, Yaroslavl; d.
October 14, 1934, Riga.

1. EdS 1/9; GROVE 6/17 (Bibliography); RIEMANN/Supp. (Bibliography).

2. RC 24/7-8 (under Sobinoff).

4. Remezov, Ivan Ivanovich. <u>Leonid Vital'evich Sobinov: K 25-letiiu
so dnia smerti</u>. Moskva: Gos. muzykal'noe izd-vo, 1960. 137,

C0602.
SOEDERSTROM, ELISABETH. Swedish Soprano. b. May 7, 1927, Stockholm.

1. EdS/Supp.; GROVE 6/17 (Bibliography); RIEMANN/Supp.

2. ON 24/7, 46/3; OPERA 20/1; OW 6/6.

3. Soederstrom, Elisabeth. In My Own Key. Translated by Joan Tate.
    London: Hamish Hamilton, 1979 [1st edition 1978]. 102 p.,
    20 illus.

C0603.
SOLA, WAEINOE. Finnish Tenor. No lexicon listing.

3. Sola, Waeinoe. Waeinoe sola kertoo. 2 vols. Helsinki: Werner
    Soederstroem Osakeyhtioe, 1951/52. 359 p., 80 illus., index;
    277 p., 68 illus., index.

C0604.
SONTAG, HENRIETTE. German Soprano. b. January 3, 1806, Coblenz; d.
June 17, 1854, Mexico City.

1. BAKER 6; EdS 1/9 (Bibliography); FETIS + Supp.; GROVE 6/17 (Bib-
    liography); MGG 1/12 (Bibliography); RIEMANN + Supp. (Bibliog-
    raphy); SCHMIDL.

2. MQ 28/1.

4. A Memoir of the Countess de Rossi. London: Mitchell, 1849
    [French translation published in Paris by Sartorius in 1850].
    111 p.

    She had secretly married Count Carlo De Rossi in 1828, and this
    idealized biography coincided with her return to the stage after
    having traveled with her husband for a number of years on his
    various diplomatic missions.

    Dilthey, Karl [pseud. for Julius Werner]. Henriette Sontag:
    Blueten und Dornen am Baume eines Kuenstlerlebens. New York, 1873.

    No copy located.

    Gautier, Théophile. L'ambassadrice: biographie de la Comtesse
    Rossi. Paris: Ferdinand Sartorius éditeur, 1850. 35 p.

    Life of Henriette Sontag, Countess de Rossi, with Interesting
    Sketches by Scudo, Hector Berlioz, Louis Boerne, Adolphe Adam,
    Marie Aycard, Julie de Marggueritte, Prince Puckler-Muskau,
    and Theophile Gautier. New York: Stringer & Townsend, 1852.
    64 p., portrait.

    Pirchan, Emil. Henriette Sontag: die Saengerin des Biedermeier.
    Wien: Wilhelm Frick Verlag, 1946. 270 p., 69 illus., genealogy,
    345-item bibliography, index of names.

Another of those extremely rare efforts which are basic.

Russell, Frank. Queen of Song: the Life of Henrietta Sontag.
New York: Exposition Press, 1964. 282 p., 29-item bibliography.

Sontag, Karl. Henriette Sontag, aus Karl Sontags Buehnen-
erlebnissen. Hannover: Helwig Verlag, 1875.

No copy located.

Stuemcke, Heinrich. Henriette Sontag: ein Lebens- und Zeitbild.
Berlin: Selbstverlag der Gesellschaft fuer Theatergeschichte,
1913. xvi, 312 p., 12 illus., annotated notes, iconography,
index of names.

Zuschauer, Freimund [pseud. for Heinrich Rellstab]. Henriette,
oder die schoene Saengerin: eine Geschichte unserer Tage.
Leipzig: bei F.L. Herbig, 1826. 174 p.

This is a libelous satire against Sontag which resulted in a lawsuit and imprisonment for the outspoken critic. An altered
French translation (Paris, 1828) exists which I have not seen.

5. SEE: autobiography of **ELISA ASZTALOS** (C0022).

   SEE: Max Maretzek under **MARIETTA ALBONI** (C0011).

   SEE: P. Scudo under **ANGELICA CATALANI** (C0107).

C0605.
SOOT, FRITZ. German Tenor. b. August 20, 1878, Wellesweiler-
Neukirchen, Saar; d. June 9, 1965, Berlin.

1. GROVE 6/17; RIEMANN 12 + Supp.

4. Schliepe, Ernst. "Fritz Soot: wie Man Tenor wird." In Berliner
   Musikjahrbuch 1926: 77-80.

C0606.
SOUZAY, GERARD. French Baritone. b. December 8, 1920, Angers.

1. BAKER 6; GROVE 6/17 (Bibliography); RIEMANN 12 + Supp.

2. GR 48/3; ON 32/5.

C0607.
SPENNERT, JENNY. Swedish Soprano. No lexicon listing.

3. Spennert, Jenny. Mitt liv och min sang. Helsingfors: Soederstroem & Co Foerlagsaktiebolag, 1946 [1st edition 1945]. 207 p.,
   28 illus.

C0608.
SPIES, HERMINE. German Mezzo-Soprano. b. February 25, 1857,
Loehneberger Huette, near Weilburg; d. February 26, 1893, Wiesbaden.

1. BAKER 6; MGG 1/12; RIEMANN 12.

4. Spies, Minna. Hermine Spies: ein Gedenkbuch fuer ihre Freunde von ihrer Schwester. Stuttgart: G.I. Goeschensche Verlags- handlung, 1894 [augmented 1905]. viii, 300 p., portrait.

CO609.
SPOORENBERG, ERNA. Dutch Soprano. b. April 11, 1926, Yogyakarta, Java.

1. GROVE 6/17.

3. Spoorenberg, Erna. Daar lig je dan. Den Haag: Bert Bakker/ Daamen N.V., 1962. 137 p., 11 illus.

CO610.
STABILE, MARIANO. Italian Baritone. b. May 12, 1888, Palermo; d. January 11, 1968, Milan.

1. BAKER 6; EdS 1/9 (Bibliography); GROVE 6/17; RIEMANN 12/Supp.; SCHMIDL/Supp.

2. OPERA 7/5.

CO611.
STADER, MARIA. Swiss Soprano. b. November 5, 1911, Budapest.

1. GROVE 6/18; RIEMANN 12 + Supp.

3. Stader, Maria. Learning the Masters: J.S. Bach's Aria "Aus Liebe will mein Heiland sterben" from St. Matthew Passion. biography, discography.

    No copy located.

    Stader, Maria and Robert D. Abraham. Nehmt meinem Dank: Erinner- ungen. Muenchen: Kindler Verlag GmbH, 1979. 460 p., 82 illus., 19-item bibliography, repertoire, discography by Hans E. Greiner, index of names.

CO612.
STAGNO, ROBERTO. Italian Tenor. b. October 11, 1840, Palermo; d. April 26, 1897, Genoa.

1. BAKER 6; EdS 1/9 (Bibliography); RIEMANN 12 + Supp.; SCHMIDL.

4. Stagno Bellincioni, Bianca. Roberto Stagno e Gemma Bellincioni: intimi. Fierenze: Casa Editrice Monsalvato, 1943. 172 p., 22 illus.

    Reprint 1977 includes both this title and the earlier 1920 edition of Gemma Bellincioni's autobiography with discography by W.R. Moran.

    Bianca is the daughter of this famous couple (b. January 23, 1888,

Budapest). SEE: EdS 1/9 (Bibliography).

5. SEE: autobiography of **GEMMA BELLINCIONI** (C0047).

C0613.
STEBER, ELEANOR. American Soprano. b. July 17, 1916, Wheeling, West
Virginia.

1. BAKER 6; GROVE 6/18; RIEMANN 12/Supp.

2. ON 11/13, 25/22, 37/17, 45/7.

C0614.
STENBORG, CARL. Swedish Tenor. b. September 25, 1752, Stockholm; d.
August 1, 1813, Stockholm.

1. BAKER 6; GROVE 6/18 (Bibliography); RIEMANN 12; SCHMIDL.

4. Flodmark, Johan. Elisabeth Olin och Carl Stenborg, tva gustavianska sangargestalter: bilder fran svenska operans foersta tider.
   Stockholm: Froeleen & Comp., 1903. [v], 201 p., 29 illus.

C0615.
STENHAMMER, FREDRIKA. Swedish Soprano. b. September 19, 1836, Visby;
d. October 7, 1880, Stockholm.

1. MGG 1/12 (Bibliography); RIEMANN 12 + Supp.

4. Stenhammer, Elsa. Fredrika Stenhammer brev. Upsala: Almqvist &
   Wiksell/Gebers Foerlag AB, 1958. 188 p., annotated index of
   persons.

C0616.
STERLING, ANTOINETTE. American Mezzo-Soprano. b. January 23, 1850,
Sterlingville, New York; d. January 9, 1904, London.

1. BAKER 6; GROVE 6/18.

4. MacKinlay, Malcolm Sterling. Antoinette Sterling and Other
   Celebrities: Stories and Impressions of Artistic Circles. London:
   Hutchinson & Co., 1906. xiii, 340 p., 16 illus.

C0617.
STEVENS, RISE. American Mezzo-Soprano. b. June 11, 1913, New York
City.

1. BAKER 6; GROVE 6/18; RIEMANN 12/Supp.

2. ON 28/17.

4. Crichton, Kyle. Subway to the Met: Risë Stevens Own Lighthearted
   Story of the Long Road from the Bronx to Bizet. Garden City:
   Doubleday & Company, 1959. 240 p., 31 illus.

She became a Director of the Metropolitan Opera National Company.

C0618.
STEWART, THOMAS. American Baritone. b. August 29, 1928, San Saba, Texas.

1. BAKER 6; GROVE 6/18; RIEMANN 12/Supp.

2. ON 32/15, 34/22, 47/17; OW 8/5, 18/8.

C0619.
STIGNANI, EBE. Italian Mezzo-Soprano. b. July 10, 1904, Naples; d. October 5, 1974, Imola.

1. GROVE 6/18 (Bibliography); EdS 1/9 (Bibliography); RIEMANN 12 + Supp.

2. ON 35/21; OPERA 3/6.

4. de Francesci, Bruno and Pier Fernando Mondini. Ebe Stignani: una voce e il suo mondo. Imola: Grafiche Galeati, 1980. 231 p., 87 illus., chronology, debuts, repertoire, discography, index of names, index of operas.

C0620.
STOCKHAUSEN, JULIUS. German Baritone. b. July 22, 1826, Paris; d. September 22, 1906, Frankfurt/M.

1. BAKER 6 (Bibliography); EdS 1/9 (Bibliography); GROVE 6/18 (Bibliography); MGG 1/12 (Bibliography); RIEMANN 12 + Supp. (Bibliography); SCHMIDL (Bibliography).

3. MGG 1/12 mentions a pedagogical book on vocal technique. Actually there are four:

Stockhausen, Julius. Das Saenger-Alphabet; oder die Sprachelemente als Stim-Bildungsmittel. Leipzig: B. Senff, 1901. 29 p.

Stockhausen, Julius. Der Buchstabe G und die sieben Regeln des Herrn H. Dorn nebst einer vocal- und consonanten-Tabelle. Frankfurt am Main: Alt und Neumann, 1880. 56 p.

Stockhausen, Julius: Julius Stockhausens Gesangs-Methode. Leipzig: C.F. Peters Verlag, n.d. [1884]. 155 p.

Novello in London published a translation the same year as: A Method of Singing.

Stockhausen, Julius. Julius Stockhausens Gesangstechnik und Stimmbildung: Ausgabe fuer hohe Stimme; Ausgabe fuer tiefe Stimme. Leipzig: C.F. Peters Verlag, n.d. [c.1886]. 115 p.; viii, 117 p.

4. Wirth, Julia. Julius stockhausen der saenger des deutschen liedes. Frankfurt am Main: Verlag Englert und Schlosser, 1927. [iii], 537 p., 22 illus., repertoire list, 112-item bibliography, index.

5. SEE: Edward Speyer under **JENNY LIND** (CO360).

    Wirth-Stockhausen, Julia. Unverlierbare Kindheit. Stuttgart:
    Engelhornverlag Adolf Spemann, 1949. 160 p., 4 illus.

CO621.
STOLTZ, ROSINE. French Mezzo-Soprano. b. February 13, 1815, Paris;
d. July 28, 1903, Paris.

1. BAKER 6 (Bibliography); EdS 1/9 (Bibliography); GROVE 6/18
    (Bibliography); RIEMANN 12; SCHMIDL + Supp.

4. Bord, Gustave. Rosina Stoltz de l'Académie de Musique (Victoire
    Noël) 1815-1903. Paris: Henri Daragon, 1909. 237 p., 3 illus.,
    list of roles.

    Victoire Noël was her real name although she first sang as Mlle.
    Ternaux, later as Heloise Stoltz, and finally as Rosine Stoltz,

    Cantinjou, Corneille. Les adieux de Madame Stoltz sa retraite
    de l'Opéra, sa vie théâtrale, ses concurrentes, son intérieur.
    Paris: Chez Breteau, Libraire-Editeur, 1847. 72 p., portrait.

    Marks her retirement from the Paris Opera and, along with the
    pamphlets by Lemer and Pérignon, is clearly an attempt to
    justify her resignation in March of 1847.

    Pérignon, Eugénie. Rosine Stoltz, Maxime, Mlle. Lavoye. Paris:
    privately printed, 1847. 51 p., illus.

CO622.
STOLZ, TERESA. Italian Soprano. b. June 2, 1834, Kosteletz, Bohemia;
d. August 23, 1902, Milan.

1. BAKER 6; EdS 1/9; GROVE 6/18 (Bibliography); SCHMIDL.

4. Zoppi, Umberto. Angelo Mariani Giuseppe Verdi e Teresa Stolz in
    un carteggio inedito. Milano: Garzanti, 1947. 403 p., 27 illus.,
    index of names.

CO623.
STORCHIO, ROSINA. Italian Soprano. b. May 19, 1876, Venice; d. July
24, 1945 Milan.

1. BAKER 6; EdS 1/9 (Bibliography); GROVE 6/18 (Bibliography);
    RIEMANN 12 (Bibliography); SCHMIDL.

2. ON 21/5; RC 12/3, RNC 4/12.

CO624.
STRACCIARI, RICCARDO. Italian Baritone. b. June 26, 1875,
Casalecchio di Reno; d. October 10, 1955, Rome.

1. EdS 1/9 (Bibliography); GROVE 6/18 (Bibliography); SCHMIDL.

2. GR 1/7; ON 19/7, 40/12; RNC 3/3.

C0625.
von STRANTZ, FERDINAND. German Baritone. b. July 31, 1821, Breslau;
d. October 25, 1909, Berlin.

1. RIEMANN 12; SCHMIDL/Supp.

3. von Strantz, Ferdinand. Erinnerungen aus meinem Leben. Hamburg:
    Verlagsanstalt und Druckerei A.-G., 1901. 272 p., portrait, 9
    facsimilies, index of names.

C0626.
STRATAS, TERESA. Canadian Soprano. b. May 26, 1938, Toronto.

1. BAKER 6; GROVE 6/18; RIEMANN 12/Supp.

2. ON 43/6, 45/8; OW 19/12.

C0627.
STREPPONI, GIUSEPPINA. Italian Soprano. b. September 8, 1815, Lodi;
d. November 14, 1897, Busseto.

1. BAKER 6; EdS 1/9; (Bibliography); GROVE 6/18 (Bibliography);
    RIEMANN 12/Supp.; SCHMIDL.

2. ON 18/10, 43/12.

4. Mundula, Mercede Busseto. La moglie di Verdi Giuseppina
    Strepponi. Milano: Fratelli Treves Editori, 1938. 321 p.,
    12 illus.

C0628.
SUCHER, ROSA. German Soprano. b. February 23, 1849, Velburg; d.
April 16, 1927, Eschweiler.

1. BAKER 6; EdS 1/9 (Bibliography); GROVE 6/18 (Bibliography); MGG
    1/12; SCHMIDL.

3. Sucher, Rosa. Aus meinem Leben. Leipzig: Breitkopf und Haertel,
    1914. 95 p., 4 illus.

C0629.
SULZER, SALOMON. Austrian Cantor. b. March 30, 1804, Hohenems,
Vorarlberg; d. January 17, 1890, Vienna.

1. BAKER 6; GROVE 6/18 (Bibliography); MGG 1/12 (Bibliography)
    RIEMANN 12 + Supp. (Bibliography); SCHMIDL.

4. Kulte, Edward. Salomon Sulzer, Professor und Obercantor: bio-
    graphsiche Skizze. Wien: Herzfeld & Bauer, 1866. 24 p.,
    portrait.

C0630.
SUPERVIA, CONCHITA. Spanish Mezzo-Soprano. b. December 8, 1895,

Barcelona; d. March 30, 1936, London.

1. BAKER 6; EdS 1/9; GROVE 6/18 (Bibliography); RIEMANN/Supp.
    (Bibliography); SCHMIDL/Supp.

2. GR 13/12, 15/10; ON 24/14; OPERA 11/1; RC 6/3, 8,2; RS 4 (Spring
    1957), 52 (January 1972).

4. Shawe-Taylor, Desmond. Conchita Supervia. London: The Gramo-
    phone Company, n.d. [1960]. 28, [1] p., 2 illus., recording
    details.

    One of a series of pamphlets for "Great Recordings of the
    Century." In this same pamphlet is a very brief article by
    Ivor Newton: "Conchita Supervia: Some Recollections."

5. Vandoyer, Jean Louis. Dédier à l'amitié et au souvenir. Paris:
    Plon, 1947. 264 p.

C0631.
SUTHERLAND, JOAN. Australian Soprano. b. November 7, 1926, Sydney.

1. BAKER 6; EdS 1/9; GROVE 6/18 (Bibliography); RIEMANN 12/Supp.

2. GR 59/11; ON 26/4, 29/2, 34/23, 47/6; OPERA 11/10; OP 6/5;
    RNC 5/8.

4. Adams, Brian. La Stupenda: a Biography of Joan Sutherland.
    Richmond [Victoria]: Hutchinson Group Pty Ltd, 1980. 329 p.,
    147 illus., discography of Joan Sutherland and Richard Bonynge,
    1st performances of operatic roles, 31-item selected bibliography,
    index.

    Braddon, Russell. Joan Sutherland. New York: St. Martin's Press,
    1962. 256 p., 16 illus., list of Covent Garden roles, USA discog-
    raphy.

    Greenfield, Edward. Joan Sutherland. London: Allan Ltd., 1972.
    64 p., 71 illus., list of debuts, discography by Malcolm Walker.
    1st of a series, "Record Masters," projected under the editorship
    of Anthony Pollard.

    Knafel, Stephen Robert. A Joan Sutherland Chronicle, emphasizing
    Her San Francisco Opera Engagements. Long Beach: M.A. Thesis,
    1977. 111p.

C0632.
SVANHOLM, SET. Swedish Tenor. b. September 2, 1904, Vaesteras: d.
October 4, 1964, Saltsjoe-Duvnaes.

1. BAKER 6; GROVE 6/18 (Bibliography); RIEMANN 12 + Supp.

2. OPERA 6/6.

C0633.

SWARTHOUT, GLADYS. American Mezzo-Soprano. b. December 25, 1900, Deepwater, Missouri; d. July 7, 1969, Florence.

1. BAKER 6; GROVE 6/18; RIEMANN 12.

2. ON 34/2.

3. Swarthout, Gladys. Come Soon Tomorrow: the S6ory of a Young Singer. Forward by Deems Taylor. New York: Dodd, Mead & Company, 1943. viii, 278 p.

    In Mr. Taylor's opinion, "this is a work of fiction, possibly colored by the events of her own career."

C0634.
SWOLFS, LAURENT. Belgian Tenor. b. March 8, 1878?, Ghent; d. April 11, 1954, Ghent. No lexicon listing.

3. Swolfs, Laurent. Souvenirs de théâtre et de coulisses. Bruxelles: Editions H. Wellens & W. Godenne, n.d. [c.1952]. 169 p., list of roles.

    Primarily recollections of other artists.

C0635.
SYLVIA, MARGUERITA. American Mezzo-Soprano. b. July 10, 1875: d. February 21, 1957. No lexicon listing.

4. Kuter, Kay E. Resumé of Notable Events in the Career of Mme. Marguerita Sylvia. New York: unpublished, 1956. 53 p., 24 illus.

C0636.
SZEKELY, MIHALY. Hungarian Bass. b. May 8, 1901, Jaszbereny; d. March 6, 1963, Budapest.

1. GROVE 6/18; RIEMANN 12/Supp.

4. Varnai, Peter. Székely Mihály. Budapest: Zenemuekiadő, 1968. 84 p., 35 illus., list of roles, 2 LP records.

C0637.
TAGLIAVINI, FERRUCCIO. Italian Tenor. b. August 14, 1913, Reggio.

1. BAKER 6; EdS 1/9 (Bibliography); GROVE 6/18 (Bibliography); RIEMANN 12 + Supp.

4. Tedeschi, Ciro. Ferruccio Tagliavini, il signore del canto nuovo idolo delle folle. Roma: Edizioni XX Secolo S.A.I., 1942. 61 p., 8 illus.

C0638.
TAJO, ITALO. Italian Bass. b. April 25, 1915, Pinerolo, Piedmont.

1. EdS 1/9; GROVE 6/18; RIEMANN 12 + Supp.

2. ON 13/10, 41/16.

4. Hastings, Ronald. "Italo Tajo." In Opera Annual 7 (1960):102-114.

C0639.
TAMAGNO, FRANCESCO. Italian Tenor. b. December 28, 1850, Turin; d.
August 31, 1905, Varese, near Turin.

1. BAKER 6; EdS 1/9 (Bibliography); GROVE 6/18 (Bibliography);
    RIEMANN 12/Supp.

2. ON 12/23, 24, 28/14; RC 7/2.

4. Corsi, Mario. Tamagno: il più grande fenomeno canoro dell'
    Ottocento. Milano: Casa Editrice Ceschina, 1937. Reprint 1977
    with discography by W.R. Moran. 214 p., 23 illus.

    There is an MS translation in English by the late George L.
    Nyklicek.

    de Amicis, Edmondo. Francesco Tamagno: ricordi della sua vita e
    aneddoti interessant. Palermo: Casa Editrice - Salvatore Biondo,
    n.d. [1902]. 23 p., 3 illus.

C0640.
TAMBERLICK, ENRICO. Italian Tenor. b. March 16, 1820, Rome; d. March
13, 1889, Paris.

1. BAKER 6 (Bibliography); EdS 1/9 (Bibliography); FETIS 2/Supp.;
    GROVE 6/18 (Bibliography); SCHMIDL (Bibliography).

C0641.
TAMBURINI, ANTONIO. Italian Baritone. b. March 28, 1800, Faenza; d.
November 9, 1876, Nice.

1. BAKER 6; EdS 1/9 (Bibliography); FETIS 2/8; GROVE 6/18;
    RIEMANN 12/Supp.; SCHMIDL + Supp.

4. de Biez, Jacques. Tamburini et la musique italienne. Paris:
    Tresse, Editeur, 1877. iii, 128 p., portrait.

    Discusses the singer within the larger musical context of his era
    with special reference to Rossini.

    Gell-Ferraris, H. Antonio Tamburini nel ricordo d'una nipote.
    Livorno: Stabile Tipografia Toscano, 1934. xv, 47 p., illus.

    Maccolini, Giuseppe. Della vita e dell'arte di Antonio Tamburini
    fino al giugno del 1842: breve commentario. Faenza: Presso
    Montanari Marabini, 1842. 22 p.

C0642.
TAUBER, RICHARD. Austrian Tenor. b. May 16, 1892, Linz; d. January
8, 1948, London.

1. BAKER 6; EdS 1/9; GROVE 6/18; MGG 1/13; RIEMANN 12 + Supp.

2. GR 17/2; RC 18/8, 9, 10, 11, 12, 19/3-4; RNC 1/2, 3, 4, 5, 7.

4. Castle, Charles and Diana Napier Tauber. This was Richard Tauber.
    London: W.H. Allen, 1971. 209 p., 67 illus., index.

    Korb, Willi. Richard Tauber: Biographie eines unvergessenen
    Saengers. Wien: Europaeischer Verlag, 1966. 187 p., 30 illus.,
    discography.

    Ludwigg, Heinz, ed. Richard Tauber. Berlin: Otto Elsner Verlags-
    gesellschaft M.B.H., 1928. 95 p., 98 illus.

    Napier-Tauber, Diana [with Ernest D. Weiss]. Richard Tauber.
    London: Art & Educational Publishers Ltd., 1949. Reprint 1980.
    237 p., 36 illus., index.

    Napier-Tauber, Diana. My Heart and I. London: Evans Brothers
    Limited, 1959. 208 p., 28 illus., index.

    Schneidereit, Otto. Richard Tauber: ein Leben -- eine Stimme.
    Berlin: VEB Lied der Zeit Musikverlag, 1974. 167 p., 84 illus.

C0643.
TEBALDI, RENATA. Italian Soprano. b. February 1, 1922, Langhirano,
Parma.

1. BAKER 6; EdS 1/9 (Bibliography); GROVE 6/18 (Bibliography); MGG
    1/16; RIEMANN 12 + Supp. (Bibliography).

2. GR 31/11, 50/9; ON 27/14, 29/12, 43/15; OPERA 6/7; OW 1/11.

4. Casanova, Carlamaria. Renata Tebaldi la voce d'angelo. Milano:
    Gruppo Editoriale Electra, 1981. 253 p., 64 illus., repertoire
    list, chronology, discography of complete operas, index of names.

    Harris, Kenn. Renata Tebaldi: an Authorized Biography. New York:
    Drake Publishers Inc., 1974. xiii, [1] p., 161 p., 30 illus.,
    discography.

    Panofsky, Walter. Renata Tebaldi. Berlin: Rembrandt Verlag, 1961.
    64 p., 29 illus., list of roles.

    Seroff, Victor. Renata Tebaldi: the Woman and the Diva. New York:
    Appleton-Century-Crofts, Inc., 1961. viii, 213 p., 28 illus., list
    of roles, discography, index.

C0644.
TE KANAWA, KIRI. New Zealand Soprano. b. March 6, 1944, Gisborne,
Auckland.

1. GROVE 6/18.

2. OPERA 32/7, 38/25, 47/12; OW 19/9.

4.   Harris, Norman. <u>Kiri: Music and a Maori Girl</u>. Sidney: A.H. & A.
     W. Reed, 1966. 62, [64] p., 86 illus., discography.

     Covers her youth up to her first trip abroad.

     Fingleton, David. <u>Kiri Te Kanawa: a Biography</u>. London: William
     Collins Sons and Co Ltd., 1982. 192 p., 59 illus., index.

C0645.
TEMPLETON, JOHN. Scottish Tenor. b. July 30, 1902, Kilmarnock; d.
July 2, 1886, New Hampton.

1.   BAKER 6; GROVE 6/18 (Bibliography); MGG 1/13; SCHMIDL.

4.   Husk, W.H. <u>Templeton & Malibran: Reminiscences of these Two
     Renowned Singers, with Original Letters and Anecdotes</u>. London:
     William Reeves, n.d. [1880]. 50 p., 3 portraits, 11 letters.

C0646.
TENDUCCI, GIUSTO FERDINANDO. Italian Castrato Soprano. b. c.1736,
Siena; d. January 25, 1790, Genoa.

1.   BAKER 6; EdS 1/9 (Bibliography); FETIS 2/8; GROVE 6/18 (Bibliog-
     raphy); MGG 1/13; RIEMANN 12 + Supp.; SCHMIDL + Supp.

3.   Tenducci, Giusto Ferdinando. <u>Instruction of Mr. Tenducci to his
     Scholars</u>. London: Longmant & Broderup, n.d. [c.1785]. 48 p.,
     portrait.

     Apparently written during his return to London for a revival of
     Gluck's <u>Orfeo</u>.

4.   Maunsell, Dorothy. <u>A True and Genuine Narrative of Mr. and Mrs.
     Tenducci</u>. London: privately printed for the author, 1768.

     Tenducci's elopement in 1767 with 16-year old Dorothy Maunsel was
     a popular subject of gossip until the marriage was annulled in
     1775.   Could Charles d'Ancillon's legal groundwork (cited under
     C0106) have been important in the decision? Angus Heriot (A0046)
     details some events in this unusual partnership (pp. 186-89).

C0647.
TEODORINI, ELENA. Romanian Soprano. b. March 25, 1857, Craiova; d.
February 27, 1926, Bucharest.

1.   BAKER 6; EdS 1/9; GROVE 6/18 (Bibliography); SCHMIDL.

2.   RNC 2/11, 3/1.

4.   Cosma, Viorel. <u>Cîntáreata Elena Teodorini: schitǎ monograficǎ</u>.
     Bucureşti: Editure Muzicalǎ, 1962. 212 p., 65 illus., repertoire,
     164-item bibliography.

C0648.
TERNINA, MILKA. Croatian Soprano. b. December 19, 1863, Vezisce, near

Zagreb; d. May 18, 1941, Zagreb.

1. BAKER 6; EdS 1/9 (Bibliography); SCHMIDL/Supp.

2. ON 20/9.

3. Ternina, Milka. An autographed MS autobiography exists. This is
   another of those historic reminiscences which should be published.

4. Grković, Mato. Milka Ternina: priredio slavko batušić. Zagreb:
   "Znanje," 1966. 430, [2] p., 21 illus.

C0649.
TESI TRAMONTINI, VITTORIA. Italian Mezzo-Soprano. b. February 13,
1700, Florence; d. May 9, 1775, Vienna.

1. BAKER 6; EdS 1/9 (Bibliography); FETIS 2/8; GROVE 6/18 (Bibliography); MGG 1/13; RIEMANN 12 (Bibliography); SCHMIDL.

4. Ademollo, Alessandro. "Le cantanti italiane celebri del secolo
   decimottavo: Vittoria Tesi." In Nuova Antologia 21 (1889): 308-
   327.

   Croce, Benedetto. Un prelato e una cantante del secolo decimottavo: Enea Silvio Piccolomini e Vittoria Tesi lettere d'amore.
   Bari: Gius. Laterza & Figli, 1946. 93 p.

C0650.
TETRAZZINI, LUISA. Italian Soprano. b. June 28, 1871, Florence; d.
d. April 28, 1940, Milan.

1. BAKER 6; EdS 1/9 (Bibliography); GROVE 6/18; MGG 1/13; RIEMANN
   12 (Bibliography) + Supp. (Bibliography); SCHMIDL + Supp.

2. GR 13/11, 18/1; ON 29/5, 35/3; OPERA 14/9; RC 4/8.

3. Tetrazzini, Luisa. How to Sing. London: C. Arthur Pearson, Ltd.,
   1923. Reprint 1974. 126 p., portrait.

   Actually about how Tetrazzini herself sang!

   Tetrazzini, Luisa. My Life of Song. London: Cassell and Company,
   Ltd., 1921. Reprint 1977. 328 p., 12 illus., index.

   This is a translation of the 1921 Milano edition: La mia vita di
   canto.

   Tetrazzini, Luisa and Enrico Caruso. The Art of Singing. New
   York: Metropolitan Co., 1909. Reprint 1975. 71 p., illus.

5. SEE: Andre Benoist under **LILLIAN NORDICA** (C0450).

C0651.
TEYTE, MAGGIE. English Soprano. b. April 17, 1888, Wolverhampton; d.
May 26, 1976, London.

1. BAKER 6; GROVE 6/18 (Bibliography); RIEMANN 12 + Supp. (Bibliography).

2. GR 14/9; ON 34/21; OPERA 3/4, 30/4; RC 9/6, 11-12.

3. Teyte, Maggie. Star on the Door. London: Putnam, 1958. Reprint 1977. 192 p., 15 illus., discography.

4. O'Connor, Garry. The Pursuit of Perfection: Maggie Teyte. New York: Antheneum, 1979. 328 p.

    Despite its recent date, I could not locate a copy.

C0652.
THEBOM, BLANCHE. American Mezzo-Soprano. b. September 19, 1918, Monessen, Pennsylvania.

1. BAKER 6; GROVE 6/18; RIEMANN 12 + Supp.

2. ON 9/6, 29/21, 36/6, 42/5.

C0653.
THILL, GEORGES. French Tenor. b. December 14, 1897 Paris.

1. EdS 1/9 (Bibliography); GROVE 6/18 (Bibliography); RIEMANN 12 + Supp. (Bibliogrphy).

2. ON 24/7; OW 22/12.

4. Georges Thill. Paris: L'Avant Scène Opéra, Septembre/1984. 114 p., 82 illus., chronology by André Segond, Discography by Georges Voisin, interview with Georges Thill by Angelo Pradier

    Mancini, Roland. Georges Thill. Paris: Société de Diffusion d'Art Lyrique, 1966. 64 p., 30 illus., discography.

    Segond, André. Georges Thill ou l'âge d'or de l'opéra. Preface by Georges Thill. Lyon: Editions Jacques-Marie Laffont et Associés, 1980. 279 p., 40 illus., selective chronology, repertoire, discography.

    Edition of 4,000.

C0654.
THOMAS, JESS. American Tenor. b. August 4, 1927, Hot Springs, South Dakota.

1. GROVE 6/18; RIEMANN 12/Supp.

2. ON 27/15, 36/5; OPERA 17/7; OW 4/8, 5/5.

C0655.
THOMAS, JOHN CHARLES. American Baritone. b. September 6, 1891, Meyersdale, Pennsylvania; d. December 13, 1960, Apple Valley, California.

1. BAKER 6.

2. ON 25/18; RC 25/1-2.

C0656.
THORBORG, KERSTIN. Swedish Mezzo-Soprano. b. May 19, 1896, Venjan;
d. April 12, 1970, Hedemora.

1. BAKER 6; GROVE 6/18 (Bibliography); RIEMANN 12.

2. ON 27/16; RC 24/9-10.

C0657.
THURSBY, EMMA. American Soprano. b. February 21, 1845, Brooklyn, New
York; d. July 4, 1931, New York City.

1. BAKER 6 (Bibliography).

4. Gipson, Richard McCandless. The Life of Emma Thursby 1845-1931.
    New York: The New York Historical Society, 1940. Reprint 1980.
    xxii, 470 p., 74 illus., chronology of concert appearances, index.

    Edition of 2,000.

C0658.
TIBBETT, LAWRENCE. American Baritone. b. November 16, 1896, Bakers-
field, California; d. July 15, 1960, New York City.

1. BAKER 6; EdS 1/9; GROVE 6/18 (Bibliography); RIEMANN 12.

2. GR 16/2; ON 25/2; OPERA 11/10; RC 23/11-12, 24/1-2; RNC 4/12,
    5/4, 5.

3. Tibbett, Lawrence. The Glory Road. Brattleboro: privately
    printed for the author, 1933. Reprint 1977 with discography by
    W.R. Moran. 70 p.

C0659.
TICHATSCHEK, JOSEPH ALOYS. Bohemian Tenor. b. July 11, 1807,
Weckelsdorf; d. January 18, 1886, Dresden.

1. BAKER 6; EdS 1/9 (Bibliography); FETIS 2/8; GROVE 6/18 (Bibliog-
    raphy); MGG 1/13; RIEMANN 12; SCHMIDL.

4. Biographische Skizze nach handschriftlichen und gedruckten
    Quellen. Dresden: K. Fuerstenan, 1868.

    No copy located.

C0660.
TODI, LUIZA ROSA de AGUILAR. Portuguese Mezzo-Soprano. b. January 9,
1753, Setubal; d. October 1, 1833, Lisbon.

1. BAKER 6 (Bibliography); EdS 1/9 (Bibliography); FETIS 2/8; GROVE
    6/19 (Bibliography); MGG 1/13 (Bibliography); RIEMANN 12 (Bibliog-

raphy) + Supp.

4. Guimarães, J. Riberio. Biographia de Luíza de Aguiar Todi.
    Lisboa: Imprensa De J.G. De Sousa Neves, 1872. 87 p.

    Luisa de Aguier Todi. Lisboa: Edicao da Revista Ocidente, 1943.
    91 p., 8 illus., 45 bibliographic notes.

    Sampayo Ribeiro, Mário de. Luísa Todi. Lisboa: S. Industriais
    Da C.M.L., 1934. 20 p., portrait.

    Sampayo Ribeiro, Mario de. Luisa de Aguiat Todi. Lisboa: Edicao
    da Revista Ocidente, 1943. 91 p., illus.

    Vasconcellos, Joaquin Antonio. Luiza Todi: estudio critico.
    Porto: Imp. Portugueza, 1873. xxxi, 157, [3], [1] p., table
    of major dates.

    This title was reprinted in an expanded edition: Coimbra: Imprensa
    Da Universidade, 1929. xxi, 183 p., chronology.

C0661.
TOUREL, JENNIE. Russian-born Mezzo-Soprano. b. June 22, 1900, St.
Petersburg; d. November 23, 1973, New York City.

1. BAKER 6; GROVE 6/19 (Bibliography); RIEMANN 12/Supp.

2. ON 34/27.

C0662.
TOZZI, GIORGIO. American Bass. b. January 8, 1923, Chicago, Illinois.

1. BAKER 6; GROVE 6/19; RIEMANN 12/Supp.

2. ON 27/22, 33/9; OW 10/12.

C0663.
TRAUBEL, HELEN. American Soprano. b. June 20, 1899, St. Louis,
Missouri; d. July 28, 1972, Santa Monica, California.

1. BAKER 6; EdS 1/9; GROVE 6/19 (Bibliography); RIEMANN 12/Supp.

2. ON 15/16.

3. Traubel, Helen and Richard G. Hubler. St. Louis Woman. New York:
    Duell, Sloan and Pearce, 1959. Reprint 1977. xiv, 296 p., 2
    illus., list of performances.

C0664.
TREBELLI, ZELIA. French Mezzo-Soprano. b. 1838, Paris; d. August 18,
1892, Etratet.

1. BAKER 6; EdS 1/9 (Bibliography); GROVE 6/19 (Bibliography);
    SCHMIDL.

4. de Mensiaux, Marie. <u>Trebelli: a Biographical Sketch and Reminis-
    cences of Her Life</u>. London: Henry Potter & Co., 1890. 66 p., 10
    illus., list of roles with first appearance.

C0665.
TREE, VIOLA. English Mezzo-Soprano. b. July 17, 1884, London; d.
November 15, 1938, London.

1. EdS 1/9 (Bibliography).

3. Tree, Viola. <u>Castles in the Air: a Story of My Singing Days</u>.
    New York: George H. Doran Company, 1926. 292 p., 8 illus., index.

C0666.
TREIGLE, NORMAN. American Baritone. b. March 6, 1927, New Orleans,
Louisiana; d. February 16, 1975, New Orleans.

1. BAKER 6; GROVE 6/19; RIEMANN 12/Supp.

2. ON 31/18.

C0667.
TUCCI, GABRIELLA. Italian Soprano. b. August 4, 1929, Rome.

1. BAKER 6; EdS 1/Supp.; GROVE 6/19; RIEMANN 12/Supp.

2. ON 30/24.

C0668.
TUCKER, RICHARD. American Tenor. b. August 28, 1913, Brooklyn, New
York; d. January 8, 1975, Kalamazoo, Michigan.

1. BAKER 6; EdS 1/Supp.; GROVE 6/19 (Bibliography); RIEMANN 12 +
    Supp. (Bibliography).

2. ON 26/7, 30/26, 34/26, 39/14, 39/20.

4. Drake, James A. <u>Richard Tucker: a Biography</u>. Forward by Luciano
    Pavarotti. New York: E.P. Dutton, Inc., 1984. xvi, 304 p., 62
    illus., discography by Patricia Ann Kiser, index.

C0669.
van TULDER, LOUIS. Dutch Tenor. b. May 22, 1892, Amsterdam; d.
October 1969, im Haag. No lexicon listing.

1. KUTSCH 3.

3. van Tulder, Louis. <u>Van kantoorkruk tot hooge c</u>. Amsterdam: De
    Boekerij, n.d. [c.1942]. 152 p., 27 illus.

C0670.
TURNER, EVA. English Soprano. b. March 10, 1892, Oldham.

1. GROVE 6/19; RIEMANN 12/Supp.

2. GR 6/3, 13/5, 37/11; ON 24/4; OPERA 1/6, 33/3; RC 11/2-3, 8, 9-10.

4. Richards, J.B. Eva Turner. London: The Gramophone Company, n.d. [1960]. 14, [2] p., 2 illus., recording details.

    One of a series of pamphlets for "Great Recordings of the Century." In this same publication are thirteen short paragraphs by the singer herself about specific roles.

C0671.
UNGER, CAROLINE. Hungarian Mezzo-Soprano. b. October 28, 1803, Stuhlweissenburg; d. March 23, 1877, near Florence.

1. BAKER 6; EdS 1/9 (under Ungher with Bibliography); GROVE 6/19 (Bibliography); MGG 1/13 (Bibliography); RIEMANN 12 (under Unger-Sabatier with Bibliography) + Supp. (under Unger-Sabatier with Bibliography); SCHMIDL.

C0672.
URLUS, JACQUES. Dutch Tenor. b. January 9, 1867, Hergenrath, near Aachen; d. June 6, 1935, Noordwijk.

1. BAKER 6 (nationality difference); GROVE 6/19 (Bibliography); MGG 1/13 (Bibliography).

2. GR 15/9; RC 26/11-12, 27/2-3, 7-8.

3. Urlus, Jacques. Mikn loopbaan. Amsterdam: N.V. Van Holkema & Warendorf's Uitgevers-Mij, n.d. [1930]. 250 p., 32 illus.

    This first appeared as a series of newspaper articles in the Algemeen Handelsblad, Amsterdam, 1928-1929.

C0673.
URSULEAC, VIORICA. Romanian Soprano. b. March 26, 1894, Cernanti.

1. BAKER 6; GROVE 6/19; RIEMANN 12 + Supp. (Bibliography).

2. ON 19/16.

C0674.
VALDENGO, GIUSEPPE. Italian Baritone. b. May 24, 1914, Turin.

1. GROVE 6/19; RIEMANN 12/Supp.

3. Valdengo, Giuseppe. Ho canto con Toscanini. Como: Pietro Cairoli Editore, 1962. 163 p., 15 illus., discography, 29-item Toscanini bibliography, index of names.

C0675.
VALLIN, NINON. French Soprano. b. September 8, 1886, Montalieu-Vereieu; d. November 22, 1961, Lyons.

1. EdS 1/9, GROVE 6/19 (Bibliography).

2. ON 36/15; OP 2/1; RC 8/3.

4. de Fragny, Robert. <u>Ninon Vallin princesse du chant</u>. Paris:
    Editions & Imprimeries du Sud-Est, 1963. 199 p., 2 illus.

CO676.
VAN DAM, JOSE. Belgian Bass. b. August 25, 1940, Brussels.

1. GROVE 6/19; RIEMANN 12/Supp. (under Van Damme, Joseph).

2. ON 45/1; OP 11/5; OW 19/2.

CO677.
VAN DIJCK, ERNEST MARIE HUBERT. Belgian Tenor. b. April 2, 1861,
Antwerp; d. August 31, 1923, Berlaer-lez-Lierre.

1. BAKER 6 (under Van Dyck); EdS 1/9 (under Van Dyck with Bibliog-
    raphy); GROVE 6/19 (under Van Dyck with Bibliography); SCHMIDL.

2. RC 5/2.

4. de Curzon, Henri. <u>Ernest van Dijck une gloire belge de l'art
    lyrique</u>. Bruxelles: Librairie Nationale d'Art et d'Histoire,
    1933. 202 p., 26 portraits, list of roles.

    There is an MS translation in English by the late George L.
    Nyklicek.

CO678.
VANNI-MARCOUX, JEAN. SEE: MARCOUX, VANNI (CO387).

CO679.
VARNAY, ASTRID. American Soprano. b. April 25, 1918, Stockholm.

1. BAKER 6; EdS 1/9 (Bibliography); GROVE 6/19; MGG 1/16; RIEMANN
    12 + Supp.

2. ON 26/24, 39/8; OPERA 9/10; OW 3/10, 13/2.

4. Wessling, Berndt W. <u>Astrid Varnay</u>. Bremen: Carl Schuenemann
    Verlag, 1965. 124 p., 32 illus., 25-item bibliography, discog-
    raphy, index of names.

CO680.
VEASEY, JOSEPHINE. English Mezzo-Soprano. b. July 10, 1930, Peckham.

1. GROVE 6/19; RIEMANN 12/Supp.

2. OPERA 20/9; OW 9/4.

CO681.
VENDRELL, EMILIO. Spanish Tenor. No lexicon listing.

3. Vendrell, Emilio. <u>El canto: (libro para el cantante y para el
    aficionado)</u>. Barcelona: Sucesor de E. Meseguer, Editor, 1955.

141 p., 6 illus.

Vendrell, Emilio. El mestre millet i jo: memòries. Barcelona: Aymà, Editors, 1953. 251 p., 26 illus.

C0682.
VERRETT, SHIRLEY. American Mezzo–Soprano. b. May 31, 1931, New Orleans, Louisiana.

1. GROVE 6/19 (Bibliography); RIEMANN 12/Supp.

2. ON 33/2, 40/11; OPERA 24/7.

C0683.
VESTRIS, LUCIA ELIZABETH. English Mezzo–Soprano. b. January 3, or March 2, 1797, London; d. August 8, 1856, London.

1. EdS 1/9 (Bibliography); GROVE 6/19 (Bibliography); MGG 1/13 (Bibliography); SCHMIDL.

4. Appleton, William. Madame Vestris and the London Stage. New York: Columbia University Press, 1974. x, 231 p., 24 illus., notes, 106–item select bibliography, index.

Memoirs of the Life of Madame Vestris, of the Theatres Royal Drury Lane and Covent Garden. London: privately printed, 1830. 72 p.

Pearce, Charles E. Madame Vestris and Her Time. London: Stanley Paul & Co., n.d. [1923]. 314 p., 18 illus., appendix, index.

Williams, Clifford John. Madame Vestris -- a Theatrical Biography. London: Sidgwick & Jackson, 1973. xii, 240 p., 51 illus., 3 appendices, 31–item selected bibliography.

5. SEE: Charles Pierce under **LAVINIA FENTON** (C0196).

C0684.
VIARDOT–GARCIA, PAULINE. French Mezzo–Soprano. b. July 18, 1821, Paris; d. May 18, 1910, Paris.

1. BAKER 6 (Bibliography); EdS 1/9 (Bibliography); FETIS 2/Supp. GROVE 6/19 (Bibliography); RIEMANN 12 + Supp. (Bibliography); Schmidl.

2. MQ 1/3, 4, 2/1; ON 43/18; OPERA 22/7; OW 15/7, 10, 16/1.

3. Viardot–Garcia, Pauline. Ecole classique de chant. Paris, 1861.

This pedagogical manual is listed in GROVE 6/19. No copy located.

4. Fitzlyon, April. The Price of Genius: a Life of Pauline Viardot. New York: Appleton–Century, 1964. 520 p., 21 illus., 210–item bibliography, index.

Another fine piece of scholarship.

La Mara [pseud. for Ida Maria Lipsius]. <u>Pauline Viardot-Garcia</u>. Sammlung musikalischer Vortraege IV. Leipzig: Breitkopf & Haertel, 1882. 18 p.

Marix-Spire, Therese, ed. <u>Lettres inédites de George Sand et de Pauline Viardot 1839-1849</u>. Paris: Nouvelles Editions Latines, 1959. 316 p., 13 illus., 240-item bibliography, index.

Rachmanowa, Alja [pseud. for Galina von Hoyer]. <u>Die Liebe eines Lebens: Iwan Turgenjew und Pauline Viardot</u>. Frauenfeld: Huber Verlag, 1952. 398, [1] p., bibliography.

Turgenev, Ivan Sergeyevich. <u>Lettres à Madame Viardot</u>. Publiées et anotées par E. Halpérine-Kaminsky. Paris: Bibliothèque-Charpentier, 1907. vi, 263 p.

5.   SEE: Erna Brand under **AGLAJA ORGENI** (C0460).

SEE: Desternes and Chandet under **MARIA MALIBRAN** (C0378).

SEE   Louise Hériette-Viardot's autobiography under **MANUEL PATRICIO GARCIA** (C0231).

Liszt, Franz. <u>Gesammelte Schriften</u>. vol. 3. Leipzig: Breitkopf und Haertel, 1880. pp. 121-136.

SEE: M. Sterling Mackinlay under **MANUEL PATRICIO GARCIA** (C0231).

SEE: autobiography of **ANNA EUGENIE SCHOEN-RENE** (C0566).

SEE: Charles V. Stanford under **JENNY LIND** (C0360).

C0685.
VICKERS, JON. Canadian Tenor. b. October 29, 1926, Prince Albert, Saskatchewan.

1.   BAKER 6; EdS 1/Supp.; GROVE 6/19; RIEMANN 12/Supp.

2.   ON 24/15, 26/6, 38/19; OPERA 13/4, 33/4; OW 16/10.

C0686.
VILLANI, LUISA. Italian Soprano. b. 1885, San Francisco, California. No lexicon listing.

1.   KUTSCH 3.

4.   Bott, Michael F. <u>Luisa Villani -- Forgotten Diva</u>. San Francisco: privately printed for the author, 1981. 12, [13] p., discography, 22-item bibliography, repertoire, genealogy.

Edition of 100 copies.

C0687.
VINAS, FRANCISCO. Spanish Tenor. b. March 27, 1863, Barcelona; d.

July 13, 1933, Moya.

1. EdS 1/9 (Bibliography).

3. Viñas, Francisco. El arte del canto: datos históricos consejos
    y ejercicios musicales para la educación de la voz. con un
    prologo de Victoria De Los Angeles. Barcelona: Casa Del Libro,
    1963 [1st edition 1932]. 388 p., illus., musical examples, index.

4. de Gregori, Luigi. Francesco Viñas: el gran tenor Catalá fundador
    de la lliga de defensa de l'arbre fruiter. Barcelona: privately
    printed, 1935. 269 p., 57 illus., chronology.

    The publication run was 9,000, but there is a limited edition of
    200 numbered copies.

C0688.
VINAY, RAMON. Chilean Baritone/Tenor. b. August 31, 1912, Chillan.

1. EdS 1/9; GROVE 6/19 (Bibliography); RIEMANN 12 + Supp.

2. ON 30/22; OPERA 9/6.

C0689.
VINCENT, JO[hanna Maria]. Dutch Soprano. b. March 6, 1898,
Amsterdam.

1. GROVE 6/19.

3. Vincent, Jo. Zingend door het leven: memoires. Amsterdam:
    Elsevier, 1955. 128 p., 16 illus.

4. Bouws, Tom, ed. Levensbeeld van Jo Vincent. 's-Gravenhage:
    Uitgeverij Sint-Joris N.V., n.d. 12 p., 3 illus., 45 RPM record.

C0690.
VISCARDI, MARIA. Italian Soprano. No lexicon listing.

4. Falzetti, Giulia and Tommaso Falzetti. Maria Viscardi: una vita
    per il canto. Roma: Angelo Signorelli Editore, 1966. 307 p.,
    45 illus., list of colleagues.

C0691.
VISHNEVSKAYA, GALINA. Russian Soprano. b. October 25, 1926,
Leningrad.

1. BAKER 6; EdS 1/Supp. (under Visnevskaja); GROVE 6/20 (Bibliog-
    raphy).

2. ON 40/3; OW 5/12.

3. Vishnevskaya, Galina. Galina: a Russian Story. Translated by Guy
    Daniels. New York: Harcourt Brace Janovich, Publishers, 1984.
    xiii, 519 p., 73 illus., list of repertoire, discography, index.

C0692.
VITTORI, LORETO. Italian Castrato Soprano. baptized September 5, 1600, Spoletto; d. April 23, 1670, Rome.

1.   EdS 1/9 (Bibliography); GROVE 6/20 (Bibliography); MGG 1/13 (Bibliography); RIEMANN 12; SCHMIDL.

4.   Rau, Carl August. Loreto Vittori: Beitraege zur historisch-kritischen Wuerdigung seines Lebens, Wirkens und Schaffens. Muenchen: Verlag fuer Moderne Musik, 1916. xii, 117 p., 86-item bibliography, list of the most famous castrati.

C0693.
VOGL, HEINRICH. German Tenor. b. January 15, 1845, Au, suburb of Munich; d. April 21, 1900, Munich.

1.   BAKER 6; EdS 1/9 (Bibliography); FETIS 2/Supp.; GROVE 6/20 (Bibliography); MGG 1/13 (Bibliography); RIEMANN 12.

4.   von der Pfordten, Herman Freiherr. Heinrich Vogl zur Erinnerung und zum Vermaechtniss. Muenchen: Carl Haushalter, Verlagsbuch-handlung, 1900. 27 p.

     Wuennenberg, Rolf. Das Saengerehepaar Heinrich und Therese Vogl: ein Beitrag zur Operngeschichte des 19. Jahrhunderts. Tutzing: Hans Schneider, 1982. 162 p., 36 illus., 63-item bibliography.

C0694.
VOGL, JOHANN MICHAEL. Austrian Baritone. b. August 10, 1768, Steyr; d. November 20, 1840, Vienna.

1.   BAKER 6; GROVE 6/20 (Bibliography); MGG 1/13 (Bibliography); RIEMANN 12 + Supp. (Bibliography); SCHMIDL/Supp.

4.   Liess, Andreas. Johann Michael Vogl Hofoperist und Schubert-Saenger. Gratz: Verlag Hermann Boehlaus Nachf., 1954. 224 p., 8 illus., list of roles, 52-item bibliography, index of names, music insert.

     NOTE: Liess lists an annonymous MS biography of Vogl currently in the collection of the Gesellschaft der Musikfreunde in Vienna.

C0695.
VULPESCU, MIHAIL. Romanian Baritone. b. December 31, 1888, Cîmpia Bărăganului; d. August 23, 1956, Bucharest. No lexicon listing.

4.   Obreja, Constanta. Mihail Vulpescu. Bucureşti: Editura Muzicală, 1967. 179 p., 36 illus., 7-item bibliography, repertoire, discography.

C0696.
WAGNER-JACHMANN, JOHANNA. German Soprano. b. October 13, 1828, Hannover; d. October 16, 1894, Wuerzburg.

1. BAKER 6; FETIS 2/8; GROVE 6/20 (Bibliography; birthdate given
   as 1826); MGG 1/14; RIEMANN 12; SCHMIDL/Supp. (under Jachmann-
   Wagner).

4. Kapp, Julius and Hans Jachmann. Richard Wagner und seine erste
   "Elisabeth" Johanna Jachmann-Wagner. Berlin: Dom-Verlag, 1927.
   237 p., 25 illus., index of names.

   There is an abridged translation (by M.A.T.) published by Novello
   and Company in London, 1944. 71 p., 8 illus.

C0697.
WAKEFIELD, MARY. English Mezzo-Soprano. b. August 19, 1853, Kendal;
d. September 16, 1910, Kendal. No lexicon listing.

4. Newmarch, Rosa. Mary Wakefield: a Memoir. Kendal: Atkinson and
   Pollitt, Printers and Publishers, 1912. 142 p., 11 illus.,
   appendix.

C0698.
WALDMAN, LEIBELE. American cantor. No lexicon listing.

3. Waldman, Leibele. Song Divine: an Autobiography. Compiled by
   Mona Sarro. New York: The Saravan House, n.d. [c.1941].
   273 p., portrait.

C0699.
WALLACE, IAN. Scottish Bass. b. July 10, 1919, London.

1. GROVE 6/20.

3. Wallace Ian. Promise Me You'll Sing Mud! the Autobiography of
   Ian Wallace. London: J. Calder, 1975. 240, [6] p., illus.,
   index.

C0700.
WALLNOFER, ADOLF. Austrian Tenor. b. April 26, 1854, Vienna; d. June
9, 1946, Munich.

1. BAKER 6; REIMANN 12; SCHMIDL/Supp.

2. RC 14/11-12, 19/3-4.

C0701.
WALSKA, GANNA. Polish Soprano. No lexicon listing.

3. Walska, Ganna. Always Room at the Top. New York: Richard R.
   Smith, 1943. 504 p., 90 illus.

   Walska was a wealthy dilettante determined to perform. Marjorie
   Lawrence expressed it best in her autobiography (pp. 73-74).
   "...Madame Gilly was forced to take as students several people
   with full purses but very minor talents. Some she discouraged
   by charging exorbitant fees, but high fees were no deterrent to
   one woman who contributed substantially to Madame's bankroll.

This was Ganna Walska, a Polish socialite."

CO702.
WALTER, GUSTAV. Austrian Tenor. b. February 11, 1834, Bilin,
Bohemia; d. January 30, 1910, Vienna.

1. EdS 1/9 (Bibliography).

4. Nunnenmacker-Noellfeld, Maria. Der Schubertsaenger Gustav Walter:
    ein Wiener Kuenstlerleben. Bilin: B., Verlag Ernst Menda, 1930.
    141 p., 3 portraits.

CO703.
WARFIELD, SANDRA. American Mezzo-Soprano. b. August 6, 1929, Kansas
City, Missouri. No lexicon listing.

2. ON 35/18, 36/6.

3. McCracken, James and Sandra Warfield. A Star in the Family: an
    Autobiography in Diary Form. Edited by Robert Daley. New York:
    Coward McCann & Geoghegan, Inc., 1970. 388 p., 33 illus.

CO704.
WARREN, LEONARD. American Baritone. b. April 21, 1911, New York City;
d. March 4, 1960, New York City.

1. BAKER 6; EdS 1/9 (Bibliography); GROVE 6/20 (Bibliography).

2. GR 32/2; ON 24/22, 39/18; OPERA 11/6.

CO705.
WATSON, CLAIRE. American Soprano. b. February 3, 1927, New York City.

1. GROVE 6/20; RIEMANN 12/Supp.

2. ON 23/22, 34/8; OPERA 21/11; OW 7/10.

CO706.
WEATHERS, FELICIA. American Soprano. b. August 13, 1937, St. Louis,
Missouri.

1. RIEMANN 12/Supp.

2. ON 31/27; OP 9/9; OW 8/2.

CO707.
WELITSCH, LJUBA. Bulgarian Soprano. b. July 10, 1913, Borisovo, near
Varna.

1. BAKER 6; GROVE 6/20; RIEMANN 12 + Supp.

2. ON 13/16, 36/18; OPERA 4/2.

CO708.
WHITEHILL, CLARENCE EUGENE. American Baritone. b. November 5, 1871,

near Parnell, Iowa; d. December 19, 1932, New York City.

1. BAKER 6; GROVE 6/20; RIEMANN 12.

2. RC 22/10-11.

C0709.
WILSON, JAMES STEUART. English Tenor. b. July 22, 1889, Clifton; d.
d. December 18, 1966, Petersfield.

1. GROVE 6/20.

4. Stewart, Margaret. <u>English Singer: the Life of Steuart Wilson</u>.
    London: Gerald Duckworth & Co., Ltd., 1970. 320 p., 18 illus.,
    6 appendices including a list of recordings and publications,
    23-item bibliography, index.

C0710.
WINDGASSEN, WOLFGANG. German Tenor. b. June 26, 1914, Annemasse,
Haute Savoie; d. September 8, 1974, Stuttgart.

1. BAKER 6; GROVE 6/20 (Bibliography); MGG 1/16 (Bibliography);
    RIEMANN 12 + Supp. (Bibliography).

2. ON 30/21, OPERA 13/9; OW 1/3, 15/10.

4. Honolka, Kurt. <u>Wolfgang Windgassen</u>. Stuttgart: Deutscher Opern-
    Verlag GmbH, n.d. [c.1962]. 62 p., 31 illus., repertoire list.

    Wessling, Berndt W. <u>Wolfgang Windgassen</u>. Bremen: Carl
    Schuenemann Verlag, 1967. 126 p., 25 illus., repertoire list,
    Bayreuth appearances, discography, chronology, 57-item biblio-
    graphy + letters and interviews.

C0711.
WINKELMANN, HERMANN. German Tenor. b. March 4, 1849, Brunswick; d.
January 18, 1912, Vienna.

1. BAKER 6; EdS 1/9 (Bibliography); GROVE 6/20; SCHMIDL.

2. RC 7/6-7.

C0712.
WITHERSPOON, HERBERT. American Bass. b. July 21, 1873, New York City;
d. May 10, 1935, New York City.

1. BAKER 6; SCHMIDL/Supp.

3. Witherspoon, Herbert. <u>Singing: a Treatise for Teachers and
    Students</u>. New York: G. Schirmer, Inc., 1925. 126 p., illus.,
    index.

    Witherspoon, Herbert. <u>Thirty-Six Lessons in Singing</u>. Chicago:
    Miessner Institute of Music, 1930. 51 p., illus.

C0713.
WOOD, MARY ANN. Scottish Soprano. b. October 1802, Edinburgh; d. July 21, 1864, Chapelthorpe.

1. GROVE 6/14 (under Paton, Mary Anne with Bibliography).

4. Memoir of Mr. & Mrs. Wood. Boston: James Fisher, 1840. 36 p., 4 inserted plates.

   "...containing an authentic account of the principal events in the lives of these celebrated vocalists..."
   Her husband, Joseph Wood, was a tenor. b. March 7, 1801; d. 1890.

C0714.
WOYTOWICZ, STEFANIA. Polish Soprano. b. October 8, 1925, Orynin.

1. GROVE 6/20; RIEMANN 12/Supp.

4. Kánski, Józef. Stefania Woytowicz. Polskie Wydawnictwo Muzyczne, 1961. 27 p., 12 illus., repertoire list.

C0715.
WUELLNER, LUDWIG. German Baritone. b. August 19, 1858, Muenster; d. March 19, 1938, Berlin.

1. BAKER 6; GROVE 6/20 (location of death different); RIEMANN 12/ Supp.

4. 50 Photos aus dem Leben und der Kunst Dr. Ludwig Wuellners sowie eine Originallithigraphie von Emil Orlik. Leipzig: Erich Weibezahl Verlag, n.d.

   Ludwig, Franz. Ludwig Wuellner: sein Leben und seine Kunst. Leipzig: Erich Weibezahl Verlag, 1931. xxxii, 253 p., 51 illus., lieder repertoire.

   Rapsilber, M., ed. Ludwig Wuellner: ein musikalisches Charakter-bild dargestellt...aus den Jahren 1896 bis 1907. Leipzig: Erich Weibezahl Verlag, n.d. [c.1930. 1st edition 1907]. 84 p.

C0716.
WUNDERLICH, FRITZ. German Tenor. b. September 26, 1930, Kusel, Rheinland-Pfalz; d. September 17, 1966, Heidelberg.

1. GROVE 6/20 (Bibliography); RIEMANN 12 + Supp.

2. OP 6/9; OW 1/7, 7/11.

5. SEE: Hubert Giesen under **KARL ERB** (C0184).

C0717.
ZANELLI, RENATO. Chilean Baritone. b. April 1, 1892, Valparaiso; d. March 25, 1935, Santiago.

1. GROVE 6/20; SCHMIDL/Supp.

2. RC 7/9.

4. Elgueta, Juan Dzazopoulos. "Renato Zanelli: el coloso Chileno". In
    Ayer y Hoy de la Opera 5/5 (1984):3-34. 4 illus.

C0718.
ZENATELLO, GIOVANNI. Italian Tenor. b. February 22, 1876, Verona; d.
February 11, 1949, New York City.

1. BAKER 6; EdS 1/9 (Bibliography); GROVE 6/20; RIEMANN 12 + Supp.
    (Bibliography); SCHMIDL.

2. RC 4/2, 5/5, 14/5-6, 7-8, 27/4-5.

4. Consolaro, Nina Zenatello. Giovanni Zenatello, tenore; ideatore
    degli spettacolo lirici dell'Arena de Verona (1913). Verona:
    Novastampa di Verona, 1976. 157 p., illus.

C0719.
von zur-MUEHLEN, RAIMUND. German Tenor. b. November 10, 1854,
d. December 9, 1931, Steyning, Sussex, England.

1. BAKER 6; GROVE 6/20 (Bibliography); MGG 1/14 (Bibliography);
    RIEMANN 12; SCHMIDL.

4. von zur-Muehlen, Dorothea. Der Saenger Raimund von zur-Muehlen.
    Hannover-Doehren: Verlag Harro von Hirschheydt, 1969. 240 p.,
    3 illus.

5. SEE: autobiography of **OLGA LYNN** (C0374).

C0720.
ZYLLIS-GARA, TERESA. Polish Soprano. b. January 23, 1937, Vilnius.

1. GROVE 6/20; RIEMANN 12/Supp.

2. ON 33/10, 39/14; OW 20/3.

APPENDIX I:
Reference Material

Apart from standard encyclopedia entries (EdS 1/2 under "Cantante";
EdS 1/2 under "Canto"; GROVE 6/17 under "Singing"; and MGG 1/4 under
"Gesangskunst"), there are a small number of other sources which I
found helpful in tracking down material by and about concert and opera
singers. Most of these are titles which would be familiar to the serious musicologist and researcher but, perhaps, not to the collector,
afficionado, or earnest dilettante.

DO001. Bernsdorf, Eduard. Neues Universal-Lexikon der Tonkunst: fuer
Kuenstler, Kunst-Freunde und alle Gebildeten. 3 vols. Dresden: (vols.
1/2) Verlag von Robert Schaefer, 1856/1857; Offenbach: (vol. 3) Verlag
von Johann Andre, 1861. 878p.; 1084 p.; 912, [2] p. supp. 1865.

   Very helpful for obscure performers. Not in DUCKLES 3 (DO006).

DO002. Bertz-Dostal, Helga. Oper im Fernsehen. 2 vols. Wien: Verlag
und Druck Minor. Herausgegeben mit Foerderung der Gesellschaft fuer
Musiktheater. 1970. 623 p., 110 illus.; 629-1132 p., index of names.

   An absolutely monumental work which includes production details
   of 1,646 television productions (1936-1970) including casts. Not
   in DUCKLES 3 (DO006).

DO003. Brockway, Wallace and Herbert Weinstock. The World of Opera:
the Story of its Origins and the Lore of its Performance. New York:
Pantheon Books, 1962 [1st edition 1941]. viii, 723 p., 32 illus.,
index, index to the annals of performance.

   One of the major features of this book is the final section which
   gives the performance history of 253 operas including the premiere
   and other historically important productions. There is a special
   index for this section. Not in DUCKLES 3 (DO006).

DO004. Brown, James D. and Stephen S. Stratton. British Musical Biography: a Dictionary of Musical Artists, Authors and Composers, born in
Britain and its Colonies. Birmingham: Chadfield and Son, Ltd., 1897.
11, 462, [1] p.

   Most helpful for obscure vocalists. Not in DUCKLES 3 (DO006).

DO005. Dabrowskiego, Stanislawa, ed. Slownik biograficzny teatru
polskiego. Warszawa: Panstwowe Wydawnictwo Naukowe, 1973. 905 p.,
numerous illus.

   Critical for Polish singers. Not in DUCKLES 3 (DO006).

DO006. Duckles, Vincent. Music Reference and Research Materials: an
Annotated Bibliography. 3rd edition. New York: The Free Press, 1974.
xvi, 526 p.

   THE basic reference for music research materials in all languages,
   DUCKLES 3 is particularly helpful in its international and national
   biography sections. There are 130 titles, many of which include
   material related to concert and opera singers!

DO007. Eisenberg, Ludwig. Grosses Biographisches Lexikon der
Deutschen Buehne im XIX. Jahrhundert. Leipzig: Verlagsbuchhandlung
Paul List, 1903. [iii], 1180, [1] p., frontispiece, 182-item bib-
liography, index of cross-referenced artists, errata.

   Enormously helpful for the period. Not in DUCKLES 3 (DO006).

DO008. Engelmuellera, Karla. Ottuv divadelni slovnik. Prague: n.p.,
n.d. [c.1920]. 944 p., numerous illus.

   Only the initial volume (A-Gatty) was published. Not in DUCKLES
   3 (DO006).

DO009. Ewen, David, ed. Living Musicians. New York: The H.W. Wilson
Company, 1940. 390 p., photo of each musician, classified list by type
of musician.

   Includes seventy-two sopranos, eighteen contraltos, forty tenors,
   twenty-four baritones, and fourteen basses.

DO010. Ewen, David, ed. Living Musicians. first supplement. New
York: The H.W. Wilson Company, 1957. 178 p., necrology [1964 2nd
printing], list of new biographies, classified list of new biographies.

   Adds twenty-six sopranos, twelve mezzo-sopranos, twelve tenors,
   and twenty-two baritones and basses.

DO011. Highfill, Jr., Philip H., Kalman A. Burnim and Edward A. Lang-
hans. A Biographical Dictionary of Actors, Actresses, Musicians,
Dancers, Managers and other Stage Personnel in London, 1660-1800.
10 vols. to date. Carbondale: Southern Illinois University Press,
1973-   .

   The Preface to volume one indicates both the scope and the nature
   of this absolutely monumental undertaking. For example, one
   memorable eighteenth century singer who did not qualify for an
   individual entry in this compliation, Francesca Cuzzioni, has a
   comprehensive entry in Highfill (vol. 4:112-118, 3 illus.) far
   surpassing anything else available. Not in DUCKLES 3 (DO006).

D0012. Hughes, Rupert. Music Lover's Encyclopedia. Completely
revised and newly edited by Deems Taylor and Russell Kerr. Garden City:
Garden City Publishing Co., Inc., 1947 [1st edition 1903]. xxv, 877,
unpaginated chart, [1] p.

   Another valuable reference for obscure performers.

D0013. Kosch, Wilhelm: Deutsches Theater-Lexikon: biographisches
und bibliographisches Handbuch. 2 vols. Klagenfurt, Verlag Ferd.
Kleinmayr, 1953/1960. [iii], 864 p.; 865-1728 p. fortgefuehrt von
Hanspeter Bennwitz.

   Hopefully someone will complete the work of Kosch and Bennwitz as
   this is particularly valuable for lesser-known performers. Not in
   DUCKLES 3 (D0006).

D0014. Mixter, Keith E. General Bibliography for Music Research.
second edition. Detroit: Information Coordinators, Inc., 1975. 135 p.

   The section on national and international biographical dictionaries would be of major help to anyone researching performers.

D0015. Monahan, Brent Jeffrey. The Art of Singing: a Compendium of
Thoughts on Singing Published between 1777 and 1927. Metuchen [New
Jersey]: The Scarecrow Press, Inc., 1978. xiv, 342 p., index.

   Lists 608 pedagogical documents, a number of which are annotated.
   The author researched seven major collections including the
   the Library of Congress, the Boston and New York public libraries;
   Indiana, Princeton, and Rutgers university libraries; and the
   Westminster Choir College collection. Not in DUCKLES 3 (D0006).

D0016. Moore, Frank Ledlie. Crowell's Handbook of World Opera.
Introduction by Darius Milhaud. New York: Thomas Y. Crowell Company,
1961. [v], 683 p.

   "The People in Opera," pp. 184-307 includes short biographies
   of numerous singers and their principal operatic roles.

D0017. Wechsberg, Joseph: The Opera. New York, The Macmillan
Company: 1972. [vi], 312 p., index.

   Note the section: "Singing and Singers," pp. 126-176. Not in
   DUCKLES 3 (D0006).

APPENDIX II:

Index to Singers in GROVE 6

This index lists the 1,439 concert and opera singers who were given an individual entry in The New GROVE Dictionary of Music and Musicians (1980) edited by Stanley Sadie. Widely avail- able, it is quite probably the reference work most frequently consulted by those seeking information on performers, both past and present, in all the various applied music specializations. Thus, a cross-referenced list should prove helpful to readers. Of the 708 individual singers accorded entries in the main body of this bibliography, some 491 of them appear as entries in the New GROVE or GROVE 6 as Dr. Sadie chose to identify it. This commonality is indicated by the appropriate code number preceding the name, e.g. C0001 (the entry number in my INDIVI- UAL SINGERS, A–Z, p. 49) before **EMMA ABBOTT** who is the first singer listed in GROVE 6.

Several things should be kept in mind when utilizing this compilation. First, all names are spelled as in GROVE 6, i.e. Shalyapin, and not as in my listing, i.e. Chaliapin. Due to space limitations, not all forenames identified in GROVE 6 are included. And, finally, some entries, i.e. Vanni-Marcoux, are listed differently in this bibliography, i.e. Marcoux, Vanni. In all cases, alphabetical order in this bibliography was based where possible upon the outstanding work of Nicolas Slonimsky who edited the sixth edition of BAKER'S BIOGRAPHICAL DICTIONARY MUSICIANS (1978). Regretfully, the eagerly awaited seventh edition was not available as my own final editing began.

It is rather revealing to note that there are two hundred seventeen singers about whom sufficient sources exist to qualify them for inclusion in this bibliography who are not accorded an entry in GROVE 6! This suggests the enormous discrepency among the various "standard" reference works as to exactly which artists are deserving of inclusion. As a matter of fact, each of the earlier editions of GROVE includes singers who are not to be found in the 1980 version; what better reason could there be to pursue the master index of singers and the biographical dictionary of singers to which I alluded earlier in my Preface. At this point the best advice would be in the form of a caution to investigate any and all sources which suggest the remotest possibility of containing information on that special artist. And remember -- no one will ever compile the definitive work.

C0001. Abbott, Emma
Abrams, Harriet
C0004. Ackté, Aieno
C0005. Adam, Theo
Adamberger, Valentin
Adami da Bolsena, Andrea
Adams, Charles R.
Adams, Suzanne
Addison, Adele
Aguiari, Lucrezia
Ahlersmeyer, Matthiew
Alarie, Pierrette
Albanese, Egide
C0009. Albanese, Licia
C0010. Albani, Emma
C0011. Alboni, Marietta
C0012. Alcaide, Tomáz
C0013. Alda, Frances
Alexander, John
Allegranti, Maddalena
Allen, Betty
Allen, Henry
Allen, Thomas
Allin, Norman
Altmeyer, Theo
Alva, Luigi
Alvary, Max
Amara, Lucine
C0014. Amato, Pasquale
Ambrosch, Joseph
Ameling, Elly
Amorevoli, Angelo
Ancona, Mario
C0016. Anders, Peter
C0017. Anderson, Marian
Andreoni, Giovani
Andrésen, Ivar
Annibale, Domenico
Anselmi, Giuseppe
Ansseau, Fernand
Antier, Marie
Antinori, Luigi
Aprile, Giuseppe
Aragall, Giacomo
Arangi-Lombardi, Giannina
Archieli, Vittoria
Arkhipova, Irina
d'Arkor, André
Armstrong, Sheila
Arndt-Ober, Margarethe
C0020. Arnould, Sophie
C0021. Arroyo, Martina
Artôt, Désirée
Atlantov, Vladimir

Austin, Frederic
C0024. Austral, Florence
Avdeyeva, Larisa
Avoglio, Christina
Ayliff
Ayton, Fanny
Babbi, Gregorio
C0026. Baccaloni, Salvatore
C0027. Bachmann, Charlotte
Bacquier, Gabriel
C0029. Badía, Conchita
Baglioni, Antonio
Baglioni, Francesco
Bagnolesi, Anna
C0030. Bahr-Mildenburg, Anna
Bailey, Lilian
C0031. Bailey, Norman
Baillie, Isobel
C0033. Baker, Janet
Baklanov, Gregory
Baldassari, Benedetto
Baldi, Antonio
C0035. Balfe, Michael
Balkanska, Mimi
C0036. Bampton, Rose
Banderali, Davidde
Bandrowska-Turska, Ewa
Bandowski-Sas, Aleksander
C0037. Banti, Brigida
Barbier
C0039. Barbieri, Fedora
Barbieri-Nini, Marianna
Bareva, Lilyana
C0041. Baroni, Leonora
Barrientos, Maria
Barsova, Valeriya
Barstow, Josephine
C0043. Basilides, Mária
Bassi, Luigi
Bastianini, Ettore
Bates, Sarah
Bathori, Jane
C0044. Bathy, Anna
Battaille, Charles
C0045. Battistini, Mattia
Bayseitova, Kulyash
Beard, John
Beardslee, Bethany
Bechi, Gino
Begnis, Giuseppe de
Begrez, Pierre
Behr, Therese
Bell, Donald
Belletti, Giovanni

C0047. Bellincoini, Gemma
C0048. Belloc-Giorgi, Teresa
C0049. Bender, Paul
Benucci, Francesco
Bérard, Jean-Antoine
Berberian, Cathy
Berbié, Jane
Berenstadt, Gaetano
C0051. Berganza, Teresa
C0052. Berger, Erna
Berglund, Joel
C0054. Bergonzi, Carlo
C0055. Bernac, Pierre
Bernacchi, Antonio
Bernasconi, Antonia
C0056. Berry, Walter
Berselli, Matteo
Bertinotti, Teresa
Bertolli, Francesca
Berton, Adolphe
Betz, Franz
Bianchi, Antonio
Bigonzi, Giuseppe
C0058. Billington, Elizabeth
Bilt, Peter van der
Bishop, Anna
C0059. Bispham, David
C0061. Bjoner, Ingrid
C0060. Bjoerling, Jussi
C0062. Blachut, Beno
Black, Andrew
Blaes, Elisa
Blanc, Ernest
Blanc, Jonny
Bland, Maria
C0065. Blegen, Judith
Boccabadati-Varesi, Elena
C0066. Bockelmann, Rudolf
C0067. Boehme, Kurt
C0068. Bohnen, Michael
C0069. Bonci, Alessandro
Bondini, Pasquale
C0070. Boninsegna, Celestina
Bordogni, Giulio
C0071. Bordoni, Faustina
Borg, Kim
C0072. Borgatti, Giuseppe
C0073. Borgioli, Dino
C0074. Bori, Lucrezia
Borkh, Inge
Boronat, Olimpia
Borosini, Francesco
Borosini, Rosa
Broschi, Giuseppe

Bosio, Angiolina
Bouhy, Jacques
Bourdin, Roger
C0076. Bovy, Vina
C0077. Braham, John
Brambilla, Marietta
Brambilla, Teresa
Brambilla, Giuseppina
Brambilla-Ponchielli, T.
C0078. Brandt, Marianne
Brannigan, Owen
Branzell, Karin
Braun, Victor
Brema, Marie
Brent, Charlotte
Brooks, Patricia
C0082. Brouwenstijn, Gré
Brown, Wilfred
C0083. Brownlee, John
Brusciantini, Sesto
Bruson, Renato
Bryn-Julson, Phyllis
Bruckman, Rosina
C0086. Bumbry, Grace
Burian, Karel
Burke, Edmund
C0087. Burke, Thomas
Burmeister, Annelies
Burrowes, Norma
Burrows, Stuart
Bussani, Dorothea
Bussani, Francesco
C0088. Butt, Clara
C0089. Caballé, Montserrat
Cabel, Marie
Caccini, Francesca
Caccini, Settimia
C0090. Caffarelli
C0091. Callas, Maria
Calori, Angiola
C0092. Calvé, Emma
C0093. Campanini, Italo
Camporese, Violante
C0094. Caniglia, Maria
Canne-Meijer, Cora
Cantelo
Cantelo, April
C0095. Capecchi, Renato
Cappuccilli, Piero
Capsir, Mercedes
Caradori-Allan, Maria
Carestini, Giovanni
Carlyle, Jean
Carosio, Margherita

C0102. Carreno, Teresa
C0103. Carreras, José
        Carron, Arthur
C0104. Caruso, Enrico
C0105. Carvalho, Caroline
        Carvalho, Léon
        Cary, Annie
        Casazza, Elvira
        Cassani, Giuseppe
        Cassilly, Richard
        Castallan, Jeanne
C0107. Catalani, Angelica
C0108. Catley, Anne
        Cavalieri, Catarina
C0109. Cavalieri, Lina
C0110. Cebotari, Maria
        Chardiny, Louis
        Charton-Demeur, Anne
        Chimenti, Margherita
C0114. Christoff, Boris
        Cibber, Susanna
C0115. Cigna, Gina
        Cinti-Damoreau, Laure
        Clive, Kitty
        Coates, Edith
        Coates, John
        Cobelli, Giuseppina
        Cochereau, Jacques
        Colbran, Isabella
        Cold, Ulrik
        Coletti, Filippo
C0117. Collier, Marie
        Coltellini, Celeste
        Conti, Gioacchino
        Cook, Thomas
C0118. Corelli, Franco
        Corena, Fernando
C0119. Cornelius, Peter
        Cortez, Viorica
        Cortis, Antonio
C0121. Cossotto, Fiorenza
        Cosoutta, Carlo
        Costantini, Livia
C0123. Cotrubas, Ileana
C0124. Cox, Jean
C0125. Crabbé, Armand
        Craig, Charles
        Crammer, Arthur
        Crass, Franz
C0126. Crespin, Régine
C0127. Cristoforeanu, Florica
        Crivelli, Gaetano
        Croce, Elena
C0128. Croiza, Claire

C0129. Crooks, Richard
C0130. Cross, Joan
C0131. Crouch, Anna
C0132. Cruvelli, Jeanne
C0133. Cuenod, Hugues
C0134. Culp, Julia
        Curioni, Alberico
        Curioni, Rosa
        Curphey, Margaret
        Curtin, Phyllis
        Cuzzoni, Francesca
        Czerwenka, Oscar
C0136. Dalla Rizza, Gilda
C0137. Dal Monte, Toti
        Dalmorès, Charles
        Dal Pane, Domenico
C0141. Danco, Suzanne
C0142. Dannstroem, Isidor
C0143. Darclée, Hariclea
        Dauer, Johann
        Davide, Giovanni
        Davies, Benjamin
        Davies, Cecilia
        Davies, Mary
        Davies, Ryland
        Davies, Tudor
        Davis, Mary
        Davy, Gloria
        De Amicis, Anna
        Dean, Stafford
        De Angelis, Nazzareno
        De Gaetani, Jan
C0150. Della Casa, Lisa
C0151. Deller, Alfred
        Delle Sedie, Enrico
C0152. Del Monaco, Mario
        Del Puente, Giuseppe
C0154. De Luca, Giuseppe
C0155. De Lucia, Fernando
        DeMezzo, Pietro
        Dempsey, Gregory
C0160. De Reszke, Jean
C0159. De Reszke, Edouard
        De Reszke, Joséphine
C0161. Dermota, Anton
C0162. Dernesch, Helga
        Derzhinskaya, Xenija
        Desmond, Astra
C0165. Destinn, Emmy
        Deutekom, Cristina
C0166. Diaz, Justino
        Dickie, Murray
C0167. Didur, Adam
        Di Murska, Ilma

CO237. Gerhardt, Elena
Gerl, Barbara
Gerster, Etelka
Geszty, Sylvia
CO239. Ghiaurov, Nicolai
CO240. Giannini, Dusolina
Gibelli, Lorenzo
Giebel, Agnes
CO242. Gigli, Beniamino
CO243. Gilly, Dinh
Giardeau, Isabella
Girelli, Antonia
Gismondi, Celeste
Giuglini, Antonio
Gizzi, Domenico
Gladkowska, Konstancja
Glossop, Peter
Glover, William
CO248. Gluck, Alma
CO249. Gobbi, Tito
Goltz, Christel
Gomez, Jill
Gordon, Alexander
CO251. Gorr, Rita
Gottlieb, Anna
Goward, Mary
Gramm, Donald
CO252. Grandi, Margherita
Grant, Clifford
Grassi, Cecilia
CO253. Grassini, Josephina
Graziani, Giuseppe
Graziani, Lodovico
Graziani, Francesco
Graziani, Vincenzo
CO256. Greindl, Josef
Grey, Madeleine
Grieg, Nina
CO257. Grisi, Giuditta
Grisi, Giulia
CO258. Grist, Reri
Grobe, Donald
Grossi, Giovanni
CO260. Gruemmer, Elisabeth
Guadagni, Gaetano
Guarducci, Tommaso
Gudehus, Heinrich
CO261. Gueden, Hilda
Guglielmi, Giacomo
Gulak-Artemovsky, Semyon
CO263. Gulbranson, Ellen
Gura, Hermann
Gyurkovics, Mária
Gyuzelev, Nikola

Habich, Eduard
Haefliger, Ernst
Haisinger, Anton
Hallin, Margareta
CO269. Hammond, Joan
Hammond-Stroud, Derek
Handt, Herbert
CO270. Harper, Heather
Harrison, Samuel
Harrison, William
Harshaw, Margaret
Hartig, Franz
Harwood, Elizabeth
Hatašová, Anna
CO272. Hauk, Minnie
Hauser, Franz
CO273. Hayes, Catherine
CO274. Hayes, Roland
Haywood, Lorna
Hedmont, Charles
Heinefetter, Sabine
Heinefetter, Clara
Heinefetter, Kathinka
Heldy, Fanny
CO277. Heming, Percy
CO278. Hempel, Frieda
Hemsley, Thomas
Henderson, Roy
Henius-Klaiber, Carla
CO279. Henschel, George
Hensel, Heinrich
Herincx, Raimund
Herlea, Nicolae
CO282. Herold, Vilhelm
Hersee, Rose
Heš, Vilém
Heynis, Aafje
CO283. Hidalgo, Elvira de
CO284. Hillebrecht, Hildegard
CO285. Hines, Jerome
Hiolski, Andrzej
CO286. Hislop, Joseph
Hoekman, Guus
Hoeffgen, Marga
Hoffman, Grace
Hoeiseth, Kolbjoern
Holm, Richard
CO290. Homer, Louise
CO291. Hoengen, Elisabeth
Horbowski, Mieczyslaw
CO293. Horne, Marilyn
CO294. Hotter, Hans
Howell, Gwynne
Howell, John

Howells, Anne
Hueni-Mihaczek, Felice
Hunter, Rita
Hurka, Friedrich
Huesch, Gerhard
Ilosfalvy, Róbert
Incledon, Charles
Ivanoff, Nicola
C0302. Ivoguen, Maria
Jachmann-Wagner, Johanna
C0303. Jadlowker, Hermann
Jakowicka-Friderici, T.
C0306. Janowitz, Gundula
C0307. Janssen, Herbert
Jarred, Mary
C0308. Jélyotte, Pierre de
Jerger, Alfred
C0309. Jeritza, Maria
Jobin, Raoul
C0311. Johnson, Edward
Johnston, James
C0313. Jones, Gwyneth
Jones, Parry
Journet, Marcel
Jozzi, Giuseppe
Juch, Emma
June, Ava
Jungwirth, Manfred
C0314. Jurinac, Sena
Kabaivanska, Raina
Kalisch, Paul
Kálmán, Oszkár
Kalter, Sabine
Kappel, Gertrude
Kashmann, Gieseppe
Katul'skaya, Elena
Kelemen, Zoltán
C0315. Kellogg, Clara
C0316. Kelly, Michael
C0318. Kemp, Barbara
C0319. Kennedy, David
C0320. Kennedy-Fraser, Marjorie
Kern, Adele
Kern, Patricia
Kerns, Robert
Khokhlov, Pavel
Kibkalo, Evgeny
C0231. Kiepura, Jan
C0322. King, James
C0323. Kipnis, Alexander
C0324. Kirsten, Dorothy
C0325. Klafsky, Katharina
Klein, Peter
Klose, Margarete

Kmentt, Waldemar
Kniplová, Neděžda
C0327. Knote, Heinrich
Knuepfer, Paul
C0329. Kollo, René
Komlóssy, Erzsébét
C0330. Konetzni, Anny
Konetzni, Hilde
C0331. Konya, Sandor
Koréh, Endre
Koernyei, Béla
C0328. Koeth, Erika
Kozlovsky, Ivan
C0334. Krásová, Marta
C0335. Kraus, Alfredo
Kraus, Ernst
Kraus, Otakar
C0336. Krause, Tom
C0337. Krauss, Gabrielle
Krenn, Werner
Kruscenski, Salomea
Kruysen, Bernard
Kubiak, Teresa
Kufferath, Antonia
Kuhse, Hanne-Lore
C0339. Kullman, Charles
Kunz, Erich
Kupper, Annelies
C0340 Kurz, Selma
Kusche, Benno
Kuusik, Tiyt
Kuznetsova, Maria
La Barre, Anne de
C0341. Labia, Maria
C0342. Lablache, Luigi
Lacy, John
Ladysz, Bernard
Laguerre, John
Laguerre, Marie-Joséphine
Lammers, Gerda
C0343. Langdon, Michael
Larrivée, Henri
C0346. Larsén-Todsen, Nanny
Laschi, Luisa
László, Magda
Laubenthal, Horst
Laubenthal, Rudolf
C0347. Lauri-Volpi, Giacomo
Lavirgen, Pedro
Lavrovskaya, Elizaveta
C0348. Lawrence, Marjorie
Lays, François
Lazzari, Virgilio
C0351. Lear, Evelyn

Lebrun, Franziska
Lebrun, Louis-Sébastian
CO353. Lehmann, Lilli
CO354. Lehmann, Liza
CO355. Lehmann, Lotte
CO356. Leider, Frida
Lemmens-Sherrington, Helen
CO357. Lemnitz, Tiana
CO358. Lenya, Lotte
Leonova, Dar'ya
Leopardi, Venanzio
L'Epine, Margherita de
Le Rochois, Marthe
Levasseur, Nicholas
Levasseur, Rosalie
Leverdige, Richard
Lewis, Richard
Licette, Miriam
CO359. Ligendza, Catarina
CO360. Lind, Jenny
Lindelheim, Joanna
CO362. Lindholm, Berit
CO363. Linley, Elizabeth
Linley, Mary
Lipkowska, Lydia
Lipp, Wilma
Lisitsyan, Pavel
List, Emanuel
Litvinenko-Wohlgemut, M.
CO364. Litvinne, Felia
Ljungberg, Goeta
Lloyd, Edward
CO366. London, George
CO367. Lorengar, Pilar
CO368. Lorenz, Max
CO369. Los Angeles, Vitoria de
Lottini, Antonio
Lowe, Thomas
CO370. Lubin, Germaine
CO371. Lucca, Pauline
Luchetti, Veriano
CO373. Ludwig, Christa
Lukomska, Halina
Lunn, Louise
Luxon, Benjamin
Maas, Joseph
CO403. McCormack, John
CO404. McCracken, James
CO405. McDaniel, Barry
McDonall, Lois
McDonnell, Tom
M'Guckin, Barton
CO406. McIntyre, Donald
CO375. MacNeil, Cornell

Macurdy, John
CO376. Madeira, Jean
Mahon-Second, Sarah
Major, Malvina
CO378. Malibran, Maria
CO379. Maliponte, Adriana
Mallinger, Mathilde
Malten, Therese
Mamedova, Shevket
CO380. Mancini, Giambattista
Mandac, Evelyn
Mandini, Stefano
Mandini, Maria
Mandini, Paolo
Manelli, Francesco
Manina, Maria
Manners, Charles
Manning, Jane
Manuguerra, Matteo
Manzuoli, Giovanni
CO381. Mara, Gertrude
Marchesi, Salvatore
CO384. Marchesi, Mathilde
CO382. Marchesi, Blanche
CO383. Marchesi, Luigi
Marchesini, Maria
CO385. Marchesio, Barbara
CO386. Marchesio, Carlotta
CO389. Mario, Giovanni
Marshall, Lois
Martin, Jean-Blaise
CO391. Martinelli, Giovanni
CO392. Masini, Angelo
CO394. Mason, Edith
Massard, Robert
Massol, Eugene
Masson, Elizabeth
Masterson, Valerie
CO396. Mastilovič, Daniča
Materna, Amalie
CO397. Mathis, Edith
Matters, Arnould
CO398. Matzenauer, Margarete
CO399. Maupin
CO400. Maurel, Victor
Mayer, Dorothy
CO401. Maynor, Dorothy
CO402. Mayr, Richard
Mazurok, Yury
Meili, Max
CO408. Melba, Nellie
CO409. Melchoir, Lauritz
Melis, Gyoergy
Mel'nikov, Ivan

Méric-Lalande, Henriette
Merighi, Antonia
Merli, Francesco
C0412. Merrill, Robert
Marriman, Nan
Mesplé, Mady
C0413. Messchaert, Johannes
C0414. Meyer, Kerstin
Micheau, Janine
Mierzwinski, Wladyslaw
Mikhaylov, Maxim
Mikhaylova, Maria
Mikhaylov-Stoyan, K.
C0417. Milanov, Zinka
Milashkina, Tamara
Milder-Hauptmann, Anna
Mildmay, Audrey
Millico, Giuseppe
C0421. Milnes, Sherrill
C0422. Mingotti, Regina
C0423. Minton, Yvonne
Miroshnichenko, Evgeniya
C0426. Moedl, Martha
C0427. Moffo, Anna
C0429. Moll, Kurt
Moncrieff, Gladys
Mongini, Pietro
Mommart, Berthe
Montagnana, Antonio
Monti, Anna Maria
Monti, Grazia
Monti, Laura
Monti, Marianna
Monticelli, Augelo
Monza, Maria
Moody, Fanny
C0431. Moore, Grace
Moralt, Clementine
C0432. Morena, Berta
Moriani, Napoleone
Morison, Elsie
C0433. Moser, Edda
Mravina, Evgeniya
C0436. Mueller, Maria
Mullings, Frank
C0437. Muratore, Lucien
Mustafá, Domenico
C0439. Muzio, Claudia
Myers, Raymond
Mysz-Gmeiner
Myszuga, Aleksander
Nachbaur, Franz
Naldi, Giuseppe
Nautier-Didiee, Constance

Nash, Heddle
Nasierova, Khalinia
Negri, Maria C.
Negri, Maria R.
Neidlinger, Gustav
Nelson, Judith
Nemeth, Maria
Némethy, Ella
Nessi, Giuseppe
Nesterenko, Evgeny
C0443. Nevada, Emma
Nevada, Mignon
Neway, Patricia
C0444. Nezhdanova, Antonia
Nicholls, Agnes
Nicolini
Nicloini, Ernest
Niedzielski, Stanislaw
C0446. Niemann, Albert
C0447. Nilsson, Birgit
C0448. Nilsson, Christine
Nimsgern, Siegmund
Niska, Maralin
Nissen, Hans
Nixon, Marni
Noble, Dennis
Noni, Alda
Nordblom, Johan
C0450. Noridca, Lillian
Norena, Eidé
Norman, Jessye
C0451. Nourrit, Adolphe
C0452. Novello, Clara
C0453. Novotná, Jarmila
Oberlin, Russell
C0454. Obratsova, Elena
Obukhova, Nadezhda
Ochman, Weislaw
Oestvig, Karl
Ognivtsev, Alexander
Ohms, Elisabeth
Olezewska, Maria
Olenina d'Alheim, Mariya
C0456. Olivero, Magda
O'Mara, Joseph
Oncina, Juan
C0457. Onegin, Sigrid
C0460. Orgeni, Aglaja
Osborn-Hannah, Jane
Osten, Eva von der
O'Sullivan, Denis
C0461. Ots, George
Otto, Lisa
Otto, Melitta

Oudin, Eugène
C0462. Pacchiarotti, Gasparo
Pacini, Andrea
C0464. Pagliughi, Lina
C0465. Palló, Imre
Palmer, Felicity
Palmerini, Giovanni
Pampanini, Rosetta
Panerai, Rolando
C0468. Panzéra, Charles
Paprocki, Bohdaw
Parepa-Rosa, Euphrosyne
C0469. Pareto, Graziella
Parly, Ticho
Partridge, Ian
C0470. Paskalis, Kostas
Passerini, Christina
C0471. Pasta, Giuditta
C0472. Pataky, Kálmán
Pate, John
Patey, Janet
C0713. Paton, Mary Ann
Patorzhinsky, Ivan
Patti, Salvatore
Barilli-Patti, Caterina
Patti, Carlotta
C0473. Patti, Adelina
C0475. Patzak, Julius
C0476. Pauly, Rose
C0477. Pavarotti, Luciano
C0478. Pears, Peter
C0479. Peerce, Jan
C0480. Pélissier, Marie
C0481. Peralta, Angela
Périer, Jean
Pernet, André
C0483. Pertile, Aureliano
C0484. Peters, Roberta
Petrella, Clara
C0485. Petrov, Ivan
C0486. Petrov, Osip
C0488. Phillips, Henry
C0489. Piccaver, Alfred
C0490. Picchi, Mirto
C0491. Piccolomini, Marietta
C0492. Pilarczyk, Helga
Pilotti-Schiavonetti, E.
C0493. Pilou, Jeanette
Pinacci, Giovanni
Pini-Corsi, Antonio
C0494. Pinza, Ezio
Piozzi, Gabriele
Pirogov, Alexander
Pirogov, Grigory

C0496. Pisaroni, Benedetta
Pixis, Francilla
Plaichinger, Thila
C0497. Plançon, Pol
Plaschke, Friedrich
C0498. Plishka, Paul
Pollak, Anna
Polzelli, Luigia
C0500. Pons, Lily
C0501. Ponselle, Rosa
C0503. Popp, Lucia
Powell, Walter
Predieri, Antonio
C0506. Prey, Hermann
C0507. Price, Leontyne
Price, Margaret
Pring, Katherine
Procter, Norma
Prohaska, Jaro
Puliaschi, Giovanni
Pyne, Louisa
Quilico, Louis
Quinault, Marie
C0508. Raaf, Anton
C0510. Raimondi, Gianni
C0511. Raimondi, Ruggero
Rainforth, Elizabeth
C0512. Raisa, Rosa
C0513. Ralf, Oscar
Ralf, Torsten
Ranalow, Frederick
Randhartinger, Benedikt
Rasa, Lina
Rascarini, Francesco
C0514. Raskin, Judith
Ranzzini, Venanzio
Reading, John
Reardon, John
Rebel, Jean
Rebel, Anne
C0517. Reeves, Sims
Regan, Anna
Rehfuss, Heinz
Reicher-Kindermann, Hedwig
Reichmann, Theodor
Reinhardt, Delia
Reinhold, Frederick
Reinhold, Henry
Reining, Maria
Reiss, Albert
Remedios, Alberto
C0519. Renaud, Maurice
Renzi, Anna
C0520. Resnik, Regina

CO521. Rethberg, Elisabeth
Reynolds, Anna
Reyzen, Mark
Rhodes, Jane
CO522. Ricciarelli, Katia
Richardson, Marilyn
CO523. Ridderbusch, Karl
Riemschneider, Johann
Righetti, Geltrude
Rinaldi, Margherita
Ritchie, Margaret
Rivoli, Ludwika
CO525. Robeson, Paul
Robinson, Ann
Robinson, Miss
Robinson, Francis
Robinson, F.J.
Robinson, William
Robinson, John
Robinson, Joseph
Robinson, Anastasia
Robinson, Forbes
Rochetti, Filippo
Roeckel, Joseph
Rode, Wilhelm
CO528. Roger, Gustave
Rogers, Nigel
Rokitansky, Hans
Roman, Stella
Romer, Emma
Ronconi, Giorgio
Ronzi de Begnis, Giuseppina
Roser, Franz
CO527. Roesler, Endre
CO531. Rossi-Lemeni, Nicola
Rossoni, Giulio
CO532. Rosvaenge, Helge
CO533. Rothenberger, Anneliese
Rothmueller, Marko
Rouleau, Joseph
CO534. Rubini, Giovanni
Rudenko, Bela
CO535. Ruffo, Titta
Rummel, Franziska
Rupin, Evan
Ruprecht, Martin
CO537. Russell, Henry
CO538. Rysanek, Leonie
Rywacka-Morocewicz, Ludwika
Saéden, Erik
CO540. Saint-Huberty, Antoinette
Sainton-Dolby, Charlotte
Saléza, Albert
Salmon, Eliza

Saltzmann-Stevens, Minnie
Salvai, Maria
Salvini-Donatelli, Fanny
Salway, Thomas
CO543. Sammarco, Mario
CO544. Sanderson, Sibyl
Sante, Sophia
CO546. Santley, Charles
Santorini, Lorenz
Saporiti, Teresa
Sardinero, Vicente
Sass, Sylvia
CO547. Sayão, Bidú
Sazandarian, Tetevik
Scalchi, Sofia
Scalzi, Carlo
Scarabelli, Diamante
G1044. Scaria, Emil
Scarlatti, Anna
Scarlatti, Melchiorra
Scarlatti, Tommaso
Schock, Benedikt
Schechner, Nanette
Scheff, Fritzi
CO550. Scheidemantel, Karl
CO553. Schick, Margarete
Schikaneder, Urban
Schikaneder, Emanuel
CO554. Schiøtz, Aksel
CO555. Schipa, Tito
Schipper, Emil
CO557. Schlusnus, Heinrich
CO558. Schmedes, Erik
CO560. Schneider, Hortense
CO561. Schnorr von Carolsfeld, L.
CO562. Schnorr von Carolsfeld, M.
CO564. Schoeffler, Paul
CO565. Schoene, Lotte
CO567. Schorr, Friedrich
CO569. Schreier, Peter
CO570. Schroeder-Devrient, W.
Schroeder-Feineu, Ursula
Schroeter, Elisabeth
Schroeter, Marie
Schubert, Georgine
Schuch-Proska, Clementine
CO572. Schumann, Elisabeth
CO573. Schumann-Heink, Ernestine
Schuster, Ignaz
Schuetzendorf, Guido
Schuetzendorf, Alfons
Schuetzendorf, Gustav
CO574. Schuetzendorf, Leo
CO575. Schwarz, Joseph

C0576. Schwarzkopf, Elisabeth
C0577. Sciutti, Graziella
C0578. Scotti, Antonio
C0579. Scotto, Renata
C0580. Seefried, Irmgard
       Seguin, Arthur
C0581. Seinemeyer, Meta
C0582. Sembrich, Marcella
       Sénéchal, Michel
C0583. Senesino
       Seroen, Berthe
C0112. Shalyapin, Fyodor
       Shanks, Donald
       Shaw, Mary
C0585. Sheridan, Margaret
C0586. Shirley, George
C0587. Shirley-Quirk, John
       Shore, Catherine
C0588. Shuard, Amy
       Sibilla
C0589. Siboni, Giuseppe
C0590. Siems, Margarethe
C0691. Siepi, Cesare
C0592. Silja, Anja
       Silk, Dorothy
C0593. Sills, Beverly
       Silveri, Paolo
C0595. Simionato, Giulietta
       Simoneau, Leopold
       Simonetti, Leonardo
       Sinclair, John
C0596. Singher, Martial
C0599. Slezak, Leo
C0600. Slobodskaya, Oda
       Smirnov, Dmitry
C0601. Sobinov, Leonid
C0602. Soederstrom, Elisabeth
C0604. Sontag, Henriette
C0605. Soot, Fritz
       Sorosina, Benedetta
       Sotin, Hans
C0606. Souzay, Gerard
       Soyer, Roger
       Spangler, Maria
       Spiess, Ludovic
       Spindler, Stanislaus
C0608. Spoorenberg, Erna
       Sportonio, Marc'Antonio
C0610. Stabile, Mariano
C0611. Stader, Maria
       Staudigl, Joseph
       Staudigl Jr., Joseph
C0613. Steber, Eleanor
       Stegmann, Carl

C0614. Stenborg, Carl
       Stepanova, Elena
       Stephens, Catherine
C0616. Sterling, Antoinette
       Stevens, Horace
C0617. Stevens, Risë
C0618. Stewart, Thomas
       Stich-Randall, Teresa
C0619. Stignani, Ebe
       Stilwell, Richard
       Stockhausen, Margarethe
C0620. Stockhausen, Julius
C0621. Stoltz, Rosine
C0622. Stolz, Teresa
       Stolze, Gerhard
       Stoppelaer, Michael
       Storace, Nancy
C0623. Storchio, Rosina
C0624. Stracciari, Riccardo
       Strada del Pó, Anna
C0626. Stratas, Teresa
       Stravinsky, Fyodor
       Streich, Rita
C0627. Strepponi, Giuseppina
       Studzińska-Marczewska, W.
C0628. Sucher, Rosa
       Sullivan, Daniel
C0630. Supervia, Conchita
       Suthaus, Ludwig
C0631. Sutherland, Joan
C0632. Svanholm, Set
       Svéd, Sándor
C0633. Swarthout, Gladys
       Szczurowski, Jan
C0636. Székely, Mihály
       Székelyhidy, Ferenc
       Sziklay, Erika
       Szostek-Radkowa, Krystyna
       Tacchinardi, Nicola
       Tacchinardi-Persiani, F.
       Taddei, Giuseppe
       Tadolini, Eugenia
       Tagliabue, Carlo
       Tagliafico, Joseph
C0637. Tagliavini, Ferruccio
C0638. Tajo, Italo
       Talvela, Martti
C0639. Tamagno, Francesco
C0640. Tamberlik, Enrico
C0641. Tamburini, Antonio
       Tappy, Eric
C0642. Tauber, Richard
       Tear, Robert
C0643. Tebaldi, Renata

Weichsell, Frederica
Weidt, Lucie
C0707. Welitsch, Ljuba
Welsh, Thomas
Wendling, Dorothea
Wendling, Elisabeth
Wendling, Elisabeth
Wendling, Dorothea
Westenholz, Barbara
Westenholz, Carl
Westenholz, Sophia
Wettergren, Gertrud
C0708. Whitehill, Clarence
Widdop, Walter
Wildbrunn, Helene
Wilmann, Magdalena
Wilmann, Caroline
C0709. Wilson, Steuart
C0710. Windgassen, Wolfgang
C0711. Winkelmann, Hermann
Witte, Erich
Wittich, Marie
Wixell, Ingvar
Wolff, Fritz
Wood, Anne
Woodeson, Leonard

C0714. Woytowicz, Stefania
Wright, Mrs.
C0715. Wuellner, Ludwig
C0716. Wunderlich, Fritz
Yakovlev, Leonid
Young, Ceclia
Young, Isabella
Young, Esther
Young, Isabella
Young, Elizabeth
Young, Polly
Young, Alexander
Zaccaria, Nicola
Zandt, Marie van
C0717. Zanelli, Renato
Zannoni, Angelo
Zbruyeva, Evgeniya
Zeani, Virginia
C0718. Zenatello, Giovanni
Zídek, Ivo
Zimmermann, Erich
Zítek, Vilém
Zonca, Giovanni
Zonca, Giuseppe
C0719. Zur Muehlen, Raimund von
C0720. Zylis-Gara, Teresa

Index of Authors

This index includes authors, joint authors, and editors. Many individual singers are not included in this listing due to the fact that they did not author published material. References are to individual entries by category: A0001–A0120 COLLECTIVE WORKS/Books on Singers; B0001–B0154 COLLECTIVE WORKS/Related Books; C0001–C0720 INDIVIDUAL SINGERS, A–Z; D0001–D0017 APPENDIX I/Reference Material.

Abraham, Hélène, C0128
Abraham, Robert D., C0506, C0611
Ackté, Aino, C0004
Acloque, Elisa, C0011
Adam, Klaus, C0328
Adam, Theo, C0005
Adami, Giuseppe, C0011
Adams, Brian, C0631
Ademollo, Alessandro, C0042, C0225, C0542, C0649
Aguila, Luis Alberto, C0233
Alavedra, Jaun, C0029
Albani, Emma, C0010
Alberti, Celso, C0471
Albrecht, Otto E., C0017
Albus, Harry T., C0017
Alcaide, Tomáz, C0012
Alcari, C., B0001
Alda, Frances, C0013
Aldrich, Richard, B0002, C0360
Allegri, Renzo, C0091
Altmann, Wilhelm, C0446
Amstad, Marietta, C0015
d'Ancillon, Charles, C0106
Anderson, Marian, C0017
Andersson, Otto Emanuel, C0568
Andro, L. C0265, C0353
Angelucci, Nino, C0122
Appleton, William, C0683
Arditi, Luigi, B0003

Ardoin, John, A0011, C0091
Armin, George, C0104, C0582
Armitage, Merle, B0004, C0232
Armstrong, William, A0001, C0450
Arnosi, Eduardo, C0535
Asztalos, Elisa, C0022
Averkamp, Antoon, A0002

Bab, Julius, C0570
Bacchetti, Antonio, C0080
Bach, R., C0030
Bădescu, Dinu, C0028
Bahr, Hermann, C0030
Bahr-Mildenburg, Anna, C0030
Bajerová, Marie, C0165
Baker, Janet, C0033
Balassa, Imre, C0545
Balatri, Filippo, C0034
Balfe, Michael William, C0035
Bamberg, Eduard von, C0304
Bannenta, D., C0069
Banti, Giuseppe, C0037
Barát, Endre, C0104
Barbieri, Gaetano, C0378
Barbieri, Paolo, C0091
Barbu, H. C0127
Bardi, Mitzi, C0040
Barker, Frank Granville, A0003, A0004
Barnes, Jr., Harold M., C0232, C0439

Reinhardt, Hannes, B0096, B0104
Reis, Kurt, C0104
Reissenberger, Albert, C0518
Reissig, Elisabeth, A0090
Rellstab, Heinrich, C0604
Remezov, Ivan I., C0601
Rémy, Pierre-Jean, C0091
Ribera, Salvador A., C0233
Ricci, Corrado, C0188
Rich, Maria F., A0091
Richards, J.B., C0670
Richardson, Ben Albert, C0017
Richter, Hermann, C0570
Richter, Karl, C0067
Ridgway, James, C0058
Rie, Therese, C0265, C0353
Rie-Andro, Theodore, C0570
Riemann, Heinrich, C0360
Riemens, Leo, A0058, A0059,
    A0060, B0121, C0091, C0355
Rigby, Charles, C0199
Riiber, Anne Marie, C0360
Ring, Lothar, C0599
Ritter, Carl, C0559
Rivalta, C., C0392
Rizzi, F.G., C0136
Roberts, Peter, C0369
Robertson, Alec, C0355
Robeson, Eslanda Goode, C0525
Robeson, Paul, C0525
Robeson, Susan, C0525
Robinson, Francis, C0104
Robinson, Ray, C0344
Robinson, Terry, C0344
Robinson-Duff, Sarah, C0232
Roca, Otavio, C0579
Rochlitz, Friedrich, C0071, C0381
Rockstro, William Smith, C0360
Rode, V. von, C0209
Roeder, Ernst, B0122
Roger, Gustave-Hippolyte, C0528
Rogers, Clara Kethleen, C0529
Rogers, Francis, A0092
Roggis, Philip K., C0570
Rokitansky, Victor, C0038
Rollins, Charlemae, C0017
Ronald, Landon, C0408
Rootzén, Kajsa, C0360
Rosenberg, Charles G., B0123,
    C0360
Rosenberg, Herbert, C0060, C0554
Rosenblatt, Samuel, C0530
Rosenfelder, Carl, C0559
Rosenthal, Harold, A0093, A0094,
    A0095, B0090

Rosner, Robert, C0242
Rossi-Lemeni, Nicola, C0531
Roswaenge, Helge, C0532
Rothenberger, Anneliese, C0533
Rouff, Marcel, C0560
Rubboli, Daniele, A0096, A0097
Rubini, Giovanni Battista, C0534
Ruffo, Titta, C0535
Ruhrberg, Karl, C0288
Rushmore, Robert, B0124
Russell, Frank, C0604
Russell, Henry, C0537
Russell, Henry (son), B0125
Ryan, Thomas, B0126

Sacchi, Giovenale, C0188
Sadko, Konstantin, C0539
Sáenz, Gerardo, B0127
Saleski, Gdal, B0128
Salvucci, Antonio, B0129
Sampayo Riberio, Mário de, C0660
Sanborn, Pitts, C0205
Sánchez-Torres, Enrique, A0098
Sanner, Jr., Howard C., C0205
Santley, Charles, C0546
Sargeant, Winthrop, A0099, C0494
Sarobe, Celestino, C0207
Sassi, Romualdo, C0462
Satter, Heinrich, C0107
Sbârcea, George, C0143, C0502
Scanzoni, Signe von, A0100
Schaefer, Walter Erich, C0426
Schaetzler, Ernst, C0548
Schebest, Agnese, C0549
Scheidemantel, Karl, C0550
Scherer, Carl, C0381
Schiavazzi, Pietro, C0552
Schiøtz, Aksel, C0554
Schiøtz, Gerd, C0554
Schipa, Tito, C0555
Schirmer, Adolf, C0360
Schliepe, Ernst, C0605
Schlosser, Anatole I., C0525
Schlusnus, Annemay, C0557
Schlusnus, Heinrich, C0557
Schmidt, Eberhard, A0103
Schmiedel, Gottfried, C0569
Schneidereit, Otto, C0642
Schoene, Marion, A0056
Schoen-René, Anna Eugénie, B0130,
    C0566
Schonberg, Harold, B0131
Schouwman, Hans, C0449
Schreier, Peter, C0569
Schroeter, Carona, C0571

About the Author

ROBERT H. COWDEN is Professor of Music at San Jose University. He has written numerous reviews and articles, appearing in such journals as *The Opera Journal, Theatre Design and Technology, Arts in Society, Opera, MLA Notes,* and *The NATS Bulletin.*